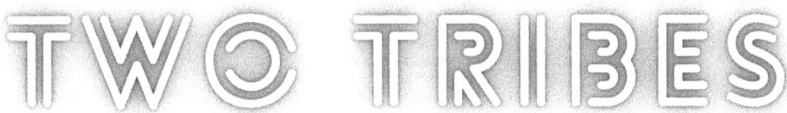

The untold story of rugby league's divided year and the birth of the NRL

STEVE MASCORD

WHITE LINE FEVER MEDIA

First published in 2021

White Line Fever Media

C37 Du Cane Court

London SW17 7JF

Mascord, Steve author

ISBN 978-1-5272-9379-3 (paperback)

Proof-read by Tony Harper

Cover design by Steve Mascord

Book design by Jahid Munshi

Dedicated to, And In Memory Of:

David Barnhill snr
Arthur Beetson
Tom Bellew
Micki Braithwaite
Ron Casey
John Chalk
Mike Cockerill
Simon Cooper
Roger Cowan
Eric Cox
Peter Deakin
Darrell Eastlake
Steve Folkes
John Fordham
Bob Fulton
Peter Frilingos
Ian Frykberg
Mike Gibson
Greg Growden
Hugh Hazard
Kevin Humphreys
Frank Hyde
Harry Jepson
Elizabeth Langley
Paul McBlane
Mick Markham
Peter McLeod
Allan McMahon
Paul Malone
Betty Mascord
Michael Moore
Paul Morgan
Peter Moscatt
Graham Murray
Barry Nelson
David Oates
Quentin Pongia
Rusty Priest
Norm Provan
Tom Raudonikis
Gerald Ryan
Colin Sanders
Arthur Summons
Glenn Tobin

Rebecca Wilson

Thank you to

NIGEL WOOD

for his support and encouragement on this project

Thank you also to my wife Sarah and to the following people who supported Two Tribes via Substack subscriptions. This is a living project that will continue to grow until December 19, 2022 as a digital installation at twotribes.substack.com

Timothy Alun

Steve Austine

Michael Adams

Muzammil Ali

Peter Anderson

Darren Andrews

Diego Arrelano

Josh Bailo

Jeffrey Barnes

Kristie Boaler

David Bolt

Brendan Bradford

Karsten Brumme

Michael Carayannis

Ian Camlett

Paul Challinor

Alex Clark

Chris Coleman

Ben Costelloe

Brendan Crabb

Shaun Cronin

James Deadly

Shannon Donato

Chris Doyle

Johnno Duncan

Daniel Eastwood

Andrew Ferguson

Eric Fleming

Andrew Foster

Matt French

Kris Gayle

Sean Gaynor

Phoebe Glover

Kyle Gray

Antony Greenall

Bevan Hannan

Russell Hansen

Aaron Hawkins

Glen Humphries

David Hundt

Brandan Ingham

Chris Isouard

Nicholas Janzen

Lachlan Jeffery

Bob Jennings

Tim Johnson

Michael Jones

Jonathan Kauri

Ben Liddicoat

David Lonsdale

Richael Liu

Phil Mayes

Bruce McGrath

Matt McKee

Reece Mahoney

Matt McKee

Paora Manuel

Greg McCallum

Chris McCormack

Stuart McLennan

Malcolm Middleton

Matt Middleton

Paul Morabito

Danny Munk

David Murray

Vivek Nayak

Brad Newman

Rory O'Hara

Jason Oliver

Daniel Payne

Bill Peters

Matthew Price

Elliott Richardson

Damon Roast

Nathan Russell

Steve Russo

Martyn Sadler

Brock Schaefer

David Sharp

Richard Shaw-Wright

Martyn Simpson

Luke Spear

Andrew Stringer

Topher Sutton

Mikhail Ushakoff

Shaun VanderDonk

Vanuatu Rugby League

Brad Walter

Alex Warton

Pat Webster

Gavin Willacy

Adrian Williams

Greg Wood

Stephen Woodcock

Richard York

Table Of Contents

FOREWORD

IF this was a movie, the opening scene would probably depict a generous-sized rock shattering the window of the Hunter Mariners' office in suburban Newcastle and a faceless functionary of BHP announcing the steelmaker would be withdrawing from the city, at the cost of 4500 jobs.

Movies require symbolism that books don't.

There was no lack of cinematic-scale symbols, portents, and even omens in 1997.

The year, journalist Bevan Hannan recalls, was full of "heavy stories … the Princess of Wales, her passing … Mother Teresa went not long after her. Pop culture wise, Michael Hutchence died … there was the Thredbo landslide with Stuart Diver, the people who didn't make it there.

"And in Canberra just before the Canberra team went to the UK for the World Club Challenge you had the hospital implosion which went wrong. All those people went out by the lake to watch the hospital get imploded and a little girl lost her life.

"It was sort of apt that the Super League year happened in that year."

This is a football story linked to a business story linked inexorably to the wider world of that era, all of it probably a significant marker in your life, too, if you're old enough and rugby league was part of it.

I was reading the opening passages of Paul Broughton's excellent autobiography, *One More Walk Around The Block*, just then and I found myself reflecting on the impact of the Super League War on the course of my own personal story.

Yes, covering the battle for control of Australian rugby league on a daily basis for the *Sydney Morning Herald* a quarter-century ago taught me more about the qualities and failings of my species than a lifetime of doing most other things could impart.

But the Super League War influenced other basic things; like where I lived, who my friends were, where I travelled.

In 1996 was looking for new digs in Sydney. I remember being at NSW State of Origin training at Coogee Oval, horribly hungover (as usual at that time of year for a Sydney rugby league writer in the mid-nineties), when the late *Illawarra Mercury* journalist Glenn Tobin told me he might have a lead for me.

No, it wasn't a Blues player carrying a secret hamstring strain. It was somewhere I might like to live.

The Illawarra Steelers' Ken Stephen Medal winning hooker, Michael Bolt, had moved to The Rocks historical district to curate the proposed rugby league museum which would be located there. But the Super League War, which had broken out the previous year when Rupert Murdoch's News Corporation had attempted to start a breakaway competition it could show on its new pay TV assets in Australia, had robbed the NSW Rugby League, which ran the ARL competition, of its cash reserves.

The money had been spent primarily on so-called "loyalty contracts" to stem the flood of players to the rebellion. The Rugby League Museum project was dead and 'Bolter' was moving back to Wollongong.

A couple of days later I fronted up to a heritage-listed building in Lower Fort Street, in the imposing shadow of the Sydney Harbour Bridge, and met Michael's old flatmate, Ross Bootle.

Ross stands out so much in a lifetime of rogues encountered that I contemplated writing a book about him. But with values already shifting away from the adoration of larrikins after the turn of the century, I soon realised the folly of that idea. Ross was - and is - a kind, irascible man but was in no way "woke".

Many of the characters in this book are like Ross - only less so. They are of another age.

They did many great things, remodelling a sport which is now the most successful club rugby competition of either code on this or any other planet. But many of them also succumbed to greed, they abused their power, they got drunk and lied and womanised. "I'll tell the truth, the whole truth and anything but the truth," one of them reputedly told fellow officials the night before testifying in the original Super League court case.

"They were days that don't exist anymore," promotions man Paul Kind - who worked on both sides - says with a certain wistfulness, "in terms of your requirement, really, to have some fun when you're out and about with your work."

In 1997, without mobile phones or social media, the currency of business and of rugby league were secrets.

And that made being a reporter back then so ineffably fun.

Back to "if this was movie": it would need a central character to guide us through the year. That character would probably be Newcastle's Roger Ramjet captain, Paul 'The Chief' Harragon, who at the start of the war drove his team-mates to the ARL on a mini-bus, and at the end played a key role in the match that made sure enough fans still cared for the sport to cling - just - to its place in Australian popular culture.

The NRL is a behemoth now and I don't think it knows how to process 1997, the year when two tribes went to war, when there were twin competitions in Australasia for the only time. This squeamishness was underscored at the start of the Covid-wrecked 2020 season when the war was referenced in the League's advertising campaign. "The Super League War is tearing the game apart", a news clip proclaimed in between verses of Tina Turner's "The Best". The reference was subsequently altered after the campaign made its debut.

How can we still be so sensitive about something that occurred so long ago? How come it still hurts?

I can identify four broad groups of rugby league people, defined by their attitudes to this chaotic - but often exhilarating and even comedic - year.

There are the zealots, still fighting in the jungle as the cliche goes, who refuse to acknowledge Brisbane won something, NSW and Queensland handed out caps that weren't Origin appearances, big crowds watched an Ashes series and 2021 saw the second grand final in Brisbane, not the first. They're still mad at Rupert Murdoch and always will be.

Then there are the trainspotters, who fetishise things like Melbourne playing a trial against Adelaide in Hobart and those jumpers with the Nike tick just below the chest. They can't get enough of Hunter Mariners v Paris Saint-Germain.

Thirdly, there is perhaps the majority of rugby league fans who find the memory of the entire year somewhat painful and confusing - like a nasty past breakup with someone who is now a life-partner - and would rather not think about it at all.

The fourth group is Newcastle Knights fans.

My objective in *Two Tribes* is somewhat lofty: I want the game to make its peace with 1997. I want to give a human face to sport's lowest point since its birth in England 100 years before; to tell how a peculiar melange of personalities, technological advances, commercial pressures and rivalries produced a season that was bizarre, eventful, side-splittingly funny and - yeah - sometimes shambolic and tragic.

The NRL also lacks an origin (small 'o') story, which is curious for an institution that carries such cultural gravitas. This is the story of the NRL's birth. "Buffoonery, black humour and broken dreams," the *Sydney Morning Herald* said on the 10th anniversary of the outbreak of the war.

To labour the break-up metaphor, your love for him or her is probably deeply rooted in what happened that year you were apart. You just need to process it, admit it to yourself, to gain a deeper understanding of where you find yourself today and what really lies at the centre of your relationship.

Some of the key figures from the period, like News Limited 'fixer' Ian Frykberg and Super League media manager Rebecca Wilson, are no longer here to tell their stories. None of those interviewed in the following pages will be around forever (Bob Fulton died shortly after he was interviewed), nor will I - one of a handful of reporters who lived that season through its crazy days and hazy nights on both sides of the world.

What started as a dry investigation into an historical event became (perhaps despite my best intentions, since my only previous book had been overly autobiographical and even self-indulgent) something of a personal journey. Visiting Ken and Barbara Arthurson on the Gold Coast, a battle scarred but feisty Maurice Lindsay at Lytham St Annes and having the honour of Neil Whittaker's first in-depth rugby league interview in 20 years, I found myself spending as much time gossiping about things that had nothing to do with 1997 as we did recording our conversations.

There was so much more that both groups in this conflict had in common than there was that separated them - and despite the odd bits of spin, lingering bitterness and gentle conceit, it was heartening to see that the main actors mostly realise this today.

How close did these Two Tribes come to killing the thing they both professed to love?

Well, as Bevan also reminded me, "even the Titanic movie came out that year."

Steve Mascord
October 2021

CHAPTER 1
October 4

AS if things couldn't get any weirder, the sun rose over Bondi Beach at 5.28am on October 4, 1996.

It was a warmish spring day, the temperature topping out at 24 Celsius. "Macarena" by Los Del Rio was dominating pop charts worldwide, John Howard was Australia's Prime Minister and Princess Diana's divorce from Prince Charles was two months old.

The game of rugby league had been played in Sydney, the continent's first city, for 87 previous winters and perhaps the most blessed working class in the world had gone about its recreation unfettered, pummelling each other in the mud, celebrating in the pubs and retiring to the beach (or to the north of England for a tour every now and then) about this time of year.

Three generations of sun-drenched lives, rolling with the waves, well spent.

But the previous winter, 1995, big business and global money had intervened.

The overseas-based Australian media mogul, Rupert Murdoch, had sought to bring pay television to his homeland and - fully realising the need for a Trojan horse - had attempted to hijack rugby's locally popular 13-a-side variant, exploiting existing internal tensions. Climbing through windows and locking out agents to sign players, Murdoch had purchased the entire game worldwide (such as it was) with the exception of those inside the Australian Rugby League fort at Phillip Street in downtown Sydney - and those they had contracted with the help of Murdoch's main domestic rival, Publishing and Broadcasting Limited boss Kerry Packer and the company to which it had bequeathed Pay TV rights, Optus Vision.

And - before the sun rose on October 4 - the inhabitants of that fort appeared to have repelled the moneyed hordes outside. A Federal Court ruling via Justice James Burchett the previous February barred the so-called "Super League" from starting in 1996 - but not only that.

Super League had to pay players to compete in the establishment ARL. All branded Super League merchandise had to be handed in. The competition's staff was legally banned from even planning for a future in which it existed. This was as humiliating a defeat as could be imagined for a corporate empire upon which the sun never set.

Hamstrung by Draconian court orders, Super League employees continued going to work throughout 1996 - but spent most of their time playing touch football in Hyde Park or drinking in city hotels.

Murdoch appealed. After proceedings were adjourned on June 6, the sport waited for a decision.

Then-Canberra Raiders chief executive Kevin Neil recalls: "I received a call about two weeks before the judgement was handed down and it was someone with information on what date the decision would be handed down - what date and what time and what the decision was.

"I answered the phone to anyone in those days. I was out the front of the Commonwealth Bank. It was anonymous. I don't know who it was. It wasn't a voice I recognised. It was two phone calls. Before anyone ever knew when the judgement was being handed down.

"I told a couple of people. I told (journalist Peter) Frilingos, I told Rebecca (Wilson) and I told (Super League chief executive John) Ribot and I think (Cronulla Sharks official) Shane Richardson.

"I didn't know whether to take any credence from it but then three or four days after that, a phone call … he rang me back and said 'the date the decision will be handed down has changed'.

"It was now on a Friday. So that was right."

Officially, on Thursday October 3, recalls Ribot, 'we were told it was all going to unfold'. It had been announced Friday would see the results of a full bench Federal Court appeal handed down … at 2.15pm, to be exact.

"I remember having a very sleepless night," Ribot, now 65, recalls. "There was really no Plan B. Where we'd gone and what we'd done and being so badly beaten on the judgement from Justice Burchett … we couldn't imagine being in a worse position.

"As I understand, there were meetings held … Rupert said 'hey, this is costing a lot of money. Are we better off cashing in now? Because if we're not going to win, I don't want to keep good money chasing bad money'.

"I remember there being a hookup, Ken (Cowley, News' Australian chief) calling in all our senior counsel and saying 'should we appeal this, because there's a lot at stake?' They were very keen to do that so he got a good vibe out of that and it was 'righto, we'll take it to appeal'.

"When we went to appeal, we felt we had a good hearing there. We never really had a good feeling with Justice Burchett. That didn't go well at all, that court case, for us and I think I had a gut feeling that this was not going to be a good day for us when he called us all in.

"We were probably put in a worse position than we thought we would be and then going to the appeal, you just never know…."

The previous Sunday, Manly had beaten St George 20-6 in the 1996 Australian Rugby League grand final at the Sydney Football Stadium before a crowd of 40,985 - the culmination of a Frankenstein-like season for which the warring clubs have been frogmarched down the aisle to reaffirm their vows … or else.

The previous Monday, Prime Minister Howard had abandoned his promise of a Royal Commission into cross-media ownership, replacing it with a low key enquiry.

"Don't listen to anyone who says 'thank goodness it's finally over'," a certain S Mascord wrote on the back of the *Sydney Morning Herald* on October 4. "It's only just beginning."

Ken Arthurson, the Australian Rugby League chairman nicknamed "The Pope" for his role in fighting Murdoch, says now: "I remember it very vividly, I really do, notwithstanding the fact it was so many years ago.

"I went there feeling quite up market because of Justice Burchett's rulings. He'd gone through it for 40 days…"

But in his biography, *Arko: My Game*, Arthurson admitted that like Ribot, "I barely slept at all on the Thursday night. I was uneasy. Something didn't feel right.

"On the stroll to the court I said … 'we can't possibly lose. I mean, the loyalty contracts for a start would have to be enforceable. They would have to be valid for starters. We're not going to lose that'."

David Gallop, a lanky former cricketer of some note and then Super League's 31-year-old legal counsel, recalls: "We obviously had a very well credentialed, experienced legal team who had been a bit shocked by the first decision and felt confident an appeal court would overturn the decision.

"But you never know until you hear it come out of the judges.

"It was a day of anxiety for a lot of people, particularly the many people at Super League who'd had to put tools down for many months while we waited for that appeal. For me personally, I was busy the whole time because the shut-down orders didn't impact on me directly.

"But I can remember I had office space right near Mal Meninga and Terry Lamb and Graham Annesley and Ian Schubert and many, many other people who had waited patiently for this day to come."

Super League referee and administrator Annesley says of News: "They kept everyone employed because they were confident they were going to win on appeal.

"We really didn't know whether we were going to have any more involvement in the game. If we'd lost on appeal, we were all effectively finished, really."

Shane Richardson, the garrulous and emotional CEO at News-aligned Cronulla and a recruiter for the rebel competition, thought it would lose at 2.15pm and he would be back repossessing cars and televisions in Brisbane before the year was out.

Name-checking his club chairman and father of supermodel Elle McPherson, he says now: "Peter Gow was there (in court) for Cronulla. I thought 60-40 the ARL would win it so I was preparing myself for unemployment again. It would have been the third time in 15 months.

"(In 1996) me and (coach) John Lang had sat in dressing rooms with our heads in our hands saying 'I hope News Limited are smarter than we think they are because they don't look that smart'."

(Lang's recollection is that he said 'you know what really terrifies me, Richo? I don't think these News Limited blokes are any smarter than us. It's terrifying, isn't it?' adding today: "They might have known how to run a newspaper company but generally, they were hopeless.")

The Shark pair's pessimism proved unjustified. Arthurson was not to feel "up market" for long.

"Yes!" Super League media manager Rebecca Wilson was heard to shout as the findings were read. The ARL's erudite and charismatic chief executive at the time, John Quayle, recalls: "I just remember how quick it was."

Justice John Lockhart, Justice John Von Doussa, and Justice Ronald Sackville found the loyalty agreements signed by the 20 ARL clubs at the outset of the war illegal under section 4D of the Trade Practices Act. The full bench did not believe the clubs were members of the

League and bound by its rules. They were not, as Justice Burchett had originally determined, in a joint venture together.

The full bench overturned all 37 of Burchett's orders.

Tom Mockridge, Ken Cowley's assistant at the time, says: "I was at Holt Street (News' Surry Hills offices) with Ken and the News Corp team and I think John (Ribot) was down in the courtroom.

"We had a smallish team that went down to the courtroom. We very deliberately kept it tight. One of them sneaked into the bathroom when the first part of the hearing came out (and) sent us a message saying 'we've won' or 'we're up'. The first message we got, to my recollection, is that someone pretended to sneak out for a pee."

Arthurson recalls: "I was sitting between Colin Love and John Quayle. I just. … they could see it on my face. They couldn't believe it either.

"Their reason was, they said, under corporate law (News) were entitled to start another competition.

"I was to say many times later that it was like playing the same team twice, under the same set of rules, with the only difference being the new referee and winning 100-0 the first week, then losing 100-0 the next."

In his book, published in late 1997 (from which the sentence directly above is drawn), Arthurson makes the point that Justice Burchett had 51 days to hear all the evidence in the case and to make judgements on who was telling the truth. He had found that News had not acted in good faith, that Brisbane Broncos had been "clandestine".

The full bench, however, had not allowed themselves to be concerned with that.

News never tried to disprove the accusations of dishonesty, Arthurson wrote. "They were prepared to cop that sort of humiliation in the interests of the bigger picture.

"This wasn't justice as I had grown up understanding it in Australia.

"I will go to my grave never understanding how the law could reward proven dishonesty and deceit."

But as Quayle will explain later in this book, he was not stunned at all. "This was a case purely on Trade Practices," Quayle told me in his interview for *Two Tribes*. "A lot of people didn't understand that. We did."

The full bench's only finding in the ARL's favour was that the "rebel" clubs did breach an annual agreement with the league by switching to Super League in 1995 and that this would entitle the ARL to damages. "Justin Burchett saw News Ltd and Super League Pty Ltd as predators," wrote legal analyst John Slee the next day. "The appeal judges see News Ltd and Super League as a service provider for the clubs and players."

Tellingly, while Burchett had used quite emotive language to describe News Limited's raid, the appeals judges made it clear their approach had been - as Quayle says - altogether more dispassionate.

"A decision as to where the best interests of the game lie is not one that lends itself to judicial determination," they wrote in their judgement. "It is quite a different question to one which asks where the best interests of THE LEAGUE lies."

To say emotions ran high as the decision was read out would be to state the bleeding obvious - but only one side was bleeding. Quayle would later be quoted as saying "the court says that as long as you do things underhand, it's OK.

"It's hard for any organisation to come to grips with the fact it's legal to secretly plot to take half a game's assets."

Laurie Daley, who would become Super League's Australia captain, was watching with his Canberra Raiders team-mates as events unfolded 280km away. Perhaps symbolically given the freewheeling era that was about to end, they were in a nightclub - because it was the club's presentation night that evening.

"We all gathered at Queanbeyan Leagues Club upstairs to watch it on the big screen," Daley, now a successful media personality, recalls.

"None of us could believe what was happening because the judgement in the first case was pretty scathing and then they overturned it and we were sitting there and we really didn't know what to do!

"We didn't know whether to cheer … we were stunned. Even the people covering it on television were stunned with the decision, you know? Kev Neil was there, he was off doing phone calls with Ribes and Ken Cowley."

(Neil had enjoyed a schooner or two in Sydney, then flown back to Canberra for more).

"I just remember us having a beer and trying to figure out how it was going to work and then they started to organise meetings with Kevin and the team at the Raiders and then meeting Lachlan (Murdoch) and Ken Cowley - mostly Ken Cowley.

"Even though it happened, it was quite surreal. It was like 'hmm, is this really happening? Is this going ahead?'."

One witness says some players even turned their backs to the big screen and bared their buttocks "in jubilation". They used to call them "browneyes".

Back in Sydney, the Australian Rugby League's public affairs manager John Brady was trying to stage-manage the passage of Arthurson and Quayle from the steps of the courthouse to the NSW Leagues Club less than 100m across the road. In the way was a boiling sea of cameras and outstretched dictaphones.

"We held them back, went to a room, talked about how we'd handle it," Brady says. "The plan was: we'd say just a few words downstairs and then go across the street. As we came down the lift, I told them to wait on the corner and I'd go up to meet the press corps and tell them that's what we were going to do … which was probably naive at the time.

"Arko and Quayley started to walk behind me and suddenly I'm in the way. I had to get out of the way. They weren't supposed to move until after I came back. That was understandable. It was hard for them to sit around. I'd realise that if I'd been through it a few times."

When I visited him at his high rise retirement apartment on the Gold Coast on New Year's Day in 2020, Arthurson seemed to remain wounded by the judgement.

"Justice Burchett, he was so definite about his findings," he said, shaking his head in the manner those of us who watched him at media conferences for years find so familiar, the loose skin on his tanned face trembling.

"He ruled very much against News Limited. In fact, his exact words were that even if they were entitled to do (what they did) under corporate law, he still would have ruled against it because of the way they carried on and the way they handled things which was totally wrong.

"He gave them an awful blast, you know? He was absolutely scathing in his views on News Limited and the way they acted.

"And then … three blokes who knew absolutely nothing about the game overturned all his rulings. I think they were from South Australia or somewhere.

"I was just devastated by that. I just couldn't believe it."

Geoff Cousins, the CEO of ARL benefactor Optus Vision, has a different take on events that day, which paved the way for warring competitions in Australian rugby league the following year.

"It wasn't News's success," he argues during an almost hour-long interview for this book. "What happened was, the … ACCC (Australian Competition and Consumer Commission) wanted to run a case on the definitions of market.

"So the reason that they did not want that original decision to stand … if it stood as a precedent, it took away a lot of their ability to determine what a market was and what it wasn't. A lot of competition law is based on that. They put an enormous effort into getting that decision overturned and that's the basis on which it was overturned: the definition of the market. It wasn't overturned on anything whatever to do with the sport or what was happening.

"It was basically (the ACCC's) Professor Allan Fells. He was a significant player in all the matters relating to the competition between us and Testra and Foxtel … and so-on.

He is one of the more impressive people I have ever met. Not many people have ever concerned me, including Murdoch and Packer. But Allan Fells did. You never quite knew what he was thinking. He was a ferocious sort of regulator and very effective, too. I have great respect for what he did. He was truly trying to protect consumers.

"We would have preferred, of course, that the original decision stood because it gave us 100 percent of everything but I wasn't dismayed by it in any sense because we were still in a very strong position."

NSW Supreme Court judge Geoff Bellew counters: "The ACCC weren't a party to the proceedings. It was News Ltd against the ARL. It's an interesting theory but it's not the way things work."

With her exclamation of "yes" - ironically, that was Optus's advertising slogan - Wilson betrayed the elation that would later turn to celebration in the News Limited camp.

News Limited executive Malcolm Noad says: "One of the things I remember about the day was how cool Ken Cowley was. We were all pretty excited and it got around the office pretty quickly, around Mahogany Row, but we went in to see Ken and it was business as usual."

And while Cousins was not as disappointed in the verdict as you might expect, nor was Ribot as jubilant. He describes his mood as he strode out of court 21A as primarily one of relief.

"…because we'd built up something and it had been going for quite a bit of time. There was a lot of emotion and the further we went into it, we just knew: what we were doing, we believed in.

"If the decision didn't go our way, I'd hate to think what would have happened. I don't think it would have been a very good period in my life.

"Someone would have got put on the cross and I think I would have been the first one there."

GOALPOSTS SHIFT BUT OBSTACLE REMAINS

By STEVE MASCORD, Sydney Morning Herald, Monday October 7 1996

IT'S funny how, even after the most cataclysmic of upheavals, some things never change.

Now that the league world has been altered forever - or at least for now - by Friday's Federal Court judgment, you'll hear people talking about compromise.

How naive. We are no closer to compromise, no closer to the interests of the game coming first, than we have ever been.

Despite the goalposts being shifted irrevocably, the same old obstacle is still there. There have been a number of occasions over the past two years when we could have had a truly "super" league - a competition which, regardless of who ran it. would do the game proud.

The single biggest reason why the ARL did not embrace the idea in the first place was not ideological. It was contractual. The ARL had a contract with Optus Vision and Channel 9 to broadcast rugby league.

When the clubs tried to jump ship and play games for someone else, they took the "someone else" to court and won. Fair enough.

But, since Friday, there are two governing bodies of rugby league in Australia. Whereas before the ARL had some justification in saying it was defending the game, because that is what it ran. any reasonable observer will tell you Phillip Street must now defend itself.

And Super League is doing its best for those who stuck by it. That's fair enough, too.

But who is left to look after the game?

The ARL still has a contractual obligation to provide programming for Optus and Channel 9 - it is so dependent on both it couldn't wave the white flag even if it wanted to.

If merging clubs and joining Super League is in the interests of the game, don't expect the ARL to do it.

Optus has shown its desperation to preserve something for its pay TV service by pledging more money to the ARL's ailing clubs. By doing so, it has indicated it expects the ARL to fight to the death.

Even if more clubs defect, the ARL must provide a product for Optus Vision, no matter what.

Super League has its own vested interests.

It might be in the game's interests to have a team in Wollongong but the Steelers sacked Graham Murray and are, therefore, persona non grata.

Super League doesn't like Manly because it's Ken Arthurson's club,and reckons the Gold Coast are a joke despite the undisputed size of their market.

As a turbulent month gets more turbulent, we are once again close to a pretty good outcome for rugby league.

A national competition, the Sydney mergers everyone always thought were necessary, the

sort of international media exposure others would kill for and the backing of a media empire. Admittedly, the death or denigration of traditional sports administration is sad and regrettable, but the law says it is legal.

Heavens above, if things developed a certain way over the next couple of months, we might even be able to sit back and look at the torment of the past two years as "a necessary evil".

Is there any chance of people putting aside their biases and vested interests and taking advantage of the second or third chance they don't really deserve?

Penrith really have no obligation to hold merger talks with anyone, and Super League needn't bother trying to give the old ARL administration a role in their competition.

But what the heck - how about you do it anyway?

CHAPTER 2

"What did you say to him?"

AS you would expect, News Limited and Super League threw a party on the night of October 4.

But first there was a meeting in John Ribot's penthouse apartment, above the breakaway's offices in Elizabeth Street, Sydney. The mood was buoyant, although Super League staffer Trevor McKewen would have been celebrating anyway - because it was his 38th birthday.

"Someone said 'we've got about 48 hours to get one of the ARL clubs'. If we'd done that, it would have been very different," Super League's marketing manager, Gary Pearse, recalls now.

A few city books away, ARL executive Greg Mitchell says, after the judgement and the brief media doorstop "it was into John (Quayle)'s office to figure out the next steps - which included seeking leave to appeal to the High Court."

Maurice Lindsay, the charismatic head of the News-aligned British rugby league, had flown the flag for the breakaway the previous year in Australia, including launching an ill-fated Super League alternative, Global League. With Aussie Super Leaguers check-mated by court orders, Lindsay took over. The former bookmaker and soccer club chairman had been watching news reports from the courtroom in a Sydney hotel suite, with former international forward and News recruit, Ian Schubert.

"Arko was the first to speak ….," Lindsay says at his home on England's north-west coast. "He said 'there will be two competitions next year'. So Schuey gave me a high five and said 'well, we've won'.

"...a big relief for Rupert but also a big relief for Ken Cowley. I love the way Australians do things quickly, within minutes. Calls went around, 'right there's a party on tonight…'."

That knees-up was on the border of the city and Surry Hills, at what is now the Pullman Hyde Park. Super League hired a function room and there were conference calls and video links to News Corporation and rugby league officials from other countries.

The revolution was underway.

"It was celebratory," says business consultant Eric Fleming, whose engagement with Super League had finished a couple of months previously but who nonetheless scored an invitation.

"People were giving each other bear hugs and slapping each other on the back. They were very happy - as they should have been."

Ribot recalls: "We partied. I remember we had hook-ups and links all around the world and we spoke to everybody and it was just an enormous sigh of relief because we'd gone so far, got beaten so badly and then got ourselves in a position to come back and prove what we were talking about, the argument we put up was valid and it was vindicated - the right decision was handed down.

"There was certainly no tomorrow that night. Everyone partied hard all around the world.

"In some ways it was pretty surreal after that. It was a great night and then the next day was … 'wow, now we've got to get this thing going' … and away we went."

Lindsay recounts: "Ken Cowley made a speech and then he came to me and he said 'right, Rupert's on the phone, he's in New York, he needs to speak to you directly.'

"(Murdoch) said 'I'm coming over at the weekend, can we have a meeting? I said 'sure'. I heard him say to Ken Cowley 'Have you been onto the (Sydney Daily) *Telegraph*?'. Ken said 'yeah'. Rupert said 'how many pages have you got?' Ken said 'seven'.

"Rupert said to him 'what's wrong with the first 27?'."

Super League junior pathways boss - an unofficial social director - Barry Russell says: "It was a big night, as you can imagine. We'd had six months where we'd come to work and we weren't allowed to work.

"Once the button got pressed, holy shit it was on. We had a really skinny crew to try and get a competition up and running. We worked hard and we played hard."

McKewen: "We still believed the dream, we believed the rhetoric from drinking the Kool-Aid. There was genuine excitement: 'now we're going to get this thing on the road, now we're going to show how it's really done'.

"It was misplaced. I don't know if 'optimism' is the right word. It's misplaced bravado."

The bravado involved a belief - shared by many fans - that the ARL was on the verge of collapse. Ribot admits even now: "I thought they were getting towards the end".

"RIP Australian Rugby League, born 1908, died 1996," read a cartoon tombstone in the *Sun-Herald*.

ARL public affairs manager John Brady: "There was stuff about 'the ARL is dead' and if you read the clippings there were plenty of people jumping on that. News (publications) were doing what they were doing. I've got no trouble with that. But there were plenty of people in there with them saying that.

"There was this huge period, I think it was the next two weeks, where there was this speculation News were going to pick off clubs. They were going to pick off Parramatta. They were going to pick off St George."

Quayle, speaking to me from his Hunter Valley winery, says: "We knew it wasn't over. We knew we'd be getting picked off, that News Limited … we knew that they had more money."

News' Tom Mockridge recalls: "I do remember going out to speak to Parramatta with Lachlan (Murdoch) in the next 48 hours or something (after the judgement). And I can certainly remember meeting Norths. Everyone was talking. There was certainly no harm in talking."

But the gripping accounts of ARL clubs preparing to jump ship were, Mockridge insists, largely overplayed. "News by then had decided it had spent enough.

"It was going to spend more but it was already committed to the clubs it had. There wasn't an appetite within News from Ken and Rupert to step up again with any big investments."

Lindsay insists: "Parramatta is one that we should have had. We lost by one vote. If we'd had Parramatta, I think they would have caved in, the ARL."

By the Tuesday, October 8, Eels chairman Alan Overton confirmed Penrith's Roger Cowan had called suggesting that, if the competitions got together, so should the two clubs.

Cowan, who died in 2017, inspired fierce loyalty at the foot of the mountains - "anything that Roger Cowan was involved in was always full of inspiration and confidence," then-Panthers media manager Rob Weaver insists - but Parra chief executive Denis Fitzgerald was no fan. "Roger Cowan organised a meeting at the old South Sydney Leagues Club, across the road from Redfern Oval, where a number of Sydney clubs went and Roger spoke in favour of staying with the ARL - but within a month he had taken the money and run with it and signed over to Super League.

"The money was a deciding factor in what he wanted to do with the leagues club and with all the amalgamations, all the (licenced) clubs they wanted to take over."

And so despite the wagons slowly circling in the ARL camp, News still had enough money to crush the establishment and prevent it running a meaningful competition the following year. Optus Vision, the broadcaster for the ARL and major sponsor, was the only realistic possible saviour.

Optus' CEO, Geoffrey Cousins - a firebrand who reputedly once threatened to throw a fellow board member out a high rise window - initially told Quayle the cupboard was bare.

"He said 'John, I can't contribute any more'," Quayle, known as the 'Canon' or, if you're HG and Roy, 'Monsignor', says. "I said 'unless we can get more money, we're not going to have a competition, we're not going to have a 10-team competition'. "

Cousins doesn't remember telling Quayle there was no more cash, "but I don't say that he's wrong. As a businessman the first thing you say to someone who asks for more money is … 'there isn't any'. Then you go away and figure out whether you need to get any.

"If I did say that, it sounds a bit odd that I did … if I did, that was just a 'we'll have a look at it and we'll give you the least amount that we possibly can.'"

Already bitterly disillusioned at the events of October 4 and on his way out of rugby league - pretty much for good - Quayle enjoyed his finest moment as an administrator during these dark days, according to Brady.

"That was the amazing thing about Quayle," Brady says. "Over those next few days, he went back to his farm - which very few people could contact him at, at the time. No doubt he was knocked around but over those three days as I remember, is when he pulled Geoff Cousins in and got the Optus money.

"…and came back and got the clubs together and essentially said he'd have the money for them. That took News and everybody by surprise."

Optus' $30 million rescue package had miraculously become $120 million in time for the first editions to come out on Wednesday, October 9. "Rubbish. Absolute rubbish," Cousins insists.

"I was the bloke who was getting the money and I never went to the shareholders and said 'give me another $120 million'. Can I remember exactly what the figure was? No. But it wasn't anything like that. That's nonsense. I don't know where that comes from.

"Not anything anywhere near that dimension. My recollection of the whole commitment we made (over the course of the entire war) was more $30 million to $50 million. Something around there. A hundred and 20 million? No way! God help me! That's madness!"

What had happened is that, in the race to inspire public confidence, Optus Vision's commitment had been dressed up as being for a much longer period than it actually was - and the sponsorship had been added to inflate the total. It would take John Quayle's successor to convince Cousins' successors to actually deliver a commitment beyond 1997.

International centre Chris Johns was Super League's player representative. His close friend Geoff Carr was a senior ARL official. When Cousins announced Optus was bailing out the ARL, Johns said to Carr: "Jesus, Freddy Krueger's back".

Whatever the details, the infusion kept the ARL in the fight and prevented some of its clubs from either going broke or being forced into the arms of Super League. When we talk of South Sydney's survival now, we focus on a march down George Street on November 12, 2000. Without Cousins, they may not have survived 1996.

"The way I got the money is I had a very supportive group of shareholders who'd backed me all the way," Cousins says. "I always met with them face to face on things like that because … I was asking an unreasonable amount from them, quite frankly, in many cases.

"I went to them and said 'this is what I need and I need it now' and they gave it to me. Part of the reason they did that was we already, with them, had a lot of runs on the board."

Cousins' fierce independence and unconventional methods had won him almost undying trust from his shareholders. "We were doing things they hadn't really expected. A lot of those shareholders had serious doubts about whether we could run a contest successfully with News and Telstra so we were building the network much faster than Telstra. We passed many more homes than they had and nobody thought we'd be able to do that. We brought both Seven and Nine in as shareholders, small ones. Five or seven per cent, something like that.

"The big shareholders thought that was absolutely impossible. They said 'that is never going to happen' because Seven was half-owned by News and by Telstra so they were

stunned by that. After that happened, they probably thought we could do things that we couldn't actually do. When I went to them and said 'OK, we won the (Burchett) court case, we have 100 percent (of rugby league)' … I had said to them when we won it 'don't necessarily believe this is going to stay like this'. So when I went to them and asked for the dough, they gave it to me like *that*. My recollection on how quickly that happened is not in any sense precise but I seem to remember it was not weeks but days."

With the funding secured, the likes of Souths and Gold Coast signed on immediately. Others, such as the aforementioned Eels and Saints, were much tougher nuts to crack.

Mitchell says: "I can recall sitting in (Quayle late personal assistant) Micki Braithwaite's anteroom there, just outside John's office, waiting for a call to come through from either Denis Fitzgerald or Alan Overton to let the League know of Parramatta's position - which ultimately was one of remaining in the ARL.

"But it was a critical one, and one people were sweating on."

St George? Publicly, the most famous traditional club wanted compromise rather than offering to support the ARL. The club's chairman, Warren Lockwood, said Super League had offered the club its Melbourne franchise.

Brady: "There's a meeting that was terribly significant where Warren Lockwood, who is often maligned, essentially got up and said 'don't worry, I'll carry St George'.

"He hadn't had his meeting yet but he said he'd carry them. That allowed Quayle to focus on Parramatta. Quayle focused on Parramatta big time. I remember watching him make calls and he was amazing, just amazing.

"It didn't come down to who was closest to leaving. It came down to where the dominos fell. They had a crack at Balmain … in that week as I remember it, Balmain were as certain as anyone could be … most of the clubs in the room were able to say they were there (with the ARL)

"St George couldn't say they were there for sure but Lockwood said they would be.

"At that stage Parramatta became the last domino in the piece. There's a lot of things I've seen written over the years about 'so and so stuck solid' … a lot of it came down to who was in the chain at the time, not who was the most or least important.

"You get to the Parramatta meetings after Murdoch's on the phone and all that … Lachlan led the team to go out and present to the Parramatta board. Then Quayle went out to present to the Parramatta board.

"I watched Quayle many, many times as a journo during my time in rugby league and saw him from the inside for a year which was a good privilege but that week was pretty amazing on his part.

"He held it together when … I can't research the other side, never really talked to them about it but there was an element of 'geez, we've won' on the other side where it should have been 'we're cactus' on our side, Quayle found a way to keep going, albeit that he was knocked around by it.

"Those were the two turning points as I remember them: Lockwood getting up and being solid … and Quayle worked hard on Parramatta."

On October 10, I wrote in the *SMH* that every club bar Parramatta had agreed to stay in the ARL. On October 11, it was front page news that the Eels had now signed on, too.

"We were never going to go with News Limited," Denis Fitzgerald says in his interview for this book.

When I ask the iconic and feisty western Sydney administrator what the vote was, he reaches into a cupboard at his home and pulls out a picture of the Parramatta board as it was in October, 1996. "I think it might have been, for the eight people, five-to-three.

"There was certainly a lot of bullshit going around. I couldn't believe anything that was coming out from the News people.

"I didn't even want to talk to them. If we had gone to News or Super League at the time, we probably would have been in the order of $20 million better off.

"And we were a key factor, certainly a key team.

"I remember at the time we didn't share in the ARL handouts that came via Optus and Packer because we were one of the few ARL clubs that had some cash reserves. From a Leagues Club point of view, of course, we had $7 million in cash.

"My view - and I had a degree of control, 'influence' might be a better word, at Parramatta - was that News Limited were trying to steal the game at its peak after it doing so well.

"And I thought 'what have News Limited done to deserve to take over our game?' Our game belongs to the people and all the clubs who had been in there, for varying years, since 1908.

"All the clubs, or just about all the clubs, were owned by the members and that translated to membership of licensed leagues clubs that supported the Sydney clubs.

"I thought 'we don't need News Limited' and the way they went about it - especially Ribot, who I still have a degree of hatred for - it was all about the money.

"We were one of the big players in terms of getting four internationals (Jim Dymock, Jarrod McCracken, Jason Smith and Dean Pay) from Canterbury, which I was pleased about for more reasons than one because of what 'Bullfrog' (Canterbury chief executive Peter Moore) had done."

Shane Richardson says Super League's talks with the ARL clubs were "taking place before" the appeal but "became more fervent" afterwards. "I thought I had two clubs over the line, three clubs over the line.

"I was sure I had the Crushers over the line but at the last minute they stayed. I thought I had North Sydney over the line but at the last minute they stayed and … neither of them survived. In both those cases, if they'd taken the money they'd still be alive today. - there's no doubt in my mind whatsoever.

"It was right down to the wire. In the case of the Crushers it was a last-minute emotional decision by (chairman Dick) 'Tosser' Turner. And the players took control (at North Sydney), like they did at Newcastle. Some of the leading players were being paid a shitload of money by the ARL, like Jason Taylor.

"They took control of last-minute proceedings and forced the turnaround.

"North Sydney would have been the dominant side north of the harbour and there's no doubt the Crushers would have survived in Queensland. We had the CEO on board. Darryl Van de Velde wanted to change. It was a lay down misère. (Brisbane business consultant) Bruce Hatcher was involved in that too. Bruce was a great supporter of the change.

(The Crushers' decision against Super League came very early in the war, in 1995).

"We had St George pretty close too. Certainly we'd met with the players. We got a few players out of St George, Jason Stevens and these guys who wanted a change."

The actual football? No-one cared.

Perth sacked their coach - the biggest news cycle story we have in modern professional sport - and it was the last paragraph of a "spill" inside the East Coast papers.

That man was Peter Mulholland, a beacon of the schoolboy and junior games who was - such was the craziness of the time - subsequently picked up by Paris Saint-Germain and had the satisfaction of beating the Reds in the World Club Challenge in June the following year.

A celebrated talent scout who has recently faced significant health challenges, he says now of his sacking: "It wasn't a surprise to me to a certain degree, in that I said if they were keeping a particular player, you know, it was either him or me.

(That player has elsewhere been reported to be enfant terrible Julian O'Neill)

"They said … 'it'll be you'.

"It was very unsavoury. It didn't come as a shock. It came as a disappointment."

Meanwhile, with Optus Vision's fightback on behalf of the ARL, Ribot's own optimism from the previous week about having the only major rugby league competition in Australia the following year evaporated.

"There was conversation … there's a guy who was in charge of Channel Nine at the time, I think his name was David Leckie," Ribot recalls.

"He was on the ARL board. I said 'David, until Kerry and Rupert get together and say 'we've got to stop this', this is going to go on. I'm going to go on. We're not blinking at the moment'.

"Rupert didn't blink once. All the bills got paid, it wasn't a matter of 'we're chasing some money, we've got to ring them up'. We put our budgets in, the money was always in the bank, the clubs got paid."

The ARL lodged its application for leave to appeal. On Thursday, it was revealed News expected its clubs to repay their investment by 2007. They're still waiting, presumably.

But twin competitions in just a few months? That still seemed more unimaginable to the general public than the Parramatta Panthers or the Melbourne Dragons.

"Even when the ARL won the first court case, there was this feeling of 'oh yeah, they'll all come together and eventually the comp will look like what Super League want it to look like and there'll be a bit of give and take'," Laurie Daley says.

"Ninety-seven, leading into that year, again most people thought a deal would get done. When it didn't … it felt quite weird, you know?"

Quayle said at the time: "Nobody wants there to be two competitions but that is what the court wanted."

According to *Rugby League Week*, "on the afternoon of October 4, construction workers were halfway through tearing down the purpose-built Super League grandstand at Adelaide Oval when word came through to down tools.

"At the same time, Hunter Mariners official Michael Hagan was whipping all comers in a table tennis tournament at Mariners headquarters - he was nicknamed Arko, the ruler of the game."

('I don't remember the story - and I don't remember being referred to as that either!' - Hagan says)

Ribot, speaking in a *Sydney Morning Herald* feature, added: "What we have to do now is put a face on Super League."

Canberra prop Luke Davico says now "I remember it was an exciting time to finally get the go-ahead because there were all these bells and whistles about Super League - what it was going to do and where it was going to go. We'd been sitting on it for over 12 months."

But Manly halfback Geoff Toovey, in the *Sun-Herald*, suggested players should strike for one competition. "Two competitions will ruin the game," he claimed. Chris Johns retorted: "I didn't see any ARL players striking when we were all excluded from the World Cup."

Forward John Cross plus utility Dave Watson, meanwhile, prepared to go to court after signing ARL contracts but then being recruited by Super League clubs.

"All the information I was getting was that it won't be a split comp, they'll work it out during the off-season," says Cross, with whom I went to school. "That's why I ended up signing with a Super League club,"

Western Suburbs chairman Jim Marsden says of the period: "I'm a lawyer. I know court cases can go either way. Which every way they go, go in and settle the damn thing! That's from a lawyer's perspective but also from a rugby league administrator's perspective, you weren't going to have two competitions running side-by-side being successful. Murdoch knew that, Packer knew that, everybody knew that. You needed a resolution."

In an interview with film-maker Brian Cobb for an unreleased documentary called *The Super League War,* Quayle recalls that during this period: "We get a phone call from Kerry saying 'Cowley wants to meet with me. You OK with that?'. We said yes and Ken (Arthurson) said 'mate, this could be good for us. Do you think this can happen?' I said 'well, it's the first time they're together at this stage'."

Could a resolution be at hand? Could those expecting a single competition in 1997 be proven correct?

"And we waited in my office for Ken Cowley to come back to us. The phone call came and it was Ken Cowley and we said 'how did you go?' And his words were 'not very well'.

"We get a phone call a little bit later from Kerry. We're both on conference phone, Ken and I, and we said the same thing to Kerry: 'Well, what did you say?'.

"He said: 'I told him to get fucked'."

Balmain chief executive Danny Munk now suggests that had Ribot answered the phone one night during this period, the Tigers may have jumped and - like the breakaway's other Sydney clubs - remained stand-alone entities today.

"There was a meeting between the club and Ribot and Cowley," Munk - still working in the licensed clubs industry - says during a Zoom conversation.

"They put a number of things on the table. We went away and had a think about it. Our board had a fairly heartful chat and said 'look, go back to Ribot and friends and put these following questions and let them know we've got a meeting coming', I think it was a Friday night.

"We were meeting at a place in Darling Harbour and we'd also organised after that meeting, another meeting with the ARL.

"For some reason or another, and I don't know why still to this day, I must have left countless messages. I think Ribot was staying at the Sheraton On The Park during that time. For some reason there were no call-backs. No response, no nothing.

"Because they didn't come back to answer questions and probably ... whether they just thought they had us. I think through following court cases and various other things, they were given the impression they had us.

"They felt us, Souths and Norths were not clubs they had to put as much effort into because we were that desperate. What they didn't understand was the value that the board put in the Tigers brand and the fact they also felt the ARL was the one that was treating them fairly.

Ribot says it was quite the contrary.

"(Iconic Tigers hooker and later director) Ben Elias had been a fan of Super League and at one stage he was the only one that voted in favour of Balmain joining us - I think the feeling was that they were no hope," Ribot laughs, before recalling a much closer call earlier in the war.

"At one stage Easts agreed to come over and it was left in the hands of solicitors. There was a very strong directive that came from Rupert: 'we're going to resolve this, we're going to bring these parties together' and there was a meeting organised with Easts because obviously of Packer (who had strong ties to the club).

"And we sat at a hotel on the park and the legal teams got together and there was a guy called Tom Mockridge.

"The deal was done in my mind. I thought 'wow, this is a great day for us' because I thought once Easts jump, it's all over. I'm thinking that happened much earlier (than October 1996).

"But the deal was done for them to come over. We had a few deals done … but the Easts thing, all the legal people were together in agreement and I gave it to Tom Mockridge and he said we're going to sit on this for the weekend and we missed our opportunity.

"I still don't know why. If you asked me 'when Easts decided to go, why didn't that happen?', the only person to answer that would be Tom Mockridge. That would have hastened everything up … once you've got Easts, with their relationship with Kerry and James, it was all over."

Responding in an email, Mockridge writes: "I've no

recollection of Easts, but it is true that in April 1995 (when Super League was hurriedly signing players) we got a directive from Ken Cowley at the end of the week after we'd signed England and NZ to stop

("we've spent enough") .

"The following year, after News Limited won the appeal, there were discussions with several ARL clubs, but by then News had no appetite to take another bite. Beside which there was always a lot more going on in the relationship between Rupert and Packer than Easts. John wouldn't have seen all those angles."

October 1996

- Eight Penrith players contested their ARL loyalty contracts. They are told their case may not be heard until after the dual competitions kick off;

- Sydney City Roosters half Adrian Lam was forced to pull out of a PNG-Kiwis Test, which the Kiwis won 64-0, because the other countries were aligned to the breakaway competition.

- In announcing their on-field structures for the following year, the ARL acknowledged its rural support with a pre-season country carnival.

- The Super League coaches attempted to right a long-standing wrong by introducing a mid-season poaching ban. The game is still trying to get that one right.

- Super League would offer $3 million to its premiers and an additional $1 million for the championship-winning players to split.

- Seven Network owner Kerry Stokes claimed Optus Vision didn't have the $120 million it had - reportedly - promised the ARL.

LET THE SONG AND DANCE BEGIN

By Steve Mascord, Sydney Morning Herald, Tuesday January 14, 1997

A MAN in his mid-20s is crossing Railway Parade, Lidcombe, in late December, proudly wearing his most treasured Christmas present a Canterbury Super League jersey.

It's the most traditional of the new competition's strip designs; the familiar blue V, albeit sharpened at the point, on a white background. The only hint of cable TV flashiness is the fact the V also extends down the back of the shirt, perhaps allowing the wearer to put it on backwards if the front gets dirty.

Clearly quite chuffed with himself, our Bulldog is taken aback when a couple of metres from the sidewalk he finds himself confronted by an angry motorist "Get it off, you mug," the driver bellows from the window of his Toyota Corolla. "You should be ashamed of yourself, wearing that thing."

Our Belmore buddy shuffles off, chastened.

The moral of our (true) story is not that people can be awfully rude and intolerant. What this rather innocuous anecdote proves is that thank heavens someone in Sydney still cares about rugby league.

One man cares enough about Super League and Canterbury to ask for a $115 jersey for Christmas and wear it proudly. Another cares enough about the ARL and its history to berate him for it.

The first time much of Sydney thought about rugby league since October 4, when Super League had its landslide Federal Court appeal victory, was on New Year's Day.

Unfortunately, it took the sight of North Sydney captain Jason Taylor being expelled from the Sydney Cricket Ground, during a limited-overs cricket match, to do the job.

With two competitions, there will be more games of league to watch in the months ahead than anyone but the most maniacal of supporters could wish for.

But as the Australian Rugby League and Super League prepare to spend unprecedented sums on promoting the sport, the biggest fear confronting both must be: "What if we hold a party and no-one comes?"

Can the financial resources of a couple of media empires undo all the harm done during the past two of league's 102 years?

We're about to find out; brace yourself for the biggest hard sell in Australian sporting history. From the end of this month, you'll have Brad Fittler, Andrew Ettingshausen, Paul Harragon and Laurie Daley staring at you from as many billboard, television or cinema screen and full-page newspaper advertisements as you can think of.

Visit your local shopping centre and you may have them staring at you in the flesh. You'll see so much of "Freddie", "ET", "Chief;, "Lozza" and their mates that, by comparison, your immediate family will seem like complete strangers.

Both sides are keeping their battle plans under wraps, but this week we tried to get some insight into just how they intend to do what some sports-come-lately types hope is impossible: get you talking about, watching and, heavens above, even going to the footy again.

PRE-SEASON: In three weeks the war will be on sans pleasantries. From January 31 to February 2, Super League's second annual World Nines will be staged at the North Queensland Cowboys' Stockland Stadium. While Super League will be showing off its high-profile Australian, British and New Zealand sides, it is interesting that the "World Vision" has its limits. Last year's financial failure in Suva has forced organisers, to rein in the number of countries represented from 16 to 12. The ARL's two-day World Sevens, a week later at the Sydney Football Stadium, will have at least 11 international teams - an indication the ARL is intent on rebuilding its empire quickly. The rival bodies' pre-season trials reflect slightly different philosophies. The ARL is conducting a two-round Country

Carnival on February 15 and 22, sending teams everywhere from Gladstone to Moruya. Two games are to be televised. Super League clearly does not want to detract from its opening night on February 28, when Cronulla meet Canberra at the Sydney Football Stadium, and is shielding its stars from the bright lights, with games in places such as Suva and Wanganui.

ADVERTISING: Both sides have recently changed advertising agencies as they prepare to splurge at least $15 million on ads beginning at the end of this month. The ARL, which is reportedly spending $5 million, switched from Singleton Advertising to new outfit Brown Melhuish Fishlock. Super League, whose account is valued between $10 million and $15 million, has moved from Mojo Partners to Foxtel's advertisers, Young and Rubicam, whose managing director Gary Kearley last year described Super League as "the biggest brand launch in Australia" for 1997. Neither side is saying much about the content of its ads, although Super League's will be "match specific", a departure from the image-building "Simply The Best" ARL commercials. Ray Beattie, Norths chairman and head of the ARL's marketing group, which includes representatives of the ad agency, Optus and Channel 9, said the ARL's promotional onslaught would not necessarily be revolutionary but would be "very, very good".

THE SALES PITCH: "Rugby league has taken a severe bashing recently and it's our job to make sure confidence is restored," said Beattie. Cronulla chief executive Shane Richardson believes the public is more confused than disillusioned: "They don't know what Super League is," he said this week. "People were asking me 'What's going on? "I think that once they can touch it, once the football is on again and they begin to understand they can go to their local ground and see teams from overseas and things like that they will be interested." At a conference in Manly in November, the ARL clubs attempted to distill what advantages they had over Super League. "We've got the real game," said Parramatta chief executive

Denis Fitzgerald. "Not something that's been made up." Richardson said he hoped the game would benefit from the competition but admitted Super League hoped its average supporter would be a little younger than the ARL's. "We've got to keep faith with our grassroots," he said, "and then go out and attract the other people. If there's 40,000 people at the SCG for a Swans game, they're not all Aussie rules supporters." Super League wants to gain some street cred.

GETTING THE MESSAGE OUT: While the rival headquarters plot their publicity blitzes, the clubs are getting involved as never before. "We need to do the advertising, the complimentary tickets to schoolkids, the personal appearances; a lot of it we've done before but we need to be more consistent," said Fitzgerald. Canberra spokesman Bevan Hannan, whose club has hired a full-time producer, underscores the resources at the disposal of Super League clubs, saying: "There is a budget of $100,000 to promote every home game. That means advertising, pre-match promotions and match-day entertainment. It's a big deal". In Sydney, Canterbury, Penrith and Cronulla players will be scouring beaches, parks and shopping malls in search of a crowd. In Newcastle, Harragon and lock Marc Glanville are drumming up sales in a TV commercial. In Adelaide, the Rams sponsor the TV movie of the week.

SPONSORSHIP: A threat by Dominion Breweries to sue the Auckland Warriors and Super League has seen the new league relent on its policy of "clean skin", or sponsorless, jerseys. At last count, Adelaide, Canberra, Canterbury, Cronulla, Hunter and Penrith were yet to secure major backers. But the Raiders are said to want three times their previous asking price. Most ARL clubs have jersey sponsorship deals continuing from last season and report other corporate support as being at, or above, last year's levels.

TELEVISION: At the time of writing, Super League's free-to-air home had not been determined. Adelaide chief executive Liz Dawson said she hoped expansion clubs would get free-to-air coverage in their home town even if the games were televised live on Foxtel and replayed on free-to-air. The future of ARL telecasts outside NSW and Queensland is uncertain. "TVNZ have a contract with the ARL for a 20-team comp including one from New Zealand," Auckland chief executive Ian Robson said. "I don't know where that leaves them." But ARL spokesman John Brady is upbeat on the issue. "When people talk about their Super League's TV, they include FoxteL and when they talk about ours, they tend to ignore Optus," he said. "Including Optus Vision, we're on everywhere."

A COMPARISON: Canberra and Newcastle: There is ample evidence that, while animosity towards one side or another did surface, it never translated into disillusionment with the sport outside Sydney. A possible exception is Brisbane, where crowds dropped markedly last year. Newcastle, faced with opposition from the Hunter Mariners, had sold 80 per cent of their season tickets by November last year. Canberra's season ticket sales are up 35 per cent and all corporate boxes are sold, with the waiting list growing. The Knights have sold well over half of theirs. Canterbury and Parramatta: Both clubs are aiming to average 15,000 spectators at home games. Canterbury have already passed last year's total of season ticket holders and are pressing on with the "CB Club" membership drive. "We called everyone who did not renew their ticket and found only 10 percent of those who have not renewed did so because they supported the ARL," said Bulldogs spokeswoman Debbie Spillane. "And most of them say they'll come this year anyway." Fitzgerald admitted season ticket sales had been "a bit slow", but added: "Once they see what sort of team we've got, there's no doubt things will pick up."

AND THE WINNER IS ... Is it possible that, rather than sink even deeper into the mire under two administrations, rugby league could be invigorated by the number of deep pockets and keen minds now being applied to its promotion?

"We've got a great product, we just have to get that message out," said Beattie. Even Brady, in the ARL's front trench for what must seem like an age, admitted some good may come out of the split.

"If you gave me a blank page and asked me to write down how to get that result, I wouldn't come up with the current situation. But it could happen."

If rugby league is to be a long-term winner, much of the interest this season will be in which side becomes the medium-term victor.

Since neither will agree on the criteria for deciding a winner (the ARL says quality, Super League leans towards ratings and attendances), you may be none the wiser on that one come the end of this year.

But according to Cronulla marketing manager Richard Fisk, there's no doubt who the short-term winner will be: the footy fan.

Fisk interrupted his latest marketing survey to be interviewed and like just about everyone we spoke to in compiling this article, sounded as though he would be happy to drive you to his team's matches this season. Maybe even shout you a meal and beer afterwards.

Footy players may have gone from being Neville Nobodies to multiple home owners thanks to this battle. But, according to Fisk, the beanie brigade will cash in next.

"Your average football supporter has never been so important; he's never had so many people seeking his business," Fisk said.

"We are always talking to our supporters. Someone who goes to the football this year, he has to be completely spoilt"

Now you may long for the days when there was just one NSW side, one Queensland side and one Australian side. But when was the last time you went to the footy and felt spoilt?

CHAPTER 3

Tour de farce

WHILE all this was happening, Great Britain was on a tour in the South Pacific that was to be such a disaster it blackened the name of Super League south of the equator even as the breakaway was being told it could finally kick off there.

After the First Test at Mt Smart, Auckland, between the Lions and New Zealand - the *First* Test (the teams had already been to Papua New Guinea and Fiji) - the RFL laid off six staff in Leeds and sent 11 players home to save money. One, who was on holiday in Australia, was subsequently asked to come back.

More of that shortly.

As a 27-year-old reporter with a strict agency background, I had rejected most overtures in my two years at the *Sydney Morning Herald* to editorialise. My coverage of the 1994 Kangaroo Tour had been criticised by *Herald* colleagues as too "wire service", with not enough features and colour.

After the Super League court case was handed down, I had holiday time owed and did what I normally did for fun - I followed a rugby league tour around and tried to get copy in the paper without being paid for it. I can vividly recall a shuttle bus dropping me at the Beasley

Avenue gates of what was then Ericsson Stadium, straight from the airport, for that First Test on October 18.

By the time the shambles of a tour was over, and with Super League due to kick-off in Australia the following year, I finally felt like I had something to say aside from reporting the news. I'd witnessed something most Australians had not. For perhaps the first time, 'I' felt confident in referring to myself, in print, in the first person.

On November 12, the following story appeared in the *Sydney Morning Herald*:

"Walking into a Wellington gymnasium during Great Britain's ill-fated tour of New Zealand last month, this reporter noted a game of American football on television monitors suspended above a bank of step machines.

"Checking my watch (2pm Tuesday), I realised it was Monday Night Football, live on Sky Sport. It was Rupert Murdoch's grand plan for world sports in action: attractions which are big domestic grossers, such as soccer in England, league in Australia, union in New Zealand, being shown in prime-time locally while time differences are the empire's biggest ally in allowing it to telecast other sports from its worldwide arsenal live at all hours of the day.

"A perfect plan, it would seem.

"But the question which lingered in the gym that day was: will fitness fanatics in Cincinnati be sweating it out to a Super League game between Canberra and London by the time next year is out?

"Given what I had seen of the Lions tour, there were more than a few reservations.

Super League will this month make one of the biggest announcements in rugby league's history: the world's first trans-hemisphere international club competition of any code. Twenty-two teams from three countries (*actually, four - ed*) will cross the equator for a tournament that is the breakaway's showpiece.

"It's a golden opportunity for league to gain some much-needed credibility in the eyes of old and new fans and the wider international business community. But Super League already has 12 months of international football under its belt and while the jury is out on whether the Euro League was a success or not, no-one can argue that the representative component has been even satisfactory.

"Disasters included playing an England-Wales game the same day as a European Cup soccer match involving England and almost no-one showing up and just 2,000 attending a Test match between New Zealand and Papua New Guinea in Palmerston North.

"Then, last month, the piece de resistance. Eleven Lions players were called home early from New Zealand to save the princely sum of $10,000. One, Tulsen Tollett, was subsequently recalled from Australia, costing around $2,000 in airfares and accommodation anyway.

"At the same time, the British Rugby League laid off six employees and it's claimed that the touring PNG players had been accommodated four-to-a-room during their earlier visit to New Zealand.

"Regardless of the fine football on show in the first two Great Britain-New Zealand Tests last month, the Lions tour to Papua New Guinea, Fiji and New Zealand was an unmitigated disaster.

"The abiding memory of the trek was not the guile of Kiwi halfback Stacey Jones, the rugged defence of Lions centre Kris Radlinski or the magnificent athleticism of New Zealand second rower Stephen Kearney. It was of Welsh prop Rowland Phillips, upon being told he was to be sent home, appearing on television after a final night out with his teammates and reciting drunken poetry like "if you think your life is dire, spare a thought for (Lions forward) Bernard Dwyer".

Viewers of TV3 found it funny. John Ribot would not have.

"The tour lost at least $1 million, more if you count the expense of sending the Great Britain Academy side to New Zealand for curtain-raisers. World Super League director general Maurice Lindsay will point out that the last tour to PNG and New Zealand, in 1990, ran at a big loss, too.

"But there were deeper concerns about just how difficult it will be to implement "the vision" outside 10 Australian stadiums.

"The vision, we're told, is all about marketing, promotion, merchandising and expansion.

Let's start with marketing. Great Britain could not find a sponsor for the tour, BSkyB, which paid £87 million ($180 million) for exclusive rights (to Super League), didn't send any commentators. As for promotions, the players barely appeared in public aside from training and games during the tour.

"There were no post-match functions after the first two Tests and no-one was presented with a cup at full-time in the third. Great Britain complained they weren't even met at Christchurch airport when they arrived.

"The crowds for the Tests were 12,000 (Auckland), 12,000 (Palmerston North) and 9,000 (Christchurch). The Auckland Warriors drew more than 25,000 to a trial match in Christchurch earlier this year.

"There was no entertainment to speak of at any of the grounds and in Christchurch the ground announcer didn't even know the players' names "C Joynt is on for T O'Connor".

"In fact, the New Zealand Maori Rugby League put its parent body to shame when it hosted the Lions in Whangarei. It laid on a band, a cultural dance group and a well-stocked souvenir stall with credit card facilities.

"Which brings us to merchandising. Put simply, the group who made the most out of merchandising during the Test series were a pair of English backpackers who printed up some T-shirts and sold them - often inside the ground - for $10 a pop.

"At most matches all you could buy from the official stand was a poster, a cap or an autograph book. In fact, travelling British fans complained they could not find a Kiwi jersey in any shop in New Zealand. By comparison, All Blacks jerseys are everywhere.

When it comes to expansion, it's more difficult to fault Super League.

"They took the Lions to Fiji for the first time and will commit a percentage of Test gate-takings to developing nations. But a percentage of a 2,000 gate still isn't much, is it?

"In accordance with the grand plan, News Ltd has bought into a big-time sport: Australian rugby league. But in doing so, it has also committed itself to push the cause of a minority sport in 16 other countries.

"That's an undertaking it never had to make to secure the rights to American football, rugby union or soccer. As well as the Brits and the Kiwis, there are league people in places like the Cook Islands, Italy and South Africa who have been encouraged to look upon Murdoch as their fairy godfather.

"If he proves to be just that, we will all look back on the past 24 months as a painful adolescence for the game.

"If he isn't, looking back may be all we are able to do."

Sitting in his lounge room watching the races from Cheltenham, Lindsay says of the tour: "I should have called that off.

"That was in the diary but they had a new chairman, the car dealer. What was his name (Graham Carden)? He drew up the financial projections and we all said 'this won't work'. I'd been a tour manager in years gone by, I knew what worked and what didn't. I thought 'this will be a catastrophe'.

"'No, no. We've got backing for this, the council here and the council there'. So, to cut a long story short, we ran with them.

"I'll never forget Neil Tunnicliffe … Neil was a lovely guy but a dreamer. He took over from me when I left. I said 'listen, this will blow up in our face. This will be a complete disaster. I want to pull out, what do you think?' Because he was sort of an amateur, a lover of the game, he said 'we can't do that, it would be terrible'.

"I said 'yeah but it will be forgotten in two or three months. Let's pull out and save ourselves a lot of cost'.

"He said 'well you asked my opinion and my opinion is no. The press will crucify us'. I said 'the press always crucify us, whatever we do'. So we did it and it was a fucking disaster, as you know."

Carden was gone by February. He is now the subject of a website specifically established to protect people from being swindled by him. Tunnicliffe, a sports consultant in 2021, has heard this story before.

"I know that Maurice has tried to, effectively, pin that on me previously," he tells me in a phone conversation.

"There's no way I had the power and authority to make it go ahead. He was the chief executive, there was a whole board of directors. There is no way that I had any level of delegated authority to make that kind of decision.

"When he asked my advice, I said yes I did think it was important that the tour went ahead. I was, and still am, a believer in the power of international rugby league to drive the growth of the game.

"I also thought at the time that the international vision was important to the future of Super League because that was one of the things that would set it apart from the way the game had always been run. It was very much a part of the Murdoch vision.

"I felt if we didn't go on tour, we would undermine all of that. It was an important statement to make at the time."

Trevor McKewen - a New Zealander seconded to Sydney by News Limited during the secretive early days of Super League - observes that despite its supposed USP, the breakaway was "very myopic in its approach, in that it was about Australia.

"The international part was an afterthought.

"Whilst they'd done the deal with Maurice, they hadn't even thought about New Zealand. It just wasn't on their radar outside the Warriors joining them."

The assistant to coach Phil Larder for the Lions on the tour was Welshman Clive Griffiths. "Before we took off, (Martin) Offiah dropped out," Griffiths recalls. "He felt he didn't have the enthusiasm to tour.

"Jason Robinson - ARL. Gary Connolly - ARL. Lee Jackson - ARL. Shaun Edwards injured, Paul Newlove injured. Steve McNamara injured."

Tollett, London-born but Aussie-raised and 23 at the time, went back to Australia when the cost-cutting occurred, was recalled to New Zealand without playing a game, and then returned to Australia.

"Whenever I see Clive, that tour comes up in conversation - always," says Tollett, now a high-profile broadcaster with BBC TV.

Griffiths was proud of himself - a rugby union lad who had been appointed to the coaching staff of a Great Britain rugby league team. He'd taken Wales to the World Cup semis in 1995 and then helped set up a new professional club that hoped to be promoted to the new Super League in 1996.

But by the time Griffiths got home, the club had been denied entry and he had plummeted from a career highlight to unemployment.

Tollett, meanwhile, was accompanied back to Sydney by Huddersfield forward Neil Harmon, who had a visa because the tour was originally supposed to include Australia.

"Without sugar coating it, we just went out every night," Tollett, who now lives in Galway, admits.

"One night, I just left him sleeping on Epping train station. He's much bigger than me, he couldn't walk and I couldn't move him. He walked a good five km to my parents' place from Penrith train station the next day."

Then came a call Tollett had not fathomed - GB team manager Phil Lowe saying Stuart Spruce had an injury and Tulsen had to go back to New Zealand.

"I didn't think much of it … it's not like you lose all your fitness and forget all the plays.

"I turned up at the airport and there were about 30 people there - cameras and all sorts of stuff! It was surreal. I'm pretty sure I looked a mess. Someone asked me what I thought, I was half asleep, and I clearly remember saying 'it will be good for my frequent fliers'.

"We trained, Stuart was fine, so they just threw me some money, 'here you go, this is for this week' and that was it. I didn't have to train. I think it was a Wednesday I got there .. and by Sunday I was heading back over to Sydney."

And back to the pub.

CHANGE OF ACCENT FOR SUPER TROOPERS

By Steve Mascord, Sydney Morning Herald, Tuesday January 21, 1997

"THEY all want to know the swear words," burly Paris Saint Germain prop Jason Sands said as his new teammates trained behind him.

"But I'm not so sure it's a good idea to tell them . . ."

A sun-baked St Gregory's College, Campbelltown, is not a place you would expect to come across a group who hold the destiny of French rugby league in their hands.

But then, 23 young Australians aren't the people you'd expect to be playing for a team called Paris St Germain. They come from Perth, New Zealand, Brisbane, Canberra, Sydney and just about all points in between.

They signed contracts with Super League during the 1995 frenzy, seeing a wealthy future for themselves in a glitzy new competition.

But a lot has happened since then.

For a start, there was no Super League last year. And with Australasian clubs restricted to just 23 "protected" players in 1997, injury, poor form or being with an ARL-aligned club has brought the careers of many to a grinding halt

Most of them are well paid; but they are contractually bound not to play in the ARL. "It's like we're castaways," says former St George prop Tony Priddle, trying to restart his career after a knee reconstruction.

"We've got four Mariners players. Last year they were in their squad, this year they're not and in-between the club didn't even play!"

Priddle will be joined at PSG this year by the likes of former North Sydney golden boy Jason Martin, talented journeyman Jamie Olejnik, former Wallaby Matt O'Connor and ex-Manly and Sydney City hooker David O'Donnell.

Their coach is Peter Mullholland, sacked by the Western Reds despite the side winning half its games in its first year.

"It's not like going to play in England," Mullholland, says of his task in preparing them for life in France. "It's the food, it's driving on the other side of the road, it's little things . . . it's an adventure. Europe is your base and the world's your oyster."

Paris play Hunter and Perth, home and away, in this year's World Club Championship. The new Paris franchise drew 17,000 at home to the first Super League game last year -and won.

But with most of the players also committed to a domestic competition at the same time, PSG's fortunes quickly waned. They only narrowly escaped relegation.

Since then, the club has suffered the loss of its public face, former French rugby union coach Jacques Fouroux, and its relationship with the PSG sports organisation is in doubt.

But Super League has clearly increased its commitment. The players will live in Paris, unlike last year when they were flown in from the south, and News Corporation will pay for their cars and rent.

The players fly out next Tuesday and Thursday. Until then, they are staying at the Narellan Leagues Club, squeezing in, between weights and drills, informal French lessons and lectures from consular officials and other Australians who've played in France.

Only three Frenchman have so far been named in the senior squad. Sands, wisely, warns this may make it hard for Parisians to accept them.

But Priddle couldn't be happier. "I said to Peter: 'If you get a few Aussies together, I'll go over.

"I didn't expect this many."

CHAPTER 4

John Quayle

Like so many aspects of the period covered by this book, the exact circumstances and mood of John Quayle's departure from rugby league have been obscured by time and the swirling emotions of the game in late 1996.

If you suggested to Australian fans that he was actually IN the Tina Turner ads, playing saxophone perhaps, many would not immediately dismiss it. "The Canon" *was* "Simply The Best", expansion, Andrew Ettingshausen, mullets…. everything about the era that seared itself into the popular imagination.

In NSW and Queensland he was as omnipresent during 1995 and 1996 as, say, Paul Keating or silverchair.

Where did he go?

"Oh, he moved on just before the NRL came along didn't he? Still a well respected guy, worked on the Olympics, probably got a tonne of footy mates he goes to the pub with to spin yarns about the time he brought the Newcastle Knights into the Premiership and went in the studio with Jimmy Barnes and Tina Turner."

Like so many things we tell ourselves about the days of two tribes, this is a convenient fairytale.

In fact, when John Quayle departed in December 1996, he may have continued as a sports administrator of some note but he cut himself off completely from the game and the community that made him a household name. For 25 years, he's not had a single tinge of regret about this.

"I've never been to a grand final, never been to a State of Origin, never been back to the game," he tells me during an hour-long interview for this book.

To understand why, it's important to dismiss another misconception: that as the man who oversaw seven expansion teams, Tina Turner, the Winfield Cup, a disciplinary crackdown and Origins in Melbourne and Los Angeles, Quayle was an avowed rugby league progressive.

This interview left me in no doubt that by most definitions of that term, he is not - and never was.

Instead, his experiences in the mid-eighties when there was pressure to oust Cronulla, Newtown and Western Suburbs shaped his views and his rugby league morals.

"... admittedly Newtown were gone, a motion brought Cronulla back in and then Wests challenged the game in court," he recalls from his Hunter Valley winery.

"That, to me, the Wests challenge ... it was my first job, my first experience in the loyalty of the game and how the law started to destroy it.

"(You heard) what the Wests club, in that court case, meant to so many people. By then I realised 'they are a foundation member of this game and they have every right to be in the League. Why would we take them out?'

"The clubs are the future of the game. Not the players, the clubs."

This attitude is frankly an anathema to many modern sports administrators. Save for the quantifiable extent of "a "franchise's IP", under the American ethos popular in Australian sport for decades, clubs are shells which can be moved around and killed off when no longer profitable.

So Quayle and Ken Arthurson believed in expansion - but not at the expense of tradition. They added Auckland, North Queensland, Perth and South Queensland in 1995, expecting Sydney clubs who failed to keep up to fall on their swords. No-one would be forced to shut or merge or move.

Academic Stephen Alomes, writing in the *Sydney Morning Herald* on December 18 1995, perhaps considered the Ancient Greek origins of the word "hubris" when he wrote: "Both the NSWRL/ARL and the VFL-AFL tried to have it both ways, stretching their empires while keeping Rome strong."

I accompanied Quayle and a group of corporates and media as buses and planes carried us from Sydney to Newcastle, the Gold Coast and Brisbane for round one 1988, and again on the epic journey from Sydney to Auckland, Brisbane, Townsville and Perth seven years later.

I was on a coach at Kings Park on the morning of March 12, 1995, when a photo opportunity overlooking Perth on game day was organised. The Roman emperors were to regally survey their newly-conquered distant capital.

Instead, they were faced with questions about reports in the Sydney Sunday papers that 'Super League was back on'.

The news was broken to the fiddling Neros that Rome was ablaze. It always seemed to me the sport's innocence was lost precisely then, 100 years after its birth in the George Hotel in Huddersfield. "No matter what happens, the game will never be the same again," Quayle said sadly at the time.

The bigger something gets, the more likely you will lose control. And so, ever since, there have been those who saw the most obvious solution as keeping rugby league small.

And in the western world's most isolated city, John Quayle became rugby league's most isolated official.

Rugby league's most adventurous, ambitious season was ruined. By September, Ken Arthurson vowed publicly that should peace arrive, Quayle would not be a sacrificial lamb. Less than six months later, though, the former Parramatta and Eastern Suburbs lock made it clear he would lead himself to such a slaughter.

The new world he had helped create was no longer one of which he wanted to be part. "The person Super League most wanted out was me … well, take me out now," veteran journalist Ian Heads quoted him as saying in early '96

Quayle tells me that shortly before the October 4, 1996, defeat in the Federal Court - where our story here begins - he told Arthurson he expected the ARL to lose and that if that happened, he was out.

"I probably always had a negative feeling towards the appeal," Quayle begins, in that erudite, soothing way you can recall if you're old enough.

"Ah… it was very brief. A lot of people then didn't understand that. We did, pretty much because we'd been involved day-to-day in the whole thing and we knew the risk in all of this, that if it was against trade practices…."

Quayle uses the phrases "I knew" and "they knew" regularly during our conversation. What does he mean? The future; what would happen.

Working on this book in the first half of 2020 and watching the science fiction reboot *Star Trek: Picard*, I eventually became unable to distinguish the character of the retired starship captain from that of Quayle; living on a winery, Shakespearean elocution, widespread respect, calmness, knowledge, experience … paucity of hair?

Whenever I transcribed the tape of Quayle, in my mind's eye I saw actor Patrick Stewart.

In the space opera, Picard is also something else: bitter. Bitter at a betrayal from his beloved but coarsened and morally compromised Starfleet 14 years before. After my conversation with Quayle, I came to question the nature of bitterness itself.. Can it be wholly internal? Or does bitterness have to manifest itself in actions and words in order to exist?

From that morning in the Perth sunshine, he says, "I knew … it was only my relationship and commitment to the game (that kept me there) but more so my relationship to my chairman.

"I remember (after the Burchett ruling outlawing Super League in early 1996) Ken Cowley had indicated 'we've got to get together, we're not going to appeal' and then it was a very short time after that he said 'no, we're going to appeal either way'.

"From that point on, I indicated to Ken that if we lose this, people like me can't stay because we're never going to get together as a league while people like me are there. There was so much animosity over what happened.

"In talking to Ken I said 'it's different for you as a statesman of the game. It's different for you as chairman. But me, as chief executive, who's fought in this … if the game is going to be reunited, it is going to be with different staff.

"I knew in my own mind - I'd made that decision long before the appeal."

Quayle, of course, was right about the result before the full bench. "A couple of days later … as we used to do, we went to White City and had a game of tennis.

"Ken said 'mate, you can't leave, you can't leave. We'll be able to do all this'. I said 'no mate, I've made my mind up' and I think he accepted that."

By November 10, 1996, speculation reached the public arena that the ARL chief executive was about to stand down. John Brady was on a river cruise with his wife when a reporter called him about it; he phoned Quayle in shock and was instructed to do nothing.

Five days after Brady's cruise was rudely interrupted, the ARL's application for leave to appeal to the High Court against the decision allowing Super League to start was declined.

Quayle stepped down. "He needed to, for his health," says ARL communications manager Geoff Car. "He worked bloody dreadful hours under plenty of pressure for a long time. I'd sometimes take his car home and pick him up in the morning. One morning I picked him up and I said 'are you alright?' He'd been to hospital that night with chest pains but he still went to work the next day."

'Arko' says now: "He just reached the stage where he'd had enough. He came and saw me and he told me he was going to resign and it was really a sad time for me because he's a good bloke, John - and not only a good bloke but did a terrific job for the game too."

To understand the depths of John Quayle's disillusionment - that's not strong enough a word, try "desolation" - it's important to note that he felt he had been betrayed not once but three times.

First, he felt double-crossed by the three of the four teams he brought into the Winfield Cup in 1995 when they climbed into bed with News. That is, Auckland, North Queensland and Perth.

And if you go back to 1988, there were the chief rabble rousers, Brisbane.

"It was us as a league who convinced the NSW clubs to allow us to expand. There were six of our clubs opposed to expansion because they knew (there's that expression again).

"It was the NSW clubs who sacrificed so much in allowing expansion - even though it was the right decision.

"It was the new clubs that dudded them when they'd been in that competition for ... some of those clubs had been in the competition since 1908 but the new clubs weren't in that competition a year and didn't repay the loyalty.

"I knew then that the loyalty that the game was built on, all those wonderful years of rugby league run by genuine rugby league people, was all over."

Then the law showed itself - to him - to be an almighty ass. "This is a case that was solely on trade practices and within five minutes he ruled the League didn't have the right to enter into the contracts that we did - that was it.

"Those last three years of knowing about it … it became a debate about the law in the end … when we were controlled by two big media players … it was very hard to then ever get out of it (the war) until the law decision was done. "

And finally, when he worked tirelessly to save the others clubs in the face of what to him was treachery and judiciary amorality, Quayle was snubbed and disrespected by them as well. In the weeks following October 4, he had brought the ARL back from the brink of complete collapse.

"It was only through the incredible support of, not the Nine Network, not from Kerry (Packer) at that time but from Geoff Cousins and the team at Optus. Geoff had played such a major role at Optus getting us the funds that he said 'John, I can't contribute any more'.

"I know (in) my negotiations with him and his team, I said 'unless we can get more money, we're not going to have a competition, we're not going to have a 10-team competition'. In the end, he committed to that $3 million, $3 million a club. "

(Here, an answer to Cousin's statements in chapter two - it was $94 million less than reported at the time!).

"I knew News were going to pay the clubs $5 million. (Cousins) rang me that day and I thought 'we're good, we're going to be able to handle this' …

"When I told our clubs, called a meeting and told our clubs what we'd achieved and two of them, the words I'll never forget were: 'oh, that's not enough'.

"And I knew I didn't want to work with them again. That sealed it all for me."

Quayle's opposite number in the Super League War, John Ribot, planned an exit to Victoria almost as soon as he walked through Rupert Murdoch's gilded door for the first time.

Quayle had no such contingencies.

"They tried very hard to split Ken and I. Ken said 'it was always about you completing what you set out to do'. I said 'yes I did. My commitment to you was to start expansion and make sure expansion happened'."

Although his farewell speech to the staff at Phillip Street has become the stuff of myth, he says he was close enough to everyone there that they knew what he was planning to say before he said it.

"They worked at Phillip Street around the clock. It didn't matter. Days of war, days when we were depressed knowing that was going on behind the scenes. They were all just genuine loyal rugby league servants. You can go through them all, whether it be Paul Broughton, Graeme Foster, Greg Mitchell.

"They knew, they knew, what had to. … they were close enough to me. I told them the priority was to unite the game at the next step but it couldn't involve me.

"We sent Paul to the Gold Coast and that sort of stuff … they knew I'd stayed and done my bit and history recorded that I represented the game. We fought for the right of the ARL, we fought for the contract that we had in place, we never wavered from that. We were loyal to the contracts we had with Channel Nine.

"I think everyone knew what my attitude was."

And so in 2011 it was widely reported that News Limited opposed Quayle being on the first ARL Commission. This prompted outrage from many, who pointed out that not only did he have no club affiliation at the time but he had been estranged from the sport for 15 years.

However, News' position becomes, perhaps, a little clearer as Quayle continues to explain why he only lasted four chapters into a book about Australian Rugby League's split season.

Quayle's attitudes, formed when Wests were expelled, remain undiluted. To put it bluntly, they are not News Corporation-friendly.

"I understood at the end how loyal those NSWRL clubs were to make the decision in the long term interests of the game (to expand) but then they were the first clubs News Limited threw out, be it Norths, whether it be combining Balmain, get rid of Souths - they didn't care," he says pointedly.

"They didn't care one bit about the loyalty of the clubs that allowed them to come into the competition.

"News Limited was all about money. Let's make more money. Our position was 'expand the game on a national level to get a greater audience, new development', as the AFL have done.

"Now with things they're going through (with Covid), 'oh this is good, we'll have less teams'. Well, who's talking less teams? The new clubs!

"… under our league it was profits back into the game, expand the game on a national level so we knew we had a new audience - which Perth gave us.

"If I'd have listened to the journalists - 'oh, you can't expand, there's not enough players'. Well, that was self-interest.

"We had coaches say 'oh no, you can't expand'.

"If we had listened to them then … a lot of them were coaches at prominent clubs that didn't want expansion. They knew there'd be less players. Oh yes, 'we're interested in the game, it will be wonderful for the game'. What a lot of crap!

"It's no different to when Canberra were broke after they won the premiership and certain clubs were saying 'nah, look, let 'em go because then I can pick up a Ricky Stuart and I can sign Laurie Daley, I can get a Bradley Clyde'.

"Why would you ever listen to anyone (in that situation)? That's why administrators are there, to act in the long term interests of the game. That's the sad part of what all that created - it was all self-interest.

"That's the sad thing even now, you look at what I read about (in England with the split between Super League and the Rugby Football League). Everyone will be loyal until they're offered a bigger deal. Self-interest will always come in.

"That was very evident then. They had a very good partner in News Limited who were going to give whatever it took in money and promises to young chief executives and new chairmen. It was hard to beat."

Quayle's comments in light of some of the public debate when the NRL was shut down by the global pandemic in early 2020 - and perhaps Australia and New Zealand's boycott of the World Cup in 2021 - provide a stark insight into the morals that forced him to hang up his briefcase in December 1996.

And his perception of the Melbourne Storm gives us an idea of why, again, his oil does not mix easily with the water of that club's former owners, News Limited.

"You listen to them now, maybe North Queensland (will close), I think they've been pretty good. Maybe Auckland. I thought they'd been pretty good. See, Auckland was (added) to challenge rugby (union). We knew it was a rugby nation. But we knew with the Winfield Cup on television, we were getting exposure.

"Once the Ruben Wikis and all those were playing here, people were interested. It was their people.

"If you take, even, Melbourne now. Melbourne would never have happened without News Limited, putting in $10 million a year, $100 million over 10 years and they haven't developed a player!

"There's all this debate now, you want to go to Perth or you want less teams? You want to take Auckland out?

"Why don't you take Melbourne out? What have they done?

"When all of a sudden you say Easts … the (2019) premiers, they don't draw many crowds … that's what happened with Norths and Souths and that's why News Limited brought Souths back. That was affecting the News Limited model, because of Souths' history. They (fans) just turned against News Limited.

"If you take teams out that've got great history, you never get it back and that's why, if you're going to expand a competition, it's going to take years.

"Look at the AFL. When the Swans came here (NSW) in '82, they weren't interested in what was going to happen in '85. They were interested in what was going to happen in 1990. When they expanded their competition, they told me: 'we're only interested in what our competition will be when we play live television out of Sydney'."

John Quayle, then, is still the same man who in 1996 could not stomach the impact of big media, the law and corporatisation on rugby league. He's still the same man who walked out on the game in disgust and has barely been back.

And so to our central question: does this ideological intransigence amount to bitterness? Is John Quayle still fighting in the jungle? Or did he just move to the jungle, where he now lives happily and peacefully?

He certainly has no relationship with most of his contemporaries from the period with which this tome concerns itself. Maurice Lindsay - reconciled with Arthurson - said he'd not heard from Quayle since the war was at its height. John Ribot, likewise.

Is John Quayle bitter?

"Look, to walk away … I was able to where Ken couldn't. He stayed there. I walked away. I never watched the game. I was fortunate to go to the Olympics. It's only recently, since David Smith asked me to come back and, after the (Nathan) Tinkler case, to try and get Newcastle sold ….other than that, I've had no involvement.

"My association with the Roosters was there but I didn't have to see anyone. There's very few of them … I've never seen any of them since I left.

"From my point of view I knew I could never walk in and be part of the same room as people that I knew had dudded me. It was easy for me. It was very easy for me to leave."

When I ask him again, gently but directly, about bitterness, he answers: "I don't think any of them are in the game anymore, who was there then and I never mingled with anyone since. When you ask me that question. I've never had to go and see them all.

"That's why I didn't have to worry. Because it was so long ago."

We can only conclude, then, that John Quayle believes bitterness must manifest itself in some way in order to be real.

He did tell the *SMH* upon his departure: "The scruples that have been lost have shattered me more than anything.

"So many of the challenges to the game came from within.

"One of my big regrets is we did not charge the new clubs a franchise fee for joining."

That, at least, is a lesson the NRL seems to have learned as it considers doing exactly that with a new Brisbane franchise in the offing some time in the next five years.

Greg Mitchell recalls: "The thing in my mind was the press conference, where John and Ken were there with the Optus Vision backdrop - just the sadness … of both of them, but obviously I was closer to John. The emotional toll his departure from the game took on him was just devastating."

John Quayle fought for something that he eventually ceased believing in. In explaining his departure at the time, The Canon was quoted as saying: "Some of the clubs are loyal to the ARL the way a cow is loyal to hay."

And yet Quayle still offers me some strange advice when I turn off the voice recorder and we discuss a few ventures in which I've involved myself in recent years, like the effort to start a Nines world circuit.

Clearly, just because he was forced to surrender does not mean he believes the battle is hopeless.

"Whatever you do," John Quayle says to me after an hour on the phone, "don't give up.

"Keep fighting."

SUPER STARTS THE SHOW

By Steve Mascord, Sydney Morning Herald, Thursday January 30 1997

WHEN Super League won its Federal Court appeal in October, some in the breakaway movement wanted to strike quickly in the public relations war with the Australian Rugby League.

At the time, Great Britain was on tour in the South Pacific. What better way for the new competition to flex its international muscles than for the Lions to visit Australia for a Test series on the way home?

Big crowds, television coverage, name players all paraded before the league world while the ARL sat mute in early summer.

So why didn't it happen?

The official line from Super League was that there was no time to organise it properly, that the News Ltd-financed league wanted to do things properly or not at all,

But there's little doubt there were other reasons for dropping the idea. With some Australian players not having made a tackle in anger for up to three months, there were fears the world title won by the ARL Aussies the year before at the World Cup would be embarrassingly surrendered by "the best of the best".

What a disastrous kick-off to Super League that would have been.

This weekend in Townsville, however, there will be precious few excuses if the Super League Australians don't win the second annual World Nines.

They were eliminated in the semi-finals in Suva last year when the players' new world appeared to have fallen in following the ARL's original Federal Court victory on the same weekend.

It was a false start for the Australians, if not for the other countries aligned with the breakaway, who put on a brave face for the rest of the year.

74

One year later, Super League is finally kicking off in this country and 14 footballers in green and gold (with a dash of blue) couldn't be under more pressure.

(Teams in Herald order of favouritism; odds courtesy of Centrebet)

AUSTRALIA: Colours: Green, gold and blue. Coach: Tim Sheens. A powerful line-up which marks only the second international appearances by Laurie Daley, Andrew Ettingshausen, Steve Renouf and Co in three years. New cap Gorden Tallis is a bizarre selection after missing all of 1996 but he'll cause havoc anyway. For sheer ability, they dwarf their nearest rivals Great Britain and New Zealand. Odds: 7-2 on.

NEW ZEALAND: Colours: Black and white. Coach: Graeme Norton. The reigning champions have been hit hard by withdrawals, with Matthew Ridge, Gene Ngamu, Henry Paul, Grant Young and Sean Hoppe all unable to make the trip. But at least Bradford's Robbie Paul, the most exciting player in Britain at the moment, earns his first cap. Shane Endacott goes from Auckland

reserves to internationals in an amazing leap. Odds: 6-1.

GREAT BRITAIN: Colours: Red, white and blue. Coach: Andy Gregory. The Lions, forced to send an under-strength side on last year's disastrous South Pacific trek, are once again well below their best. The side has been limited to one player per club because the Challenge Cup kicks off this weekend. Players to watch include new Wigan signing Stephen Holgate, a second rower, and Auckland's Denis Betts, who bounced back to his best during the New Zealand series last year. Odds: 8-1.

WESTERN SAMOA: Colours: White and blue. Coach: Mark Graham. With 1996 finalists Papua New Guinea, Western Samoa are dark horses. Australian audiences will get their first taste of explosive St Helens forwards Apollo Perelini and Vila Matautia. Odds: 12-1.

PAPUA NEW GUINEA: Colours: Yellow, red and black. Coach: Gabriel Kiluwa. PNG enjoyed one of their best moments on the international stage by making the final of last year's Nines.

Unfortunately, the Kumuls squad has been weakened by the emergence of a rival, ARL-aligned league in that country. Canberra's David Westley, Adelaide's Bruce Mamando and Hull KR's Stanley Gene are their key men. Odds: 33-1.

FIJI: Colours: White and black. Coach: Waqa Etuwabe. Fiji have a long way to go in 13-a-side football, as evidenced by last year's 72-4 Test loss to in his tracks, centre, and Laurie Daley looks for support. the show Great Britain. But it's in truncated football that the Bati shine, although a suspension to star Noa Nadruku won't help their prospects. Watch for speedy winger Jo Tamani, who starred with Bradford last year and will turn out for Adelaide, in '97. Odds: 8-1.

COOK ISLANDS: Colours: Green, gold and white. Coach: Paul McGreal. The reigning Emerging Nations World Cup holders are determined to justify their new status as full members of the International Board. Big Kevin Iro returns to lead the land of his forebears, while the halves combination of Craig Bowen and

Ali Davys should play a major role. Odds: 150-1.

FRANCE: Colours: Red, white and blue. Coach: Ivan Greseque. The French and South Africans will have match fitness on their side; their domestic competitions are reaching their climax. Three players - Pascal Bomati, Pierre Chamorin and Fabien Devecchi - already have full-time contracts with Paris St Germain and coach Peter Mullholland or another representative will be checking on other players' form. Odds: 20-1.

TONGA: Colours: Red and white. Coach: Duane Mann. Interestingly, the Tongans have chosen not to recall players from Australia and Britain, deciding instead to field a mostly home-grown squad. Barring late changes, the only survivor from the World Cup is utility back Willie Wolfgramm. The Tongans are an unknown quantity but always dangerous in this sort of football. Odds: 100-1.

SOUTH AFRICA: Colours: Gold and green. Coach: Paul Matete. The Republic is finally able to cash in on the number of rugby union stars who have switched to league. Tiaan Strauss (Cronulla) is captain, with Andy Marinos, Kevin Schraader and Hannes Venter (all Canterbury) also on board. These combine with World Cup players such as Mark Johnson and Tim Fourie. Odds: 20-1.

UNITED STATES: Colours: Red, white and blue. Coach: Dan McAffey. The Americans were split in two last year, with half their top squad going to the Nines and the other half to the World Sevens. Despite this, they exceeded expectations in Suva. This year, the side is reunited. David Niu will direct play, while Duke Ieriko is a surprisingly strong and quick backrower. Odds: 100-1.

JAPAN: Colours: White and red. Coach: Max Mannix. Along with the US, the only non-International Board country to be included in this year's tournament. Japan have also been split by the Super League war, with the East Japan Rugby League formed by the ARL. And there is still no regular competition there. Odds: 100-1.

CHAPTER 5

Welcome Or Commiserations?

"LOW and behold, I'm told by the head hunter that I've got the job."

Malcolm Speed, now one of Australia's most decorated sports administrators, is just getting started on one of the most incredible 'sliding doors' moments of rugby league's Year Of Living Ridiculously.

"The job" was the ARL chief executive's post, replacing John Quayle. The time was the end of 1996.

"I was in Melbourne (where) I was involved in basketball," Speed says from the same city, shortly before the completion of *Two Tribes*.

"I'd done some consulting work with John and I knew him reasonably well. I'd had a bit to do with Ken (Arthurson).

"It was a high point of the war. I was a reluctant starter but the head hunter got me interested. He interviewed me, I can't remember who else interviewed me, whether Ken was involved in that.

"I'm told by the head hunter that I've got the job and I just need to come to Sydney at nine o'clock on a particular morning - I think I had a couple of days' notice - and I was going to be interviewed by the full board.

"So I'd spoken to John in the meantime and he confirmed 'yes, you're the choice, you're going to get the job' and it was all a bit mysterious … the head hunter told me he was authorised to tell me yes, I had the job. I just needed to turn up.

"I head to Sydney, I caught the early plane and I'm in a taxi heading to Phillip Street and I hear on the radio an announcement that I'm the likely new chief executive. I thought 'shit, they haven't kept that very close'.

"I look in the *Daily Telegraph* and there's a little article there saying I'm going to be appointed as the chief executive of the ARL. I'm surprised at that too.

"So I get to the ARL and I'm told that I have to go in the back door … because there's press out the front, or there might be press out the front.

"And I sit there in reception for about 40 minutes, thinking 'this is a bit strange' because I'm right on time.

"John and Ken come out after 40 minutes, an hour, whatever and John in his typical blunt form says: 'G'day mate, we've got some bad news for you. The chairmen of the clubs met last night, they had dinner, and they decided they don't want you for the job'.

"'They don't want someone from fucking Melbourne, they don't want a fucking lawyer and they don't want someone from fucking basketball!'

Quayle recalls now: "The person who was right for the job at that time was … the (later) head of cricket, Malcolm Speed. He was a lawyer and he was the pea. There was a concern then that he wasn't a part of league. It was said then, and yes Ken was about this … he said 'don't you think it's a time to have a league guy?'

"That's when Neil (Whittaker), who was at Balmain … I rang Neil and said 'what about you coming into my job?'. That's how all that happened.

"But Malcolm Speed was the one that was recommended and the one that would have got the job other than that concern that we'd just gone through a Super League War that had brought other people into the game that we thought at that stage, and I know Ken wanted at that stage, a league person."

Although he had delivered the expletive-laced bad news, Quayle - it seems - would have been happy with Speed. "I felt that we needed somebody that was new and independent, that wouldn't have a history with either group. Yes, I know when Neil took the job I offered him full support but I felt we needed independence at that time.

"Malcolm was a sports administrator, he'd been involved in basketball, he was from Melbourne but he understood … he was new and I thought if we were going to unite this you needed somebody that's not been part of any of this."

Arthurson, though, denies playing a big role in championing Whittaker. "I would have been asked about him. I hadn't had a great deal to do with Neil over the years but I think, you know, he was a pretty good appointment and I think he did quite well when he was there."

Geoff Carr has the story from the other side. "The chairmen went to dinner with Arko and the chief executives and the League staff went to lunch with Quayle. We sort of met up afterwards and Ken

Arthurson said to me 'I think we've got our man' and he was alluding to Neil Whittaker."

On the same day Quayle departed, New Zealander Liz Dawson was appointed Adelaide Rams CEO - but even before twin competitions got off the ground, there was a clearing of the decks at administrative level.

On November 14, it was announced that Tom Bellew would not seek re-election to the NSWRL board. He remained on the ARL board. "He had been diagnosed with leukemia," his son, NSW Supreme Court judge Geoff Bellew, says now, adding that Tom thought his Gold Coast Chargers were being set up to be culled under a peace deal.

"He was quite angry. He stepped down because I think he thought - quite rightly - that he had personally been quite badly treated given what he had done over a number of years.

"When you look at the circumstances in which my father took over back in 1983, I never thought he'd been given proper recognition for what he did. The model of management they (the NRL) are using is the model introduced by my father almost 40 years ago."

Broncos co-owner Paul 'Porky' Morgan, an architect of Super League, was next out the door - quitting in mid-November. Geoff Cousins also resigned. John Singleton was let go as the ARL's advertising account holder.

At the end of that month, the Super League clubs dropped their nicknames, to become Super League Canterbury, Super League Penrith, Super League Cronulla etc. This nomenclature was eventually phased out and quietly forgotten.

Rumours of a peace meeting between Rupert Murdoch and Kerry Packer in London swirled at the start of December 1996 and overall, the mass departures made it look like the sides were suing for peace.

In fact, the off-field battle lines that would endure for the next 13 months were being drawn up. Ian Frykberg, a long-time Nine employee, was appointed News Limited executive director of sport - recalling him from Britain.

While there is no doubt Frykberg was appointed to make peace with the ARL and offered a success fee to do so, Super League's marketing manager Gary Pearse says his first job was to do a TV deal.

That was the bear-like South African's forte - he was often to be found in Seat 1A on Qantas flight QF1 to London, where he would negotiate a sports television contract and then come straight home again.

"I was very pro Frykberg coming in," says John Ribot. "As I said to News, I've never done big TV deals. I understand TV but not to the point of sitting down and … what's the real value of something?

"News brought Frykberg in and I think that was good for a period but I don't think it was totally great for our game.

"He was able to get some TV money in there but he wasn't big on our game. He was very much a rugby union person. But he got us into a position where he could balance our books a lot better because of the money that was generated so from a TV point of view he certainly got us out there and then he wasn't a long-term player anyway.

"I think he only stayed 12 months after I left. "

Between 1995 and 1996, the NSWRL had turned a $14.2 million profit into a $9.7 million loss. In early December, Roosters chairman Nick Politis was elected to the NSWRL board for the first time.

Taking up the story of what he describes as one of the most bizarre days of his career, former International Cricket Council chief executive Speed says: "And Ken's standing there quite stoney faced about it. I said 'that's not what I've been told but if they don't want me, they don't want me. What does the board think?'

"(Quayle) said 'oh, they've found another guy. One of the chairmen of the clubs is an engineer, Neil Whittaker, and they want to appoint him so we're going to appoint him'.

"I thought 'I've got out of bed early, I've come to Sydney, it's in the newspapers, people in basketball are going to be very grumpy with me because I'm seen to be trying to leave'."

But wait, there's more.

"John says 'oh, anyway, the board wants you to come in and they want you to talk to them. They want you to tell them what you think they should do'.

"I said 'what's going on? You've just given me the arse, you know who's getting the job. What does the board want?'

"I thought 'I'm here, I might as well go in'. I remember David Leckie was there. I don't remember who else was there but they were a pretty formidable sort of group, the board of the ARL.

"I should have walked out of there and said 'you can get stuffed, I haven't got the job, sort it out yourselves'. I can't remember what I said aside from 'you'll have to find an out, there's no easy way out of this. You're going to have to fight it out and then try and find some sort of peaceful solution within a couple of years'.

"They ultimately did. It was quite funny."

A political assassination followed by a brain-picking shakedown of the victim? "It was very typical of rugby league in those days, wasn't it?" says Speed.

December 11 was a big day with Whittaker, the former Balmain hooker and president, announced as the new CEO of the ARL.

"I was working with a company called Metal Manufacturers in Moorebank, living at Collaroy and I was chairman of Balmain," says Whittaker, 63, sitting across from me in a mid-city consultancy office in Sydney, with the Harbour Bridge visible over his shoulder.

"They did a search. I mean, I wasn't interested in the job at all. They did a search for people to do the job and that search sort of went down a path, they ended up in a place where they weren't comfortable. They wanted someone within the game.

"Then they - they being Quayley and a couple of others - approached me.

"I think I said 'no' three times and in the end my wife said 'you'll regret not doing it'. I went and talked to Quayley and whoever the search firm were, and then very quickly it happened."

As November rolled on, the ARL indicated it was challenging Super League's agreements with foreign leagues as a restraint of trade. It's easy to forget how many rule changes were trialled during this period. Some, like the 40-20 rule, caught on. Others, like the use of four touch judges, did not.

Super League was not as well advanced in planning for dual competitions as they would have had us believe.

Young promotions man Paul Kind had the previous year snuck into a Hunter Mariners media conference posing as a reporter to spy for the ARL. Now he was on the other side of the fence, working for Foxtel on a loose assignment of "sports promotion".

"I shared an office with Rebecca Wilson, I was sort of up to my neck in Super League and trying to fulfil Ribot's vision," Kind, who went on to have a senior role at the NRL, says.

"I remember not too soon after that (successful appeal), sitting on the ninth floor of that building they had in Elizabeth Street, working out how they were going to make a draw happen.

"While they talked a lot about creating a league, they actually hadn't done a lot of preparation on that, that idea of actually running a competition. They'd all been working out of that building and doing nothing for 12 months. They'd all been running in the park at lunch. It was the dawning of a reality that I don't think anybody had really considered: that they were going to need to create a whole operating competition within a reasonably short time frame.

"Suddenly rugby league needed to be presented bigger, brighter and better than it had ever been presented before. Who's going to perform at the opening round? There had been all sorts of names thrown around over a two year period. One of the things we did over that summer was plan the opening round entertainment acts that were going to be blowing people's minds."

Barry Russell recollects: "You can imagine the logistics of bringing kids in from all around the country to try and pull a comp together and travelling every week. It was huge."

As the breakaway prepared to unveil its draw in mid-month, the ARL toyed with some of their own novel rule change ideas. One was that a team scoring a try could eschew a conversion attempt and instead get a tap from the 20 metre line and three tackles to score again.

What became the 40-20 rule - if you kick the ball into touch from within 40 metres of your own line to the opposition 20-metre zone, you have a chance to get it back - was also tossed up by ARL coaches at this time, as was the idea of the scoring team having the choice of kicking off or receiving from the restart of play.

In the 1997 Country Carnival, it was planned that scrums would become a contest again and striking at the play-the-ball would be banned.

"We actually came up with a draw with stand-alone Origins in it for the first time and, low and behold, I remember some marketing genius came up with the idea of changing the NSW jersey for the next year as well - which was one of the great weird calls of all time," says John Brady.

"Whittaker, he comes in and changes the draw. He wasn't going to take risks with the draw. He undid some of the draw things we'd announced … which was smart at the time, when you think back.

"Quayle was half-thinking about throwing a team in from Melbourne. He was bold, he was having a go at that, he was really thinking outside the square. (Whittaker) settles the clubs down in a lot of ways but also talks about the challenge we face from within.

"He had a meeting with them where he said 'we've got to watch it, we're our own biggest problem here - if we hang tight, we can do things'. Some of them got offended at that but he was entirely right.'"

With Whittaker's arrival, Ribot was already preparing to decamp to Melbourne and start a new team. He had been planning it since the very earliest days of Super League. "I knew I was going to go to Melbourne," says Ribot.

"The Broncos ... when I left there, my 2IC there at the time was Shane Edwards and I thought it would be totally unreasonable for me to go back there. He should have his moment in the sun. He'd done a really good job there so for me to go back wouldn't have been the right thing. That's where you negotiate your 'out' when you negotiate your 'in'.

"When we were talking initially ... life after, I said that this was not going to go on forever. I was realistic."

Whittaker, for whom rugby league had previously been a part-time job (including during his 118 games for Balmain between 1979 and 1985), was engulfed in the maelstrom. When I ask him if he encountered a lot of emotion at Phillip Street, he looks back incredulously.

"Encountered? There wasn't anything else. All there was, was emotion.

"The Phillip Street vibe, anyone could describe it. Anyone could think it through. Quayley had gone, Arko was going to stay on for a bit but he ended up leaving in early January. I wasn't meant to start until the first of February.

"I think my appointment was announced in mid-December or something - it's a long time ago - and I didn't ever go back to my place of work. They packed my box up and sent it to me. I was on remote control from that moment.

"All the people there had worked through the lead-up to that 1997 season with Arko and Quayley and were part of it. So the emotions were really raw, about a) them leaving and b) what was gonna happen next.

"The only thing on my agenda was to get the comp going as quickly and as well as we could. Because the real asset we had was the players and the clubs and the game. "

On December 10, the ARL announced it was adding a Melbourne team in 1998. The next day, Super League launched its World Nines in Townsville. It would be a three-day tournament from January 31, 1997.

It was during the New Years period that a group of North Sydney players, including captain Jason Taylor, got into trouble at a day/night cricket match.

Taylor was ejected from the ground; players were accused of urinating in a cup and throwing it in the air, putting tomato sauce on a fellow spectator's back and making obscene comments to a woman.

And thus was born a new core skill of anyone in charge of rugby league in Australia: dealing with the off-field behaviour of young men with too much money and time on their hands. With a friendly media and in a less-vigilant society, Quayle had been spared what - by David Gallop's time - would become an almost daily chore for the game's top official.

"Everyone wants a united league and I think he has the capabilities of doing that," Quayle said of his successor. "(But) I don't know if it is 'welcome Mr Whittaker' or 'commiserations'."

Malcolm Speed, meanwhile, returned to Melbourne embarrassed after rugby league had jilted him at the altar.

"The head hunter rang me later and apologised for everything," he recalls.

"I think that was December '96. I got approached for the cricket job in March '97. I think what had happened - and the head hunter said this to me - 'oh, you'll get the next job that comes up because people now know you've put your flag up that you're looking for a change, you're looking for a job'.

"I met Neil a bit later when I was in the cricket job, probably towards the end of '97 I think. I remember him saying to me 'any chance of swapping jobs' or something like that. He was doing it pretty hard at the time.

"I remember slinking out of rugby league headquarters feeling quite rejected and dejected … but it didn't take me long to cheer up once I realised what I'd missed."

A RAM CALLED ROCKET

By STEVE MASCORD, *Sydney Morning Herald*,
Friday January 31 1997

ROD REDDY first walked onto Kogarah Oval some time very early in 1972, as an 18-year-old from central Queensland.

He doesn't remember much about the training session; there was certainly very little that night to indicate he would go on to play 16 Tests for Australia, or star on two Kangaroo Tours, or play a part in the birth of State of Origin.

Just a few drills, a few laps of the oval and a few drinks at the pub afterwards. But Reddy, now 45, recalled this week being taken aside by legendary Saints secretary Frank Facer towards the end of the same season, a debut year which exceeded his wildest dreams.

"I remember Facer saying to me, 'Son, you'll coach this club one day'," Reddy said from Adelaide, a long way from Kogarah.

"At the end of 1995, 1 remember hearing his words in my head. I had plenty of flashbacks. It wasn't easy."

Reddy hasn't spoken at any length in public about the events of November and December 1995. For a start, he was legally bound not to do so until at least March last year.

He fulfilled Facer's prediction on August 8, 1995, when he was named St George first-grade coach for the following year. Brian Smith had left for Bradford, the club had abandoned merger talks with Sydney City, and chief executive Geoff Carr was on the way to being "let go".

What was to unfold over the next four months made Reddy one of the most controversial figures in the famous club's colourful history. By the end of the year, Reddy had departed for the still nonexistent Adelaide Rams, leaving Saints without a coach just two months out from their first game and in the greatest period of uncertainty the club had ever known.

"When Saints took me to court, they put a clause in my contract that I wasn't allowed to say anything about my departure until March," Reddy said.

"I think they were worried I'd go around bagging them. I don't want to bag the club; I'm proud to have played there and proud to have coached there."

But listen to "Rocket" tell it now, and Saints officials gave him little alternative but to leave.

"It wasn't me who started talking to Super League; it was the board," he said, "or at least a third party co-opted by someone on the board."

Reddy claimed he was told by "a very influential member of the Saints board" that the club would not have a rugby league team in two or three years' time.

"That meant I was going to be laid off; I had to look for another job," Reddy said. "Five days before I left, I was still very much a part of the St George club."

Somehow, Reddy ended up at the Rams, and Saints stayed with the Australian Rugby League. And then Super League was outlawed.

"There were times when I wondered if I made the right decision," said Reddy, who watched last-minute stand-in David Wake take the Dragons to the grand final last year. "It hurt a bit when people said I'd made the dumbest decision of the year. But I just had to bite my tongue and hang in there."

Rupert Murdoch answered only three or four questions after News Ltd's annual shareholders meeting in Adelaide late last year.

So it's easy to understand how unpopular one shareholder made himself with journalists when he asked: "Will the Rams be on free-to-air?"

Murdoch, apparently taken aback, began talking about an American football team before he was nudged in the right direction by one of his aides.

Still, the answer to the question remains unclear.

The day the *Herald* visited the Rams training camp in suburban Oakden, Adelaide was baked in the sort of desert heat that makes the Gobi seem like a tropical paradise. Under a tree on a training field adjoining the Rams' administrative complex, Reddy tossed a ball in the air as he addressed the day's training group halves and hookers. New recruit Kerrod Walters, Papuan bar-fridge impersonator Elias Paiyo, stocky halfback Stuart Topper and versatile Queenslander Dean Schifilliti looked on, swatting flies.

The difference between Reddy's old club and his current employer are striking reminders of the contrasts between the old league world and the new. St George are funded by a poker-machine palace and have their headquarters within the leagues club, while the Rams, funded by pay television, are based in a massive office block which boasts a mess hall, weights room, accommodation for juniors and more floor space than the headquarters of Super League and the ARL combined.

There are people whose full-time job it is to make sure the players are comfortable. All relocation costs were met by News Ltd, former Cowboys first-grade coach Grant Bell is the full-time junior development officer and Reddy refers to training as "coming to work".

Schifilliti, raised in sweltering north Queensland, said he had been looked after and liked the place.

"But it's bloody hot," he said, sucking on a water bottle.

The chief executive is Liz Dawson, the 38-year-old former Auckland Warriors marketing chief and only the second woman to head a rugby league club in recent memory.

She said the Rams were just like any other News Ltd enterprise - Ansett, the Adelaide Advertiser or Foxtel.

"Our charter is to move into profit as soon as possible," Dawson said in her air-conditioned office.

"Being a franchise situation, I would imagine there is eventually an opportunity for private ownership in the place.

"News, being a business organisation, would have to look at that when the time comes." But are the Rams even recognisable as a football club, or just a provider of programming for a television network?

"I think that's fair comment, but would you say the same of American sport?" Dawson said.

"I think if you watch something on television and there's no-one in the stadium it isn't a good event for television. But if you hear the crowd in the background then it's more exciting."

The club that TV rights built? "You're really harsh," she replied, without disagreeing. The novelty of going to Adelaide Oval, under lights, to see a new sport is one plus for the Rams.

"They don't understand ARL v Super League down here," said Reddy, "they just know they're getting a rugby league team."

On the other hand, the Rams have an extra competitor this year with Port Adelaide joining the Australian Football League.

And then there are the persistent doubts about the Rams' playing depth. A quick look at the Rams' roster shows what appear to be some significant imbalances. Three hookers Schifilliti, Walters and Paiyo, no recognised five-eighth and very little depth in the three-quarter line.

"The club was thrown together in a rush, and the best job was done with the available players," Dawson said.

But many players have at least enhanced their reputations during the past 12 months: Marty McKenzie and Rod Maybon both had a good year with Parramatta, Kevin Campion made the grand final with St George, Joe Tamam was a revelation with Bradford and Mark Corvo played much of the year in first grade for Canberra.

Only 14 players are contracted for 1998. Reddy, who left a number of spots open last year in case there was a flood of players from the ARL, still has the door ajar.

"We're not going to win every week," said Dawson. It may turn out to be the understatement of the year.

The Rams begin their belated debut season next Thursday with a game against Auckland in Nuku'alofa, Tonga. Before Justice Burchett called a halt to everything last year, they pushed Canberra and flogged Perth m trials.

The club's marketing department is negotiating with some multinationals for naming rights and sleeve sponsors.

Utility Chris Quinn, a former Dragon, has been named club captain. And Reddy could be excused for not giving much thought to what St George supporters think of him

But he has a fair idea.

Believe it or not, he went back to Kogarah Oval last year. It was round 16, the Dragons were at home to Western Suburbs and "Rocket" was a guest at an "Internationals Day". He was paraded around the oval in a open-top car. The crowd reaction?

"What do you think?" he said. "It was . . . mixed.

"Obviously some people don't like the decision I made, but I have to think of my family and my future.

"No-one can take away the fact that I played for St George, that I coached there and I'm proud of what I achieved there.

"Some of the people who've been critical, if they were brutally honest with themselves and they were placed in the same position as me, they may very well have made the same decision."

Reddy is satisfied he can look old Frank Facer in the eye on Judgment Day and say he did what he thought was best.

"He made me feel special that night, when he said one day I'd be coach," said Reddy. "Then again, for all I know he could have said that to every kid who showed up at the joint"

CHAPTER 6
Betrayal

HUGH Marks had been legal counsel at Channel Nine for two years when he was called in to negotiate a deal that would rock the ARL.

His is a name that will resonate much more recently in the minds of rugby league fans; the 54-year-old is the man who in April 2020 as Channel Nine's chief executive attacked the NRL as bloated, called for clubs to be given more power and threatened that the sport's long-time free-to-air broadcaster would walk away from from it during the Covid-19 lockdown.

Marks' comments led directly to the departure of CEO Todd Greenberg; 23 years earlier the deal he did with Super League hastened Ken Arhurson's exit from the game.

"(It's) so long ago I can hardly remember any detail," he wrote to me in an email.

"The bust up was my first day on the job at Nine and the peace deal obviously post-that but not sure I've got much interesting for you, sorry."

(By the end of 2020, Marks had departed Nine after admitting a relationship with a staffer 16 years his junior)

When Kerry Packer in 1995 insisted on enforcing a pay TV clause with the NSWRL even though he had no pay TV outlet, and threatened to "sue the pants" off any club that did business with News, the ARL went to war on his behalf.

Surely Packer wouldn't then put Super League on his TV stations, would he?

"I had heard the rumours on this but had defended our 'allies'," Arthurson wrote, perhaps insisting on the inverted commas with his co-author, Ian Heads.

"'Not when the chips are down, they won't do it to us', I had said to people who suggested that treachery was in the wind."

Sure enough, On January 17 1997 it was announced Nine, until then the staunchest of ARL allies whose chiefs had handed out cheques at Phillip Street like 'how-to-vote' fliers at a polling booth, had taken a bet each way by signing a deal with the breakaway. Monday Night Football would be the domain of Super League and it would be on Nine. "Ken felt betrayed," Maurice Lindsay says.

Explaining their decision at the time, the channel said in a statement: "We believe that the Nine Network telecasting both the ARL and Super League will increase the prospect of a unified rugby league competition, which we believe to be in the interests of the public, viewers and all parties.

"If the Nine Network had not secured the rights, another network would have and this would have made the prospects of one competition remote."

David Gallop, the youthful legal counsel for Super League, recalls: "I was there (at Nine's Artarmon studios) with Hugh Marks ... and

I remember we were there until 1am doing the deal that meant Channel Nine would now cover Super League games.

"It was urgent enough that we stayed there until we got it done and yeah, it was at least one o'clock in the morning. I remember getting a cab back over the Harbour Bridge with Tom (Mockridge)." (Mockridge was assistant CEO at News who went to Foxtel at the end of 1996).

Arthurson looks grim, even today, when the episode is raised. He insists that there was no mention of Monday Night Football when James Packer called him, just that Nine were going to show Super League matches.

"It's very, very clear in my memory and I was disappointed that Kerry hadn't rang me personally because we'd had a good relationship over the best part of 20 years. We always got on well and each of us had always honoured our agreements with the other.

"The phone rang and it was James, his son. He got James to ring me. I can always remember his words. He said 'it gives me no pleasure to say what I've got to say to you now Ken' and he told me they'd reached an agreement.

"I said to him 'I can't tell you how disappointed I am, James'. I said 'you've let us down badly but in any case I at least expect you to honour the financial arrangements you've made over this (with us)', which he did.

"James handled it as well as he could. It wasn't news he wanted to give and it wasn't news I wanted to hear. I was surprised that James and not Kerry himself had passed on that message."

Gary Pearse observes: "It showed the true colours of the media in regard to loyalty. There was a war between the two of them and one of their generals had basically gone across straight away and bought the rights to the opposition."

John Ribot added: "You could see a few cracks coming into negotiations (for the ARL). I really respected Kerry Packer. With cricket and all those things he's done, he was just a leader. Rupert said to me one day, when we did the deal (to launch Super League)… 'you know, this is going to be a very difficult thing to do here because Kerry Packer owns Sydney. I'm very well placed internationally, off-shore and that, with a head office here in Sydney. This is going to be quite a battle' but he said 'geez, it's going to be a lot of fun'.

"He shook my hand and walked out and I thought 'bloody hell'. "

In the wake of Packer doing a deal with Ribot, Arthurson effectively demanded ("offered the opinion" in his words) that Nine CEO David Leckie could no longer sit on the NSWRL board - and Leckie duly resigned. Between this moment and the release of his book many months later, Arthurson did not speak to anyone at Channel Nine.

"Channel Nine's move dragged me down about as far as it was possible for a fundamentally positive person like myself to go," he wrote.

South Sydney patriarch George Piggins wrote: "Business and the bottom line had won - and it was a huge disappointment. Kerry Packer had seemingly been rock solid with the ARL since the February meeting in 1995 and then suddenly bang! And he's over the fence."

But, true to form as a pragmatist-come-lately, Neil Whittaker was unfazed even by one of the most ruthless acts of the entire Super League War.

"There were a lot of disappointing things that happened," Whittaker says, very early in our chat. "That each-way bet was disappointing but I just couldn't allow it to distract me from getting the comp going and at the end of the day, that's what won us the outcome, was the competition.

"James (Packer) was more worried about the discussion than I was. I don't know who made the decision within their organisation but it was a decision he was very anxious about.

"It's interesting, I remember very clearly the meeting I had with James when he told me about it. You know, things were so bad that my reaction to it was really surprising. He expected me, I think, to go off the planet over it. Arko and everyone, we'd got this far and we were about to start the comp and they'd taken the Super League rights.

"So I just said to James 'it's already done, you've told me you're doing it, there's nothing I can do so I'm just going to get up and walk out and get out of here and get on with something I can do something about'.

"And that's what I did.

"A few years after, after the Super League War when you bump into James, I always had the feeling that he respected the way I approached that meeting, that I saw it as a business decision they had to make. Everyone was making business decisions to suit their organisation. No-one knew how it was going to go, everyone was placing bets.

"I've never spoken to James about it but I suspect that worked towards building the relationship that I had with him and I got on fairly well with Lachlan (Murdoch) as well. We had two youngish executives in the middle of it, caught up emotionally. One on either side, it wasn't easy to manage."

Ribot recalled: "The Americans had Monday Night Football and it became the family night for their game.

"We had a conference in Los Angeles with all the clubs from around the world (in December 1995) and we had keynote speakers and we all went down and saw San Diego on a Monday night. It was an unbelievably good night. Everyone enjoyed it, had a great time and I think … if you had the networks wanting to do it, and having seen it in America I had no issues with that at all."

But Shane Richardson believes the TV deal between Nine and Super League was actually much more than a TV deal. If not for Optus Vision and its combative CEO Geoffrey Cousins, Richardson believes, it would have been the beginning of the end of the fight. "I'm sure Murdoch and Packer had come together and the real saviours of the ARL were Optus and Geoff Cousins," Richardson says.

"He's never got enough recognition for what he did to save the ARL. The same goes for (saving) the traditional clubs."

And so as our year in question dawned, 1997, Super League had all the running. It looked like being the "juggernaut" it had promised to be.

But the competition hit choppy waters when Nine conceded it would be contractually unable to televise the opening game of the breakaway's season - between Canberra and Cronulla - on a Friday.

Its arrangement with the ARL precluded it showing any other competition on that day of the week - so the kick-off of the new league was put back a day (Brisbane v Auckland at ANZ Stadium) and the Raiders-Sharks game moved to Monday at the Sydney Football Stadium.

But in a compelling sign of the game's malaise at the time, Nine didn't judge either competition worthy of live prime time coverage. MNF and the ARL's Friday night match were kicked back to a delayed 9.30 time slot; cop drama *Water Rats* was considered a stronger ratings bet at 8.30 with *Friends* and the Lotto draw also airing while the matches were being played.

Journalist Ian Heads wrote: "From the beginning, the struggle has been about hidden agendas unconnected with the game at the heart of it.

"...the two sides have just got to hope there are enough people around who still care."

And in the wake of a significant body blow to the ARL, Arthurson made comments that led the public to think he was heading the way of Quayle - out the door. "I would have bet my life on Nine standing by us but I guess I'm naive. I'm bitterly disappointed.

"When all this started and we were approached by News, we told them we would not, and could not, do what they were asking because we had a legal and moral obligation to Nine.

"I've been friends with Kerry Packer for a lot of years and I vividly remember being at the International Sevens in February, 1995, when he gave me an assurance that he would not make any deal with News without coming to me and getting the approval of the ARL.

"If they are going to reach an agreement now, the Packer and Murdoch families, why the hell didn't they reach that agreement in the first place without putting us all through this trauma we've been through the last two years?

"It certainly would have added a few years to my life."

Ribot, in the same story, said: "If we can enhance the product, while there's a coming together of the parties, then that's good for the game and it's good for Super League."

Another alliance seen as unholy in many circles: Saturday Super League on the publicly owned ABC.

"There was a friend of mine called Gerry O'Leary who actually pursued the rights," says journalist and presenter Debbie Spillane. "She was acting head of sport at the time.

"She was a mad rugby league fan. She still doesn't get much kudos, she was the first woman to be producer of ABC live rugby league. She was the person in charge of the coverage, in the van calling the shots.

"She told them what Super League needs more than anything is national coverage but coverage with a traditional base, some cred.

"She put a good argument: we can't afford to give you any money for it but ….

"A lot of people were disgusted with the ABC for that. Those people were mainly from NSW and Queensland. But we were always getting tackled by the ABC board because rugby league wasn't a national sport and it was the national broadcaster.

"So Super League (with a wider geographic spread) actually fitted the ABC criteria a lot better than the ARL had.

"She talked (Ian) Frykberg into the deal and then she gave me the job of fronting it. She impressed Frykberg so much they offered her a job at Fox Sports."

'Aunty' broadcasting Super League was targeted on the ABC's *Media Watch* program, with Spillane's dual roles with a club - she was Bulldogs PR - and on the coverage, highlighted as potential conflict of interest.

January opened up ahead of a divided game; early in the new year, Whittaker told the *Sydney Morning Herald:* "We've got to accept that there are too many teams in Sydney".

At the time, there were 11: Cronulla, Manly, North Sydney, Parramatta, Penrith, the Bulldogs (then known as Sydney Bulldogs), the Roosters (then known as Sydney City Roosters), the Tigers (then known as Sydney Tigers), South Sydney, St George and Western Suburbs.

As Michael Adams, the host of a recent podcast series about the Super League War - *Rugby League Digest* - noted, it's a fallacy that maintaining the same number of teams in the Emerald City is "traditional". In fact, talk of cutting them had become a tradition of its own - and that remains to this day. When Illawarra and Canberra joined in 1982, it had not been called "expansion", an American buzzword. It had been referred to as "decentralisation".

The news cycle trundled along. Players outside each club's top 20 in Super League were told they'd have to pay their own medical insurance, a backflip on a previous understanding.

And Super League's plan of "clean skin", or sponsorless, jerseys was abandoned after a threat by Dominion Breweries to sue the Auckland

Warriors for breach of contract if they were removed. In England, David Howes resigned as a director of the RFL.

Canberra announced plans to float the Raiders on the stock market. At a mid-month media conference in Brisbane, senator Graham Richardson predicted a united competition in 1998.

And - inevitably - on the evening of January 22, Ken Arthurson resigned along with executives Greg Mitchell and Graeme Foster.

Arthurson had originally intended to stand down only as NSWRL chairman and stay on with the ARL, but concluded that resigning twice was more than he could bear. "I don't know what the scoreboard will say," Arthurson mused at the time. "I hope it says 'he gave the game his best shot. He never sold the game out'.

"Super League kept talking about a partnership. But what they really meant was a two-tier system where News Ltd ran the elite tier of top clubs and we looked after juniors, referees and ran coaching courses."

Mitchell now says his own decision was actually taken much earlier, in response to the departure of his close friend, Quayle. "When I knew that he was going .. to SOCOG (Sydney Organising Committee for the Olympic Games) with Michael Knight recruiting him., the minister in charge of SOCOG, I had a meeting with John. I said 'if you're going, I think I might move on.'."

Quayle helped Mitchell get a job at the Australian Rugby Union.

Arthurson's resignation was to take effect the day Super League was scheduled to kick off, February 28. Perhaps unlike his friend Quayle, Arthurson has let the circumstances surrounding his departure from Phillip Street fade with the passing years. The betrayal by Channel Nine hurt at the time, but not now.

"I'd always said that I was looking forward to retiring when I turned 65. I'd said that since I was 40 years of age, you know?

"I'd reached 67, John had gone and I thought probably the time had come for a fresh start and to have some fresh points of view in there. That influenced my decision, very much so. One, I thought probably it was in the best interest of the game to have a fresh start take over and also I missed the fact I wouldn't be working with John.

"I only went to 67 because I hung on because of the Super League War."

Having lamented that Packer and Murdoch had taken years off his life - Arthurson moved to the Gold Coast and set about getting them back.

"Many kind words were spoken," Arthurson wrote in 1997, "including a nice tribute in the media from John Ribot. I appreciated that. I'd always liked the bloke.

"…just wish he hadn't done what he did."

The relationship between Ribot and Arthurson is a touching and compelling one, like the heads of warring houses who only briefly paused the breaking of bread. It was Arthurson who separated Ribot and Quayle at Phillip Street in 1994 when the latter confronted the former about rumours of a rebel competition.

Ribot says now: "It's probably worth mentioning … Ken Arthurson gave me an opportunity. I broke my neck when I was playing football. I laid in hospital for a few months and what was I gonna do?

"I was semi-committed to a contract at Wests and he rang me up and said 'would you come over and Manly would like to take you on. We think you're a great winger and we'd love you to play in our club'.

"So I went over there and he fundamentally changed my life. He gave me an opportunity to play at a level and it was well before Super League but the money I was on, to the money I got, was multiplied by three.

"I was able to do things for me and my family that you never forget.

"I can't say anything bad about Ken Arthurson. Ken, he's a colourful guy and you could write books on some of the things they did, but for me, I've always had a great relationship with him. We see each other, we get on well."

Ribot had an almost visceral understanding of how hurt his friend had been by Nine's betrayal. Like Quayle, there was an old world code to the way Arthurson saw the world and did business. That code had been eviscerated.

"I don't know if you can recall but if you went into Ken's office … a bit of an insight into why he would have been taken aback by that … there was a photo behind his desk, on the wall, of him and Kerry Packer shaking hands.

"I think they both had their arms around each other. It was a really nice photo.

"When it all went a bit pear shaped, I said to him once 'you see Kerry as a good friend of yours. He's a businessman and he'll make business decisions. It will be interesting to see where this goes. If he sees an opportunity, he's going to go for it' and I think that probably highlighted it to Ken.

"Everything Ken had done, he'd put all his eggs in (Packer's) basket and all of a sudden he looked and a few of the eggs had been taken out."

Cousins was unruffled and unconcerned by the change in the balance of power in free-to-air TV. Whatever Packer and Murdoch did, he knew he still held the cards.

"I wasn't in any sense surprised about Kerry hedging his bets," he tells me. "That's what he'd done with Rupert all his life.

"He was a bit in awe - frankly - of Rupert, Kerry. I don't think he was in awe of anyone else."

Tom Mockridge, when I tracked him down in Italy for this book, summed up Nine's 'deal with the devil' simply: "It was part of the peace plan."

SUPER LEAGUE: THE VERDICT

By Steve Mascord, *Sydney Morning Herald*,
Monday February 3, 1997

AFTER two years of talking the talk, the question that hung in the muggy Townsville night on Friday was: Could Super League walk the walk?

After all, it's one thing to pay players sums resembling telephone numbers, command an army of lawyers, put out press releases and make promises

But a year after first intended, Super League finally happened in Australia at the weekend.

And there couldn't have been a better forum for Rupert Murdoch to parade his new world order for rugby league than at the second annual World Nines.

Wingers from Warrington, centres from Carcassonne, toilers from Tokyo, marines from Michigan and drop-punters from Paris gathered to illustrate rugby league really was going somewhere.

ARL chairman Ken Arthurson believed Super League couldn't sell rugs in Alaska.

Maybe not - but could they flog rugby league to Townsville?

CONCEPT

The new world order isn't that new. Many of the 12 countries which attended began playing league through Colin Love's ARL aligned World Sevens.

The idea of having an Australian team, rather than just local clubs, seemed to be a winner with spectators. They cheered the Australians and regarded even the most inept opposition as an enemy

Super League deserves credit for not simply cashing in by inviting its crowd-drawing club teams.

The whole concept isn't bad but the breakaway is yet to make it its own.

Rating: 3 out of 5

ENTERTAINMENT

Super League planned to have international acts at many of its domestic games this season

Yesterday, Australian pop singer Christine Anu entertained the crowd, while there were cultural dance groups at every half-time break - and around town - throughout the tournament

The timing of the fireworks - at the end of play on Friday and Saturday - seem ill-conceived, however. Most spectators were already on their way to the exits.

Rating: 4.
CROWDS

This area was the disappointment - 10,530 on day one, 12,360 on Saturday and 13,423 yesterday.

Aside from Brisbane, North Queensland is the best-supported league club in the country, but locals didn't turn out in force.

Admittedly, it rained overnight on Friday and Saturday and during play yesterday.

"Townsville has a population of 100,000 and we got close to 40,000 over the three days," said Super League chief executive John

Ribot. "I think any sport can be proud of that."

Rating: 2.5.
NEW TOYS

The video referee didn't have good Australian debut. On Saturday, Western Samoa's Joe Galuvao was award a try, although Australian winger Michael Hancock clearly forced the ball in-goal beforehand.

Referee co-ordinator Graham Annesley admitted the wrong decision had been flashed on the big screen.

There were also glitches with the referees' radio microphones and cameras mounted on the caps of trainers failed to work.

Rating: 2.
RULE CHANGES

Few of the Super League rules that will be used in 13-a-side football this season were applied Players who gathered possession from an opposition kick or mistake won an extra tackle for their team, but rules pertaining to bail-stealing and bomb-saking weren't used

In Super League the scoring side kicks off, but in Nines the team scored against was given a tap on half-way.

Rating: Not applicable.

VENUE

Stockland Stadium is simply a showpiece. An excellent surface, spacious dressing rooms, conference facilities, a press centre, an auditorium and a recovery pool make the Cowboys' home a monument to Super League. If promoters can attract bigger crowds, Townsville should become the Nines' permanent home.

"I think the tournament should have a permanent base because people need to know where and when something is on so they can make long-term plans," said International Board director general Maurice Lindsay.

Rating: 5

ORGANISATION

Super League's Elizabeth Street staff was determined to make the most of its active debut after two years of pen-pushing

Everything was minutely planned, with enough security employed to staff an Olympics

But while the thoroughness was impressive, there's no doubt there are a few areas in which it'll be looking to improve

The breakaway league promises to give the sport the same type of statistical focus as does American football, but for the second year running there was no official scorer at the Nines.

The last day was also a little anti-climactic, with the program going for just five hours after a marathon nine-hour session on Saturday

Rating: 4.

THE FOOTBALL

Lastly and most importantly, what sporting administrators now refer to as the product" Most observers agreed that Nines was slightly more attractive than seven-a-side league, with the two extra players giving the game more structure.

Desperate defence was more evident and the 1997 Nines will be remembered as the scene of South Africa's greatest strides forward in the other rugby code.

Japan was outclassed, but the other 11 nations were competitive and entertaining.

But some of the humour of the Sevens was missing, with back flips, forward rolls and American football huddles sadly rare.

Rating: 4.

VERDICT

Super League did just about everything asked of it on the weekend with a tournament run smoothly and professionally. Some believed the new league would try too hard to manufacture atmosphere and spirit but there were no signs of such hype.

Because of the heat on Friday and Saturday and the rain yesterday, the carnival atmosphere of the Sevens wasn't quite matched.

But as is the case with the TV networks and the ARL. Super League seems content to go about its business and wait for the crowds to come to it.

Overall rating: 4.

CHAPTER 7
Ken Arthurson

"OH, he still says that all the time!"

Ken Arthurson's wife Barbara laughs gently. We are on the 28th floor of a luxury apartment block just north of Surfers Paradise. As I gorge on Tim Tams and tea, having travelled by bus from 1.20am on New Year's Day to get here, I apologise in advance before enquiring about the 90-year-old former ARL chairman's most colourful expression, used often during the Super League War.

"I'm so busy I'm surprised they didn't shove a broom up my arse to sweep Pitt Street on the way here," he would say, entering a media conference at a fast clip. Imagine the chairman of a giant sports organisation proclaiming that to rolling cameras today….

An hour before, wearing loose-fitting trousers and a smart pullover, Arthurson had greeted me at the lift. He's an iconic figure in rugby league history, I'm just an old beaten up reporter - so the brief hug resonates with, and surprises, me.

- ◆ During the course of our conversation in a sun-drenched kitchen, Arthurson says:
- ◆ "Thankfully, that's over now. It's all been put to rest and we've all got to get on with trying to do the best we can for the game";

- "Things have settled down and I just don't hold any grudges, of course. Not for one moment."

- "I must say that it was a very difficult and worrying time."

"Ultimately things settled down and it finished up a 50-50 split but …"

With a view over a pool that seems big enough to be requisitioned by the government in case of drought, and the Gold Coast Hinterland in the distance, Arthurson seems as content with his legacy as any man can hope to be.

"People stop him in the street all the time," says Barbara. "They say 'are you Ken Arthurson? Thank you for what you did for the game, sir. Even here in Queensland!"

Perhaps Arko's serenity is a result of his escape from circumstances that could have left him much worse off. In April, 1953, he suffered a fractured skull playing for Parkes and was in hospital for three weeks. He never, to quote a popular cliche at the time, "laced a boot" again.

Returning to Sydney, Arthurson coached Manly to the 1957 grand final while still just 27.

He took over as club secretary there in 1963 and stayed in the role for two decades, wielding ever-increasing influence and presiding over the period when Manly became 'silvertails' by purchasing the best talent from other clubs.

It's fair to say that before the Super League War, it was not certain that Queenslanders or anyone but Manly fans would be stopping Arthurson in the street to thank him for his services to the game - although that is not to say they shouldn't have.

But Sydney rugby league is all about agendas, vendettas, politics and personalities. Even though he coached at Manly, the decorated New Zealander Graham Lowe was one of few who spoke publicly about the influence wielded by the Northern Beaches club in the eighties and nineties.

And as a young reporter, it was made quite clear to me there was a danger in quoting Lowe. There was definitely an informal cartel that controlled the game back then and those who pointed it out were denied a voice.

Lowe's battles were, in fairness, more with Manly's Machiavellian coach Bob Fulton than with Arthurson, of whom the Kiwi says now: "The whole thing would have been a scrambled mess without Ken because he was the shining-through identity."

But the Super League War changed things dramatically and permanently for Arthurson's public persona. He became a crusader, a hero, the old club jealousies melting into the past.

Lowe recalls: "The Super League-ARL thing, while a lot of people have got different views on it now, it required someone who was an iron fist in a silk glove but still had the compromise in him. Arko had the compromise.

"I'm sure it broke his heart but without his vision, which required compromise, I don't think the game would be anywhere near where it got to."

Arguably, Quayle left a part of himself in the trenches, while Arthurson was created there.

"As you can see, I'm not in the first flush of youth and I've spent my whole life, since I was probably 12, 14 years of age, in rugby league,"

Arthurson says when I ask him what 1997 meant to him. "It's just been my whole entire life. I really ... at the risk of sounding corny, I really do care for the game. I want to see it succeed so ...

"In all the years I was in rugby league, the Super League War was the only really bad time that I went through. All the great years of pleasure I've had out of the game far outweigh those things."

The end of Arko's reign, then, does not define it in his own mind - even if perhaps it does in the imagination of the game's public.

"At that time, pay television had just come in and of course Murdoch wanted pay television and that was the whole thing. Kerry Packer had the rights. He had the free-to-air rights and the pay TV rights," 'King Arkos' begins from across the kitchen table.

"All that was required was for him to give Mr Murdoch the (pay TV) rights. It meant nothing to him (because Australian Consolidated Press, over which Packer presided, had no pay TV arm) but he wouldn't do it and it went on, and on, and on and in the end, unbeknownst to me, an agreement was made between him and Murdoch and that's how it all finished.

"Once that happened, the fight was over."

One perspective he does share with Quayle is that expansion was simultaneously an achievement and a regret.

"Well, I was gone when that happened, when they decided to get rid of Perth and South Queensland. Funnily enough, they were only in the competition because of us. I mean, we got them and bought them into the competition. I must say that at the time I was very, very upset about the fact that (Perth) sided with News Limited on the issue.

"Because they really owed it to us to stick with us in those circumstances. Anyway, they didn't.

"Of course, one of the first things Super League did: they got rid of Perth. Perth probably would have still been in the competition if we'd been there."

International expansion initiated just before the war has stood the test of time, however. In late 2019, Tonga became the first new nation to topple Australia in 68 years.

"I'm really delighted about that. As a matter of fact, we were instrumental in bringing Tonga in. Bob Abbott, we used him as our man to look after the advancement of the game in the Pacific and he did a very good job of it too.

"Tonga is one we brought in. I was really pleased to see them do well. I wasn't pleased to see them beat Australia… I am never pleased to see Australia lose anything.

"But I'm really delighted at the progress the game has made in that area."

I wonder how Arthurson viewed that bastard child of Manly and North Sydney, the Northern Eagles. Based at Gosford and Brookvale, the joint venture lasted just three seasons, from 2000 to 2003, before collapsing.

Turns out, Arthurson was far from a spectator in this. He reveals he came out of retirement to quell a Bears-led rebellion that could have killed Manly. He ensured it instead killed North Sydney

"At the time … I've got a high regard for the North Sydney club, funnily enough, because before Manly came in (in 1947!) I used to follow their progress," he begins.

"But it was destined to be a failure because Manly had the rights. We had the rights to be in the competition. North Sydney had been taken out, they had no rights whatsoever. We bought them in and later on I found out that they were trying to get rid of Manly and take over the license themselves.

"Once that happened, that was the end of it for me.

"We found out and we went to the League. I'd retired by then but I came out of retirement to go in and put the case to them because I knew all about it. I know that they knew that I knew all about it. Naturally, they had to agree because it was quite legal, what I said.

"We had a legally-binding agreement that if the joint venture fell over at any time, the license would revert to Manly. They did try to dispute that but I ... went in and said 'don't try and dispute it because it's in black and white and we'll take it through every court in the land if you decide against that'.

"I do know that after I left the meeting, whoever was there - I won't name him - at the time said to them 'he is right, you know'. And I was right. So naturally they restored the license back to Manly - which was, in black and white, the agreement anyway.

"Look, honestly, it was a couple of people in Norths at the time who were the top administrators. They tried to do it on a personal basis - get rid of Manly - and that was the rock on which they perished because had they not done that I don't think we would have taken any action at all."

A bonus for a book about 1997, then: why the Northern Eagles died in 2002. "It was always Manly's licence, it was part of the merger agreement," says former Northern Eagles chairman Geoff Bellew.

"I did the chairmanship of the first year of the joint venture and I thought 'I can't do this anymore because they're all completely and utterly mad' and I got out.

"North Sydney started trying to flex some muscle the following year and my recollection is that Arko did step in … by reminding everybody that 'if this goes pear-shaped, we get the license back'. And that's exactly what happened.

"The North Sydney side were never really committed to making it work. That could have been a really powerful club. When you've got Mark Cannon and Terry Randall sitting opposite each other across a board table, threatening to take it outside…."

So, Ken Arthurson: who won the war?

No pause at all.

"I think it turned out, probably, a draw. That's how it's happened. They've reunited, they've made an agreement, they've got the competition up and running. All the things that Super League wanted certainly never happened but look, the big thing they wanted was to just get rugby league because of the pay television.

"It turned out pretty even, Stephen, in the long run."

GOLDTHORPE DROPS QUEENSLAND IN A THRILLER

By Steve Mascord, *Sydney Morning Herald*,
Tuesday May 20, 1997

AS compromise between league's warring parties nears, Super League last night contributed its first game to the sport's annals of great matches.

Halfback Noel Goldthorpe booted a field goal after 104 minutes of often exhilarating and almost always gripping rugby league to clinch the first and maybe last Tri-Series with a 23-22 win over Queensland in the final.

The ANZ Stadium game was already the new competition's best when Queensland replacement winger Michael Hancock crossed and fullback Darren Lockyer converted to tie the game up with 11 minutes remaining in regular time.

There had already been feats of individual brilliance: NSW centre and man of the match Brett Mullins had scored three tries and Queensland centre Steve Renouf bagged two in his first game back from injury.

And there had been controversy. Mullins had a fair try disallowed shortly before half-time and, after the break, NSW was awarded a try that shouldn't have been.

What followed in the next 34 minutes, which made the match the longest on record, was almost impossible to catalogue.

There were seven missed field goals, two disallowed tries and NSW captain Laurie Daley told reporters afterwards he thought, shortly before Goldthorpe's match-winner, he would have to toss a coin for the title.

"You think the game is struggling and then something like that happens," an emotionally drained NSW coach Tim Sheens said.

"It was just a great game to be part of. For two groups of athletes to go through more than 100 minutes of that . . . they're just playing on emotion."

"I thought that for-and-against might come into it after the second 10-minute period of extra-time, but obviously the crowd wouldn't be happy with that."

The game was littered with near things, unlucky misses, moments of genius, unfortunate decisions, all of which may have decided the match.

Mullins pulled off a remarkable tackle on Peter Ryan in the 69th minute, only to watch forlornly as Hancock crossed off an Allan Langer bomb moments later.

Both coaches admitted their players had no idea what would happen if the scores were tied after extra-time. Some probably had no idea what would happen next at 22-22 at full-time.

Under Super League rules, there were 20 minutes of overtime and, when it was still tied, they played on until someone scored.

After 80 minutes, the drama of extra-time included:

- 86th minute: Mullins having a try disallowed after stepping into touch;

- 89th: The video referee denying Maroons replacement Paul Green a try after he appeared to touch down within milliseconds of Blues replacement Robbie Ross getting to the ball;

- 91st: Maroons fullback Darren Lockyer missing with a penalty goal attempt after NSW prop Glenn Lazarus was penalised for a high tackle;

- 93rd: Maroons centre Tonie Carroll being held up over the line ;

- 95th: Ross missing with a field goal;

- 94th: Green missing;

- 95th: Goldthorpe missing;

- 96th: Goldthorpe missing again;

- 101st: Queensland failing to take a chance at a field goal.

"The first thing you like to do in any game is win," said Maroons coach Wayne Bennett. "But the second thing is to be part of something special. That was special tonight."

The game see-sawed during regular time with replays showing that Mullins touched down fairly after the ball was tapped back to him from behind the dead ball line in the 35th minute.

But referee Bill Harrigan ruled Lockyer had safely defused the bomb although he appeared to quickly drop it.

Bennett refused to blame the loss on the failure of touch judge Keith Gregg to detect NSW winger Ken Nagas's foot on the touchline before Mullins's 45th minute try: "Refereeing mistakes happen: we had our chances to win," he said.

NSW 23 (B Mullins 3, M Ryan tries; D Furner 3 goals. N Goldthorpe field goal) **bt QUEENSLAND 22** (S Renouf 2, T Carroll, M Hancock tries; M Rogers 2 goals, D Lockyer goal) at ANZ Stadium. **Crowd:** 35,507. **Referee:** B Harrigan.

CHAPTER 8

Gone Troppo

ON the first day of the Super League World Nines in Townsville in 1997, colleague Tony Adams asked me in the press box if there were "pornos" available in my South Bank hotel room. "No," I answered, "but I think they make them there."

The comment made the next day's paper, as did the ground announcer describing the executive director of the new "World Board" - each member of which showed up to a meeting that weekend in Super League-issued Hawaiian shirts - as "Boris Lindsay".

As the press pack was making its way down to the dressing rooms after a match on the final day of the tournament, the same ground announcer boomed over the public address: "To the correspondent from the *Sunday Mail*, I did not describe Maurice Lindsay as Boris Lindsay yesterday!".

Super League kicked off in Australia with a tropical holiday, complete with video referee stuff-ups and visits to the Santa Fe Gold strip club. See my review from the *Sydney Morning Herald* in these pages.

For the second year in a row, Australia failed to even make the final - something they only managed in a full scale international Nines tournament for the first time in 2019.

"We took it seriously - we were there to win it," says the Kiwis' coach, Graeme Norton. "Great Britain beat us, which really helped us to reset. We hadn't been beaten before (in Nines)."

Some of the World Board's announcements on the Saturday, meanwhile, were a little on the optimistic side - an eight-team competition in Japan, "an increased focus on development in the US"- but also the introduction of a seven-tackle set after a turnover, and free coverage of the sport on US television.

The seven-tackle set is still with us today, as is the consistently unfulfilled ambition in the US.

Australia were eliminated 12-10 in the semis by New Zealand ("We flew at them. We probably didn't give them a chance, actually," recalls Norton, perhaps ignoring the flightlessness of kiwis), who went on to win the World Nines with a 16-0 final win over Western Samoa. The second Super League World Nines (the first had been held the previous year in Suva) attracted crowds of 10,530, 12,360 and 13,423.

"The idea is that it is to become the Melbourne Cup of north Queensland," Ribot said at the time.

And, as mentioned previously, rugby league's fourth official made a comical debut under referees boss Graham Annesley; Samoa's Joe Galuvao was awarded a try on the Friday night even though Australia's Michael Hancock clearly forced the ball in-goal beforehand.

"It was a complete stuff-up and it was my stuff-up, to make matters worse," says Annesley now. "We'd gone down the path of making the video process very complicated and very technical.

"There was a thing that they nicknamed the yellow submarine because it was a whole bunch of equipment that came in a whole range of yellow boxes that was unpacked and put together.

"Effectively, what we had set up, with the technical advice that we received, was a mini television production suite. We were controlling our own replays, as opposed to the replays that came from the broadcaster. That was very complicated and what it did, of course, was completely distract any operator from what they were really focusing on, which was making the right decision.

"…because they were too worried - I was too worried - about trying to operate the technology.

"It was out of that trial in the Nines that we modified it significantly so we relied more on the broadcast feed than on our own feeds.

"But I remember distinctly having to go down to the pool area at Townsville behind the grandstand, in the Cowboys complex, and address the Australian players and apologise to them all."

As an aside, consultant Eric Fleming believes the fact the Australians didn't blow up publicly was down to cultural change he'd help implement.

"The introduction of the video referee was a complete disaster," Fleming maintains. "The coach would go 'you've got to give it a bit of time, it's going to take some work. It'll bed in'. No dummy spits. That's because they (coaches) were involved in developing it. It was their baby."

Another innovation in Townsville included the red zone being painted … red. They liked the idea so much in England that Salford adopted it without approval for a game against Wigan on April 25 of the same year.

Lindsay recalls: "I ran the original Nines which was in Fiji. I stayed in a crummy little hotel where the team was staying where the room was about as big as my balcony to the bedroom and I remember …. (International development officer) Tas (Baitieri) came in and he said 'are you staying here?'.

"I said yeah. He said 'fuck me mate, you're chairman of the international board. I said 'so what?' I'm not about being a big shot'. He said 'Arko wouldn't do this, he'd march out'. I said 'it's just because they're used to suites and all that. I don't give a shit'.

"(In 1996) We had the Gary Connolly affair. Gary Connolly had taken the shilling and signed for the ARL.

"He went right up to changing for the game and they came into the dressing room and said 'you can't play' and he was gutted. He just loved playing rugby, Gary. To cut a long story short, yeah I like the Nines. I like anything that's a gala, anything that's promoting rugby league."

While a good time was had by all, "I can't recall any significant atrocities taking place, which is quite unusual for those days," Annesley says.

Two days after the Nines, one representative of each team - along with one each from the domestic Super League - fronted up for a launch at Sydney Showgrounds' Hall of Industries which Paul Kind estimates cost $750,000 - making it the most expensive promotional event in the sport's history.

"We constructed this giant globe," Kind recalls. "It turned a bit like a mirrorball, it spun throughout the course of the night. It was the centrepiece.

"We built this 60-metre long … it was like a catwalk or runway and it was hidden behind a wall with the big 'S'. For the speeches and the start of it, that was what you saw.

"Jon Stevens sang 'Two Tribes' and then the wall opened and this catwalk, this runway, lit up and the players started coming down in procession and they had their positions on the stage.

"Then Laurie (Daley) was the last one, representing Australia. So you had all the teams of Super League plus all the international teams. It was at a level of expense that the game wouldn't even dream of today.

"All of those things had to be done. The thing with all that was 'what are the ARL going to do?' That was the theme of the entire key moments of the year - the 'other league'.

"The approach taken by Super League was just to throw money at it, to throw money and make it deliver on its promise. It all came back to that."

Roy Masters' wrote of the night's spectacle: "It employed thunderous music, laser beams, bow-tied dancers and slinky dressed women to demonstrate rugby league's thong-and-singlet days are over."

The news cycle continued to trundle along as the twin club seasons grew closer, all hope of compromise having evaporated. Another innovation out of division: Lebanon fielded its first rugby league team in the ARL Sevens.

That tournament - a week after the Townsville event - was won by Parramatta, who beat North Sydney 32-22 in the final. The Eels had to get past those well-supported Lebanon Cedars, however, in the quarters.

An ARL Melbourne team featured former Sydney Swan Leon Higgins and sprint champion Shane Naylor. Inevitably Higgins kicked for Naylor who chased, on the Saturday. Sure enough, Naylor arrived first - and dived straight over the ball.

One of the banners in the crowd read "$uper League $ux".

The pre-season was sometimes chaotic; the Mariners were left with the prospect of living up to their name when a plane that was supposed to take them back to Newcastle after one trial was unable to land in Rarotonga, where they had played Perth.

But even this early in 1997, there was something weird happening in Newcastle.

On one hand, the club at the very centre of the community was broke. Newcastle Council demanded $138,000 in back rent from the Knights. On the other, when Nine said it did not want to televise the ARL's pre-season Country Carnival, Newcastle station NBN stepped into the breach.

Also in the Steel City, a certain Andrew Johns was trying to kick-start his career in 1997 after - by his own admission - "going off the rails" the previous year at the tender age of 22.

"That dream soon ended in Coffs Harbour in a pre-season match against Manly when I tore the ligaments in my right ankle and had to have an ankle reconstruction," he wrote in his biography.

"I missed the first 10 rounds of the competition and my replacement, Leo Dynevor, played out of his skin. There was talk that I was going to play reserve grade when I returned."

Dynevor played 17 games that year, Johns only nine. "Leo was pretty instrumental in getting us where we got in the end," recalls Knights doctor Peter McGeoch, "because in subsequent years we didn't win a lot of games when Andrew wasn't playing."

Danny Munk has a favourite story about the pre-season. "We've got a trial game (in Queensland), (Club chairman) John Chalk is going 'we can't lose any players, we can't embarrass the ARL. No-one can misbehave. Make sure you've got everyone'. No worries.

"So we played the game, my memory is the result wasn't great. The boys went and had some dinner, had a few beers, everything was fine. I'm at the bus. 'One, two, three, four… 'Everyone's on the bus and I thought 'sensational, we've done this trial game, we've got everyone on the bus and we're getting them back to the hotel. No embarrassing stories from us'.

"Mobile phone rings. It's Chalky, going 'how'd you go? Get everyone on the bus?' 'Yeah, yeah, everyone's on the bus'. 'You sure?'. I said 'why are you ringing me?'

"He says 'you fucking idiot, come back and pick me up'."

Favourite to replace Arthurson, Queenslander John McDonald, told newspapermen he favoured a Super Bowl-style play-off between the winners of the two competitions at the end of 1997. Super League, meanwhile, had planned to give its 1997 premiership-winning coach the national post for the tour of Great Britain - Tim Sheens had coached them in Townsville - but that system was abandoned

On February 5, Super League's challenge to the ARL loyalty agreements began in court.

As part of the evidence, it was claimed James Packer told Anthony Mundine Super League was"absolutely fucked" and that Quayle boasted at a meeting "we own representative football".

Justice Burchett returned to proceedings when he heard a case about whether the intellectual property of clubs belonged to them or the ARL.

But there were still incongruous examples of detente that wouldn't happen even today. ARL-aligned Newcastle released Craig Bowen to the Cook Islands Nines side in Townsville and Super League's Canterbury allowed Hazem El Masri to play for Lebanon in Sydney.

On February 12, Neil Whittaker "predicted the code would one day have its own TV channel".

Incredibly, Super League announced it would allow members of the public to lodge complaints against players for foul play. While that never came to pass, the system of demerit points with discounts for guilty pleas is now commonplace in the NRL. Each 100 demerit points amounts to a one-match suspension with each offence graded between one and five.

One feature of the system which did not last was 20 demerit points for each stint in the sin bin, meaning a one-match ban for five yellow cards.

The ARL revealed in mid-February it planned to again ask clubs to sign five-year loyalty agreements. But the *Sun-Herald* reported that Manly and Sydney City were - to coin a popular phrase at the time - "ready to jump".

ARL clubs also discussed a 'payments floor' - a minimum they must spend on players - of $3 million. Interestingly, Illawarra, South

Queensland and Gold Coast were all said to be below that level and in a murky crystal ball, the fate of all three became apparent.

Bernie Fraser, a former governor of the Reserve Bank, was announced as having been approached to head an ARL "peace mission" to Super League.

For my part, I was driving around rural NSW covering trial matches, filing previews from roadhouses, staying in motels and drinking with players after matches.

There were more hiccoughs with the video referee during the Country Carnival when whistler Kelvin Jeffes thought it wasn't working, made a decision himself to disallow a try, and then the green light flashed after play had resumed.

Super League said players would be encouraged to display showmanship. "It's OK to show you are happy after scoring a try, as long as you're not disrespectful to the opposition," said Cronulla CEO Shane Richardson.

Perth chief executive Brad Mellen was forced to resign on the eve of the new season, having joined the club from a divided Knights.

John Cross and Jack Elsegood offered to repay their $150,000 ARL signing-on fees if they could suit up for Penrith and Canterbury respectively. Their offers were rejected.

"I had the offer of sitting out the year," says Cross. "Whatever the period of my Penrith contract was, it would be extended out.

"But I also had a contract with the ARL. I ended up just coming back and playing a year down here (in Wollongong). First game, I started off on the bench for reserve grade and ended up playing first grade later that same day!

"I don't think (CEO) Bobby Millward was that keen for me to come back. I think it was more (coach) Andrew Farrar who said 'we'll have him back here for sure.'"

Masters wrote: "The reality of the Super League-ARL war is that resources are now being diverted to previously neglected areas."

But they were also being stupidly duplicated. The Northern Territory Rugby League and the Darwin Rugby League shared an office - despite one being aligned with the ARL and the other with Super League. We had Super League Japan and the East Japan Rugby League - but no actual rugby league being played in Japan.

On February 19, the internal tensions at the Warriors claimed the scalp of the club's founding chief executive, Ian Robson. Robson and coach John Monie were staunch supporters of Super League but their board was divided.

"It was always something of a mystery to me how a couple of hired hands, albeit senior hired hands, could go so diametrically opposed to the publicly-expressed wishes/instructions of their 100 per cent owners," journalist Jim Marr ponders.

"I'd been on the board of the Mt Albert league club when they'd applied to join the New South Wales Rugby League. Everyone told us it was a pipe dream and it wouldn't work.

"I was only there for a couple of years but the people who conceived it and birthed it, they were dyed-in-the-wool footy people and they were looking for pathways for New Zealanders, rather than what's transpired which appears to be the wholesale plunder of a gene pool, really, by the NRL.

"They (Robson's administration) came in and they immediately - I guess this was a commercial decision - set about distancing themselves from the rugby league community, the core rugby league community which was undoubtedly working class, undoubtedly brown and not very attractive to potential sponsors, you would have to say.

"I found, as a New Zealander, that there was a fair bit of dog in what they did."

Recalling the day of his firing, Robson says: "I had a fairly nervous board.

"I got called into a meeting with the board one Saturday morning. Inevitably, if you stick around in sport long enough, you get a sixth sense about these things.

"I had David Howman as my lawyer. He went on to run WADA and is still a great personal friend of mine, he's now back in New Zealand.

"It was meant to be a confidential meeting, the resolution out of which was that we agreed to have a separation. A settlement was negotiated. Agreements … I don't know if we actually signed on the day but we shook hands. This was all meant to be top secret.

"And when I walked downstairs out of the building, there are photographers and journos from the two New Zealand Sunday papers waiting for me. Outside this confidential meeting.

"I still get the clippings to show my kids. The next day I was front and back page, my resignation, my sacking, of both New Zealand Sunday papers - which again shows the disproportionality of interest in sport."

Asked for his thoughts on the reasons behind his dismissal, he says: "It's worth noting that (club chairman) Peter McLeod once went on record as saying the worst decision he made as chairman of the Warriors was hiring me.

"I think I was clearly seen as someone who was attached, committed to News and if the Warriors were ever to take a position that was slightly more objective in that regard, that was going to be a problem.

"Of course at the time, it was confronting. I'd moved my life over there, I felt very committed to wanting to stay there and we'd been a part of something that was incredibly exciting and now we were just starting to deliver.

"I'd been a part of the club from the beginning, I was the first full-time employee so it's something that was always going to be …. in gallows humour, it's a reverse KPI. I was the last for the foundation CEOs, of those four expansion clubs, to get the sack.

"When you're in a room and you're being told it's time … you want to maintain your professionalism and you want to maintain your professional dignity. I was getting great counsel from David Howman who was just a really wise person to have in my camp. I was still really young when that happened too. I went there when I was 31. This was 1996-97, I'm 35 years of age.

"I'm shrugging my shoulders. I'm disappointed. I've invested a lot in this place. I'm sure something will come next.

"I hope you can hear it in my voice, I've got no ill-will about all that. It's 20-odd years ago. I just had the most extraordinary adventure. You look back at it now. How on earth did I get the opportunity to go and do it with my age and experience? I hadn't come from the game, I wasn't a New Zealander, you think 'how does that happen?'.

"Those two years were just an incredible, incredible ride."

So, just a day before Super League was to kick off, Telstra was unveiled as its naming rights sponsor. In the process of being privatised at the time, the telecommunications giant's decision to back the News Limited competition was threatened with a parliamentary airing.

"It was a really hard deal to get across the line because of the diligence and the people at Telstra," said Gary Pearse - the man Robson would replace.

"On the surface at the end it looked like an easy deal because of its investment into Foxtel. Nike was the other one that was hard to get across the line. The Australian Nike guys backed us all the way to Portland in America."

Super League, the *Sun-Herald* reported, had faxed radio stations banning them from giving score updates at Monday night games because they were being shown on delay.

A media empire trying to censor the news; there were multiple examples of this. Workers lower down the food chain at News Limited regarded Super League as their competition and a chance to settle old scores with rivals at opposing newspapers and TV stations.

Conversely, ARL loyalists thought Fairfax should become a default mouthpiece for the establishment.

Fox Sports tried to cover Super League media conferences exclusively, ignoring the fact that a "media conference" is by definition for all media and - philosophically - the success of the competition depended on bipartisan acceptance as a serious sports league.

The early stages of the rebellion had been deliberately leaked to Fairfax reporters for precisely that reason.

At a very early Super League media conference, I was told by one Fox cameraman to get away from players because I was ruining his shot and his station owned the competition.

I referred him to Rebecca Wilson, who feistily gave the 'cammo' short shrift.

SECRET TALKS POINT TO UNITED COMP IN 1998

By Steve Mascord, *Sydney Morning Herald*, **Wednesday May 21, 1997**

RUGBY league's warring factions have taken their first steps towards a 12- or 14-team united competition next year.

Although neither camp was prepared to go on the record yesterday, it appears an informal meeting between Australian Rugby League chief executive Neil Whittaker and News Ltd's executive director of sport, Ian Frykberg, was held last Friday.

The fact that both men adopted the same stance on the issue, neither confirming nor denying a meeting had been held, can be seen as a compelling pointer to their having had some contact.

"I'm not going to make any comment on the matter," Frykberg said.

Whittaker's version was: "I've decided I'm going to talk about the State of Origin and football.

These sorts of rumours seem to come up all the time."

But several other highly-placed sources last night confirmed, each also on the condition of anonymity, that there had been a meeting, although someone other than Whittaker might have represented the ARL.

The timing of initial peace talks is interesting: today, the hearing of Super League's challenge to the ARL's player loyalty contracts ends in the NSW Industrial Court. A decision is expected within eight weeks.

A victory for Super League would give it the upper hand in further negotiations.

And tonight, both Whittaker and Frykberg are expected to attend a benefit dinner for former Cronulla and Parramatta prop Adam Ritson at Randwick Racecourse - the first function they have attended together since assuming their current positions.

Few of the game's officials were willing to be quoted on the issue of peace talks last night but the *Herald* established that Frykberg most likely held some discussions with a leading ARL official, in person, last Friday afternoon.

The 22 clubs have been kept in the dark about the nature of the talks. Super League favours a 12-team Australasian competition, while the ARL isn't willing to countenance less than 14 at this stage.

Whittaker yesterday gave scant details about the meeting when he met board members of the NSW Rugby League, which runs the ARL premiership.

Super League clubs were told on Friday, and ARL clubs on Thursday, that there had been no talks. The rival Leagues have said nothing to their clubs on the issue since. The News Ltd-backed competition will continue to court ARL clubs interested in jumping ship but the potential traffic may not be one-way.

Any peace talks between football officials were largely unrelated to the changing face of pay television and likely mergers in that area.

Frank Stanton, on secondment from Manly as the ARL's business manager, last night denied it was he who spoke with Frykberg. That scenario would have explained why the matter was not discussed in any great detail by the board. Stanton is not on the board.

South Sydney chief executive Darrell Bampton, whose club is a potential casualty of peace talks, said he expected to be informed the minute talks began and therefore insisted there had been none.

But a high-ranking NSWRL official said: "In the agreement all the clubs signed recently, they gave Neil and/or the board permission to negotiate on their behalf." Super League officials believe a 12-team "hyper league" would be profitable enough to finally free franchises from being at the mercy of their licensed clubs. New poker-machine taxes in NSW have hit leagues clubs badly.

Whatever the current situation, it appears extremely unlikely that any meaningful negotiations can be undertaken until Super League knows whether it is legally free to raid the ARL's player ranks.

Whittaker told the Herald's Roy Masters at the NSW State of Origin launch yesterday: "When I've got something important to say, I'll say it."

In other news, touch judge Keith Gegg has been dumped to reserve grade after incorrect decisions during NSW's double overtime win over Queensland on Monday night.

Youngster Russell Richardson has forced Queensland Tri-Series centre Geoff Bell onto the bench for Cronulla's game against Penrith at Shark Park on Saturday night. Auckland's New Zealand Test prop Grant Young is in reserve grade for Monday night's clash with Canberra at Ericsson Stadium.

CHAPTER 9

Up, up and away!

THIS book draws its title from a Super League advertising campaign fronted by Noiseworks singer Jon Stevens, the centrepiece for which was his especially-commissioned cover of the 1984 Frankie Goes To Hollywood hit.

It was 11 months into my research before I discovered this campaign played a key role in the tragicomic - and even absurd - story of Super League marketing manager Gary Pearse's sacking after just one round of the competition.

It is at first an alluring 'column item' - a curious tidbit. It's only when the layers are peeled back that a real glimpse of life inside the breakaway's Elizabeth Street 'bunker' becomes apparent. None of the participants, as it transpires, knew the entire story.

The first cracking yarn of the actual season went like this, according to a prominent Super League employee who first reminded me of it: "There was the infamous story of Gary Pearse. Rugby union international and head of marketing (at Super League).

"He sort of fell out of favour and wasn't long for his role when, on the opening night of Super League, he decided to go to the opera….."

Pearse had played nine Tests for the Wallabies between 1975 and 1978. I track him down in Covid-19 lockdown at Bermagui on NSW south coast, where he says he feels blessed to be in isolation with his children and grandchildren.

Pearse says he's the man, while working for Winfield, who came up with the idea of Norm Provan and Arthur Summons (the latter died during the compilation of this book) on the premiership trophy. Pearse had a few jobs before applying for the Super League marketing gig and was happy to get it.

"I felt If we had got our competition going in 1996," he says, "we would have just steam- rolled everything. We had that much momentum, even without that much preparation going into it.

"The thing about rugby league is that the leaner and the tougher it is for league players and clubs, the better they are. The Super League teams in that combined comp in 1996 had gone soft on money.

"They weren't super. They didn't perform. If you were going to start a comp and show you were super, we should have had the top four spots."

During the 'down' year, Pearse confirms, pay television started to think it owned the competition that was running and, in the case of Super League and Foxtel, the one that might be held the following year. TV, he claims, and "started to dictate".

"Their influence was becoming … we were being consumed. We were becoming less a sport and more content."

This was the beginning of the end for Pearse; he raises the great Patsy of 1997, the World Club Challenge, as one concept with which he vehemently disagreed. He describes the WCC as an "absurd situation".

"We researched it here and nobody wanted that at all but the people paying the money wanted it as content rather than a sport. I had a number of arguments with the pay (TV) people over that … I wasn't getting on well with the pay guys.

"They changed our advertising agency and took us into their advertising agency. Just dumped ours. It was like getting shackled. I wasn't really happy. It wasn't a great place to work.

"We started to get home phone calls and people abusing my wife and kids leading into (the '97 season). We had to have security guards at our house for the month leading into the start of that comp.

"In early '97, we parted ways."

OK, here's where we need to do a bit of digging. Not so quickly, Gary. Opera? Hello?

"In the middle of all that, I got set up, to be honest … I don't know how you're going to write this," says Pearse, hesitantly.

"There was the opening game in Brisbane and on the same night the opera was in Melbourne and News Limited invited me and my wife to go.

"I probably shouldn't have made the decision. I said I'd take my wife because she'd been under a fair bit of pressure that month. She was keen, she actually had to work at the opera.

"We went down at News Limited's invitation and got on a five o'clock flight the next morning and went to Penrith.

"I think it was a left jab ready for the right cross. It brought it to a head and we just had a discussion. Things weren't working for three months before that.

"I'm being totally honest with you here, that's how it happened. I look back and I just let my guard down. Then again, I didn't really want to be there."

But if that sounded like a ruthless double-cross, it wasn't even a double-cross. It wasn't even a triple-cross, as we are about to discover.

Pearse describes Ian Frykberg as someone he'd known for a while from his time in rugby union, "a good operator".

But John Ribot reveals: "Frykberg wasn't big on him.

"I liked Gary. He was a rugby (union) guy but he was a good bargaining guy. He played a part in the Telstra negotiations and when he got that, Frykberg didn't like him and he said he was going to get rid of him.

"I said 'I don't agree with that' and he said 'well that's what's going to happen'. I said 'if it's going to happen, I'll do it and just explain it to him'. So that was one of those not-pleasant things because I really liked him and I thought he had real capacity."

Why didn't Frykberg like him? Over to Ian Robson - who would replace Gary Pearse as Super League's marketing manager.

"What was the precursor to me being given an opportunity was the spectacular failure, certainly in the eyes of Ian Frykberg, of the marketing campaign that Gary Pearse put on the table for "Two Tribes Go To War"," Robson says from Melbourne.

"Nah, didn't want to have a bar of it.

"So Gary exited stage left and I got a tap on the shoulder. It happened inside of a week. We literally, within a matter of days, appointed an agency called VCD and George Betsis and Simon Reynolds took over the campaign."

Finally, who were the "pay TV guys" with whom Pearse wasn't getting on? We can start with the CEO of Foxtel, Tom Mockridge.

"I might have got him to go," says Mockridge. "I sacked one of the agencies myself.

"There was a lot of financial pain. There were a lot of people who got burnt through the process. There were a bunch of other people who made a quid on the process.

"The sense was that someone else should do that job but it's certainly true that Foxtel was waiting for that to happen because Foxtel didn't have the AFL and through 1996 didn't have the league.

"That makes it a pretty thin offering in Australia."

Onto the footy.

Saturday would later become a bit of a lost day for rugby league before bouncing back in the last decade with the prefix otherwise discredited: "Super". But Saturday March 1, 1997, is when Super League launched in Australia. The first actual match was to be Brisbane v the Warriors at ANZ Stadium followed a few minutes later by North Queensland v Adelaide at Stockland Stadium.

Another taste of the ridiculous; the entertainment - featuring Yothu Yindi and an Olympic-style opening ceremony - ran overtime at the venue of the 1982 Commonwealth Games so the first game of the competition was not the first game at all - North Queensland-Adelaide kicked off first! A pre-match 'good luck' video shown in

Brisbane featured controversial politician Pauline Hanson, film critic John Hinde and shock jock Stan Zemanek.

After Brisbane beat the Warriors 14-2 in front of 42,361 people at ANZ Stadium, Rebecca Wilson tried to get Broncos coach Wayne Bennett to sit down at the media conference, as would be the new professional standard that season, imported from sports leagues overseas.

Previously, the almost exclusively male press corps would crowd around the coach in the dressing room while players showered and changed nearby.

"I've been standing up and doing it this way for years, Rebecca, and that's the way I'm going to do it now," Bennett said, rebuking the PR in the room just off the tunnel, set aside for the post-match media conference.

Bennett's reticence about post-match media conferences would be a recurring theme the following years. That night, Wilson was probably more concerned when he said to journalists - the fancy backdrop sitting useless a few feet away - "We all know it's not the best of the best because there's not one competition."

The game had featured 42 errors; the Gilbert balls were blamed and replaced in round two by training balls - but not in time for Monday, when Cronulla were hoping Canberra dropped the pill as often as possible.

Warriors fullback Matthew Ridge tried to kick one of the faux pigskins from the grasp of Broncos prop Glenn Lazarus as he scored a try, knocking him out. The practice would eventually be banned from rugby league. Another controversial St George-Brisbane transfer, Anthony Mundine, suffered a leg injury.

"Now we can get on with putting this game of rugby league on the world stage," Lazarus told Fox Sports at full-time.

Although he had played in the Nines, Gorden Tallis marked his comeback to club play that night. Tallis had sat out the 1996 season rather than return to St George, with whom he had a contract. His decision had cost him a grand final appearance.

During his year off, he had begun to date a woman who became his (now ex-) wife.

"I had got to know Gorden as a kind, gentle person," Christine Tallis said in the forward's biography, *Raging Bull*. "Obviously I was interested to see this guy I had been dating for a year play football.

"I'd have to say it was a shock. You'd have to describe him on the field as being the complete opposite of the Gorden I'd got to know.

"I still can't see how a genuinely soft person can be so aggressive when he plays football."

Mundine, played in the centres for the Broncos. "I was actually quite happy that we'd signed Anthony because he was a very good footballer," said Kevin Walters, with whom "The Man" was competing for the no.6 jersey.

"Everyone loves a challenge as a player, as well. I loved his time in Brisbane. We always got on well and I certainly appreciated his skill and personality. He actually fitted in well at the Broncos. He ended up playing in the centres and was a good team fella. He was a great asset for us."

The next day at the Ansett check-in counter, I clearly recall pop star Belinda Carlisle collecting her boarding pass. The former singer of The GoGos had performed the previous night in front of 42,000 but was in for a culture shock later that day at wet and muddy Penrith, where 8398 saw the Panthers beat Perth 30-20.

"The one I will never forget is her getting out of the helicopter at Penrith," says Paul Kind, "literally almost staggering to the stage, getting blown away with high heels in the middle of a footy field... to sing 'Heaven is a Place on Earth' to a rugby league crowd at Penrith."

Promoter Andrew McManus, who decades later told a court he had lied to police over a deal to borrow $200,000 from an organised crime figure, had been charged with sourcing international acts. "There was no Bruce Springsteen and that is what had been openly discussed in media going back 18 months before," Kind recalls

"They bought every ground that didn't have a sound system, a sound system. You're dropping these artists and these sound systems into suburban grounds, many of which aren't that different today.

"Without being disrespectful to the talent, you wouldn't call it world class. But it cost money. It wasn't cheap. It was an expensive exercise in doing the best you could do in a short timeframe."

This was the debut at Penrith of Sydney Kings basketball stadium announcer Rodney Overby, whose American-accented exhortations of "east side!", "west side!" were never truly embraced by rugby league traditionalists.

Afterwards, Perth's Mark Geyer took exception to a question asked of coach Dean Lance at the media conference and seemed to challenge a local reporter to a fight. The journo had asked if the Reds had played better when 'MG' was off the field.

"That's a fair bag," Geyer said from the back of the room - he was not involved in the media conference until then. "Is that me you're bagging? Talk to me about it, what do you think?"

Our fourth estate roundsman was not cowed, repeating the question to Lance. "How can you say that?" Geyer responded, before storming off.

"MG had walked in just as he said it," Rob Weaver recalls. "He got to within six inches of this bloke's face. We all thought he was going to lift him up and put him on one of the clothes pegs.

"I went after him. He came back and attended the conference."

Many people interviewed for *Two Tribes* contended that Penrith had only joined Super League so chairman Roger Cowan could escape spending money generated by his ever growing empire of licenced clubs on football.

His son, former Panthers marketing manager Max, argues strenuously to the contrary.

"A complete myth," Max argues, saying one of the primary motivations behind the early acquisitions of licensed clubs around the state was a fear that teams would be judged on their TV ratings in a rationalised league and more locations would generate more viewers.

"He spent so much time on working out what to do in that situation, that war, that crisis, where we thought no-one wanted us. It's not that he didn't want football. He didn't want football to send us broke.

"He played for the Panthers, 60 years of his life was spent at the club. He loved the football. A lot of the people you speak to will say he hated it. It's not true."

In the other Sunday game, Canterbury beat the Mariners 20-16 in Newcastle, fullback Rod Silva stealing the result with a 77nd minute try. The fireworks before kick-off (in the daytime, right?) reportedly caused a herd of cows to stampede.

"I thought there would be a half a dozen people watching," recalls Malcolm Noad, the Mariners' chairman. "But we ended up with a pretty good crowd and I remember thinking 'wow'. They were pretty enthusiastic."

"A disastrously poor standard of game," journalist Tony Squires wrote on Monday of the weekend's fare. The average round one crowd was 18,769.

But Penrith's Royce Simmons countered: "I know at coaches meetings we've talked about entertaining people. People were getting sick of the old 'hit up for six, kick for the corners'."

And so on Monday, when Super League made its prime time debut with the MNF clash between Canberra and Cronulla at the Sydney Football Stadium. Despite events at the Mariners the previous day, "they spent a lot of money on fireworks … and they forgot about daylight savings," recalls Kevin Neil. "You could hear a lot but you couldn't see much."

John Lang goes as far as to describe the first big televised Super League game as "business as usual" but Laurie Daley recalls: "We didn't know how many people we were going to get, whether they'd boycott it, what were the Sharks doing playing at the Football Stadium and not at their home ground?

"It was a bit of a weird build-up but one where we thought 'this'll be good, we'll see what Super League is all about'. I don't know if we expected it to be a totally different competition to what we were used to.

"There was a bit of trepidation, I suppose: what do we expect? In the end it was just a tough game of football."

Shane Richardson says: "You've got to remember we spent '96 being spat on. I remember up in Newcastle, I didn't think we were going to get to the bus. I think it was the first game of the '96 season. There was a lot of violence, a lot of spitting, a lot of anger.

"So it was quite different when we came to the Football Stadium because we were playing someone who was on the same side of us with friendly fans. Canberra fans were never going to travel down to Sydney anyway so it was our own fans and our fans were never known to be great travellers.

"Here we are playing the first game at the Sydney Football Stadium to make a statement but it was a bit like coronavirus. We didn't know who was going to turn up."

Cronulla flogged Canberra 26-4 after leading 22-0 at halftime. "It's a game we're probably all disgusted in," Ricky Stuart commented. Mal Meninga's coaching career was off to a rocky start. A month into the season, he still hadn't won a game.

"Mal was sort of thrown in late," Daley recalls. "Tim Sheens went to the Cowboys so he was thrown in the deep end.

"He was very well prepared. There was no real panic except maybe after the first few weeks. You lose and all of a sudden you're under the pump.

"We probably got a bit carried away with it, 'oh, this isn't going to be too hard. There's only half the teams in the comp, a couple of new teams'. Then you lose a couple of games and you're behind the eight ball and you think 'oh shit, we'd better start ripping in here'. Results started to turn from there."

Brett Mullins remembers: "It was a big change. I always had Tim Sheens as my coach from day dot. My role changed under Mal as well do it was a very frustrating time for me.

"Don't get me wrong, I love Mal to death. He's the greatest player I played with and a great coach. But he'll attest to this as well: it was his first year as a coach and he was a bit lost as well. We had wingers … my role at the time instead of playing my own game was to make sure I covered their mistakes.

"Instead of being an older player and mature, I was kind of pissed off with that, saying we were playing first grade. Why would have I to cover their mistakes? They shouldn't be making that mistakes. I sort of carried that through that year."

Luke Davico offers: "I put on too much weight and I was way too slow. That's reflective of where we were as a team at the start of the '97 season. We lost to Canterbury and Mal just came in and tore strips off us. I can remember him saying 'the papers aren't going to read Canberra can't play. The papers are going to read Mal Meninga can't coach'. And anyone who half had a chuckle got the look off Mal. They quickly avoided eye contact.

"I remember having an honest appraisal with Mal later and from the first day he coached until the last, he was on a different scale. I drew a graph."

Kevin Neil recalls: "After we lost at Belmore one day, I had a bit of a chat to the team that 'Mal was the coach and that's the way it is, he's not going anywhere'. A few of the players weren't great fans at that time of Mal.

"But he's proved to be a great, excellent coach. At that time it was difficult. It was his first year."

The ARL - which would give seven of 12 teams a finals berth - kicked off the following Friday. In the opening match , Parramatta drew their biggest home crowd in 11 years, 25,000, to see a 10-8 win over North Sydney.

"Parramatta fans, it could be argued, were the most fanatical of all - the battlers from the west," said Denis Fitzgerald.

"They didn't want a privately owned company - it would have been publicly owned at the time - (owning the sport) and they voted overwhelmingly with their feet by coming along to the games in 1997."

Balmain-Manly attracted 18,247 to Leichhardt. Adam Ritson, the poster boy for the ARL the previous year, was presented to the crowd after 14 brain operations following a high tackle.

"It's genuinely exciting that Parramatta got 25,000 people to their game," Ribot was quoted as saying.

Asked today why Balmain fans also responded so positively to a fair-to-middling season (crowds at Leichhardt were strong all year)

Danny Munk says: "When people thought they'd lose us, they started coming out.

"That was one of the problems a lot of Sydney clubs were facing up 'til then, the apathy. 'I can go to the game when I feel like it'. 'I can watch the game on TV, I don't really have to go to the ground'. They (the club) were always going to be there.

"Well, the reality was … the story involving the costs of the game and what was involved in getting professional athletes on the paddock …. When you talk '97, that was more professional than '87 and that was more professional than '77 - but in comparison to what they do now, we were babes in the woods.

"I don't think the message was getting out to the community that if you really want to watch these teams, there's going to be a cost. I think the AFL did that message a lot better and moved a lot quicker to start moving things around.

"If you remember we had a period for two years where we were called Sydney Tigers. That really disenchanted a lot of people. That was '95 and '96.

"We morphed back to the Balmain Tigers in '97 and we moved back to Leichhardt Oval in '96 because the whole Parramatta Stadium thing started working against us.

"The other thing that worked very well was, because of the actual Super League split, there were more tribal games. There were games against Manly, there were the games against Parramatta, there were the games against St George. There was the game against Souths.

"There was a real tribalism in those games and at a place like Leichhardt Oval, you could smell the game. Leichhardt and North

Sydney were great places to watch rugby league. You had the hills, you had your breezes, you got your pies, you rubbed shoulders with people.

"You didn't have big corporates sitting up in the stands and all the rest of it.

"The thing was, what people didn't realise was that looked good but didn't raise you a lot of money because the ones who had big sponsorship bases … were starting to already erode what was happening in Sydney

"And Sydney was really bipolar.

"You had Panthers and Parramatta and the Dogs and you had Easts. And everyone else was honestly sucking air."

Perhaps this explains why George Piggins commented in early '97: "If Optus Vision had not given us the $1.8 million every ARL club received as part of a funding package, we would have been forced to withdraw from the competition. Super League saved the day for our club. We have money in the bank for the first time in 20 years."

The ARL's round one, in which Neil Whittaker told the media Sydney fans "voted with their feet", was rounded out by Manly winning 14-10, Gold Coast downing Western Suburbs 24-16, Illawarra flogging South Sydney 50-10, Newcastle edging out St George 11-6 and the Roosters beating the Crushers 34-10. It was later reported the Roosters had distributed 30,000 free tickets to the Sydney Football Stadium but only 8,475 turned up.

Knights chairman Michael Hill had returned to the club during the off-season after playing a very different role in the Super League War:

helping Kerry Packer fire a shot back at Rupert Murdoch by signing rugby union players from under his nose.

He knew better than perhaps anyone else that footballers, officials, player agents and media people were just unknowing foot soldiers in a much bigger game. And yet under his rule, the Newcastle Knights would become the pawns - pun intended - who jumped up off the chess board to punch the big players in the nose.

The club he returned to was "healthy from a playing talent point of view, as you could imagine - but it wasn't healthy from a financial point of view."

During his absence, Hill had seen directors appear to favour News Limited because of the financial incentives including a new stadium - only for the players to go the other way. The officials "were disappointed - that's my gut feeling," Hill says now.

The first weekend the two competitions went head to head, Super League drew 77,073 over five games while the ARL had 75,412 over six.

"The ARL had a big weekend for sure," wrote *Rugby League Week* editor Norm Tasker.

"With Parramatta and Balmain turning on some top fare in front of packed houses, it gave the ARL a warm, fuzzy feeling it hasn't felt for quite a few years.

"Super League had a much less inspired start … although anything completely new takes longer to wind up. Super League's hype had made expectations extremely high and reality was always going to bite sooner or later.

"The certain thing is that it's a far better season than last year, when all we had was bitterness and uncertainty."

Tasker added: "Sydney has swung back brilliantly behind the ARL. The sort of support available to Balmain and Parramatta has not been there for eight or nine years at least."

After Cronulla edged out Canterbury 13-12 in the second Monday Night Football game of the season, Sharks coach John Lang said: "People are coming back to the footy on both sides, which is good.

"It's not about being petty on either side. It's about footy."

Robson had been sacked by the Warriors as a News Limited man - a view perhaps proven correct when he was appointed Gary Pearse's replacement. The club, which had strong ties to the grassroots local league, was wavering - as was the national governing body.

Newly elected NZRL chairman Gerald Ryan upset Super League by offering to meet Whittaker. The NZRL received $1 million from Super League, compared to the Rugby Football League's $187 million.

And Ryan gave the young season its best quote when he said: "I know blind people, aged 106, at the bottom of the South Island who could referee better than some of the Australians".

Kevin Neil summed up the first month of dual competitions with disarming simplicity. "Pretty much from the first weekend, I think everyone realised we needed to have a united competition."

MARCH 1997

- On March 9, journalist Paul Kent wondered whether a merger, under the same interpretation of the law that allowed Super League to proceed, might be deemed anti-competitive and therefore illegal.

- Adelaide's first home game, against the Mariners in round three, attracted a massive crowd of 27, 435.

- By March 19, no clubs had signed the new ARL loyalty agreement tying them to the organisation until 2000.

- When video referee Ian Bissett is asked after a Monday Night Football game whether the video refereeing system is infallible, he answers: "Yes, I think it is." Warriors coach John Monie counters: "I hoped we were going to get 100 per cent of the decisions right. It may only be 90 per cent."

- When the late Quentin Pongia fronted the new Super League judiciary, his representative argued his ARL record should not count. The hearing was adjourned to have the question answered .. it did count.

- Summing up the mood early in the season, Norm Tasker wrote: "New voices in the ARL are calm and conciliatory. Super League, for their part, seem to be concentrating on getting their own game right."

- In the same edition of the magazine, it was reported that a player had asked for a "walking around allowance".

- On March 24, Roy Masters wrote in the Sydney Morning Herald that one distinct trend the first few weeks of two competitions had shown was that the days of Sunday football were limited. "Fans prefer night football," he said.

♦ Ribot described the ARL's plans to stage its own internationals as "an act of desperation" and defended Super League's inferior crowds.

♦ On March 26, Super League judiciary chairman Jim Hall gave conflicting accounts as to how an incident - Warriors prop Grant Young elbowing Adelaide back rower David Boughton - came to his attention. He told the New Zealand Herald an "official source", "not a member of the public", reported it but he told the Sydney Morning Herald he found it on video himself. The issue was relevant because of Super League's open-ended policy on how on-field incidents were reported.

♦ Columnist Phil Gould predicted fans in Sydney would get back into the habit of attending live matches because most of their teams' away games were in easy travelling distance.

♦ Super League (Europe), meanwhile, signed up with PR firm M&C Saachi and Wigan - in one of the saddest days in the club's history - sold Central Park to Tesco. Chairman Jack Robinson had been found not guilty of setting up a phony transfer deal in a bid to defraud the *Wigan Observer.*

MERGE OR DIE: SUPER LEAGUE OFFICIALS WARN ARL CLUBS

By Steve Mascord, Sydney Morning Herald, Monday May 26, 1997

PENRITH assistant chief executive Mark Levy last night warned Sydney's ARL clubs they faced "extinction" if they continued to resist Super League's push for club mergers under a united competition.

Levy joined Canterbury Leagues Club chairman Gary McIntyre yesterday in offering to take part in any discussions that might lead to the rationalisation of Sydney football. But ARL club officials Ray Beattie of North Sydney and George Piggins of South Sydney said on radio yesterday their clubs had to survive.

Beattie, on 2UE, likened merging Norths and Manly to closing a McDonald's franchise, while on ABC Piggins said he would take legal action the minute Souths were told to discuss amalgamation.

"I think any club in Sydney, regardless of what competition they are in, who refuses to even consider merging, is facing extinction," Levy said last night.

"Once the current funding runs out from Optus and News, and with the new taxes on poker machines, they are going to find it very hard to survive."

Levy's comments came two days after Sydney Super League franchises the Panthers, Bulldogs and Cronulla agreed in a meeting with News Limited executive director of sport Ian Frykberg that a reunited competition could not support the current 11 city clubs.

While ARL chief executive Neil Whittaker tries to stay out of the debate completely, his clubs seem to be divided on the issue.

St George and Parramatta, South Queensland, Manly and Gold Coast officials have given some indications they are prepared to contemplate talks but North Sydney, South Sydney and

Illawarra have fiercely decided to stand alone.

"I think the decision is going to have to come from above," Levy said.

"The ARL clubs have agreed to let the League do the negotiating on their behalf anyway.

"What we need is Mr Frykberg and Mr Whittaker to get together and say, for instance, that us, Wests and Parramatta, should merge to form a Western Sydney franchise and then it be handed to us to see whether it would work."

Levy said the success of the NSW Waratahs in rugby union and the Sydney Swans in AFL was proof that fans in Sydney would become quickly attached to a new team if it was successful, regardless of its past.

Brisbane chief executive Shane Edwards said "the sums add up to four" teams in Sydney but "other factors like emotion and tradition would probably result in there being six".

In other news, at a media conference in Brisbane, NSW coach Tom Raudonikis has reiterated comments comparing State of Origin football and war.

The NSW squad arrived yesterday for Wednesday's night's opening encounter with Queensland at Suncorp Stadium and Raudonikis told reporters he hated Queensland. "I know you're not supposed to say this but it is war," he said. "I hate them and I know they hate us."

The only injury doubt for the game, Queensland prop Craig Wilson, yesterday had his second run with the Maroons and was rated a certain starter by team doctor Roy Saunders.

Two players are in tribunal trouble following weekend matches.

Super League judiciary commissioner Jim Hall last night said he expected to charge Cronulla prop Jason Stevens with a high tackle on Perth's Robbie Kearns in the 49th minute of the Sharks' 32-2 win at Shark Park on Saturday night.

South Queensland replacement forward Danny Nutley was cited yesterday for lashing out at Sydney City prop Jason Lowrie with his feet during the Crushers' upset

28-14 win at Suncorp Stadium on Friday night. He will face the ARL tribunal tonight.

Adelaide have been left with a long list of injuries following Friday night's 42-22 loss to Canterbury at Adelaide Oval.

Back-rower Andrew Pierce (knee) is out for four to six weeks, forward Andrew Hick (groin) will miss two to four weeks and halfback Stuart Topper (abdominal wall) will miss up to a month.

And wingers Joe Tamani and Jason Donnelly and Queensland Tri-Series forward Kevin Campion are in doubt for Sunday's game against Canberra.

Western Suburbs will check the fitness of centre Brandon Pearson after he suffered a 75 percent tear of a hamstring in Saturday's 26-10 win over Gold Coast at Carrara Stadium

Chargers coach Phil Economidis is set to make several changes after the loss.

CHAPTER 10

Maurice Lindsay

IN ENGLAND's windswept north-west, Maurice Lindsay lives just off a street called Victory Boulevard. In terms of the Super League War, he is in no doubt at all that this is a piece of serendipity.

"Really, they lost the war - let's be honest," says the 78-year-old former chief executive of the Rugby Football League, in between jumps races from Cheltenham, watched on a television in a grand lounge room decorated with modern art and with a view of the receded Irish Sea.

"They had to come back on bended knee."

Lindsay is recovering from a couple of falls at home and gets around with the help of what he describes as "a buggy". Yet his razor sharp mind negotiates the controversies of 1997 adroitly, his narrative on the events of the year as persuasive as a quarter century earlier.

Maurice is not just protective of his legacy but almost aggressively colonial about it. Reporters hand out and withhold "credit" for things without a second thought, but "credit" determines incomes and how people are remembered, things that are very central to many lives.

Of the war, he says simply: "It was a financial disaster for both but of course News Corporation could carry it, ARL couldn't. Arko told me he felt he'd been let down by the Packer family. He resigned immediately, Arko, didn't he? Went to Queensland and he's been there ever since."

When Super League was outlawed by Justice Burchett at the start of the 1996 season and its Sydney staff sidelined by court orders, Lindsay became the breakaway's frontman - without being able to admit that's what he was. Ever the showman, Lindsay seemed to relish the media spotlight Down Under..

"Global League" - a competition involving Super League clubs from both sides of the world - he would have had us believe at the time, was his idea.

(Arthurson called Global League "one of the greatest pieces of bullshit it has been my misfortune to run up against in half a century in the game. For those who believed in the tooth fairy, the Easter bunny and goblins at the bottom of the garden, this was to be run by Maurice Lindsay on behalf of the players, with no involvement from Super League")

Lindsay says: "I chaired the (Global League) meeting and after that they interviewed Rupert and he said 'what? I've never heard of that, I've never heard of Global League'. He said all the right things.

"Global League never got off the ground, of course. But we went through the motions. We got every council to allocate a ground to us and we had a budget and we were sponsored by one of News Corporation's satellites.

"And I had some great people supporting me: Bullfrog (Canterbury chief executive Peter Moore), a good man to have on your team. I had some big hitters helping me."

When Super League was cleared to begin, while Lindsay was in Sydney, he suddenly wasn't required there anymore

"I was advising them on the International Board because I got the French and I got the Polynesian countries and got everyone together," he says.

"I had to concentrate on the International Board because without international football, Australia, the old ARL, would still be in charge. They had nobody to play. We got Fiji, France, everybody, on the International Board and I was elected as chairman.

"The ARL were isolated - which was a shame because Ken didn't deserve that. But as he said, he got let down by some people.

"So I arranged a calendar. The Polynesians played each other and then Australia and New Zealand played us."

John Ribot says now: "I remember when (the ARL) went over there, Maurice had a very emotional moment. He was saying 'I know you're in a fight but, shit, I'm over here on my own like I've got a pop-gun'. If you ever pull a cartoon out, they had a drawing of him with all these blokes coming over the hill with all these missiles and tanks and all that. They had Maurice in the trench and he had a little hat on and he had a pop-gun there. He had a cork on the end of it. "

Arthurson used many an epithet to denigrate Lindsay in the press during 1996 and 1997 but they are friends again now, the British game's switch to summer on the back of an £87 million investment by News now a full 25 years ago.

"They were totally influenced by money, totally influenced," Arthurson said of Lindsay and the RFL, three months earlier in his own retirement apartment 17,557 km away.

"Look, I always had a very, very good relationship with Maurice and I had a high regard for his ability too, actually. But we did fall out for a long time because he was involved in Super League and I was very much against it. We probably said a few things about each other from time to time, I can't quite recall now.

"But since then, Maurice has been out here and I've been out with him and we're quite good friends again now, which I'm very pleased to say because I was really disappointed we were on opposite sides of the fence and we were always quite good friends and we still are now.

"All that's water under the bridge."

Lindsay though, in his own inimitable way, still has a very definitive view on which way that water flowed.

His rugby league history is one where there is a direct line from what was established between 1995 and 1997 in Super League and the gigantic NRL we have now, in which the ARL are almost brushed aside.

"(It) was hard to deliver all that from scratch. We were going to places like Adelaide where they only had a little amateur team and it took a while to get going.

"Perth was difficult. It was hard work but eventually we persevered, eventually we ended up where we are now."

(Which, it must be stressed, is NOT in Adelaide or Perth. And the Western Reds pre-dated Super League by more than a year.)

It is also a history where, had he not listened to the likes of Neil Tunnicliffe and Nigel Wood, disasters such as the 1996 Lions Tour and the 1997 World Club Challenge would never have happened.

When I put it to Lindsay that Paris Saint-Germain - which lasted three seasons from 1995 - was full of problems, with players in France on tourist visas, he retorts: "Listen, there wasn't a drama. Who complained?"

I point out that the team travelled to Britain and Australia not knowing if they would be allowed back into the country. "Did they come back?" he responds defiantly.

Peter Mulholland, PSG's coach, is happy to provide Lindsay with the requisite complaint. He says he ended up staging a sit-in at Hotel Forest Hill, Bougival, in north-central Paris in August, 1997, to get out of his contract.

"When they took all my furniture over, they took over $26,000 worth of furniture and it sat on the docks at Le Havre and it wasn't unpacked," Mulholland says.

"They wouldn't give us any assistance to find accommodation, we were living in a hotel. Only one player ended up going out and getting accommodation and that was Jason Martin through his partner Charlene who spoke fluent French.

"My wife went around Paris by herself looking for accommodation for us, I had my son with me, for a period of about a month. Upon realising that they weren't doing anything, I thought 'well, this could be a short-term venture'.

"Insofar as the visas were concerned, I was OK because (wife) Mel was a British citizen so I was able to live and work in Europe. A couple of the players had British ancestry and they were right.

"But mate, we were on tourist visas. We were living in France, being paid out of the UK. It's alright for Maurice Lindsay, he didn't travel with us. Every time we went through either Manchester or London or back to Charles de Gaulle, one or two players would be pulled up by immigration.

"I had to try and explain in my pidgin French what was going on and get them through it. We bluffed our way through it on each occasion.

"When 23 players and their families suddenly find they are living in a hotel on the outskirts of Paris, there's something that says this is a tad sketchy. If that wasn't a concern for Maurice Lindsay….

"We had four cars between us. It was OK, it was novel to start with but it wears you down.

"I had a blue with them and Andy Goodway took over. I wasn't prepared to continue this charade. We got pulled up, I had three guys detained at Charles de Gaulle. There were all sorts of promises and nothing got delivered.

"I rang Maurice Lindsay and said 'mate, I can't continue to do this'. It wasn't improving. I spoke to old (RFL official) Harry Jepson and said 'I want my pay' and Maurice Lindsay refused then on a settlement so I stayed in the hotel … not on strike but I stayed on the hotel (tab) until I was getting some sort of settlement.

"They still had about four weeks of competition to go after that. I had to take a stand somewhere. I had a family and everything else. I had players there who were living in ridiculous circumstances."

Lindsay argues Paris Saint-Germain didn't fail - it just shifted to Perpignan and became a Challenge Cup- and League Leaders Shield-winning powerhouse.

"When we had the opening game of Super League, Sheffield versus Paris, everyone kept saying to me 'what are you doing in Paris? Rugby league is played in the south!'" he comments.

"But those who did or didn't know should have known that the head office for the French Federation was in Paris. Nobody asked why. You know the French have strange laws? It was a stupid law in France that whatever sport it was, If you wanted funding from the government, the head office had to be in Paris.

"So the French Federation head office was one man, the secretary, in an office the size of my bathroom, in Paris. That's why we had to kick off with Paris Saint-Germain. We persuaded Paris Saint-Germain to lend us the name. Everybody thought that they owned it (the club). They didn't own it.

"It was owned by the French Federation who were fucking useless. But two cities - Sheffield is a city, Paris is a city ... we marketed it as a battle of the cities and we got 17,450 people, marvellous crowd.

"That ran for a year and then I met Jean Paul (Ferre) and his mate from a fishing village near Bordeaux...Jacques (Fouroux)... we agreed that we would collapse Paris Saint- Germain into the south. We'd got going by then. So all went to Perpignan and it broke from there."

Catalans entered Super League in 2000, two years after the collapse of PSG.

Lindsay says the Super League War was won internationally, under his watch as director-general of the Super League World Board.

"Oh yeah. The International Board was the one that got it across the line. If you've got New Zealand, Great Britain, France, Papua New Guinea … you've got one team on their own.

"They might be the greatest team in the world, Australia, but they've got nobody to play and no support… what's the point? Australia could never play international rugby again. They wanted to.

"Also, financially, Australia were broke. I remember Ken saying to me, I was handling the finances for the (1995) World Cup, and I was pestered by all these Polynesian nations saying they wanted to have all these international training camps and they had no money.

"So I sent them all £100,000 each and Ken rang me up and said 'this £100,000, I know it sounds as though we're hard up, the truth is we are. Can you send our £100,000 today?' I said 'yeah mate, not a problem'.

"I didn't want to hurt Australia. I love Australia. I nearly married a girl from Australia. I was 53 and she was 31. It may not have worked. Fabulous, she was."

Although he lives on Victory Boulevard, Lindsay insists he does not cherish the memory of the war years.

"That is a ropey time and a ropey period and I wasn't happy then because blokes like Alfie (Allan Langer) were denied a cap they would have been a certainty to get (at the 1995 World Cup).

"To have to watch them (the all-ARL Australian team) play knowing they should have played must have been terrible. The Australian selectors and committee didn't give a fuck about the players at all. I did. I've always cared about the players.

"That was a difficult period. We still managed to get 60,000 into the final down at Wembley when Australia won it.

"Australia were always isolated. They had to come back on bended knee, in fact they came back on a good deal. I wanted them back and they wanted to come back. They knew they had to put a broken competition back together again. They did and it's marched on from then."

Our interview in Lindsay's home took place on Tuesday, March 10 2020 - right at the start of the Covid-19 pandemic. I'd driven from London the previous night, attended a New York Rugby League launch in Liverpool in the morning and travelled onwards to Lindsay's home afterwards.

Given the unfolding global news, I had thought about offering to cancel our meeting as Maurice was clearly in the vulnerable group - but he seemed happy for me to visit. I was greeted by a fist-bump, not an Arthurson style hug, which was actually relieving.

At the start of '97, Lindsay was on a short-list to be chairman of the Tote, the official British government bookmaker. At the end of 1997, according to the Rothmans Yearbook, Lindsay's "powers as the RFL's chief executive were reduced considerably".

Clubs had voted 29-5 in favour of Sir Rodney Walker's proposals for a new board.

At the end of our chat in front of the races, I asked Lindsay for a few quotes on more recent events, for a weekly magazine feature I was committed to do. He was withering in his assessment of the game's current British administration.

"I think the English administration has gone backwards," he said. "I think they wanted to punch above their weight. Australia let them in, which was great because in the old days when I used to go it was a question of 'do as you're told'.

"They actually didn't say that but we knew those were the rules. We rode on the coat-tails of Australia.

"Rodney Walker, followed by Nigel (Wood), got too pushy and instead of being smooth with Australia, and getting power into our hands at the behest of Australia by acknowledging that Australia was still miles ahead, we didn't. 'We're England, we're big, we're here now'.

"And I think as a consequence our administration went backwards which is why the clubs over here have rebelled against Nigel and got him shifted, in fact, and fought with the English administration and got certain things bequeathed to them like money and deals with Sky and all this.

"…which could have been handled much better. "

(Wood will respond later in this book)

Lindsay went on to say the RFL were "in the Dark Ages". I turned off the voice recorder on my iPhone, we fist-bumped again and I headed off on my six hour road journey back to London.

That weekend I warned Maurice by text that the piece was running in *League Weekly* and because he was an older man living alone in hazardous times I then tried to engage him by SMS on several occasions and by sending him a copy of my previous book.

He didn't respond.

I was left wondering if he had coronavirus or just a fit of rage against a perceived sleight - me reporting his words exactly as he had uttered them and occasionally comparing them to established fact and the accounts of others.

I still don't know.

My worst nightmare at first was that I had given a frail 78-year-old Covid-19. As I write this, I've still not heard from, or of, Maurice Lindsay since the day we last met.

MULTICULTURAL BASH OVERSHADOWS GAME

By Steve Mascord, *Sydney Morning Herald,*
Tuesday June 3, 1997

PENRITH 28
CANTERBURY 20 at
Belmore Sports Ground

A POLICEMAN was put in a headlock, a touch judge was threatened and several spectators were arrested as Canterbury's annual multicultural day descended into violence at Belmore Sports Ground last night.

Penrith's 28-20 win over Canterbury and controversial refereeing decisions were overshadowed by crowd unrest, with scuffles continuing 20 minutes after full-time. Reports put police numbers at more than 100. Touch judge Michael Thompson said a spectator jumped the fence three times late in the game.

"This person was standing near me and he was quite threatening," Thompson said. "He said things like, I'm going to get you, touch judge'."

Referee Brian Grant, who made two controversial decisions against the home side in the final seven minutes, responded by stopping play for about two minutes until security men arrived on the scene.

"We had one policeman who was slightly injured when he was placed in a headlock," said Sergeant George Georgiou of Campsie police.

"It had been on the boil all night but it was relatively minor. Two people were arrested for anti-social behaviour. They were both male."

Georgiou said about 10 police had been on duty at Belmore at the start of the night including mounted police, who later tried to disperse the surging crowd of about 2,000 and that reinforcements from "a number of other stations" were called in.

"Missiles were thrown at horses," Georgiou said of riotlike scenes which lasted for half an hour.

The disturbing incident comes just two weeks after crowd violence marred a national soccer league semi-final at Parramatta Stadium.

Canterbury chief executive Bob Hagan said the crowd unrest was "very unfortunate" and the club would conduct a full investigation.

The touchline assailant, who escaped back into the crowd, wasn't the only pitch invader.

During the chaotic final stages, Lavini Haumono, the mother of Canterbury second-rower Solomon, rushed onto the field sobbing when her son was knocked out Coach Chris Anderson said: "She wanted to make sure no-one kicked her son when he was down."

Anderson said enough in his post-match media conference to dominate headlines for days in normal circumstances, slamming Grant as "not up to scratch".

The referee made two crucial decisions after Canterbury had clawed their way back to be within six points of the Panthers, who were striving for their first win in five matches.

First, he ruled that Canterbury fullback Rod Silva had kept running after he called 'held' and awarded Penrith a penalty in front of the posts, which Girdler kicked to give his side an eight-point buffer.

And then he disallowed Canterbury hooker Robert Mears a try and awarded Penrith a penalty after a scuffle involving Panthers captain Steve Carter and Canterbury halfback Craig Polla-Mounter 40m away.

"I thought the refereeing for the whole game was fairly below standard," Anderson said. "I don't see why they don't give the best referees the TV game.

"Sharing the games around, I don't think some of the referees are up to scratch. The referee struggled to keep up with the pace of the game all night."

Penrith second-rower Tony Puletua is out of the World Club Challenge with a medial ligament tear in his knee, while Test hooker Craig Gower has a jaw injury and is in doubt for next Monday's clash with Bradford.

Haumono is expected to be fit for Monday's Belmore clash with Wigan, but prop Darren Britt will miss two or three weeks with a shoulder injury.

PENRITH 28 (D Farrar, M Adamson, J Gall, R Girdler tries; R Girdler 6 goals) bt CANTERBURY 20 (D McRae, H El Masri, D Halligan tries; D Halligan 4 goals) at Belmore Sports Ground. Referee: B Grant. Crowd: 12,431.

CHAPTER 11

Murdoch's Court

WHEN the Rams took on Perth at Adelaide Oval on Thursday, March 27 in front of 16,294 fans, Channel 10 Sydney reporter Tony Peters called it a "local derby".

The 2,694 km between the cities notwithstanding, relations between the sides were anything but neighbourly. Rams forward Cameron Blair was booked for a high tackle but, in one of the most famous cases in the entire history of Australian rugby league's judicial process, Rams fullback Chris Quinn - a try-scorer during the match - accused Reds hard man Mark Geyer of eye-gouging him.

"I had no idea who was opposing me when I got up to play the ball," Quinn, now living back in Sutherland Shire, told me in an interview for this book. "When I looked up and saw that MG was there … the fact it was him … it wouldn't matter who it was, I would have gone through and done the same thing. I felt I'd been over-zealously attacked around the eyes.

"When I spoke to (referee) Brian Grant, he didn't understand what I was trying to say. He was going to penalise me for walking off the mark because I was trying to get his attention to have a bit of a whinge about what had gone on with MG.

"I'm not sure who our captain was at the time. I think it might have been Kerrod (Walters). I had to grab him and say 'listen, I've got a bit of an issue'."

Grant placed the incident on report and left it in the hands of Super League's gleaming new match review system. The Reds edged out the Rams 18-16.

As the weather cooled in April, we settled into the weekly routine of two competitions. "I'll go out on a limb here," Mal Meninga said after another Canberra defeat. "I think they should change the balls. I think the balls are too slippery. They're not ideal, they're not conducive to the quick play Super League wants.

"They're sweating a bit now the game has quickened up. There's been a lot of mistakes."

At the *Sydney Morning Herald*, we mixed all the games and all the news together as we always had, in order of importance rather than according to what competition the players and officials happened to be in. Overall, the space afforded to the sport was up on the previous year, when the paper seemed to have given up on rugby league and devoted just one broadsheet page to it on a Monday.

"The Herald's become a Super League paper," Bob Saunders had said to me. In the paradigm of the early 21st century, the echo chamber of a deeply divided society, Saunders' perspective was correct. News was the Herald's corporate enemy, so Super League should have been the enemy of the *SMH* sports section. Journalism wasn't (always) like that back in 1997.

Many years later at Fairfax's Darling Park offices. I recall the lift stopping on one of the corporate floors and a suited gent entered, discussing News Corporation. "I can bear what they've done to The Souths," he said with a cultured clip. "The Souths". He didn't know much about rugby league but he knew he disliked Murdoch.

During the year of two tribes, other sports were grabbing more column inches; rugby league games in both competitions were on late at night and footy politics outranked on-field action in terms of interest. I was working as a sideline commentator for Optus Vision and I can remember being flown to the Gold Coast by the station but getting zero interest from the *Sun-Herald* in filing a match report from the same game. Eventually they printed eight paragraphs, in between splashes on what officials were doing - and I was not paid for those eight pars.

April started with more bad news for the ARL on the Channel Nine front. The network announced it would show two Super League games on Friday nights - the ARL's time slot - during the ensuing weeks. The two games were rep fixtures - NSW v Queensland and Australia v New Zealand. April 11 was, in fact, an early glimpse of what we have now - the Friday night television double header - with NSW v Queensland at 7pm followed by Wests v Newcastle at 9.30.

The Anzac Test was set down for April 25.

A couple of weeks before it, New Zealand coach Frank Endacott floated the idea of picking ARL players for the Kiwis, while it was reported the ARL's Rothmans Medal would be scrapped. It was replaced by the Nokia Provan Summons Medal, which led to sportscaster Ron Casey becoming embroiled in a racism row when he first described the new sponsors as Japanese and then corrected himself by dubbing them "Ayran".

Nokia is Finnish.

Above all this, Optus Vision was in the process of being bought out and closed down. Optus Communications, its 46.5 percent shareholder, was attempting to buy out the other owners and get rid of the television arm. Football is inestimably more interesting but it was at the complete mercy of these machinations (and, although I didn't know it at the time, so was my part time gig).

As already recorded, Geoff Cousins - Freddy Krueger to Chris Johns, who pledged enough money to keep the ARL afloat - had left. Despite the good crowds in the ARL, there are also reports the clubs were holding merger talks, with Manly heavily linked to Norths. "Just because everything is warm and fuzzy in the ARL at the moment, it does not mean you should not think about the future," said Danny Munk.

In a *Sydney Morning Herald* column, Phil Gould said Super League lacked passion on the field, which prompted the sort of outraged response - once again - we have come to take for granted in mainstream media today but which was not so common then. Wayne Bennett said after Brisbane played Cronulla at ANZ Stadium: "Anyone who saw that game out there tonight would be able to tell you that the author of that article is way out of touch with reality. If jealousy and bitterness are a part of his makeup, that's his problem. He looks a bit of a goose today."

But April 1997 gave us two off-field soap operas that put that tiff in the shade.

The first unfolded when Geyer was subsequently charged with eye gouging and a high tackle over his visit to the City of Churches. He was summoned to Super League's Elizabeth Street headquarters for its first big judiciary hearing, where his counsel was colourful Sydney solicitor-about-town Chris Murphy.

"I had to sit there and dob on him, it was quite bizarre," Quinn recalls. "They sat me next to him in the hearing, which I found a bit odd. I'm only five foot 11 and MG is seven foot or whatever he is and intimidating at the best of times.

"You go to the judiciary and … I thought 'I'm not going to come all this way and not tell them what happened'. I had to do the right thing by myself and I did that.

"All the time I was in fear that MG was just going to turn around and put one on my chin. It was quite a scary time.

"I remember MG said some things along the lines of 'if you find me guilty of being an eye gouger, you might as well find me guilty of being a child molester'. It was a really weird stretch."

The judiciary panellists that evening were ex-players Col Bentley, Darrell Williams and Mal Cochrane. A former Penrith team-mate of Geyer's, Bentley makes a number of intriguing revelations when I track him down by phone.

"I wasn't supposed to be on the judiciary that night because of the conflict with MG being an ex-team-mate," he says.

"Ian Schubert said 'oh Col, can you fill in' and I felt uncomfortable about it. I don't know who else was on (the panel list) but they were sick or unavailable so I filled in at the last minute.

"The head of the judiciary (Ian Callinan), he always said 'if you're unsure, you've got to go like a jury. You've got to give the benefit of the doubt'. I was not quite sure, I wasn't 100 per cent and I went with what my gut feeling was.

"The allegation was gouging. I didn't think MG did that. My recollection was I said 'no, I don't think he did'. The outcome was that they said he was guilty. It was guilty or not guilty, they didn't say whether it was unanimous."

When Geyer was suspended for seven weeks on a charge of eye-gouging, he was heard to tell his legal representatives - by me, I covered the hearing - "I want to speak to Mr Murdoch. New game, new image, fucking bullshit. I've been bankrupted."

Geyer later told reporters: "To be labelled an eye-gouger is like being called a pedophile."

Murphy went on to provide perhaps the most dramatic performance by a legal counsel in the history of rugby league disciplinary hearings. "I think you're incompetent: grossly incompetent," he told the panel. "It's an utter joke, a disgrace, a kangaroo court and an idiotic process. I think having three football players decide this matter is a total joke. This is Mr Murdoch's court. I don't know how much commercial interest is in this place but I'm going back to the ARL. Goodbye."

Outside the hearing room, Murphy described the judiciary as "corporate cowboys" and threatened to challenge the entire Super League judicial system in the Supreme Court. He, in fact, walked out after Geyer was banned for eye gouging, leaving the player to defend a separate high tackle allegation alone!

The Reds subsequently warned Geyer they would not pay his legal costs if he retained Murphy - but Geyer chose to keep him for the appeal nonetheless. He was eventually denied leave to appeal.

Nevertheless, the Super League judicial code remains one of the war's most positive and lasting legacies. "In hindsight, that has proven to be a good system," says Geoff Bellew.

"I didn't like it at the start because I'm a bit of a fan of having a proper hearing and not being subject to fixed penalties … but 20 years down the track that's one of the things that came out of it that's a positive."

The second great controversy of the month surrounded the Anzac Test. Like many innovations of Super League, the idea of Australia and New Zealand playing each Anzac Day had been kicking around for a while. In the minds of business analysts, Super League was a corporate take-over but in the imagination of veteran agitators within the game, the money on offer from News came at the perfect time to enact a suite of concepts previously stonewalled by the Phillip Street establishment.

The Returned Servicemen's League (RSL) of NSW accepted a $20,000 donation from Super League, to complete a memorial, in return for endorsing the Test, to be held at the Sydney Football Stadium. "Super League has turned Anzac Day into a marketing exercise," wrote Roy Masters.

Masters' column caused such a stir that John Ribot - his old winger at Wests - and a very close friend - was given a page-leading response in the *Sydney Morning Herald*.

"Nothing has angered me as much as reading that headline and the accompanying photograph," Ribot wrote. "To insinuate that a group of diggers would sell themselves and their name is insulting in the extreme to both parties."

In a recollection of the spat provided to this book, Masters writes: "The phone at my Surry Hills house rang early on the morning of April 16, 1997.

"It was John Ribot, one of the players in my 1980-81 Western Suburbs team who went on to play for Australia. But he wasn't calling to say hello. He was phoning in his position as Super League chief executive and there were no niceties in his opening remarks.

"Ribes was furious at a piece I had written which appeared that day in the *Sydney Morning Herald*. Basically, I had attacked Super League for hijacking the Anzac spirit to promote their upcoming Test between Australia and New Zealand.

"Ribes had done a deal with the RSL to use military insignia on the players' jumpers in exchange for a donation of $20,000 and their support for the game. My objection wasn't scheduling the match on Anzac Day.

"After all, many of the teams I coached had played on Anzac Day, with a dignified ceremony before kick off, including a bugler. Rather, I was opposed to transferring symbols of the Ist AIF, such as crossed rifles, onto football jumpers.

"I called it a cynical marketing exercise and, given the war at the time between News Limited/Super League on the one side and Fairfax/ARL on the other side, I concede I overdid it.

"I recall Ribes was particularly incensed I had compared Lachlan Murdoch, whose News Limited was funding Super League, with his grandfather, Keith Murdoch whose dispatches from Gallipoli helped ignite the Anzac flame.

"Only two years earlier, I had upset ex-diggers with a piece in the *SMH* regarding the 1995 grand final between Manly and Canterbury, referring to the Sea Eagles' half duo of Cliff Lyons and Geoff Toovey.

"Lyons's uncle and Toovey's grandfather were in the same World War II unit, a famous battalion.

"When I made a link between the spirit of the Lyons-Toovey soldiers and Manly's "brothers-in-combat", it appalled old diggers.

"They wrote letters about sportsmen's battalions which never saw action; claimed footballers in World War II units were more interested in running gambling games than the gauntlet and made the point that nothing in peace-time sport can compare with the horror of battle.

"So, maybe that was also in my mind.

"In fact, one old fellow from Newcastle called after the Anzac piece wanting to belt me, believing somehow that I had equated war with football.

"Yet I should have also considered Ribes' own father, who served in the merchant marine during World War II. A photo of him, in his naval uniform, sat above Ribes' desk in his office. He would have been proud that his son was honouring the fallen, as much as promoting the Test match.

"It took Ribes and I a few years to get over our differences but we are closer together now than we ever were. In fact, neither of us would let a week pass before a phone call was made.

"That's the cost of an emotional war. I had more friends on the other side than in the ARL but my strong belief was that a media company should not own a game, particularly one which evolved on the sacrifices and labour of so many volunteers over nearly 100 years.

"Looking back over the past quarter century, I agree with every innovation Ribes promoted and which has become his legacy – judiciary reform, video referee, night grand final, Nines, even zero tackle and moving scrums infield.

"At the same time, I suspect Ribes would probably accept it is not wise for a media company to own a game."

I went to the Super League Anzac luncheon and remember it as one of the most moving rugby league functions I had ever attended, with veterans and local Papua New Guinea "Fuzzy Wuzzy Angels" - the name given by Australian soldiers to PNG war carriers who were recruited to bring supplies up to the front and carry injured Australian troops down the Kokoda trail during the Kokoda Campaign - interviewed on stage. The fact few of them remain gives the experience added resonance; I still have the boxed coins given to guests that day.

Ribot says his own childhood ensured he would never commodify the Anzac legacy.

"I understood his position but the thing that really disappointed me, he didn't understand my position," Ribot said in his interview for this book.

"He didn't realise my old man came from the Second World War and it gives you an understanding of all those great warriors and the Anzacs. We talk about a game of football. It pales into insignificance when you look at all the things people have done for this country to keep us alive.

"From my point of view there was no way ... it's just not in my DNA to try to bastardise through a commercialisation of the Anzacs. It was an extreme view from me - I had a great upbringing but sometimes when people go to war, they come home and sometimes the war starts at home too.

"As a family, we experienced that and it was something that I….

"News were really good with me on that too. I just said we should look at some of the great moments … even great moments during war. They'd still go out and have a game of football. It was in their competitive nature. It's the mateship, a great thing about our game.

"They could live in the moment and not reflect on maybe getting shot the next day.

"They were finishing off a memorial, out in the western suburbs. I got to know the guys, Rusty (Priest) the NSW guy from the RSL. We had a good relationship. I think the Anzac Test is one of the legacy pieces. If we did anything, we put a lot of time into that game and promoting it. That trophy between Australia and New Zealand, it was absolutely fantastic. "

North Queensland coach Tim Sheens subsequently wrote of the Super League administration: "Some of the controversies have probably caught them unawares but I don't necessarily think the drama is a bad thing."

Other debate around the Test was of a less philosophical nature and followed the usual partisan lines. "So far the Super League Australian team has been arseholed out of the semi-finals of the Nines a couple of times. Things aren't looking good," said Ken Arthurson.

The game? Australia's first home Super League Test resulted in a 34-22 win over New Zealand in front of 23,829 fans. Arthurson called it "a joke team, a false team and nothing more." Australia captain Laurie Daley claimed afterwards: "It's the hardest Test I've played against New Zealand - and I've been beaten by them. I'd like to see (league) like rugby union and played in as many countries. I know that won't happen when I'm a player but when I retire I'd like to help make that happen." Endacott called it "as good an Australian performance as I've ever seen."

Paul Kind recalls: "We just didn't sell tickets to that Test and it had to be a success; 20,000 people went to that game. They had a fantastic time. It wasn't a success. It looked successful because 20,000 people took the opportunity to come along and not pay.

"My view of that is I'd rather have managed that, fulfilled that outcome, than not. But it was false. It wasn't real. Whereas two year before that, we were taking over Melbourne and travelling to two different cities and the game was flying."

Up the F3 on the same night in the ARL's first representative game of the year, Country beat City 17-4 in Newcastle. The result marked Country's first back-to-back wins in 25 years. This was a portent of the grassroots-focused year ahead in the ARL, where the game didn't buy back the farm so much as up sticks and move there.

Oh, the 'real news' continued to be off the field.

Two spectators sustained burns when struck by fireworks at a Penrith-Hunter game on April 4. I covered the match; as soon as it happened I got to my feet and walked to the eastern side of the stadium to interview a "victim". "We are very embarrassed about what happened and obviously wish to offer our apologies to the people involved in the accident," said Ribot.

The Warriors on April 30 sacked coach John Monie with 18 months remaining on his contract. "I made the comment to a reporter that I wasn't surprised as that's the way they treat Australians over there now," Ian Robson recalls.

"I received a call from Ian Frykberg telling me to shut the fuck up."

But back to man of the moment Geyer, who proceeded with court action against Super League and its judiciary chairman Callinan. "I note that our judiciary process, which was so heavily criticised by Mark Geyer's lawyer, is not the subject of the challenge," said David Gallop at the time. But the day after the report he was pressing on with the action. Geyer dropped it. "Basically, I can't afford it," Geyer said. Murphy later told a different story - that Geyer would be paid for six of his seven missed games for eye gouging, in exchange for dropping the action.

The length of the ban had a foreboding implication for Chris Quinn - it meant the so-called Towering Inferno would make his next appearance in the return clash with the Rams at the WACA on June 29. "He was quoted as saying he wants to kill me," Quinn recalls. "I've never been quicker.

"Fair enough, he had the shits with what had gone on. If I'm honest, I was a bit worried because I'm not a big guy and he's a big tough dude and if there's a place you can always get square it's on the field rather than off it.

"There was a bit of verbal throughout the whole game, more from him than me. I was just trying to avoid him and keep playing the opposite side of the ruck. Luckily we got the result on the day and I had a decent game and I was quite happy we finished with a win and I finished intact. It was one of those games where I was glad when the full-time siren rang and I could walk off."

In that comeback game, Geyer was reported for a high tackle....

Quinn was recently surprised to receive a call from radio station Triple M, where Geyer was a breakfast announcer. They were playing an on-air game called the Wheel Of Apology. With tens of thousands listening in, Geyer was ringing to say sorry.

"I did that, that was all good. At that point in time (1997) he was probably bigger than life and a bit loose and probably having a great time over there in WA and probably just got a little bit over-zealous and tried to give me a little bit of a tickle-up.

"He played tough and hard, which a lot of guys did. When you're a big, intimidating back rower or front rower as he is, you're walking a tightrope a lot of the time in terms of how far you push the envelope.

"You know there's guys who, when they get on the field, they become someone that they're far away from when they're off the field. I'm pretty sure MG was like that too."

Does Quinn believe that Geyer had admitted the wrongdoing to himself? "In hindsight now, I'd say he would know (he did it) but back then he might have thought he was hard-done-by. You look at me, I turned up at the judiciary. I've got no scratches, I've got vision in both eyes, no damage done and he's probably going 'well what's he going on about?'

"He was pretty rough and tumble growing up out in Penrith district around Mt Druitt. Out there, it's catch and kill or it certainly was way back when MG was a young fella coming through.

"It's still true today that out Penrith way, out in the west, that football's a great way to go a big step along in your lifetime, you know? If you can get a footy contract ... there's a lot more people living out west and they do it a lot tougher than most so .... You're pushed to do well and sometimes you probably cross the line a bit. "

Of course, neither Geyer nor Quinn are aware - until they read this - that one Penrith boy on the judiciary that night believed Geyer was innocent.

"I've never spoken to MG about it," Col Bentley says. "I wasn't concerned. If MG ever wants to give me a call, I'd talk him through what happened - but he never did. I went with what I thought. I've seen him at a couple of reunions and different things and functions."

I finish by asking Chris Quinn what, in his mind, really happened that night at Adelaide Oval - and why.

After a short pause, he answers: "We'll put it down to an eye gouge gone wrong".

APRIL 1997

♦ ARL clubs offer, in a media conference intended to shore up public and corporate confidence, to act together in any amalgamation talks.

♦ Illawarra chief executive Bob Millward tells The Sun-Herald: "We want to reinforce the message that geographically and historically we must be part of the future, as a separate club."

♦ Columnist Gladys Craven reports that of the 40 chairmen and chief executives in those roles at the beginning of 1995, only 15 occupied the same jobs a couple of months into the 1997 season.

♦ Wayne Bennett wanted touch judges to feed the ball into scrums. The Commonwealth Bank, meanwhile, dropped its sponsorship of the national schoolboys competition after an all-in brawl.

♦ Living legend Tom Raudonkis is named NSW State of Origin coach on the same day that the ARL clubs each signed a document declaring their "availability" to play in a 1998 competition run by that administration. There were reports that early in the season, the ARL gave away 50,000 tickets for one round.

♦ ARL captains, at a meeting, gave qualified support to the return of a draft.

♦ Parramatta changed their jerseys to light blue in a promotion for then unknown "new line of chocolates" called M&Ms.

♦ Ryan Girdler was Super League's first player to 100 points during a 35-20 loss to Perth at the WACA.

- It was announced Wigan would play Canberra in South Africa; the game never happened.

- Irish millionaire Tony O'Reilly announced a Super League team in Dublin. We're still waiting.

- After Canterbury-Hunter at Belmore Sports Ground, Simon Gillies: "It's the way people coach now, they coach to score tries rather than hold tries out."

NEXT STOP: MELBOURNE

By Steve Mascord, Sydney Morning Herald, Wednesday June 11 1997

RUGBY league officials in Australia started talking about Melbourne almost as soon as they started talking about rugby league.

A group of officials stopped in Melbourne on the way back from the first Kangaroo Tour of 1908-9 and held talks with the Victorian Football League about merging the codes.

The biggest development since the creation of the new version of rugby in northern England 13 years before failed to eventuate because of irreconcilable differences.

In 1997, league has enough irreconcilable differences of its own but for some reason its officials believe after expanding their competitions to every other mainland state that it's time to talk Melbourne again.

Regardless of the attendance at the Australian Rugby League's State of Origin match at the Melbourne Cricket Ground tonight, Super League says it will go into Melbourne next year and the ARL reckons it probably will too.

The question being: is league strong enough on home turf at the moment to be spreading its wings so extravagantly again?

"I think there is room for one team in Melbourne," says Ray Duncan, a marketing expert who is general manager of the ARL-aligned Victorian Rugby League.

"There is an awareness down here of the game. Sure, people know the game has been damaged but they love their sport.

"The only thing is that the team has to be competitive."

League in Victoria has a colourful history. In 1990, the Melbourne grand final had to be abandoned because of brawling.

Although VRL officials have just about expunged the game from their records, last month first-grade side Altona scored a world record 212-0 win over Dandenong

(38 tries, 30 goals and the top scorer got 68 points).

And, of course, Melbourne was the scene in 1978 of a violent exhibition game which reputedly started the long-running rivalry between Western Suburbs and Manly

But Duncan is claiming major strides since the first top-flight representative game - a 1990 State of Origin match was played at Olympic Park.

"At primary school level, we've got 100 teams," he said. "And we have 78 in our junior competition in Melbourne. We've also got strong leagues in Gippsland and Goulburn-Murray.

"But obviously I wouldn't envisage any Victorians being in our first-grade side to start with."

The reason Super League and the ARL are now racing to be the first into Melbourne is because it is the proverbial jewel in the crown of Australian sport. The 87,161 who saw Origin II in 1994 made that obvious.

And the difference between the approaches of the two leagues in setting up their teams sums up the differences in culture between the ARL's Phillip Street bunker and Super League's headquarters in nearby Elizabeth Street.

The ARL's public affairs manager, John Brady, said his 'organisation had concentrated on "doing work on the ground".

That doesn't refer to signing leases for Docklands Stadium or Olympic Park but rather employing full-time development officers Andrew Simons and Len Mason, who have successfully expanded junior numbers.

And ARL chief executive Neil Whittaker has held lengthy talks with prospective sponsors. Carlton and United Breweries and Reebok are believed to be ready to get behind a new team, as is the Victorian sports ministry.

Super League, on the other hand, has done things big.

Chief executive John Ribot and the former chairman of News Ltd, Ken Cowley, went straight to the top when they visited Melbourne to discuss their plans for expansion, meeting Premier Jeff Kennett.

Soon after came the announcement that Super League would definitely have a team in Melbourne next year and, later, tacit confirmation that Ribot would head the new franchise.

But indications are that the former Brisbane chief executive will not hold a similar role in Melbourne. Instead, he will use some of the reported $1 million salary he attracted at Super League to buy into the new club as either its only owner or as part of a consortium.

Former international Chris Johns, who was earmarked as Shane Edwards's successor as Brisbane CEO, is set to be Ribot's choice as Melbourne chief executive officer.

How much will all this cost? "For every dollar you spend on players," ARL communications manager Geoff Carr said yesterday, "you have to spend one on organisation and infrastructure."

That means at least $8 million a year "and maybe more in the first year to attract players".

Which brings us to the biggest problem facing both parties in their push into Melbourne. As the World Club Challenge has illustrated, there is a worldwide shortage of top-class players in a sport which has experienced a boom inspired by media moguls.

Throw as much money as you like at it, there aren't enough players to go around the 34 professional clubs in Australasia and Europe.

So where will they get enough to make one and maybe two more expansion clubs "competitive".

Players like Tim Brasher, Paul McGregor, the Johns brothers Matthew and Andrew, John Hopoate and Jim Serdaris, who are off contract at the end of the year, will no doubt be targeted by ARL Melbourne.

"Our clubs are in agreement that they must co-operate to assist in setting up a team in Melbourne," Whittaker said.

"We are looking at every avenue as to how it might work, but I couldn't speculate on it." One thing's for sure: Melbourne does not want a transplanted club.

But one option open to both sides is a partial relocation - the transplanting of players. Western Suburbs this year held talks with Collingwood about a new club but

193

Duncan said: "Collingwood had their fingers burnt with the soccer. I don't think they'd want anything to do with another code now."

Super League has been widely reported to be planning to relocate the Perth Reds. Sources say the Reds' fate depends on the Industrial Court challenge to the ARL's player loyalty contracts.

If the contracts are overturned, the league may be able to staff its Melbourne team with ARL converts.If not, the Reds may be heading east.

Both leagues are confident of more than 15,000 fans attending most home games in Melbourne. The Adelaide model in Super League this year suggests this is entirely possible.

Looking into a very cloudy crystal ball, Chris Johns as chief executive and John Monie as coach appear under the Super League banner.

And the ARL? How's Geoff Carr as chief executive and Paul Vautin as coach sound? "No, I don't think so," Vautin said yesterday.

"Too cold."

CHAPTER 12
Geoffrey Cousins

TWO meals, each shared by Optus Vision chief executive Geoff Cousins and Publishing and Broadcasting Limited mogul Kerry Packer, neatly encapsulate the poorly understood truth about the year of Two Tribes and the Super League War itself.

The first meal, Cousins' recollections date at Friday, March 31, 1995.

"The rumours were around that Murdoch was going to try and take away - really, that was the idea, take away - the television rights to rugby league by starting a new competition," Cousins, now more famous as a 'corporate eco warrior', tells me from his plush home in the Byron Bay hinterland.

"I asked Kerry at this luncheon; 'do you think that's likely?' And his response was 'there's no chance at all'. I said 'but that's exactly what you did with the cricket'. He said 'no, no, you misunderstand. With the cricket all I had to do was to get a couple of teams - the West Indies, Australia, Britain (England) or something like that, and I had a competition. Whereas with rugby league, you'd have to get probably eight full teams and that can't be done.'

"That was his wisdom."

The very next day, News Limited operatives rented private jets and climbed through windows to sign dozens of players in a blatant raid on an Australian Rugby League competition that had only expanded west to Perth and east to Auckland the previous month.

And on Monday, Cousins started work at the company that would hold the pay television rights to the besieged ARL - and would therefore be chiefly responsible for its survival in the face of the raid he'd been assured just four days before would never happen.

"I signed on as CEO and basically the first thing that landed on my plate was the Super League," the 78-year-old recalls, not at all ruefully.

"And my immediate response was 'this is just fundamental to our business plan'. People don't really understand that the Optus business plan at the time was a combination of, yes, pay TV but more importantly fixed line telephony. The cable that was carrying the pay TV signal was also going to carry fixed line telephony so it would be the first time in Australia that there had been any competition to Telstra in fixed line and then of course the mobile business which was already operating.

"So I looked at it.

"When you're looking at a subscription service, it's totally different programming to free-to-air television. News doesn't really matter. Current affairs doesn't really matter. It's sport, number one, for your subscribers and number two movies and other stuff. I said 'well, we've got to win this thing. We simply have to be in it'.

"That's really why … it was nothing to do with rugby league which I thought was disgraceful. I thought the whole thing was dead *wrong*.

It was nothing to do with sport. It wasn't some clubs wanting to leave and others wanting to stay. That's a complete misunderstanding of it. It was Rupert Murdoch wanting to take away the pay TV rights for which we had a contract. Nothing else.

"I think everything that happened in the Super League was *wrong*. It was corrupt. Of course in the first court case, the judge made comments to that regard. Even though that was overturned on appeal, that doesn't overturn the comments he made. They were about the evidence that was given and the behaviour. They were running around to people in the clubs that they hadn't signed and wanted to bring over saying 'if you don't get your husband to sign then no-one's gonna talk to you and your family in the supermarket or your kids at school'. This sort of stuff.

"I hated that. I thought that was absolutely the opposite of what sport should be."

So, without putting too fine a point on it, Cousins immediately agreed to fight. Phil Gould called him "the gun that turned out to be a cannon". I put it to Cousins that there was indeed discontent among the clubs and within the game and that many innovations from Super League, still with us today, had been given the cold shoulder by Phillip Street. News did need willing co-conspirators and they found them with ease.

"Yeah, well you'll always find that. If you go to the rugby league now and run around the clubs, you'll find a group. But if the money hadn't been there, that discontent wouldn't have led to anything much other than 'we're going to change the CEO'. It would be like the rugby union is now, internal politics. It was the money that changed the whole deal and there was a helluva lot of money around, most of it from News.

"I love sport, all sport. My real football game is rugby union but I always watch rugby league as well. The quote I made when it all started was 'Rupert Murdoch came like a thief in the night to steal the people's game' which was widely reported and I still feel that way."

So while Packer v Murdoch dominated headlines, the lower profile Cousins increasingly spent his days in the early part of the war at Phillip Street. He advised John Quayle and Ken Arthurson and helped sign players. "One of the things that Optus had to do was convince the ARL that we were actually a business. I mean, we weren't. There were six of us! We hadn't built anything at that time. I had to convince them first - and then the clubs - we were real. On the other side you had this great world superpower, News Limited."

One of Optus Vision's investors was Channel Seven, which in turn was part-owned by News Limited. This should have made waging war with News very difficult. But Cousins had already worked out how to turn such fearsome barriers into mere inconveniences. His tactics in dealing with the ACCC (Australian Competition and Consumer Commission) - while they may sound like dry business journalism to rugby league fans now - were a key reason Cousins' backers were willing to hand over money to the ARL when he asked for it.

"Most businesses, when you get a regulator like that who is looking at all kinds of aspects of your business, you try to push them away," he explains, with understated but discernible pride.

"If they ask for certain documents, you read the sentence very carefully and you only give them precisely the one document that relates to the wording of the question. What I did was to say to that body 'look, I'll give you an office in our offices. You can have one of your people in there. You can look at anything you want to look at. Everything that we are trying to do is an attempt to bring competition into both telephony and pay television so I want you to see everything we're doing'. And they couldn't believe that. They said 'OK, we will but we bet you don't give us all the documents' I said 'you can walk around and pick anything up off any desk you like' No-one will stop you'.

"We did do that and that's why, and this is very, very important in the whole rugby league situation, we were allowed to have both Channel Seven and Channel Nine as shareholders in Optus. And everyone said 'how can that possibly happen because the ACCC wouldn't allow it'. Well they did allow it."

And here we get to the crux of the main narrative we can glean from this hour-long interview with Geoffrey Cousins, the founding chair of Sydney's Museum of Contemporary Art, advisor to prime minister John Howard, director of Telstra. The history of this period, certainly within rugby league, records Packer and Cousins as having been allies in the fight against Murdoch.

One only need talk to Cousins for a short period to understand this was far from the case.

"I'd known Kerry for a long time, a long time. When I was in the advertising game, we were his biggest client. So I wasn't someone who was in a position of working for him, needing to bend a knee. I'd been getting him for money! Not the other way around! We had a very good relationship until he died. I never had a row with Kerry and he never, ever was in any way rude to me or any of the other things that he did to a lot of people."

And so to the second meal, in mid 1996 after the ARL had won the Burchett case and Super League had been outlawed.

It's a revelation that should irrevocably alter all our understandings of the Super League War.

"It was in Packer's home in Sydney. He rang me. I was having dinner with my wife. I very seldom socialised with Kerry. I always kept distance. So it was very unusual for him to ring me at that hour of the night and he apologised for it. He said 'look, I've got Ken Cowley and Lachlan here and they want to make a deal with you and would I come over'.

"I said 'sure', I went over and by the time I got there I think they'd all figured out that I wasn't going to cave in to anything.

"Everybody thought we'd end up with nothing - including Kerry Packer, incidentally, who said to me 'you can't ever beat Murdoch …. everybody knows that … give up!' No, no, he did. Just in those words. He tried to - and I'm not sure this has ever been reported - get me to give up.

"The reason, and if they'd thought about it, the News Limited people … particularly Lachlan who I don't think had a clue what was going on to be perfectly honest with you ….

"…if they actually figured out what our business was all about … they had News and Telstra as the partners in Foxtel. Our business case was based on pay TV yes but also on fixed line telephony. So if some deal was going to be made, it wouldn't just be made about the pay TV rights for rugby league. It would have had to have something to do with telephony and that was impossible. It would have been in breach of the law and every other Goddamn thing.

"So I don't think, really, there was a helluva lot of intelligent thought given to what they were doing. I met several times with Lachlan at his request, including once at Murdoch's house in Sydney.

"He rang me and asked me to go over there and I met with him and my impression was he had absolutely no grasp whatsoever of the issues involved.

"I think that News Limited always assumed that I was a sort of creature of Kerry Packer and that he would give me an instruction or something and that's the way it would work because that's the way it always had worked for them. They'd talk to Kerry and he'd give someone an instruction and it would come out to their benefit normally, to News' benefit and it did to Kerry.

"I went over and by the time I got there, they all looked very glum. I knew Ken Cowley. I used to play tennis with him and whatever. I said 'you fellas aren't looking full of enthusiasm, how can I help you?' There wasn't a big laugh. We had a bit of a chat and then they got up and left. Kerry said 'stay and have dinner mate' which I did. (One-time Fairfax chairman) Brian Powers was there too."

The podcast host Michael Adams, who has studied the Super League War in detail, sees Cousins as something of a villain because he kept the war going even after Packer and Murdoch had done a deal. Cousins' recollections here confirm that - if it was a real war, he had stopped the atom bomb from detonating, extending hostilities another 18 months.

But in this metaphor - and forgive the insensitivity - what was the likely devastation that a collapsed ARL would have wrought? Which clubs would have disappeared had Cousins surrendered? What would the competition have looked like? If News had taken over the running of rugby league for 1997, what would we have now?

Cousins perhaps influenced the look of the National Rugby League more than any other individual - even though he was gone months before its advent.

Cousins left Optus Vision around the same time as Quayle and Arthurson departed Phillip Street, to care for his terminally ill wife Gayle. "The bloke who came in to replace me, Ziggy Switkowski … he certainly didn't know anything about sport or like sport. It was quite clear to me. Maybe he didn't value those things.

"Look, I don't want to misrepresent what we were doing. We were doing it for commercial reasons. There's no question about that. However I was able to talk very passionately about it to the clubs and so-on, which was very important because basically we were pitching for their business.

"I mean, Lachlan would go in and he was the pitcher for News Limited. I think that was a fundamental error, incidentally, because I thought of him as a sort of boy scout. In fact, I remember … I think it was a *60 Minutes* (TV) interview. It might have been a bit later where they were doing a programme about Lachlan and James. The interviewer said to me 'how do you compare them?' And I said 'well I think when Lachlan gets his first pair of long trousers…'

"That's what I thought of him. I'd turn up at Manly or somewhere to give my pitch and Lachlan would have just finished. He'd be walking out and I had to go in. It was a pretty bizarre situation.

"But I was able to talk passionately, not only because of the commercial reasons but I also thought that rugby league was the people's game. That was the way it started. It was the working man's game and yes, now it was good that there was lots of money there and all that. But it wasn't a game where some business should come in and own the bloody thing, which was basically what News wanted to do. They wanted to own it."

And so to that underlying truth: "It was all about pay TV" has become such a cliche regarding the Super League War yet we have wilfully ignored the main implication in that statement. Kerry Packer, scary cigar smoking Australian business icon, was largely a spectator. It wasn't Packer v Murdoch at all.

"It was about pay TV," Cousins says. "Kerry … he had about five per cent of our company. He was a very small shareholder. He didn't put up a lot of money. Optus put up 95 per cent of the money, even at the start.

"How could he win (or lose)? All he owned was five per cent."

After Cowley, Murdoch and Powers left the Packer residence and peace was firmly blocked with a court appeal underway, Packer sat down to dinner with Cousins. I ask if that means he got two meals that night, given his own dinner with Gayle had been interrupted by the invitation.

"I don't think I ever got to the first one. It would have been a lot better than the second one. Kerry wasn't a great lover of food. "

WHY ARL REJECTED SUPER PLAN

By Steve Mascord, *Sydney Morning Herald,*
Friday June 20, 1997

NEWS Ltd's director of sport, Ian Frykberg, last night outlined Super League's plan for peace - a plan he said the Australian Rugby League had rejected.

In his most candid comments since his appointment, Frykberg revealed he and ARL chief executive Neil Whittaker had met twice but had reached a deadlock on who would run the elite competition under a compromise.

Frykberg said that unless that issue was resolved, News Ltd would be prepared to fight on indefinitely.

"We have reached a stalemate - something neither of us was willing to surrender ground on," he said.

"If necessary, we will go it alone. We can do that, our funding is in place.

"But our door is always open and, hopefully, further talks will take place."

Frykberg's comments mark the first time he has confirmed holding talks with Whittaker - who was unavailable for comment last night - and the first time he has expanded on how a peace deal might work.

Under the plan:

- Super League would run the premier Australasian competition, with the ARL having a say through board representation;

- The ARL would control the game at all other levels in Australia, with Super League having control through representation on its board;

- Mergers would create an Australasian League of 12 or 14 teams, with Sydney clubs involved in mergers retaining their identities by fielding teams in a secondary competition run by the ARL;

- The ARL would run the State of Origin and pick the national team, with all players available;

- The ARL would be readmitted to the International Board, repairing the game at that level.

Frykberg said the plan did not take into account which television networks would have access to which games because the pay-TV industry was undergoing rationalisation of its own.

He said the ARL would be "properly funded" but that News was determined to protect its $300 million-plus investment in world rugby league by having a controlling interest in the premier Australasian competition.

This view will be greeted by officials of ARL clubs as confirmation of their long-held belief that Super League is only interested in compromise on its own terms.

But Frykberg insisted both sides had surrendered ground during discussions.

"From News Corp's point of view, we need to retain control of our investment," he said. "We need to be in control of the finances.

"News Corp has invested hundreds of millions of dollars into the game and the idea is that the clubs should eventually become profitable.

"We are prepared to continue funding rugby league but we need to have some control over how that funding is spent."

Asked who would pocket the profits from ARL clubs that joined the new Australasian League, Frykberg replied: "What profits? I don't think any clubs have been making profits. They were relying on handouts from licensed clubs, the rich were getting richer, the poor were getting poorer.

"We believe, if they are run properly as businesses, football clubs can make money. That is our aim."

While both sides are eager to be seen as conciliatory, Frykberg's comments make it clear that compromise will occur only if boardroom and courtroom events go News Ltd's way in the coming months.

Optus, the ARL's financier, has pledged $120 million over five years to the 12 establishment clubs, but the telecommunications company's appointment of a new chief executive, Peter Howe-

Davies, has caused nervousness among some clubs.

And the ARL player loyalty contracts are also being tested in court, with a decision expected in the coming weeks.

"It is true that if that decision goes our way, then our position may be strengthened," said Frykberg.

CHAPTER 13

State Of Confusion

This is the story of the Tri-Series and the State of Origin, told through the eyes of two men whose profiles and hard-toiling careers crested respective waves during mid-1997 - only for each to be caught in the cruel backwash of the Super League War in the years that followed.

This is the story of Noel Goldthorpe and Jamie Goddard.

NSW halfback Goldthorpe kicked the winning field goal in the longest game of top flight rugby league in history, the 104-minute Super League Tri-Series final. Queensland hooker Goddard gave Immortal Andrew Johns a gash requiring 27 stitches after an iconic brawl during the third State Of Origin game, initiated by the signature Tom Raudonikis call-to-fists of "cattledog!".

They did great things afterwards, but nothing so widely celebrated. In a united competition, it's likely each would be home watching interstate football on television.

(Even Queensland's captain in the '97 ARL series, the celebrated Adrian Lam, says he's "grateful" for the Super League war as he may not have even been in the squad without it)

While the experiences of Goddard and Goldthorpe during the rival leagues' interstate series have many parallels, each introduction to what would become the two tribes of 1997 couldn't be more different.

"They targeted the key blokes in each club - and I mustn't have been one of them," Goldthorpe, born in Botany on Christmas Day 1969 and playing for St George in '95, says.

"I never got any contact from anyone at the ARL. At the time I was with (agent) Wayne Beavis and he asked me if I wanted to have a chat with Super League.

"I was happy to sign right there on the spot. I was a young bloke and my wages jumped by five times what I was getting at Saints. I just said to Wayne 'let's sign, fucking sign!'."

Three years younger than Goldthorpe, Mt Isa product Goddard recalls: "I was at the Gold Coast Seagulls and we were an ARL club then.

"Not many many people know this but when it all went down in 1995, there was a core group of us that met with Super League at Jupiters Casino. There was Kevin Campion and myself - we are still best mates to this day and Godparents of each other's kids - Peter Gill, Craig Coleman, a number of blokes, we all went.

" … and basically we all signed contracts with Super League.

"They pulled us in individually, they gave us a cheque that night and the next day you cashed it to sign on. I went home, I had two small boys and my wife and I showed her and it was 'wow'. It was surreal. The way they worked it, whatever your yearly contract was, they gave you that up front. 'Here, sign now' and they tripled or quadrupled (your salary).

"If you're on 50 grand, they're giving you a 200 grand contract and they'd increase it for three or four years.

"When it got around to '97 I still had a contract with Super League but I flew down and met the bosses, Ribot and Chris Johns, and on compassionate grounds they let me out of the contract. Similar to Goldy, Kevin Campion … they moved them all on, they wanted me to leave and uproot my family.

"I managed to get out of it and get another contract with the ARL and stay at the Gold Coast."

And so to mid-1997. Ian Robson is now Super League's marketing manager and is facing one of his hardest sells, the Tri-Series.

Like many of the breakaway's concepts, the Tri-Series was based on a trope of expansionists and progressives - that no matter how successful the game in future years became in its quest to expand, the strongholds of NSW and Queensland would continue to hoard the money and spotlight via the wildly popular Origin brand, then only 17 years old. Adding New Zealand to Origin was one of the favourite ideas of a certain group of southern hemisphere rugby league contrarians.

"What's the most prized asset for rugby league?" Robson says from Melbourne, where he is now based as CEO of Rowing Australia. "With all due respect to the grand final, with all due respect to internationals, it's State of Origin. Then you try and replicate that and copy it?

"Good luck! That's exactly the challenge we had."

Trevor McEwen said: "It was poorly thought-out and it also messed with a tradition, it tried to fix something that wasn't broke.

"Once they figured out they needed to get New Zealand Rugby League in place … I facilitated them meeting up with (Graham) Carden and he was pretty easy to get across the line .. basically New Zealand dug their heels in and said 'we've got to have some content'

"To this day I still don't know who came up with the Tri-Series concept.

"I went to the very first State of Origin match in 1980. I was there when Artie (Arthur Beetson) belted Mick Cronin. I basically went to every Lang Park Origin game from 1980 to when I moved to New Zealand in '87.

"Despite being a Kiwi, I understood what it was about. I am still surprised so many people went along with the Tri-Series without knowing how hard a sell it was going to be. It was going to be a pale imitation.

"I was given the task of trying to make sure it got as much airtime as it could. Mate, it was hopeless. I could see that from day one."

Wayne Bennett, however, recalls Super League's 1997 answer to Origin as "a tough series" and still thinks the inclusion of New Zealand "worked well". And Brett Mullins was ecstatic to be back playing under his favourite coach, Tim Sheens.

Glenn Lazarus, like fellow cantankerous prop of the same era Martin Bella, had a mind of his own. When I asked him at 1996 Blues media opportunity what he thought of Super League's Tri-Series, he said it would be better without New Zealand in it. The competition's office was apoplectic.

The Tri-Series was to take place between April 11 and May 19. The difference between the New Zealand team in it and the New Zealand

Test team were as follows: a different jersey, no European-based players in the TS side and a different coach, Graeme Norton (not the talk show host).

Norton was an outsider in a group of seasoned professionals but recalls: "One of things we did do, which was unusual at the time, was we used a lot of the senior players to help in establishing things. When we arrived to play, everyone was happy with how we were going to go about it.

"I'd also got to know the players from the Nines. We'd had success there so I wasn't a complete stranger."

Laurie Daley says he privately agreed with Lazarus from the start and any time someone suggests overseas players should be allowed to take part in Origin, he harks back to 1997. "It was certainly different - it had a different feel when you played against the Kiwis," Daley ponders. "I think they wanted to include the Kiwis to make them feel a part of it because they'd sacrificed plenty coming into the comp.

"I felt it was never going to work. Obviously I was prepared to give it a go then but if they ever tried to do that or tried to allow … I've heard them say 'allow Sonny Bill (Williams) and some of these better Polynesian players to play State of Origin, they should be allowed'. I don't think that would work. I just think you've got to keep State of Origin as it is. That was a unique time for them to try something differently and see what everyone thought of it. They were certainly tough games but I don't think that type of Tri-Series works. If someone asked me I would definitely say 'don't go down that path again.'"

But Norton counters: "There was huge interest in New Zealand. One of the most popular shows at the time was the Paul Holmes Show.

They had highlights of the game and then they had him shooting the goal to see if he would have kicked the goal to win the game."

The ARL's State of Origin series, meanwhile, was set down between May 28 and June 25 with the second game in Melbourne. Insubordination was not restricted to the Super League camp; before the ARL series started, Brad Fittler wrote in *Rugby League Week*: "How on earth did the designers of the new State of Origin jumper come up with the strip they did? It's a fair dinkum shocker."

The design re-surfaced for the first Origin of 2020 in Adelaide - and got a similar response.

The first game of the Tri-Series between NSW and Queensland at the Sydney Football Stadium attracted 26,731 fans. But up to 17,000 tickets were reportedly given away. They were distributed outside cinemas, added to half priced movie tickets, given to pay TV subscribers and school kids. Robson recalls: "We found a whole bunch of fervent fans for the Blues. We bussed them in from Penrith, we gave them t-shirts, caps, scarves, clappers, streamers…

"We gave them everything we could because we needed to, effectively, manufacture some degree of passion and tribalism about this. In terms of tickets, it used to be you'd go to the movies and get two for $10 on a Tuesday night?

"Well - you get two for $10 and you get *10* free Super League tickets! We were doing anything and everything to try and populate the market with tickets. But as we all know, there's a misnomer about free tickets. You've still got to want to go. You've still got to allocate the time. You've still got to get yourself there."

When NSW fullback David Peachey asked for some tickets for his family, he supposedly was handed 80. The TV ratings in Sydney for that game were 450,0000 - compared to 1,115,000 for the opening match of the previous year's Origin series.

And New Zealand's involvement in the Tri-Series threw up plenty of complications – the NZRL did not want to release players back to their clubs between games. They were subsequently forced to let the players affected, Canterbury's John Timu and Hunters' Tony Iro, go home. In the second Tri-Series match on May 9 at Ericsson Stadium, Queensland beat New Zealand 26-12.

This was also the month in which the outspoken Anthony Mundine - later a celebrated boxer - offered one of his most famous quotes: "Laurie Daley is running on old legs … it's time for the new generation, brother." In the same edition of *The Sun-Herald,* Mundine also reckoned his Brisbane Broncos would be "more creative" with him at five-eighth instead of Kevin Walters.

Daley says of the affair now: "When I first read it, I had a bit of a laugh and thought 'geez, he knows me pretty well' because, mate, I had bad knees so I was running on old legs!

"But that type of stuff didn't worry me. I just thought 'who's the brash young kid? He probably needs to zip his mouth if he's ever going to reach the heights because he's putting a target on his head'.

"He'd say that motivated him to play better football and if he believed that, that's great.

"But for me, it never worried me. I've got a good relationship with him. If I do run into him, I say 'g'day' to him, we'll have a yarn. I'm pretty casual and pretty laid back. If it had have been 'you're a fucking dickhead' or this or that, you might have taken it a bit more to heart.

"But those types of things, water off a duck's back"

At the other end of the audacity spectrum: after NSW beat New Zealand 20-15 at Bruce Stadium to eliminate the Kiwis, shy Blues winger Ken Nagas told a media conference: "We knew they were pretty ordinary up the middle". His startled captain Simon Gillies retorted: "That'll be your last press conference".

In that match, a touch judge was subsequently found to have blundered in ruling NZ winger Sean Hoppe offside before he claimed a try which could have won the contest. Referee Steve Clark said at the time: "I got a call instantly from the touch judge and upon hearing that call I called on Sean Hoppe to stay out and he kept going so I felt with the information I had at the time, I had no option other than to penalise him."

Super League needed a Blues win if the final was to be anything like a success. The New Zealanders' coach, Norton, finished the series without a win and never coached adults again.

Asked if his career would have taken a different turn had the Kiwis progressed that night, if the touchy had not raised his flag, Norton answers: "Yeah. Maybe there would have been other roles for me later on but, yeah…"

The Tri-Series final epic, won 23-22 by NSW at ANZ Stadium (Brisbane) before a crowd of 35,570, was described as Super League's first (and perhaps only) contribution to the sport's annals of great matches. "You think the game is struggling and then something like that happens," said NSW coach Tim Sheens at the time. "They're just playing on emotion.

"It used to be said Australia could pick two or three sides which could win most Tests. Since these players have come through in both leagues, we could now pick maybe three or four. That means Australia will be ahead of the rest of the world for another 20 years unless we help the other countries lift their intensity with things like the Tri-Series and World Club Challenge."

And so back to one of our central characters here. Noel Goldthorpe ended the longest game in the sport's history in dramatic fashion, recalling: "Previously I had two attempts at field goal and missed. They were really hunting up on me so I said to Laurie 'you get on the other side this time and have a go'.

"We didn't realise that Robbie Ross, he went to dummy half for that play instead of (Craig) Gower, for whatever reason. I'm looking at Laurie thinking 'OK, you'll get this' and I turned back to the dummy half and … I've seen the ball floating at me! I thought 'oh shit' … I just dropped it and hit it and I knew straight away it was sweet.

"But it wasn't even supposed to come to me."

Mullins had scored a hat-trick of tries. "At fulltime, 'Alfie' Langer got man of the match!" he laughs. "I thought 'how did they come up with that? If it had have to anyone, I'm glad it was Alfie because he was a legend and a great player."

Recounting his own memories of the footballing marathon, referee Bill Harrigan said: "I was aware of what happened if it's tied at fulltime, that's something you have to know before you go out on the field. The players weren't really aware. They were like 'what the fuck happens here, Bill?'

"Both teams were all going down to …. (nightclub) City Rowers (afterwards). I remember the boys said 'c'mon Billy we're going' and I remember I was that rooted mentally, physically absolutely shattered … they had a few drinks afterwards at the ground… I left and went back to my room and I said 'I can't boys, I'm absolutely stuffed'.

"I woke up about 2.30 with the lights still on, still in my gear, with my jeans that I'd put on, laying on top of my bed. I'd passed out. I was gone."

Upon hearing the story, Goldthorpe calls Harrigan "soft". "We got on the piss all night! What's his problem? NSW and Queensland at City Rowers, both teams were there drinking together. It was so funny. We were drinking like we'd all played together."

Across town at the ARL, It emerged Origin players would receive 33 percent less than the previous season. Coca-Cola agreed to sponsor the series for three years. The ARL promoted Origin with the slogan: "Right arms, eye teeth and left nuts are no guarantees of a ticket." Frank Hyde, the legendary radio commentator then aged 81, was unimpressed: "These are not the words I would use to promote the outstanding event in rugby league's calendar. This is gutter language."

Only 28,222 fans saw the opening match of the 1997 State of Origin series at Suncorp Stadium. Andrew Johns had been selected after just one club game back from that ankle reconstruction. "That was my introduction to Origin," says Goddard. "It sounds like a cliche but as a boy from Mt Isa - it's every kid's dream in Queensland to run out for your state." NSW won 8-6 and went to Melbourne to win the series.

Tom Raudonikis' appointment was on-message as part of the ARL's back-to-basics marketing in contrast to Super League's aspirational sophistication. "I felt like I'd known him my whole life," Paul Harragon, Blues prop for all three games, recalls. Tommy, according to his club captain Paul Langmack, loved his new post, too.

"He said 'how good's this? We're getting paid, we're in camp …'. He said 'mate, I won't be coming to training. You can train the side all week'.

"We were playing the Gold Coast up at the Gold Coast. He might have rang me once. Or not even once, I rang him.

"He said 'oh Paully, I'm having a ball here with all these legends. I'm getting paid being on the piss', he said 'how are they training?'. I said 'good'. I said 'when are you getting to the game?' He said 'I'll get there an hour before kick-off'.

"Tommy comes in an hour before kick-off and I say 'what's the game plan?' and he says 'same as usual - we just bash the halfback'. And we won the game!"

That year Raudonikis, who we lost in 2021, immortalised the term "Cattledog" - a code word which instructed his charges to start a brawl. "I barred that," said team manager Geoff Carr.

"I found out and I said 'under no circumstances, Tommy!' He certainly took a lot of notice of me! I said 'we're in the middle of a war. We can't be seen to have the coach - when you're trying to win hearts and minds - sending the team out there to try and bash another team'."

There in Victoria, the Queensland coach Paul Vautin told his players the series might be the last ever due to looming compromise.

"Tommy had to go down (to Melbourne) for a promotion," recalls Blues physio Liz Steet, "and early in the morning he rings my room. 'Lizzy, can you find my teeth? I can't find my teeth. I need you to come and find my teeth'. At about five o'clock in the morning."

Harragon says: "Tommy could deliver bad news or tell a ribald story and get away with it because he had this magic twinkle in his eye. He was magnetic.

"While the coaching dynamics and specifics and tactical side of things was at a bare minimum, in respect to 'who are you, why are you here, what's that jumper meaning to you' ... it was just amazing...

"...and hilarious. We had a great team that had been well drilled by Gus (Phil Gould) for years."

NSW's 15-14 MCG win in front of only 25,105 fans ("pretty hollow but once you're out there having a go, it's a tough game," says Goddard) was the scene of a memorable controversy, with Blues selector John Raper's son Aaron chosen and left on the bench for the entire game.

(As an aside, Blues captain Geoff Toovey was studying accountancy and sitting for tests while in camp).

But even before the game, there was drama, with Manly's omitted Jim Serdaris claiming Raudonikis had held against him the fact he left Western Suburbs for the Sea Eagles. Andrew Johns withdrew before kick-off through injury, meaning Raper should have gone into the side. But instead, John Simon was promoted.

My memory is that John Raper did speak to Raudonikis - quite aggressively - about the snub afterwards at the team hotel and that the words "my son" were heard. The affair cut to the heart of old school rugby league's problems when it comes to what we now call "optics". The chairman of selectors is involved in selecting his son, who the coach then snubs for a starting spot and leaves on the bench. It was an alcohol-fuelled atmosphere at what is now the Pullman Melbourne On The Park. John Raper was subsequently investigated and cleared.

"I was at training at Melbourne Uni (before the match) and Tommy came up to me, took me into his confidence about how Aaron wasn't going to play and asked me not to write it," journalist Brad Walter recalls. "I felt compromised so asked (AAP Brisbane reporter) Wayne Heming what to do. He said to leave it and at Queensland training the next day Fatty said he wasn't expecting Raper to start so I got the story."

Stuart Raper, Aaron's brother and the coach of Castleford at the time, recalls: "I was over the moon when Aaron got picked in the Origin side … sat up that night and watched the game, sat there for friggin' 80 minutes and stupid Tommy Raudonikis forgot to put him on so…

"I was shattered and quite pissed off to be honest. As a coach, it was wrong. It was wrong that someone with an opportunity to play Origin and you don't give it to them.

"When you look at the situation … there would have been plenty of opportunities to put him on. They needed a defender and Aaron would have done 20 tackles in 10 minutes.

"Chook (their father) was ready for him, that's for sure."

So did Raudonikis "forget" or, as Brad Walter suggests, pre-meditate leaving Aaron Raper on the bench that night?

Geoff Carr nonchalantly ends a 25-year-old mystery. "Tommy took the blame for that but that was actually my fault.

"I used to sit next to the coaches in those days. There wasn't a lot of other staff. If I felt there was something important I should remind the coach about, I would.

"On this occasion, it was a tight game. Tooves was playing dummy half and Johnny Simon was playing halfback. Tommy said to me 'I've got to get Raper on, I'll move Toovey to halfback and and I'll put Raper on at hooker'.

"I said 'Tommy, Johnny Simon is the only one who can kick a field goal. This is going to come down to a one-pointer. If you take him off, who's kicking?' We didn't have one."

Simon duly kicked the winning field goal. "Tommy had all the intentions in the world to get Aaron on, he wanted him on, but the state of the game didn't allow it," says Carr.

"When we go to the Hilton Hotel after, Chook was quite emotional about the whole thing and tore into Tommy. Tommy, to his credit, took the full brunt of that and took the blame for it but in actually he could have had a strong defence in saying he was desperate to get him on - which he was."

Queensland won the 'dead rubber' Origin III 18-12 at Lang Park in a game best remembered for the stand-up brawl between Johns and our other central character here, Goddard.

"Joey was on fire, he was young and just coming through," recalls Goddard. "Geoff Toovey was at half. Fatty obviously told us all we've got to get Joey, make sure he doesn't dominate .

"A set or two before that scrum, I had had the ball. We're attacking their line. I passed the ball, Joey hit me late. We had a scuffle. My fault, I give a penalty away while we're attacking, which is stupid.

"(Mark) 'Spud' Carroll takes a hit-up and knocks Clinton O'Brien out straight off the tap, basically. Clinton O'Brien gets carried off on the opposite side of the field, NSW do a shift attacking into our half and then they drop it. Spud had just knocked out Clinton O'Brien, Spud's going off his head walking to the scrum.

"To be honest, I didn't hear the 'Cattledog' call but I could tell from Spud … I said to the boys 'it's fucking on here'. Poor old Craig Smith, if you watch the tape, Craig Smith literally got on for that scrum. He packed opposite to Spud Carroll and Spud didn't even pack and punched him straight in the head and knocked him out as well!

"Then it was obviously just an all-in blue. Joey and I came together again. We got broken up. I was held back by my team and then he came around the touch judge and then we got into it again. It was a pretty full-on scrap.

'When we got sent off (to the sin bin), which I thought was a bit rude, getting sent off ….. Spud Carroll knocked out Craig Smith clean-as! It wasn't good. Joey's still carrying on."

Afterwards, Geoff Carr scrambled behind the scenes for Newcastle coach Malcolm Reilly not to make a big deal about the fact that Johns had been instructed - via the 'cattledog' call - to use violence. One employee of the NSWRL was forcing Johns to do something which got him in trouble with another branch of the game.

The renown surrounding their respective successes in Brisbane would stay with Noel Goldthorpe and Jamie Goddard for the rest of their lives. But they would only be able to enjoy it for a day or two.

For everyone else, it was back to club football as the ARL and Super League continued their courting dance while they tried to win over those hearts and minds that remained available in a war-torn season.

Hunter Mariners became the highest scoring losers in premiership history when beaten 48-36 by Canterbury at Belmore. Two weeks earlier, Manly and Illawarra had played out the highest scoring draw – 34-34. Mariners coach Graham Murray said: "I think people would be happy with 20-18 … 48-36, I don't think is what they're after."

But by then, Noel Goldthorpe was largely a spectator. His fall from the giddy heights of that night in Brisbane had been merciless and swift.

"Muzz (Murray) said 'come into my office, we'll have a chat'," he says. "I went in there and he told me the news and I looked at him and I went 'fucking really'?"

While he was away on representative duty, a 20-year-old called Brett Kimmorley had played well for the Mariners. NSW's 'field goal hero' was being dropped. Goldthorpe said at the time he was "humiliated" and "embarrassed" by his demotion.

He says now: "I told him I didn't agree with it but you're the coach of the team. That's it. Our relationship, between Muzz and I, went pear shaped. I wasn't in his plans anymore.

"He said to me 'you're not going to England (for the World Club Challenge)'. 'Yeah, righto, whatever'. I think at the time I needed an operation anyway so I just went 'I'll have the operation'."

That one winter in '97 of rival interstate series soon faded from the popular memory, just as - for a while - did Noel Goldthorpe. But, in a unique way, they keep each other's memories alive - Goldy and the Super League Tri-Series - on YouTube and in pub trivia competitions.

"I never got to play Origin but for me, being in the same sort of team of players like Laurie and Robbo (Ian Roberts), Brad Clyde, greats of the game, Glenn Lazarus, it was the greatest buzz for me to do that," he recalls.

"A lot of people say 'it wasn't really State Of Origin, you got New Zealand in….' You go back to the one the ARL had, all those boys, they get recognised as having played a State of Origin game. Probably like myself, if everyone was together 50 per cent of the players don't get that opportunity.

"For me, it's not marked down I played State of Origin which … I don't really give a fuck anyway."

Goddard, likewise, is aware of the sneers from rugby league purists. "I know you're talking about '97 but in 1998 I got called into the deciding game of Origin to start the game at hooker and Wayne Bennett was the coach. That, to me, I'm proud of that. I got selected on my merits. We won that game, we won that series in Sydney and I got to play alongside Alfie Langer and Kevin Walters and Steve Renouf was in the centres. You look at the '98 team. I roomed with Gorden Tallis who was a north Queensland boy.

"I'm proud of the '97 … no-one can take it away from me. My family came to every game that year, from Mt Isa … '97 was something like a dream. But then to win it in '98, man, that was the best feeling.

"No-one remembers that."

They just remember the punch-up with Joey Johns.

From their highs of mid 1997, from receiving cheques that quadrupled their earnings, Jamie Goddard and Noel Goldthorpe each went on to have front row seats for the pain and sadness of the war's toxic wreckage. Between them, they played at five clubs which died as the game paid for the excesses of media barons.

Goldthorpe saw the Mariners collapse in 1997 and the team he joined the following year, Adelaide, followed them into the abyss. "I'm thinking 'is it me? Is it me sending these bastards broke?'

"Looking back, I would love to have stayed at St George my whole career. It would have been ideal for me but obviously it didn't work that way. But I went to Super League for the money. Don't let anyone tell you otherwise about what they did back then."

Graham Murray died in 2013 without the pair ever making amends. "But I have a friend who was pretty close with Muzz and he said to me Muzz was a bit disappointed with how it went down. We all make decisions at the time that's best for ourselves or for the clubs or whatever.

"In the end, I've got no hard feelings towards Muzz. It is what it is and it was what it was. It looks like he probably made the right decision with Noddy because Noddy ended up playing for Australia and NSW, he was a great halfback."

Goddard became a similar Jonah.

Gold Coast (1998), North Sydney (1999) and Northern Eagles (2002) all died on his watch. He lives on the NSW Central Coast because "the kids were in school and we didn't want to move"

Now 49, he says: "I was actually our players union rep at the time and we were filthy because the Gold Coast folded with money in the bank and were sacrificial lambs. Obviously the Mariners were (too). At the time, in '98, Adelaide Rams were as well.

"Players had to move on, players went over to New Zealand or went to England. You had Dessy Clark, one of my best mates, he went to England. It was sad, it was sad. The '99 season was horrible with the Bears. They folded after that.

"I still talk to guys from up the Gold Coast and guys down here…. For instance, I'm selling a house for a guy who is an old North Sydney Bears fan. He said 'mate, I haven't watched a game since Super League'. What are we, 25 years on?

"So we've lost people from 25 years ago that have not watched a game of footy. The Bears are a foundation club. I just can't get that: 1908 and they let the Bears go. When South Sydney got back into the comp, everyone was rejoicing. I think that was tremendous. To let the Bears go, and the Gold Coast … there are still blokes up there who are filthy that the Gold Coast Seagulls folded and then the Chargers folded. I wish the Titans all the best and you need them to succeed. It's a tough gig.

"The game needed a change. It helped the players. But it needed to become more professional as well and grow, even though it's taken a bit of a backwards step again."

At the back of a cupboard in Terrigal is Jamie Goddard's number one souvenir of the night he became a household name, even if he regards it as "embarrassing" and far from his career highlight. It's Andrew Johns' Origin III jersey, which was almost immediately cleansed of the 'claret' he was responsible for putting there.

"It's a collector's item. What happens on the field, stays on the field. He likes a beer, I like a beer. It's a game of footy really."

And although he played Origin a year later, like Goldthorpe, Jamie Goddard was brought back to earth suddenly after the 1997 interstate series. "Joey and I actually went to the judiciary together and Geoff Bellew represented both of us! Yeah, right?

"I said to Paul Broughton, our CEO … he said 'Geoff Bellew's going to represent both of you'. I went 'how the fuck does that work?' We're having a meeting before the judiciary, together the three of us, and I said to Geoff 'mate, how is this going to work?' He said 'don't worry, we'll be right. No-one ever gets suspended in Origin for fighting. Y'know? You'll get a slap on the wrists'.

"Mate, we got two weeks each! "And Spud Carroll didn't even get 10 in the bin! He knocked two blokes out in a minute!

"I looked at Joey and went 'fuck, that went well'."

May and June

- It is reported Neil Whittaker did not want to partake in any more peace talks because he feared no-one would watch either competition for the rest of 1997 if an agreement was done before the season ended.

- On the last day of May, the Federal Court blocked a deal between Optus and Australis Media for the use of a satellite – seen as a blow to the ARL by proxy.

- The ARL launched legal action over $600,000 it claimed it was owed by Britain's Rugby Football League for its involvement in the 1995 World Cup.

- In June, Optus Communications chief executive Ziggy Switkowski and chairman Russell Fynmore resigned.

- Former New Zealand Prime Minister David Lange wrote in a newspaper column that the ARL had a better competition than the one in which the Warriors competed. "For whatever the reason, the arrival of Super League hasn't enhanced the product," he wrote. "Its Australian rival is playing better, harder, more competitive football. Beer barons and media magnates are welcome supporters of rugby league but they can't run the game."

- News Limited director of sport Ian Frykberg responded: "The comments made by David Lange and the comments made about the Tri-Series should be taken as robust comments by our New Zealand colleagues. The fact is, we do have an agreement and we're entering into a long-term agreement. There's no disciplinary action. We resolved that Ken Cowley and myself would go to New Zealand and sort it out."

- Perth tore up fullback Julian O'Neill's $2 million contract due to off-field misbehaviours. Rather ironically, given O'Neill forced his departure from Perth, Peter Mulholland left PSG around the same time. Mulholland left after the visit of a special administrative group - former Super League CEO Robert Elstone plus Tony Gale and David Beanland. John Monie turned down the opportunity to be his replacement.

- Also in May, the RFL launched its first website.

- It emerged that Whittaker and Frykberg had met on May 16.

- Super League announced its plans to put a team into Melbourne in 1998, with John Ribot reported to be chief executive. The next day, the ARL stepped up its own plans for a team in the Victorian capital, backed by Carlton & United Breweries and Reebok.

- Frykberg told Channel Nine: "I would hope the war is over. I would think it's been over for a few weeks now. What we want is a lasting peace."

- On May 24, Rupert Murdoch was reported to have flown in to oversee just such a peace deal. Frykberg and Whittaker met again on May 22.

- A new tax on poker machine profits in NSW was a key factor in the background. The pokies were moving into pubs and the giant licensed clubs - effectively casinos by many international standards - which had financed rugby league for decades would never be the same.

- On May 23, Canterbury, Cronulla and Penrith were warned by Frykberg they may be forced into mergers. Penrith chief executive Mark Levy said: "Any Sydney club that refuses to even consider amalgamation is facing extinction." But

Souths' George Piggins vowed the Rabbitohs would seek legal advice if even asked to consider merging and North Sydney's Ray Beattie railed against the idea of the Bears getting together with Manly. Piggins told Rugby League Week: "Mergers aren't going to work. After sitting down with Eastern Suburbs and Balmain, I think merging falls into the too-hard basket. Unless the existing members on the boards are replaced by young blokes without the same emotional attachments, I can't see it happening."On Wednesday June 11, the *Telegraph* nevertheless carried the headline "Wedding Bells" - predicting the merging of Manly and North Sydney. Speaking about teams in Sydney, Brisbane chief executive Shane Edwards offered: "The sums add up to four but other factors like tradition and emotion would probably result in there being six (today there are eight and a half)."

- Graham Lowe, Dean Lonergan and Malcolm Boyle emerged as likely new owners of the Warriors.

- Canterbury's annual Multicultural Day clash, this year against Penrith, was tainted by violence with a policeman put in a headlock, a touch judge threatened and several spectators arrested. The Bulldogs won the game 28-20; this was the night on which Solomon Haumono's mother Lavini rushed onto the field when her son was injured.

- "She said she didn't want me playing any more and asked me to stop playing the game," Haumono later revealed. Super League's Rebecca Wilson responded to the violence by saying: "We have security in place at matches and we believed that was adequate security but after this we'll have to address that and see if it is adequate security."

- After beating Souths' 28-4 on June 7, Gold Coast officials said they wanted to know within 10 days if they would be in the competition the following season. On June 8, The Sun-Herald reported that Ribot would be officially released as CEO of Super League to head to Melbourne.

- Frank Stanton moved from Manly to the ARL. Veteran NSWRL ground manager Eric 'The Bosun' Cox quit in protest at no longer being allowed to take his wife, on expenses, to State of Origin games.

- Reflecting on the bare-bones operation at South Queensland, Crushers CEO Eric Laakso said: "The players knew at the start of the season that if they didn't attract good crowds, their match payments would be withheld."

CANBERRA MISMATCH A SUPER BLOW

By Steve Mascord, *Sydney Morning Herald,*
Monday June 23,1997

CANBERRA 56 WIGAN 22 at Bruce Stadium

CANBERRA and Wigan yesterday provided further evidence that in 1997, it's best for rugby league officials to hope for the best and expect the worst.

Nearly two weeks ago, ARL officials were hoping for a big crowd and a good contest in Melbourne for Origin II, one of their highest-profile events of the year.

Super League bosses had earmarked big-name Canberra versus reigning world champions Wigan on June 22 as such a major attraction it was originally scheduled for the Sydney Football Stadium.

Origin II attracted a disappointing crowd in Melbourne, but at least the ARL got a contest. Super League got 9,098 fans and a mismatch in Canberra yesterday.

Great Britain Test winger Jason Robinson admitted being "ashamed" as he and his Wigan teammates trooped into the dressing-room down 42-6 at half-time.

And although they outscored the Raiders 16-14 in the second half, Wigan's 56-22 shellacking must surely be the biggest blow to Super League's World Club Challenge concept yet.

It's one thing for the likes of Halifax to be run ragged. But Wigan are allegedly defending the title they won three years ago.

It was an unfortunate end to their three weeks in Australia, especially after a meritorious 22-19 win over Canterbury and a deceptively competitive performance in the 34-0 defeat by Brisbane, who were in top form.

"We are not used to playing at this level every week and we have to play at this level every week," said a seemingly masochistic Wigan coach Eric Hughes.

"As you know, we don't have the same number of players in England as you do here, so that is not always possible.

"If we have to come to the other side of the world to get that competition, if we have to get our backsides smacked a few times, then so be it.

"It might take two, three years for us to get to the level, but we need this competition, we need it."

Hughes correctly observed that his side had "gifted" the Raiders their first two tries. The Lancashiremen seemed certain to score in the third minute, only for Canberra centre Brett Mullins to snatch an intercept off Wigan five-eighth Henry Paul and race 90m to score.

Tongan fullback Paul Koloi then slipped over as he tried to gather a kick near his tryline, had another go and fumbled just in time for Canberra centre Ruben Wiki to arrive and score.

But then it became a procession, with five more Canberra tries before the break.

"It wasn't disappointment," Robinson said of the mood of half-time, "most of us were ashamed at how we performed in the first half."

Raiders coach Mai Meninga described his team's first-half performance as the best of the year and some of its attack as "freakish".

Tries like Wiki's second in the 24th minute, would have been scored against just about any team.

Second-rower David Furner was named man of the match perhaps as consolation for having got to within six of Michael Cronin's record for most consecutive goals, only to miss shot No 22.

Canberra have averaged 63 points during the world challenge, but captain Ricky Stuart, who with winger Noa Nadruku made a comeback from injury yesterday, said: "What I'll be saying at training this week is to forget the last three weeks.

"It would be very easy for us to go in the next three games now and get our bums smacked. They're three very hard games against Hunter, Canterbury and Brisbane and it will be completely different to the last three games."

Former Wigan international Joe Lydon, now a troubleshooter for Britain's Rugby Football League, arrived in Australia late last week to launch an investigation into the alarming gulf in standards.

Hughes yesterday applauded the investigation. But unlike others in charge of remedying the game's woes, Lydon cannot use the fall-back line of "it will be better when there's one comp in Australia".

For the Brits, that eventuality will only make things worse.

CHAPTER 14

Here for a holiday

"ONE of the great untold stories of that whole thing was the flight over," says journalist Mike Westlake, discussing the most maligned rugby league competition in history - the 1997 World Club Challenge (or Championship).

"The World Club Challenge was most certainly that - it was a 'challenge'," recalls Super League operations manager Ian Schubert.

In a rugby league version of *Almost Famous*, 21-year-old Mike had been in his job as Cowboys roundsman at the *Townsville Bulletin* for all of two months when he got the call to cover the team on their WCC trip to the UK in the first round of the overblown cross-hemisphere league. Things got a little bit too much for Mike's taste like Cameron Crowe's 2000 movie about a rock journalist - just 15 minutes out of Brisbane.

"There was just this big bang and the whole plane just started shuddering," Westlake recalls from his home on the Gold Coast, where he now works for the Titans.

"Then it started going down with that brrrrrrr. We're all looking. We're all just going 'what the fuck's going on?' The stewardesses are just running up and down the aisle, just in a mad panic.

"The pilot comes on the radio and says 'ladies and gentlemen we've had a bit of an issue, we're going to have to return to Brisbane Airport. I was travelling with the Cowboys. They've started shifting all the front rowers, all the forwards, to the exit rows, and then the stewardesses came over and addressed us all as a group.

"They said 'as able-bodied people, you have a responsibility to help those that can't help themselves'. Someone turned around and said 'holy fuck, we're gonna die'.

"So anyway, they've done this big u-turn out over Moreton Bay and dumped all the fuel and we're coming in to land and we've had to do the whole brace position and everything like that.

"Remember (halfback) Andrew Dunemann? Great guy. He was sitting in the seat beside me across the aisle and he starts taking off his pants and his shoes. We're all sitting there going 'what are you doing, Junior' and he says 'well I'm not going to be able to swim in the bastards, am I?'

"He was just terrified of flying. We've turned our heads and gone back to the brace position, thinking we were fucked and we're coming into the airport looking out the window and all you see coming past are fire engines and ambulances.

"They got it down, got us back in the airport and we're there for a couple of hours and then we got back on and started the 20 hour flight to England all over again.

"And everyone obviously paid attention to the safety announcement, about where the emergency exits were located, the second time around."

The WCC was that sort of competition. It was high farce, even on the ground. The first WCC match had been played in 1976, when Eastern Suburbs took on St Helens at Sydney Sports Ground but Graham Lowe remembers its rebirth, the 1987 game that put us on the road to rugby league's greatest money-incinerator a decade later. "I was coaching Wigan at the time and I remember Maurice (Lindsay) saying 'how do you think we'd go against the Australians sides?'" Lowe says from Auckland.

"I said 'I think we'd beat anything' because we had a really good side at that time. A few more drinks and we rang Ken (Arthurson) from the pub and put it to Ken about 'why don't, whoever wins over there, play the best team here?'.

"Ken said 'oh the guys here will want X amount of money' and what-not but I'll tell you within about 30 minutes, the whole deal was done. That took vision from Arko. Arko could have knocked the whole thing on the head then and there but he stood up and made it work."

Wigan ground down Manly In 1987 before 38,895 fans packed into Central Park. In 1989, Widnes beat Canberra 30-18 at Old Trafford, in 1991 Wigan downed Penrith 21-4 at Anfield, in 1992 Brisbane eclipsed Wigan 22-4 at Central Park and in 1994 the cherry-and-whites memorably upset Brisbane 20-14 at QEII Stadium in Brisbane.

The mid-season 1994 event was pivotal in the history of Super League in Australia; I paid my own way north on a day off from my very new job at the *Sydney Morning Herald* and the next day the visiting officials and media along with representatives of the Denver NFL team were invited aboard a Brisbane river steamer by the host club. I'll be honest: I drank too much and have no recollection of these events but apparently John Ribot let slip some time during the afternoon that a rebel competition was in the works!

By the following year, of course, that project was well in progress and no WCC was played. And by 1997, the shark had been well and truly jumped; the WCC under Super League would not just involve the champion team in each league playing each other but all 22 sides from both competitions. The 1982 and 1986 Kangaroos had not lost a single game on tour; British rugby league clawed back some pride by takingthe 1990 and 1994 Ashes series to deciders. But still the gulf in standard was apparent to most.

Not, it would appear, to those who decided to go ahead with the 1997 World Club Challenge, which George Piggins labelled "one of the greatest farces ever perpetrated upon the Australian sporting public."

Maurice Lindsay recalls: "First of all, we did a stupid thing - it's (then Halifax CEO) Nigel Wood's fault. I was in Australia and I persuaded Ken Cowley to fund the top three clubs in Australia (playing) the top three clubs in England. The English clubs would have been Wigan, St Helens and Bradford.

"After the meeting of English clubs, (Bradford's) Chris Caisley rang me and told me 'oh mate I've just had absolute drama at the meeting'. I said 'what?' And he said 'well, Nigel Wood got up and said we all play, all 12 clubs, or nobody plays'. 'Fucking hell,' I said, 'they'll get destroyed. I said 'can you imagine Halifax playing Brisbane? It will be 100-0 after 10 minutes!'

"He said 'I'm only telling you what the vote was'. I said 'you should have stood up and told them to fuck off'."

Caisley says now that Wood may have spoken at the meeting concerned, but that most of his rival CEOs and chairmen agreed with him.

Lindsay continues: "Anyway, he didn't so I went back to Ken Cowley and he said 'how will the competition be?' And I said 'it will be one-sided'. He said 'what will it cost?' And I said 'well, you've got to fly six teams over there and six over here…'

"It nearly bankrupted them. It actually caused Ken and Rupert to fall out. Now, they'd been schoolboy friends together on the banks of Melbourne (sic) growing up, living in a tent (Cowley and Murdoch were already publishers when they met in 1962, the former having just completed a tour of the latter's paper - and Cowley's family denies the rift, saying the pair still speaks every Saturday morning and has never fallen out. There are no records of them living together in a tent, either.).

"I hated the thought of it so … the first (prime time Australian) game was thankfully Wigan and Canterbury Bankstown and Wigan beat Canterbury Bankstown … only because Jason Robinson went everywhere. What an exceptional player he was.

"Apart from that, the Australians embarrassed us and Nigel Wood still didn't accept it. He thought we were going to make money out of it. To cut a long story short, it was a disaster - but the original World Club Challenge was Wigan and Manly which I designed as you know and we managed to swing it around eventually and bring it (back) to that. "

Halifax conceded 204 points in just three games Down Under during the first leg of the WCC. "Nigel Wood, he brought out 1000 Halifax jumpers," says Ian Robson, "and he took home 998 - and I reckon one of the two, he lost.

"I do remember the launch. It was great - we got Visa on board. They'd never really done anything in Australian sport so that was really pleasing.

"If you look at what Super Rugby have since tried to do, which looks to have imploded … you were trying to do it with new clubs in a new league …. It was all well intended."

Wood laughs along with Robson when it comes to the jerseys - but takes Lindsay's comments a little more seriously.

"I wanted to explore the opportunities to try and build the club brand whilst down there," said Wood. "It wasn't the best decision I've ever made and I think those shirts are on a container ship in the South China Sea even now.

"If they're not, I'm sure they'll have been put to good use by the community clubs around NSW. There's a lot of clubs playing in Blue Sox replica gear. It was a triumph of enthusiasm over experience."

On Lindsay's comments, he says: "I think Chris (Caisley) has a better recollection than Maurice, frankly.

"I would be surprised if a relatively young and inexperienced CEO of a middle-ranking club like Halifax would be able to carry the day on a matter of profound strategy.

"Once the Super League competition started in Australia, there was a general appetite to cultivate strong relationships and I think that was mutual. The Australian Super League competition saw its alignment with the British game as a positive and something that needed to be cultivated. They were pushing at an open door.

"I think it's a bit disingenuous to try and nail one person and say 'yes…' I know that's some people's style but the reality of the situation is that it was a democratic process and the clubs proffered a view.

"To be very fair to Maurice, I do remember him rubbing his chin and saying 'just be very careful because the standard of the Australian clubs is a lot higher than the British game and you need to be aware'.

"Maurice was urging caution but the British clubs, universally, wanted to participate."

On opening night, London Broncos led their big brothers Brisbane 18-12 at halftime before eventually losing 42-22 at ANZ Stadium. Josh White remembers the London side was still jet lagged and players were captured yawning during a national anthem that was actually foreign to them, since they were all Australian. Northern hemisphere teams won just three of 30 matches in the first half of the competition, which the RFL and News spent £500,000 ($A900,000) promoting.

Greg McCallum, then head of match officials in England, recalls: "I used to like to go and stand with the speccies before the game. You'd have some banter with them and they were pretty pissed off at the time.

"And once the games started, we got flogged. I remember going to Knowsley Road, St Helens were the top side in Super League and they got absolutely smashed in the first game. Then Bradford got smashed in their game.

"Within one weekend, the arse fell out of it and they never recovered."

Despite five pastings to open the WCC, Frykberg said it would be part of a united competition the following year.

But the real stories of the 1997 World Club Challenge were off the field.

Then-Canberra hooker and current Huddersfield coach Simon Woolford describes the second round of the WCC, when the Raiders travelled to England, as "the best time of my life". Having lost early to Wigan, Canterbury were effectively out of the competition and "we were blind by the time we got off in the plane in Singapore", recalls prop Barry Ward. "We had our golf clubs. Poor old North Queensland won their first three games and they were drinking juice and water". The high jinx weren't always harmless. Paul Davidson of Salford was given a suspended jail sentence for assault while in Adelaide. Martin Hall, Craig Murdoch and Gary Connolly were all fined for misbehaviour. Leeds coach Damian McGrath was injured in a dingy accident. Wigan's Neil Cowie was sent home after missing training before the match against Canberra.

Memorably, Raiders players went to an Ashes cricket Test at Headingley in drag and, reputedly, stole a baggy green cap from the Australian dressing room.

Michael Hagan reflects: "Pauly Marquet had never been out of Raymond Terrace and/or Newcastle. Next minute he's on a flight going to Paris. And Brad Godden. The two most knockabout westie type blokes in Newcastle. Timmy Maddison would be in that category. It just painted a picture where here's a bit of sophistication being brought into that group."

Hagan went on to coach Newcastle to a premiership and also Parramatta, along with Queensland. Without the WCC - like a couple of marriages and therefore a few children - it may never have happened. Hagan was the Mariners' media manager!

"I ended up getting invited to help Graham Murray with the team in the middle of the season back then because they didn't have any other genuine support to help him," he explains.

"...(and) going on the World Club Challenge to England and that's where the coaching interest sort of started."

Gorden Tallis at least had the honesty to repeat one of the great urban myths from the cross-competition league that turns out not to be a myth at all. "…my first time in England," he wrote in his biography, "our second game was against the London Broncos and when we'd been in London for a day, John Plath told me he'd been to have a look at Piccadilly Circus. I said to him "the Piccadilly Circus, where is it?". He told me it was a couple of stops on the train and that he'd been and seen all the monkeys and elephants and clowns and their little exploding car.

"I said I was really looking forward to going and all the boys joined in, telling me about the great bear act they had there. When I got there I was a bit disappointed it was just a big street with lots of buildings."

While the slogan to promote the WCC in Australia was "Visa World Club Challenge: We're not here for a holiday", the opposite was the case for many players. Wilson told me that one British-based star had expected News to cover the cost of a prostitute when he was flown out to the series launch.

"Most of them went fishing," Tom Mockeridge said of visiting English players, begging the question "for what?" (Mockeridge, as the Aussie rights holder for the WCC, does not look upon it ruefully, saying it "added flavour" to the season).

On June 22, Brisbane hosted Halifax at ANZ Stadium. "All of the forwards packing into the scrums, they just could smell the grog coming out of these Halifax forwards!" laughs Broncos five-eighth Kevin Walters, a 76-0 winner on the day.

When the ABC's Craig Hamilton was asked on air to assess the crowd at a Hunter Mariners home fixture, he responded: "Do you want to know how many are here or do you want to be introduced to them?"

"One of our directors got caught running nude down the hallway of the Crowne Plaza," says Shane Richardson. "One of our strength and conditioning staff, there was a fire drill at two in the morning and he arrives back with this girl.

"After the game, everyone would be back in the bars. We were staying in the same place with Canberra."

Wayne Bennett rhapsodises: "That was probably one of the best three weeks I spent in my life, in the UK, when we went over for the World Club Challenge. It was outstanding. I loved it. We all loved it.

"I did love the concept of it. I thought it had a lot of merit. In terms of fun and enjoyment, that three weeks in England are as good as I experienced.

"We (effectively) won the (Australian) premiership over there. We left Australia after the Origin (tri-)series and we were struggling a bit. We'd had a tough game in Canberra the night before we flew out to the UK.

"We played Wigan. A pretty tough game and we managed to beat them. I think Glenn Lazarus broke his leg that night. Alf (Allan Langer) did his groin. Then we went to London and played the London Broncos and beat them in a tough game.

"Then we played Halifax and they weren't a top side at that time and Steve Renouf scored four tries that night. He just needed to get a bit of confidence back. It didn't matter who he was playing.

"He brought that home to Australia with him."

Walters says Bennett should take much of the credit for the Broncos' Northern Hemisphere success. "We played Canberra on the Friday night and then we had to get on the plane from Canberra to Sydney. We'd all had a few drinks the night before, we were looking forward to the flight to London.

"Wayne's grabbed us all as a group and said 'that's it - we're having a clean trip, no-one's to be having a beer or anything'. I guess that was our saving grace because we arrived in a healthy state. It was a good call from Coach Bennett.

"We went on to win the '98 premiership and the 2000 premiership and no doubt that '97 year with the travel in the Super League and playing over there, it just brought a lot of us together and that team was very successful over a three or four year period because of the '97 Super League and the World Club Challenge."

Daley says now that maybe a few players on both sides of the equator were on the lookout for a holiday. Canberra scored 136 points in their first two games but so lopsided was the competition that a single loss for a southern hemisphere side meant certain elimination.

That's because under the rigged structure; the finals had to feature four sides from each league.

"We were lucky … well I don't know about lucky," Daley says. "But we lost our first game so we were straight out of the tournament!

"So the following two weeks was a game of footy for us on the weekend, knowing we couldn't make the semi-finals. So we treated it as a bit of a holiday, a couple of weeks' away trip."

London Broncos' 38-18 win over the Raiders on July 21 is regarded as one of the highlights of that club's entire history. "A lot of us were young enough to play in Australia but Super League split us all up," says Josh White. "We were still ambitious and we still had fight in our legs and beating Canberra proved that we've still got it."

London traffic made the Raiders very late to the Twickenham Stoop - and then things got worse. Daley and Woolford each admit the preparation wasn't the best, even if they don't recall some of the wilder stories kicking around at the time, like one player 'surfing' on the back of a black cab and another spending the night in a police lock-up.

Woolford says: "Mal was the coach and he liked a drink so we pretty much got straight off the plane and got on the beers for the next two or three days."

Luke Davico, who seems to have been unofficial entertainment director for the trip, describes the first night as "crazy". Daley recalls: "The first night we arrived … we went out into Covent Garden or somewhere like that and a couple of boys got into a blue.

"I can't remember who. We just went there, got on the drink and a bit of trouble happened. The boys got into a stink with someone."

Davico: "Someone was on the back of a cab. Someone said (a player) had beaten a cabbie. We got out. Next thing there were police everywhere. The bobbies started pointing at us and I was like 'go, go!'

"They grabbed us and the brought the taxi driver over to ID us. It's the closest you get to being in a lineup! He looked at three of us and said 'no, it wasn't none of them' and he said 'you guys can go'."

Of the game, Daley says: "We were stunned that they beat us but it was funny. We were disappointed but we weren't that disappointed. Looking back now, we didn't really treat it like a serious competition. You treated it like a competition … if you had the opportunity now, you'd be saying 'this would be pretty special'.

"It was just trying to give the English clubs something to look forward to from signing with Super League, you know? It was something extra. For us it wasn't the comp we wanted to win. The comp we wanted to win was the Super League premiership. Once we lost and we knew we were out of it, we were just over there having a good time."

Woolford adds: "Our leaders were real characters. Ricky (Stuart) and Laurie, they trained hard and they drank hard."

The competition may have been an overblown disaster but the life experiences it afforded were priceless to young working class men. Newcastle Herald reporter Ben Drzyzga had to take holidays and pay some of the expenses himself to follow the Mariners on the WCC but certainly has no regrets.

"I was lucky, we were lucky, we had Paris Saint-Germain so you had a week in Paris," Drzyzga recalls.

"You've got a whole bunch of young guys including myself. (Club chairman) Bob Ferris, he was pretty keen at the time that the boys got some culture.

"We went up the Eiffel Tower, we went to the Louvre. All these footballers who might not have travelled too much in their time … all of a sudden you're in Paris for a week.

"The French Open was on at the time and we went to a bar afterwards and John McEnroe was playing in a band."

Stuart Raper came up with a novel way to prevent his Castleford players from becoming too unhinged on their big trip Down Under.

"St Helens and Wigan had come over and they'd stayed on the Gold Coast and I'd heard they created all sorts of dramas, got on the piss, done all sorts of things and I thought 'oh shit….'," says Raper, who had only just travelled to England for his big break as a head coach when the WCC required him to come back.

"I'd already told them 'I don't care how we go, I just want to play good footy and get close'. I thought 'these guys are going to go mad'.

"We stayed at Brighton. We trained really hard one afternoon. I took them out with a few of my mates around here, we went to Northies, a couple of pubs, I ended up getting a bus and dragging them into the Cross, got them out on the piss until five or six in the morning.

"I was sick, we got them up at nine the next morning, we trained again, had a barbecue in the afternoon, I made them drink again. This is three days off the plane and we had to play that weekend. We had a week and a half after that.

"I said to Mike Ford, who was the captain and halfback and didn't drink: 'Fordy this is what I'm doing. If we just let them go berserk…' We did it in a controlled environment … it actually brought us really tight, it brought us together which was great.

"Dean Sampson, he said 'I'm not drinking ever again'. So it was good. They were well behaved after that. Most of the blokes, they couldn't drink then for the rest of the trip!"

Stuart had a proud moment when his father John, a staunch ARL man, actually attended a Super League game - the WCC clash with Hunter on July 20 - to support him "which is the big thing for him. I was really happy and really proud that he did that."

Cas's Adrian Vowles reflects: "That trip saved us from relegation. We came back a much tighter team".

I know of at least two marriages from the competition; England prop Andy Platt met his wife in Townsville and moved to Magnetic Island when his career was over, while Westlake, covering the North Queensland Cowboys on tour in the UK, met his partner in Leeds.

"I had just turned 21, I was single in the north of England covering rugby league for a regional newspaper on £100 ($A180) expenses a day," Westlake says now. "It was terrific fun. Tim Sheens was coach and I got along well with him and the players were fantastic. There were guys like Steve Walters, Ian Roberts, Johnny Lomax, Scott Mahon, Reggie Cressbrook was a guy I got along with super well. There were quite a lot of guys around my age so it was a pretty easy gig to cover."

That is, until the Cowboys' hooker, Jason Death, was sent home for exposing himself to members of the Australian cricket team in a hotel bar. "Twice in one night in front of the Australian cricket team's wives - that was a highlight of the trip. Quite funny. You'd get locked up for that these days and suspended for 12 months," Woolford recalls. 'Doctor' Death was fined $10,000 for 'doing the helicopter'.

"You wonder how things would play out in the modern world if something like that had happened," Westlake says. "I stumbled across it by accident. They'd been at the cricket all day. Rabieh Krayem was the CEO at the Cowboys at the time and I was talking to him in the foyer about it.

"It was not the full-on ultra-professional era we have now … but it wasn't the fun-filled boys-having-a-laugh 1980s either. I was travelling with the group, I didn't feel under any pressure about having to (not) report the story. I think Jason himself sort of took exception to the fact that I did but, you know, players always get upset if you have to write a bad story about them.

"It was just the job I was sent there to do. I was told he was being sent home. If I didn't write it, someone else was going to. The official line from the club was that he'd been involved in an off-field incident; there weren't many details."

Trevor McEwen was at the Warriors when Death later joined, becoming something of a folk hero.

"We signed him and he might have even had a clause that he wasn't allowed to do the helicopter (we'll leave the details to your imagination). He did it twice in our first six weeks but he was such a character and everybody loved him and he was so good for the club we let it all go."

The Death incident was the same day the Raiders went to the Ashes Test at Headingley, which we touched on briefly earlier in this chapter. Daley doesn't recall the baggy green cap being stolen but does remember many drunken misadventures with the cricketers.

Davico says: "I went and got outfits for everyone. We got ladies singlet tops and wigs. You'll see photos. We stormed the pitch as they won, then we got back into the sheds and celebrated with the Aussies. It was unbelievable.

"There was a whole heap of signed bats. One of the players said 'you can take it, no worries at all'. I was geeing up saying it was Glenn McGrath's bad and I walked out with it. The manager chased me out and grabbed it and said 'Glenn McGrath did not give you that bat!'

"I think Michael Kaspairwich's cap might have gone missing but it wasn't from any of us.

"We had Jason Croker sitting next to Shane Warne in the sheds, just going 'well done guys' and then I picked up someone's bat and Toots (Croker) is blind and said 'hit me across the head' so I hit Toots across the forehead with this bat.

"And the cricketers are looking up going 'what's going on here'. Toots is going 'c'mon, hit me harder!' so I just started hitting him across the forehead. He took his false tooth out and took Warney's hand and put his false tooth in Warney's hand and then stood up and said 'c'mon hit me!' so I'm smashing him across the head while Warney's holding Tootsy's false tooth!

"Out of control - and there's so many of those!

"Then we went back to the hotel and we welcomed the Aussie cricketers back to the hotel."

Daley: "I remember singing the song (John Williamson's 'Hey True Blue') and they were using bat handles and poking holes in the roof, pushing the roof up. What some of the boys did was they gee-ed the security up to go and grab Mal like they were kicking him out, to the roar of the crowd. It was all good fun but Mal had no idea what was going on.

"What I do recall of that night was Mal … we were getting pissed with the cricketers and a few of the boys thought they could tackle Mal. We were geeing Mal up, going 'these blokes reckon they can give it to you' and we were saying to the cricketers 'you'll bash him, he's soft, he's quite easy'

"So we had this comp where Mal had to run with a can of beer in his hand and he had to score a try at the other end of the room. There was a couple of the cricketers, it might have been the Waugh brothers and Michael Bevan, Slats (Michael Slater) or someone. I just remember a couple of them going into tackle Mal and Mal's just dropped the hip and shoulder and 'bang' they've all gone flying off him and hit their heads and fell over and Mal's just slammed the can down and goes 'try!' Hahaha.

"I remember waking up the next day and finding out Deathy was chucked on a plane."

Woolford: "They reckon Steve Waugh had a crook shoulder for months after that. I think Jason Croker, he picked up Michael Bevan and threw him through the roof I think.

"I was wearing Steve Waugh's baggy green back at the hotel for about an hour. I actually got a photo of Steve Waugh wearing my wig and him wearing my baggy green.

I think it was (Michael) Kasprowicz. I'm not even sure he got that (baggy green) back.

"In the dressing room afterwards was unbelievable. Luke Davico had a big fat lip, he had a big scab on his lip. He got knocked around the day before against Halifax. He lost a tooth. It went through his lip.

"He's there in the motel and Shane Warne's there with a smoke hanging out his mouth and Luke Davico just grabbed the smoke and had a drag of his smoke and gave it back.

"I remember Warney just looking at him, having a look at the lip … he didn't know what was wrong with the lip and he said 'nah, nah mate. You can keep that'.

"I remember I tackled Luke at the bar and he's knocked into (television journalist) Jim Wilson and Jim Wilson had a glass of wine and that went everywhere and he was filthy. He wanted someone else to buy him a glass of red wine."

Davico: "I've still got video of Jim Wilson. Before we went over I said 'this is gonna be the trip of a lifetime'. I bought a new video camera. The video camera got passed around like a cricket ball the day they won the Ashes.

"I vividly remember picking up the video camera the next day in the hallway and it was in bits and pieces. We salvaged the video and we've got some great footage. The footage there with Jim Wilson is hilarious. We kept going up to Jim going 'Jim, give us a report of the Ashes!"

'Statue" Davico remembers the Jim Wilson incident slightly differently to 'Germ' Woolford - but the prop has the footage to prove the accuracy of his version.

"There's one bit where Jim is going 'what a fantastic day in the Ashes - we shoved it up England's arse' and you can see Simon Woolford coming from behind. He cuts him in half, tackles him, and the glass of red flies everywhere and Jim and Simon are rolling around on the ground. He's going 'where's my red! Get me another red!"

Wilson ("I grew up on the Gold Coast where people loved to party but I never experienced the helicopter") recounts another hitherto untold story: how the affair became big news back home.

"My father Bruce Wilson was also a journo and who was in the London Bureau for News Corp ," says Wilson, who insists "nothing nasty" went on at the Crowne Plaza that night.

"He was a great journo. Loved his cricket, loved his rugby but also covered wars, spent time in the White House press gallery, Singapore, you name it…

"Anyway, I had a conversation with Bruce the day after that. He was in London, I was in Leeds.

"I said 'a bit of a funny old night last night' and he said 'what do you mean?' Bruce, being a typical journo, kept on asking me a few other questions and I'm thinking 'are you asking me as my father or are you asking me as a journo?'.

"All of a sudden, a day later, it's front page news around Australia with Bruce writing for the Herald-Sun, the Telegraph, Courier-Mail - everywhere!

"So I rang Bruce and I said 'Dad, what's that all about?' He said 'isn't that what went on?" I said 'well, no I was talking to you in jest, having a bit of a laugh.

"It was a front page splash everywhere!"

Raiders CEO Kevin Neil had left for home early. In Singapore he received a call from Ian Fykberg asking what the hell had happened, after photos of Meninga "in drag" at the cricket appeared.

Bevan Hannan was asked to prepare a report on the affair for Super League. "There were a lot of rumours - (what happened) wasn't what was being said in the papers back at home," he says now.

"You've got Super League being run by a media company - it drives some of the responses."

Paul Kind, who tried to promote the 1997 World Club Challenge, draws a blank when asked for amusing anecdotes. "I remember it being, from my point of view, a bit excruciating.

"We had come up with all of these ideas to try and get people interested and the reality was that these English players arrived looking for a good time and got trounced.

"Like everything, we threw money at advertising, we threw money at promotions, we threw the book at these things to try and drag them up beyond what we all probably knew they were.

"...which was a mismatch in the middle of the season with a lot of potential trouble on our hands regarding how people would view it.'

The WCC structure involved three rounds being played between June 6 and June 23 and three more between July 18 and August 4. The finals were at the end of the domestic seasons. Beaten by Sheffield in the first round of the World Club Challenge, Penrith went back to domestic football and remained winless until they met the Eagles in the second group of matches six weeks later.

English sides fared better at home in the second round, Leeds and Salford beating Adelaide, Wigan upsetting Canterbury and

Oldham downing North Queensland. "There was massive rejoicing when Leeds beat Adelaide," recalls historian Tony Collins, who describes the competition as an "heroic failure". "Adelaide? They'd been playing the game for a few months." It remained a hopeless mismatch almost every time the teams crossed the sideline. When Penrith beat St Helens 32-6, the winless Saints proceeded in the WCC while undefeated Panthers were eliminated. To get people onside, Murdoch had appealed to the dreamers in rugby league - and the dreamers were usually internationalists and expansionists who not only wanted the northern hemisphere game to be stronger than it was, but actually believed it to be stronger.

I was one of them.

"What we could never come to grips with was how the World Club Challenge was going to pan out," said Richardson, involved in the planning of the tournament. "None of us really knew, outside of Australian arrogance, about the standard of their game over there. Playing in St Helens and these areas, I would have thought they would have been far more competitive than they were because they were playing at home and they had a lot to play for. But they weren't. They were miles behind."

The finals were even stranger than the competition proper, which many players had treated like an end-of-season trip. That's because it actually WAS an end-of-season trip.

Brisbane mascot Buck The Bronco would do a lap of ANZ Stadium (formerly QEII) every time they scored. On October 4 when they beat St Helens 66-12 in one of the semi-finals, the next day's paper calculated how many Melbourne Cups Buck had run and animal rights campaigners complained.

"We played a grand final and some of the things that happen after that and the atrocities that always happen after grand finals, then we had to jump on a plane and go to England and play the London Broncos in a bloody quarter-final," Richardson recalls.

"We had injuries. Tawera Nikau decided he didn't want to go away from his family so he didn't go. Nick Graham, we had to run around on Sunday morning trying to get a passport for him. He came in for Tawera.

"The amazing one was, people don't realise, the Rat (Mat Rogers) played hooker that day. He started at hooker (against London). We had a week after the grand final then we flew out the following Monday to play the following Saturday in England. Then we had to fly straight back to play the Hunter Mariners at Shark Park. The Hunter Mariners weren't a bad side but they were also fresh because they hadn't played in the finals series. We would have played Brisbane four times that year if we'd made the World Club Challenge final."

Ian Schubert says: "The idea of halting the season to have this thing in the middle of the season really (reminded us) of the common sense of Origin. We don't stop the competition for Origin. We reluctantly make it work inside the season. You can't stop the season just for a two or three week period here and there to play another competition."

The Mariners' last ever game was a final for a World Championship. On October 17 at Ericsson Stadium before 12,000 people, the Broncos beat them 36-12.

The competition was, according to Neil Tunnicliffe, "a shambles from a British perspective.

"There was a point when Joe Lydon and I were sent out to Australia to get a little bit closer to the competition and find out exactly how far apart the British game and the Australian game were and find out why all the British clubs were being beaten by the Australian clubs like a drum. …and to come back with a bit of a blueprint for what the football side of things should look like in the brave new world. I think that just underlined how far apart the British game and the Australian game were at club level at that time in pretty much every respect.

"… coaching standards, training standards, support services, facilities, the whole nine yards really. From a British perspective the way the World Club Challenge panned out was an absolutely eye opener.

"…and quite a scary one as to how much work needed to be done to try and close that gap."

A concept revived by Maurice Lindsay and Graham Lowe in a pub was almost completely killed when it expanded to 400 rugby league players in 150 pubs. The WCC would not be contested again until the following century.

But at least the North Queensland Cowboys are still around to tell the story. They seem to have been so traumatised by their emergency landing in Brisbane that none of them mentioned it when they ran into the festive Bulldogs in transit at Singapore's Changi Airport.

Ward only learned of the incident when interviewed for this book 25 years later.

"Ha!" he said. "If it had happened to us, we wouldn't have remembered it."

ELUSIVE ROBINSON DISPLAYS HIS FAMOUS SIDESTEPPING SKILLS

By Steve Mascord, *Sydney Morning Herald*,
Friday July 11 1997

WHEN journalists requested Jason Robinson for a post-match media conference in Canberra three weeks back, they did so as a joke.

Robinson, after all, doesn't speak to the media.

The British press, in fact, seem to treat probably the finest winger in the world as if he were some sort of airborne disease, maintaining a five-metre distance at all times. Exactly why is not clear.

Some say he had a run-in with a tabloid a few years back, others reckon that he - or his manager - expect to be paid for interviews.

So there was some surprise when an impeccably dressed Robinson not only showed up to discuss Wigan's 56-22 loss to the Raiders at Bruce Stadium, but provided the day's best quote when he said that players had been "ashamed" of their first-half performance.

Yesterday, squinting in the Queensland sunshine after a training session with the Rest of the World, Robinson said: "It's not me not wanting to talk to the media. I find it funny the media don't seem to want to talk to me.

"It's the opposite way around. I don't reject anybody if they want to talk to me because we all want to promote the game. It helps my profile as well. It's just that I never get asked."

Perhaps the dashing, diminutive Robinson has the same effect on reporters as he has on league defences all over the world.

They don't know what he's going to do, they hesitate, and before they know it, he's gone.

Robinson and his Wigan and Rest of the World teammate, Gary Connolly, are rugby's great "sliders", moving through the game's parallel universes and back again.

Last northern winter they played rugby union, putting themselves at the forefront of that "game's move iinto open professionalism.

And tonight, they slide between Super League where they play for Wigan and the ARL, where they have long-term contracts.

No other players in the world can have a schedule like this: London in London, the ARL Australians in Brisbane, and Brisbane in Wigan all in the space of three weekends.

For an athlete with a low media profile, Robinson is remarkably well rehearsed with his answers to the obvious questions: which ARL club will you join? Do you want to stay at Wigan despite your ARL contract? Will you be allowed to play in the November Ashes series?

His answer to each is: "I'll see what happens today and let everybody else worry about tomorrow."

Watching the 22-year-old one of the game's genuine superstars chat with Gold Coast's intensely shy Papua New Guinean flanker Marcus Bai yesterday, it became apparent that tonight's game had the potential to be anything but a waste of time.

In rugby union, Barbarians matches are perceived as upholding the game's true spirit For some reason, similar exercises in league are labelled farces.

"No matter what anybody says," Robinson concluded, "tomorrow night I am playing in a game with some of the best players in the world. What can be better than' that?"

CHAPTER 15

John Ribot

JOHN Ribot doesn't answer immediately.

I am halfway through my third long conversation with the architect of Super League, the man whose frustrated ambition for the sport came to a head just as pay television descended on Australia, creating the once-in-a-century climate for insurrection.

Yet Ribot, the former Test winger, Brisbane chief executive and founder of the Melbourne Storm, is hard to pin down on matters of history and his role in it. Getting him to ruminate on his own legacy is surprisingly difficult despite more than two hours on the phone across the course of a whole year.

And so I pose the following hypothetical: if John Ribot had never been born, would North Sydney, Western Suburbs, Balmain, St George and Illawarra still be around as stand alone clubs?

"That's a really interesting question," he replies.

If the pause isn't pregnant, it has pee-ed on a stick to make sure.

"They'd all be stand-alone clubs, but in different competitions," he answers finally.

It's a round-about way of getting the 66-year-old to admit his own nuclear impact on the course of a sport's history. Earlier, he had offered: "They call it 'cradle to the grave'. People support Collingwood. Why? 'Because my father did'. 'My mother did'. 'My grandfather'. 'My great grandfather'. 'My great great grandfather'. They're the things we've got to get back to, to allow all parts of our community to participate."

This is a gigantic contradiction, of course. The Super League era was one in which the IP of clubs was poorly understood and therefore subverted. Inner-city clubs like the AFL's Collingwood were precisely those which suffered. Sure, the ARL were looking at reducing numbers too but the original Super League model was pointedly oriented towards the one town, one team North American model.

That's why I put that hypothetical to Ribot - to highlight the contrast between the way we saw things then and the way they are understood today..

No-one represents the Super League era in the popular imagination quite like him. "Vision", "China", "John Ribot" are three phrases you'll hear in short succession from thousands of Australian rugby league fans who followed ARL clubs, whose view of the war between 1995 and 1997 was shaped by non-Murdoch newspapers, magazines, TV and radio. Ribot departed Super League on February 24, 1997, to head up what became the Melbourne Storm.

No longer in charge of the rebel competition, he had no say over his legacy in relation to it. Peace was brokered without him and, like Arthurson and Quayle, his visage in the popular imagination froze at one moment in time. And so while Ribot is rarely credited with Melbourne's success, he is always blamed for what has been simplified and characterised as Super League's failures.

To many, he's become a caricature, a cartoon villain.

Long serving Parramatta chief executive Denis Fitzgerald has a story about Ribot, who played nine Tests for Australia between 1981 and 1985, that he tells with particular relish. Parramatta were at home to Melbourne on April 19, 1998 - the opening few weeks of the NRL.

"I said to our ground announcer 'I just want to make an announcement myself on the PA' as the players went on the field," Fitzgerald, now 71, says. "I read out the Melbourne team and then I said 'I'd like all the Parramatta fans here to give a really big Parramatta welcome to the CEO of the Melbourne Storm, JAHN REEBOW!

"All the boos came and it was 'how good is this?' He was absolutely howling crooked on me after that. I don't know why! He actually came over to the leagues club. I don't think he was there for very long."

Asked about Fitzgerald's incitement of the crowd, Ribot laughs: "It worked!" (Perhaps symbolically of this entire dynamic, the Storm won the match, 32-22).

In previous chapters devoted to the leading figures of the war, I've tried to give you a glimpse of each living in third decade of the 21st century, with the benefit of two and a half decades' rumination about the fissures that opening in the sport in the mid-nineties..

The enigmatic Ribot's is the most difficult story to tell; he's the hardest fellow to figure out.

He recalls a stranger saying "here he comes, the man who tried to kill rugby league!". But if you're wondering how all that affects Ribot now, the best answer I could give you is: it doesn't.

"It's all good now," he says. "I have well and truly moved on.

"That's part of what we took on. You're going to get some of that. It probably drives someone like me, it just drives me more to say 'hey we've got to stay focused here' because at the end of the day hopefully history is going to record all this happened… it's not for me to say…

"What we did, the intentions of what we did, was for all the right reasons. It was about taking ownership."

Aside from his now-resolved falling out with Roy Masters, discussed in detail earlier in this book, "I never lost friends over this period. … probably not the same with John Quayle. I don't see him, however I've always had a lot of respect for him. He was a good rugby league administrator and came through an environment with Packer which I understand."

Presented with Murdoch's millions, Ribot took the opportunity to build something that he saw in his mind. That was Super League. When it became apparent Super League would only last one year, he built something else. That was the Melbourne Storm.

And the Melbourne Storm is the only truly successful expansion club - in non rugby league territory - since those obstreperous blokes rocked up to the George Hotel in August,1895.

The Storm, like Super League, have polarised the sport's fanbase. So, clearly, you can't be John Ribot without having a very, very thick skin. Revolutionaries aren't famous for their feelings being easily hurt.

"I came out of an environment when I was younger … I thought it was a privileged environment but it was a tough environment. My father went to war and he came home as a pensioner and we didn't have the best of times.

"My parents gave me everything. One of the great things they gave me was rugby league. I was able to play the game, I was involved with the game, I understood at a very young age.

"I'd see volunteers running around, people helping each other and all that. They were little DNA things that were put into me. When we got to a stage where the ARL … where I thought we were at an impasse … for all those qualities to stay - you've got to have them - it's important we are successful too.

"When Kerry Packer became involved and stood over everyone and said 'I'll come after you guys personally', I said 'shit, that's not what our game's about' - and they were the ones saying 'the media can't own your game'.

"Well hang on, he's sitting there with Channel Nine. He owned our game. He was the one that stipulated 'that's what you're going to do'."

In one way, Ribot is different to Quayle. That's no surprise. Quayle was so hurt by his experiences described in this book that he put considerable distance between himself and the sport for 20 years, Stolid Ribot, on the other hand, went and started a new club so Fitzgerald could get 15,000 people to boo him.

"The Super League period we went through was not a good period for anybody. The true supporters of our game, we didn't walk away from it. I wasn't going to run away. We were proud of what we achieved and who's playing the game … the way the game's evolving now, and because of that conflict it's forced us into getting to a position of understanding the finances and not relying on false economies because you rely on other secondary sources that aren't directly involved in our game to fund our game."

Before I get onto how Ribot and Quayle are alike, a brief detour. This is one of Ribot's key points during the third of our conversations, shortly before *Two Tribes* went to press. It's a point none of the other interviewees made. Yes, the Super League War was about pay TV - but Ribot believed if rugby league was driven by pay TV, then was living off its own merits and not off the gambling addiction of people who had little interest in it.

The Super League War - and the schism that perhaps would have happened between the expansion clubs and the Sydney teams anyway if there had been no Super League War - was about ridding the sport of its dependence on leagues clubs, he argues.

"They created these leagues clubs and they became huge generators of income," Ribot says. "But the income was generated through a different type of entertainment.

"All of a sudden you didn't have to go out there to connect with the supporters to raise money and make the whole thing work. There was this easy way to do it: go to lunch each year and talk to the secretary-manager of the leagues club and he would supply the funds.

"When we started the Broncos, we started a leagues club. We were licensed with 36 machines. Those were the days when Sydney clubs would have had 600 or 1000 machines.

"We had to get out there and connect with people and make our supporters feel they had ownership of the club and always represented ourselves (as) 'we're just the caretakers of the club and we need your help. If you don't turn up, your club is not going to work'.

"That's where I'm a believer in private enterprise. It was an environment where we were challenged to succeed in everything we did and mediocrity was just not acceptable and we wanted to win and that was a good thing. It was good for the game."

All professional sports undergo upheavals in order to progress, he argues. "Whether it's the NFL, basketball, baseball, premier league soccer, they all had conflict. And they had conflict at what sometimes they think is their greatest point, when people don't realise the real value of what they've got."

OK, to take up my earlier point about the differences between Ribot and his nemesis Quayle, they are also much, much more alike than either would wish to admit.

All these years later, one holds onto his disappointment and belief in the sport's club-based traditions while the other clings just as grimly to his idealism and conviction rugby league is destined for a loftier place. In their own way, they are each still emissaries of 1997.

Mocked for the 'vision', Ribot still has it; he makes a point of insisting Super League was "not just about Australia but about Great Britain, New Zealand, Tonga, Samoa, France and other fledgling league nations". Ribot enthusiastically recounts - with zero irony or self-deprecation - bringing in Mandarin-speaking commentators.

"The DNA that was set in Super League over 20 years ago was going around to those Pacific Nations and all of a sudden they were funded and had appropriate equipment, apparel and a suitable playing field."

Assigning political importance to developing countries seems as out of step with the times as enthusing about Mandarin commentators.

The 2021 World Cup debacle showed us that even as those countries have become more competitive on the field, as boardroom players they have gone from very significant in 1995-97 to almost worthless in the face of the modern NRL's brutal commercial pragmatism. No-one now would use having France or Samoa onside to win any argument in rugby league today.

He reveals that even as he shook hands with Rupert Murdoch over Super League in 1994 after the media baron said "I like the idea, good luck", he was planning his exit.

He knew too much about rugby league politics to expect to be still on the evening news in 2021.

"I knew I was going to go to Melbourne," Ribot says. "That's where you negotiate your 'out' when you negotiate your 'in'. The Broncos, when I left there, my 2IC there was Shane Edwards and I thought it would be totally unreasonable for me to expect to go back there. He should have his moment in the sun.

"This wasn't going to go on forever. I was realistic there.

"Did I aspire to be Ken Arthurson or something like that? It certainly wasn't my aspiration. I have always enjoyed being involved in club administration. Seeing the development of admin staff, players, coaches and their families has always been a highlight for me."

In an unreleased interview for a documentary, Quayle begrudgingly accepts some good came out of the war, but not $800 million worth of good. Ribot disagrees.

"… on balance when you look back and say 'that's what it cost for their investment', I think it's been a fantastic investment for News and Fox. I really do believe it's been a great investment for our game. I think we're still learning from some of our mistakes and we're still making some of them today but our game is in so much better shape because of the advent of pay TV and other platforms that have been created and how we've been able to talk about those things, globalisation and getting exposure into other areas.

"It's been a no-brainer.

"To your point of who won, I don't know how they come up with an argument (that it was the ARL), to be blunt. We had every other nation in the world involved in Super League. (But) I don't think it has any relevance. It is now about where we are and how we go forward."

And furthermore, when Ribot watches the NRL - and the wider sport of rugby league - today, he sees vindication.

"In the short period of Super League, we were able to introduce … night grand finals, ANZAC Day Test match, Tri-Series … World Nines competition … the Oceanic Cup….

"You look at where we are now with the Pacific nations and the way they contribute to our game, it is significant.

"We got criticised. Remember we had the unlimited interchange? That was all taken on wellbeing and the injuries to players.

"Look at the scores now. They used to be 28-24 and we used to get criticised by certain people in the media, that the game should be 10-8 and all that sort of stuff … that it was Mickey Mouse.

"The game (in 1997) was played, I think, in a really good spirit. We believe where our game is now is where we were then. If you look at the scorelines, they're very similar. We professionalised referees, again a thing that our game had to have.

"Electronic scoreboards and replay boards, we were responsible for all that. We hired them so people could be engaged at the game.

"We engaged with Disney about the experience of going to our games. We went there and said 'how do we make this experience so good that we take all the difficult things out'. How do we train our staff to say you're welcome into the stadium? They all had uniforms on. The old days of blokes just fronting up and being gatekeepers - I came though all that. How do we modernise our game to a standard where it's going to be mums and dads,they can come to our game? It was still accessible financially for them but they have an experience they've never experienced before. We paid a million dollars for them to come and do our campaign. They designed outfits, all the point of sale material so we got a constant.

"The other thing is Terry Lamb as a player came on the board and gave them a direct voice and things that they needed from a player welfare point of view.

"(But) I think we went over the top with the entertainment. We didn't get the mix right there. I deserve a black eye for that!"

To the suggestions of people like Geoff Carr and Paul Kind that the game was "flying" before the war and that a better judiciary and uniformed stewards came at far too high a price, Ribot counters that the "boom" of the early nineties was more about appearances than commercial reality.

"That was more a marketing thing, with 'Simply The Best' with Tina Turner, that was a great period in our game," he says. "But financially, it wasn't a great time for our game because the money that came through wasn't growing our game in the right areas.

"You look at pathways, junior development … we weren't doing the things that we should have been doing there. The AFL does that a lot better."

And so to return to the chronological narrative of this book, between February and Steve Anderson's recollections of September, the Melbourne Storm was just John Ribot. He built the club himself. Typical of his density of epidermis, he does not particularly care about those who say the Storm was just his gold watch from a grateful media empire.

But he does say that they are comprehensively wrong.

"If you know News, it doesn't work that way. They get you there but once you're there, you're on your own. You've got to go and get your sponsors and get your crowds, your TV deals, do your deals with the stadiums. They throw it up and say 'oh yeah, an inside run'. We didn't get an inside run in those areas. I challenge anyone. Have a look at the books.

"Ask (NRL salary cap commissioner) Ian Schubert. He did us no favours. We tried to get compensation to relocate players and have it not come within our salary cap. They agreed to do it - then they reneged on it. We used to cop fines. There was no easy ride for us.

"I had to deal with News Corporation to set up a new football team. When they came back together, remember they had the criteria that ran for the first two years? If you weren't ranked in the top

18, the bottom two fell out. The ARL had an opportunity to go to Melbourne. They elected not to go..

"The only guarantee (News) gave me initially was that 'you have to conform with the criteria'. Our costs were bloody crazy.

"We had two years to get it right. They (critics) said 'they'll never survive down there'.

"All I could give you was a two year contract, whether it's Glenn Lazarus, Robbie Ross or whoever. If it didn't work, we all knew that it was going to fold. I was up front with them. Chris Johns, Chris Anderson, Greg Brentnall, their families and other members moving and coming down, they were all chancing their arm but were all up for a challenge.

"That is one of the most exciting things I've ever done, and will probably ever do in my career, because the adrenaline rush on that was happening all the time because we just had so much .. 'hey, we can't get this wrong'

"We had to start a team up, get it successful, get it winning. You got so many points if you won, so many points depending on how much money you generated from corporate support.

"Except for the TV and newspaper, News didn't give me any sponsorships. We got our own sponsorships. Honda ended up (one), the employment company (Adecco) were the first ones to go on the jersey. We tried to get a sponsorship at Channel Seven.

"The way the people of Victoria responded, the players responded, Chris and his coaching team .. I still reflect in awe on the way they took up the challenge and had a crack with us. We won a competition in the second year. If we didn't win a competition or make the semis, we were no chance to fulfil the criteria."

Still working in the sports venue and hospitality sector, Ribot is fascinated by the challenges facing rugby league today. "Free to air might be watched by, sadly, people who can't afford to buy pay TV," he muses at one point.

I speak to Ribot the day after James Maloney's 40-metre field goal secured the Super League Europe minor premiership for Catalans. He says the new "made my day" and recalls launching Paris Saint-Germain in 1996.

One commenter on a series of interviews published by News Limited papers with Ribot during April 2021 asked if his name should, in fact, be 'John Robot'. How can one be described on Wikipedia as "generally regarded as the most hated man in the Australian Rugby League (capital 'r' and 'l' perhaps significant) fraternity due to his involvement in the Super League War" seem cocooned from such a perception?

The answer, it seems to me, is that Ribot is - it not a visionary - then definitely an idealogue. The opinions his detractors have of him are, in his mind, patently based on a flawed understanding of the issues concerned and therefore not worth worrying about.

He tells the story of the Super League logo being tabled in a meeting with Murdoch at Holt Street, only for a trademark attorney to warn that owners of Superman's IP might litigate. Murdoch picked up the phone and called one of the owners of the trademark on the spot, getting an undertaking not to sue.

"I hope no-one's got kryptonite because we're in a really strong position here," Ribot said to the group, attracting zero laughter.

But 25 years later, no-one has come up with a Kryptonite equivalent capable of weakening the resolve and single-mindedness of rugby league's Super man.

"The resume is there if someone wants to look," he says. "Someone had to make the decisions to get there but I don't want a pat on the back - it was an amazing team effort.

"It's not for me to reflect on whether I've done a good job or a bad job but I know what I've tried to do.

"Knowing what we did and being involved in it, that was always going to be one of the hardest things I've ever done

"When you grow up in the game and you understand the passion that's involved in the game and the loyalty of being a member of a certain club - it can go back generations. You're never going to win that argument.

"(But) I've always seen myself, whether it's at the Broncos, Storm or even running Super League … while we had enormous financial support … as a caretaker of the game. I didn't want anything bad to happen to the game.

"I wanted it to go in the right direction.

"But I wanted it to realise the real value of what's in our game."

And if there is one truism at the heart of this story, it is that those on the outside got far more emotional, and held much more vengeful grudges, than those who worked in the furnace.

Twenty six years and a handful of days after the outbreak of the Super League War, Ribot found himself in the same room as Arthurson and Quayle once more.

It was the funeral at Sacred Heart Catholic Church at Clear Island Waters on the Gold Coast of Tom Raudonkis. Wests and Newtown had traded Ribot for Raudonikis at the end of the 1979 season. Unthinkable then, Raudonikis and Ribot had gone on to outlive both clubs' tenures in the premiership, leaving very different - but indelible - marks on the sport during its most turbulent period.

"We were outside," Ribot recalls. "Ken Arthurson was there.

"I went up and we gave each other a hug and I said 'I'll never forget what you've done for me'.

"It was a really nice moment."

EVEN LOSING 32-0 DIDN'T MEAN IT WAS THE LAST TANGO FOR PARIS

By Steve Mascord, Sydney Morning Herald, Monday July 28, 1997

HUNTER 32 PARIS 0 at Topper Stadium

YESTERDAY's game at Topper Stadium was always going to be the match *of* the season.

Not the match of the season, of course. The emphasis is on "of" because, for an occasion which summed up the wacky world of rugby league, 1997-style, you just couldn't go past Hunter v Paris St Germain.

Be you the game's most virulent critic or its most anal anorak, there was no better place to be yesterday than a couple of hundred metres from the grazing cattle at Birmingham Gardens in suburban Newcastle.

Consider the following:

- A crowd of 2,210 was entertained by John Paul Young singing "Love is in the Air" for a young woman who insisted on proposing to her boyfriend on a stage at half-time;

- Before kick-off, two gymnasts, suspended by a flying saucer (cynics suggested it, in turn, was suspended by a crane - such negativity) performed all manner of tricks above the Topper bog without a net;

- The game involved two teams which may cease to exist by Christmas, but which are each still well in the running to be world champions;

- The Paris squad included more Australians than Hunter's (and an equal number of players with French ancestry, if you count the Mariners' Beauchamp and Marquet);

- and PSG remained the most successful European side in the World Club Challenge, even after losing 32-0.

Even the conditions made it ideal for a match that will live in the memory longer than your average preliminary semi-final.

The field started as a mud heap, then a blazing sun came out in the second half and by full-time it had almost attained "dustbowl" status.

Then, of course, there are the well-documented woes of the 17 antipodeans in the PSG squad, who have been found to be living in Paris on tourist visas and who are not certain to be readmitted to France after next Saturday's clash with Perth.

To them, it really is the Visa World Club Challenge - with the biggest challenge being the visa.

But adversity tends to galvanise and Paris were behind just 4-0 at half-time yesterday.

The decisive moment, perhaps, came just after the break when PSG halfback and one-time Molly Meldrum protege Jason Martin burst into the clear and had just Mariners' fullback Robbie Ross to beat.

Had there been support inside, a try and the lead would certainly have resulted. But there wasn't and while Martin was contemplating whether to look outside, he was crunched by Ross.

Around 10 minutes later, Mariners five-eighth Scott Hill scored the first of his two tries. His second came in the 62nd minute, settling the result.

Then, winger Gavin Thompson crossed twice and heart-breakingly for the visitors Western Samoan Willie Poching managed a four-pointer after full-time when a Noel Goldthorpe bomb bounced off the goalposts.

That try was converted by prop Tim Maddison, who coach Graham Murray later championed as a contender for the Australian tour of Britain and France in November. "There's no Rodney Howe, there's no Glenn Lazarus," said Murray, referring to the injured Test props.

"To me I don't know who the go-forward person in the representative sides is but I don't think much better than him."

The Mariners need only to beat Sheffield next Sunday to make the quarter-finals, with fellow Pool B Australasia clubs North

Queensland, Adelaide and Perth each having been beaten during the tournament.

Paris are on the top of Pool B Europe but even if they stay there, they will have to play-off, away, to the fourth-placed Pool A side for a spot in the finals.

It's a situation which does not please coach Andy Goodway.

"Surely that's the idea of the competition," said Goodway, who reckoned his side didn't play smart enough yesterday. "If you finish top, you're top.

"Those are the rules and we'll abide by them. But as I say, we'd prefer we didn't have to play an extra game in an already tight schedule when we're trying to avoid relegation."

The Mariners will have half Brett Kimmorley available next week, leaving Murray with another difficult choice between he and Goldthorpe.

PSG's former New Zealand international lock, David Lomax, missed yesterday's game because of a death in the family but will be back next week, while centre Jamie Olejnik is racing the clock to overcome a shoulder problem.

CHAPTER 16
The Days Of Two Tribes

IAN Robson well remembers the days of Two Tribes. "I moved into the apartment upstairs with Ribes … I'd get in the lift in the morning on level 10 and I'd go down to level three and get out and go to work. At night, I'd get on at level three to go home and go to level 10. It was a surreal time in so many ways."

Each side of the war had a bunker. Some nights, people slept under their desks. "What both sides did that year was work incredibly hard .. because every week was a competition," Paul Kind says. The ARL boasted only a skeleton staff, fighting a global media empire. On the Super League side, the bonds were further solidified by accusations of disloyalty from hardline traditionalists; spitting, death threats, abuse in the streets….

But, Shane Richardson reflects, "We had some amazing parties.

"I never got so many t-shirts in my whole life as that year. Every time you went to a party there were t-shirts and a bag given out. We'd been through so much and got smashed together. There was camaraderie among the Super League clubs that we didn't know we had - and a friendship.

"A whole range of people from that Super League era, we're still friends today - the Malcolm Noads of the world.

"We were in communication, none of us were talking negative. They were paying the bills. At the end of the day, the losses must have been horrendous because the crowds weren't there.

"Not only were they paying the bills, they'd also made commitments to upgrade grounds like Shark Park with seating and lighting which cost a fortune and they kept their promise.

"I've got to say this about News Limited: they never did not complete one promise. Everything they said they'd do, they did.

"I still remember Rebecca Wilson saying to me, we were speaking about Peter Gow, 'he's nutty as a fruitcake, he's a crazy guy, you never know what he's going to do - but he's our man'.

"That's the way everybody felt. We had The Riddler (Bob Ferris) at the Hunter Mariners, we had a lot of people who hadn't been involved in rugby league before.

("The Riddler had a briefcase the same colour as his suit and he wore a different coloured suit every day of the week," Ian Schubert recalls Here, I must let Ferris interject. "I never heard the nickname Riddler. I don't remember it. And I've been called lots of things.")

"It was strange times but I do think with Kevin Neil and these guys there was a strange bond of camaraderie because we'd been through so much.

"There were people sleeping in our lounge rooms with guns protecting us from all sorts of crazy people, fingernails being sent through the mail saying my hands and fingers were going to be cut off at one stage."

Super League operations manager Schubert admits: "It was all about business. We thought we were right all along and that was our justification but the reality was, we were just trying to get a comp running."

Raiders media manager Bevan Hannan told the *Rugby League Digest* podcast in late 2020: "We worked a lot together in a collegiate way.

"We were regularly having hook-ups with all the media officers about some of the things we could do and how we could improve things.

"Some of the things might have been misguided but it was all about trying to do things better and trying to get exposure and partnering with the media to try and give the players profile but it was just hard to do that when you were in this constant day-to-day trench warfare.

"There was definitely a better effort to use marketing. I remember we were lining up players to do things with Sony on Sega games and things like that to try and reach a new audience and connect with the kids that way."

But, says then-Penrith marketing manager Max Cowan "Super League over-paid for everything they did".

The purpose of this chapter is to examine the days of two tribes through the eyes of different groups working within the game. And camaraderie forged amid adversity was even the key within that most divided of subcultures, refereeing.

"We talked about turning refereeing culture into a supportive culture. Prior to that it was fairly blame-focused," said Super League consultant Eric Fleming. "I did a lot of work with Graham Annesley, who is a particularly nice fellow."

Bill Harrigan explains: "When we came in on a Monday after the rounds, we made a pact between ourselves … and this had never happened before … if you had little idiosyncrasies or you had little things that you did to make you a better referee, you never shared that with another referee.

"And yet here we were on a Monday, Annesley, Grant, Mander, Clark and myself, and we said 'righto, we share everything because we want to be better than that mob. When we do things, let's share it amongst ourselves so we're not competing against ourselves here, we're competing against the ARL referees'.

"And there was a lot of animosity between us now - especially coming from their way because they reckoned we broke ranks and left and we should have stuck together.

"We went back and said 'we got offers. You blokes didn't get offers'. They only needed so many referees and it all comes down to the same old argument the players say: 'I've got to look after myself and do the best for my family and myself as far as the career goes'.

"But jeez, some of them … especially some of them who thought they should have got an offer to come over, they were filthy. Some of the touch judges, we did approach and we made offers but they stuck together. So we went on a recruitment campaign for all the touch judges who recently retired and we brought them all back."

Greg McCallum says: "There were friendships within the referees association that were never mended. People saw this very few number gain significant financial benefit out of refereeing.

"Bill was pretty much ostracised out of the referees association at the time. Graham (Annesley) sort of flitted in and out with different roles that he's had.

"But look, a lot of the people who were involved then, who were anti-Super League, have passed on now."

For player agents, the real action had been the atom bomb of the April 1, 1995 raids. In 1997, they began dealing with the fallout.

"It was deadset mayhem," Sam Ayoub says. "Fortunately mobile phones had not long before that come in. It was important because otherwise we wouldn't have been able to deal with it all.

"There was no regard for contracts during the war. Whether you had a contract or not was irrelevant because the other party were more desperate and anxious to coerce you into not adhering to your contract.

"The administration of both leagues and both sets of clubs … it became very antagonistic. It was hardcore. There was a great deal of hatred for some reason.

"Because there was no cap - there was no *policed* cap - the wealthy clubs had a bit more of a free reign. It favoured the clubs like the Broncos and that because they had the resources and the backing,

"I guess that's why they had more success."

Players? Things were different for them too - or at least the Super League players. Parramatta and NSW hooker Aaron Raper told me the aspect of 1997 that stood out most for the ARL's stars was "we weren't playing all the teams". Aside from that, then 19-year-old St George utility Steve Price says, "it just felt just usual. We were playing North Sydney. Greg Florimo was playing, David Fairleigh …

the Bears, Illawarra, those sorts of teams. There wasn't much banter in the changerooms talking about Super League as I recall."

On the ARL side, the money had gone to the players - leave some clubs existing on a shoestring.

"I felt we were slightly under-resourced compared with what was going on with Super League as well," says then-South Sydney hooker Shannon Donato, who recalls first graders being asked to pick weeds at Redfern Oval before training.

"They're getting all these flash trips and being flown everywhere and all this World Club Challenges and because the (ARL) had used all their money to sign people up … particularly clubs like Souths who were struggling, we were still running on the smell of an oily rag.

"We had two training singlets, two training t-shirts, a polo and a tracksuit."

Paul Kind puts it as bluntly as he can: "The Super League guys were made to feel like they were better than the other guys … they definitely were led to believe they were in a superior code doing superior things."

Super League media manager Judith Coen says: "It was very exciting and it was very big. The players became hugely wealthy and famous out of it.

"I've always found most athletes to be good to work with.

"Obviously it was very well run, it was very professional, there was no money spared for anything (but) I watched them just get given so much. Any sport I've been involved in, I've never seen so much money spent.

"If someone left a pair of training boots at home, at a training session there'd just be a Nike rep standing there and they'd get another pair out of the car and off they'd run onto the training paddock.

"I'd be thinking 'why don't they fine them? Send them home?' I did think 'this is going to create a nightmare, they're going to expect stuff'. Entitlement came with it.

"At airports, I remember picking up jackets they'd left on seats and getting on the plane behind them all. They just never thought to pick them up."

Gold Coast coach Phil Economidis, who once lamented "coaching's like juggling three balls and hoping two of them aren't yours", remembers: "These young blokes, they're backing four horses in the one fucking race. They've never gambled before, they've been given $100,000 by Super League, they thought it was Christmas."

Malcolm Noad: "One of the all-time great players, who became a Super League player, I was talking to him about what changes he noticed in the game and what has it meant to him and he said the thing that was most difficult for the players to appreciate right from the start was going from being semi-professional to professional.

"And how it took them all a while to realise that if the coach said you had to be ready to run out on the field for training at eight in the morning, then you didn't turn up at five to eight and then get out on the field at 10 past."

Peter Mulholland theorises that players who were "intrinsically motivated" kept up their standards, while those "extrinsically motivated" became lazy and worried more about buying new four-wheel drives.

"It's like any walk of life," Richardson says in response. "When you've been paid nothing and I give you a cheque for $30,000 and I give you a contract for $80,000 … that was the minimum contract … there were guys who were getting five and 10 grand working part time. Of course it's going to change some of those guys.

"But once you cross the white line, mate …. you might have all that, you might change your car, but you're still out there bashing the fuck out of people and you're still out there putting your body on the line and you're doing it for one reason and one reason only - 'cause of your mates.

"People didn't go over the top in World War I with a bayonet because they wanted to. They went over the top because their mates went over the top and they were never going to let them down. It's the same in Super League. Very few clubs broke up in Super League. For example at Cronulla, despite where we were, we only lost two major players. We lost Adam Ritson and we lost Aaron Raper. We lost Aaron Raper because his dad was an ARL guy. He didn't want to go.

"We lost Adam Ritson because he was 17 years old and had never seen so much money in all his fucking life.

"Players stuck together. Why did they do that? Because the money was virtually the same. Even when it was better in some cases, they knocked it back. They did it because there is a genuine camaraderie amongst players. When they cross the line they cannot help themselves."

While it was "business as usual" for rank and file ARL players, in Super League, there were new rules, new competitions, a new head office to contend with.

Laurie Daley recalls: "When the comp got going, it was good but you knew it wasn't the same as what you'd been playing in previously.

"Obviously when you trained and played you were giving it your best. I found the rule changes pretty good. The one with defending where you had to release straight away, that was quite weird and I think they changed that as we went through the season because it was just too fast early on. The one where (the scorer) kicks off, I didn't mind that. It felt like a faster game."

Kevin Walters: "The competition was strong, it was well-organised. The players appreciated the professionalism that Super League provided."

Danny Munk is less charitable about the standard of the football across the two leagues. "You had people making first grade who honestly wouldn't make the cut for a reserve grade team. The quality of the games was heading down with a bullet."

The ARL grand final and Tri-Series final may have been great contests, as Munk concedes, "but I'd also say there were a number of games that were pure crap. We were involved in a couple of them and you just went 'why are we here?' It was a tough time for clubs like Wests and Souths, they were just getting bashed.

"The players themselves had become disillusioned."

Eventually, the officials were too.

Trevor McKewen recalls: "I enjoyed the journey, as tough as it was, because they were heady days. You just didn't know what was going to happen each day. And it was exciting. It was intoxicating almost. In the early days you really did feel like you were changing the world.

"(But) it became pretty apparent pretty quickly that the acrimony was only going to get worse and that neither comp was lining up.

"I started to dread coming to work. The days were so full of acrimony and spin. I found myself doing stuff that I used to hate when people were doing it to me when I was a journo - and being able to see right through it.

"I found that pretty uncomfortable and mate, it just started to become a grind. I wasn't the Lone Ranger. I think there were a lot of people who felt that way.

"It was just a contest of who could spin the most. Your approach was determined by who was on the other end of the line. So with a News Limited (reporter), you're pretty much good to go to some degree … with maybe the exception of (Greg Prichard) who was at *The Australian* then and was pretty straight up and down like he's always been.

"But if it was Roy (Masters) or somebody you knew who actually got it and wasn't being told by the paymaster the tone that they needed to take, mate … I'd be incredibly careful.

"I was living in the Manly area and 'Super League' - they were incendiary, those words. Probably only twice in my life have I tried to conceal what I did. Once was in my younger days on the Gold Coast and I was a surfer and surfers were considered hippies and drug-takers so you didn't tell people you were a surfer.

"I would fudge the subject if I was meeting new people on the Northern Beaches and they asked me what I did. There's no way I'd say 'I work for Super League in the media department'. That was another bit of reinforcement for me that this has gone badly wrong, this is not good."

McEwen liked most of the people he worked with - but not all. "There were some that were just out-and-out opportunists ... massive egos, who believed Rupert could do no wrong and they had his imprimatur around this so .. there were some questionable attitudes and behaviour."

While Hannan says there was a "collegiate" spirit of cooperation between clubs, his Canterbury counterpart, Debbie Spillane, says not everyone saw it that way.

"There hadn't essentially been media managers," she explains. "Taking you back a year, the reason I got the job, or that I was offered the job, at the Bulldogs is they thought they were playing Super League in '96 and Super League insisted every team have a media manager.

"Garry Hughes literally told me that they didn't want me but Super League had told them they had to have a media manager so they were stuck with me.

"Rebecca decided we were going to have this Monday afternoon conference call with all the media managers.

"It used to be three o'clock and they'd call and say 'this is your Telstra conference call, please hold for Ms Rebecca Wilson at Super League' and one-by-one you hear all the media managers come on line.

"And she just wouldn't be there!

"I used to put it on hold and just go about my work because after a while I realised it was just a joke. It would be just 20 minutes, listening to muzak."

Penrith media manager Rob Weaver remembers that when he was appointed, Wilson "said that she was having a meeting of media managers in town. I turned up and I was the only one there. All she wanted to do really was check me out."

Reporter Jim Wilson says he tried not to be the one to "poke the bear" by bringing up Super League at family gatherings with his sister Rebecca.

Paul Kind recalls other machinations at Super League HQ which appear delightfully comedic in retrospect.

"Frykers used to have this meeting every week which was about how we were travelling on promotions and success, basically. One of the Pacific nations had given him this club. It was like an ornate club that he used to hold in his hands and tap it on the desk as he was contemplating how this whole thing was actually travelling. He was a giant of a guy and I always remember sitting there thinking 'how are we going, how is he tapping this club on the desk?'"

Max Cowan says working with Super League was "like a breath of fresh air for our organisation because we were on the periphery, really, of the League as it was. For us it (the ARL) was almost a feudal system."

But the Panthers and Super League soon butted heads - over crowd figures and ground announcer Rodney Overby.

Overby recited his PA schtick when we contacted him. "East side! West side! Family Hill!"

He recalled: "There were people who liked me and there were people who didn't. I incited some feelings - good, bad and indifferent. I remember walking through with my partner at that stage, which was (basketballer) Trish Fallon, and some people calling me some names. Some bad names, actually. But that shit didn't really bother me. It was like water off a duck's back.

"There were a lot of ordinary people, there were no airs or graces. They were "Aussie! Aussie! Aussie! Oi! Oi! Oi!' types. I fitted in. I'm from the streets. Penrith got some rough areas. They're real, they're raw, there's nothing fancy about them. I gave them the real deal."

Max Cowan says: "Ian Robson decided that he needed to take all the Super League marketing managers to Adelaide for a game and while we were down there, I got a phone call saying 'hey Max, there's a new ground announcer arrived and Rodney's been sacked',

"I said 'there's no fucking way he's been sacked'. That was all a scheme to try and get rid of Rodney. I said 'that's not happening'."

Overby responds: "I don't remember people trying to sack me but I don't doubt it. There were probably people talking behind my back trying to get rid of me."

Cowan also refused to fudge crowd figures.

"At that first game against Perth, I was told to issue the crowd figure at … probably 15,000. I said we'd made a resolution a few years before that we wouldn't be telling lies about crowds because we wanted to run a fair dinkum game and we wanted to know what we were up to.

"I fought with them - the Super League guys - about that too. We were the only club not making up our crowd numbers."

Just south of Penrith, argues Western Suburbs chairman Jim Marsden, "Campbelltown was starting to get behind the Magpies. Tommy (Raudonikis) would go up and down the main street of

Campbelltown at my instigation on the back of a ute with a loud hailer spruiking about the game the next week!"

That's players, referees and officials. What about the media? There was a new media platform - the club website, which Weaver insists Penrith built first, beating Brisbane. "We were getting over a million hits a month," he boasts.

Then-2UE reporter Damien Kelly reminisces: "We were banned from going to Super League games and I tell my kids this - this was pre social media so radio was such a key component in getting information out there.

"I used to go and sit or stand on the hill at Super League games and ring in with score updates. I remember I got busted one time on the hill at Shark Park. They used to look for us.

"They were Nokia bricks or Motorolas. The technical team developed a backpack sort of thing. I could put it over my shoulder so I could watch and talk.

"I think there was a legal requirement where I couldn't go live but I could ring in and someone like a Jimmy Dolan or someone who was back in the studio … I could say "Andrew Ettingshausen has just scored' and he could broadcast it on air."

In Newcastle, the 1997 season soon took on a gothic visage. If the Knights are the centrepiece of the movie you are now watching, then the lighting is moody and menacing and there are raindrops on the lens.

"It was just a wet year," says journalist Brett Keeble. "The Knights were supposed to play Souths and the game was washed out because the car park flooded. There was no drainage in the car park. You couldn't get TV cameras and crews into the car park so they postponed that game.

"I remember watching a heap of wet Knights games. They played the Roosters on a really wet night in Newcastle. I think even when they had the replay of the Souths game it was wet. What Bevan said about the dark year."

Coaching? It was far from the science it is today, Michael Hagan stresses.

"To put it into perspective of where the coaching support staff sat back then, and this wasn't just the Mariners, this was across the Knights and other clubs: Graham Murray was the head coach, Peter Harding was the strength and conditioning coach, Maxy Winkler was the second grade coach, you might have had an Under 19s coach, that might have been Mal Graham. But the support staff and the entourages we've seen develop over the last 25 years - that was it.

"So there was the playing group of maybe 25, it might have been a stretch of maybe 27 or 28 full time guys, and then there were all part time guys - a bit like what it used to be.

"It was a pretty lean operation even though there was a lot of dollars being talked about for players. The actual operational stuff was fairly conservative."

At Canterbury, says Spillane, "the Moore-Hughes faction fighting was still really big. That's where my difficulties in not travelling with the team and so-on came about. I was seen as ... I didn't know the depth of it until I was in the middle of it.

"I had been labelled on the Moore team because it was Lynne (Anderson) and Peter (Moore) who approached me about the job.

"Chris and Garry Hughes were at loggerheads a lot of the time. Garry (Hughes) had complained about the flat attack thing that Chris (Anderson) had going. There was this big row between Chris and Glen Hughes at the Leagues Club and he (Chris) got banned from the Leagues Club for three months.

"It was not a pleasant atmosphere - at all. I kept getting told by Garry I wasn't allowed to talk about football because I hadn't played."

Another of the few females in either competition was Roosters physio Liz Steet. "You were never discriminated against as such but it was always just a little bit awkward, I'd guess you'd say. You had to find your place.

"I always thought it was important not to make a big thing about being there and just sort of do your job in the background.

"One of the things I used to say to girls coming through is 'don't over-glamourise yourself, dress appropriately to be in that environment'. Dress yourself down, if anything. Not a lot of them took a lot of notice in some respects.

"It was always a bit awkward going away, they'd have to find a separate room for you and all that sort of stuff."

Of course the number of women involved had nothing to do with the war and many of the other seismic changes sweeping the sport would have happened anyway, Munk insists. "Between '95 and the end of '97, the game changed radically. The expectation of the media, the expectation of the community all changed and everyone wanted to know everything.

"I remember talking to (veteran Balmain administrator Keith Barnes) when I was there in '95 and '96 and saying 'did you get all these reporters wanting to talk about numbers and this and that?'. One of the things Barnesy said was 'if a footballer did something wrong, yeah, you got a phone call'. But he said 'your problem is: they want to have it on the news by a certain time, they want to talk to you about where you are, they want to know finances, they want to know about the players and you've got to be ready for it'.

"Keith ran a football club where the total budget was under a million dollars. Within two years, I was running a football club - and we were on the cheap end - that was five to six million dollars. That was within 24 months and now, of course, it's $20 million."

On June 11, 53 per cent of players in *Rugby League Week*'s annual poll said the ARL was the tougher competition. The same number said Souths was the team that should be cut from a united competition. Forty-seven per cent wanted Neil Whittaker to run a united competition.

"Ninety-seven was very much about 'is the game stuffed, can it survive, is there enough talent?'" says John Brady, part of a small team at Phillip Street that included Neil Whittaker, Geoff Carr, Chris Turner, John Coates, Greg Mitchell and Mark Levy. "Obviously News pushing for what News was pushing for, all the rumours of people behind the scenes doing deals, how things were going to come together at the end of the year. It was mayhem - and everybody, absolutely everybody, with an idea and a proposal for how to put the comp back together. You would spend hours and hours every night writing back. I made a point of writing back to everybody, (to) people with weird and wonderful ideas for how you merge this club with that club."

Brady became used to Super League making big announcements on the day of the ARL's most significant events, noting rugby union used the same tactic.

"News … had a newspaper and the *Herald* were trying to prove how independent they could be and not give anyone one side or the other, in their own view. News was being News. Clearly it was a challenging situation.

"We took the view that there was no point getting into a slanging match. I talked to the Newcastle guys once. I said 'everything you read in the paper about the Mariners is someone taking space that used to be yours. Each time you talk about them, you're giving them space. So talk about you.'

"It's not that hard. Rugby league has difficulty doing that. If you go to Melbourne and say 'rugby league's going to take over Melbourne', Melbourne would just say 'bugger that, let's talk about Collingwood on Sunday and what the hell are you talking about?

"In rugby league, 'aw geez, we're dead!' All they would do is talk about it. It's just the nature of how the game operates."

Hannan recalls: "Our first home game, Belinda Carlisle was the talent. One of the big stories around town was that she'd had a big night out the night before and lost her way and went to the studios of 104.7 which she recognised from the promotional material that she must have had.

"She hit the buzzer there and whoever was on early in the morning there and said 'I'm lost, how do I get home?".

Paul Kind ("It was a pretty torrid time to be a young person on the game too. In '97 I was 26, I guess") had booked Carlisle and many other international acts. "The Village People were given the curator's room (at Shark Park) as their dressing room," he recalls.

"(Cronulla official Richard Fisk) ended up arguing with them because the only room under the stand at Shark Park was the greenkeeper's office. You can imagine that then. I have this very funny image of them standing in the greenkeeper's hut at Cronulla, arguing with Fisky about their facilities.

"We bought a Harley Davidson in Perth to give away on a Friday night. I'll never do that again."

The minimum $10,000 spend on entertainment per home game "did a bit to put all the clubs on notice to do better but there was nothing transformational about it," Kind reckons.

"Throughout the year, it was all chasing your tail a bit to reach this unattainable level because we just don't have the market. We don't have the stadiums. We don't have the number of people to pay at the gate. It just doesn't make any sense at all.

"I felt at times like we were just propping up a promise rather than adding value to the game. Did we prop the promise up? Yeah we did."

Meanwhile, Kind feared, other sports were catching up.. "In 1995 when I worked inside the ARL, I was very passionate and that was a far more natural place for me to be because I'd grown up in the country, I'd fulfilled a dream of mine which was to work in rugby league in that sort of role and I felt very strongly about fighting that fight.

"I think in '97, having been out of the game 12 months and having worked on rugby (union) which didn't fit well with me and Super 12 was really successful, and that worried me.

"Like, I remember, we had real momentum around Super 12 and I was like 'what's going on here?' Is this code going suddenly going the grow legs and take over?'"

In contrast to all these very interesting manoeuvrings and personality nuances in the rebel camp, Western Suburbs captain Paul Langmack says simply: "There was no interest in Super League in Sydney.

"I think the ARL could have survived. People in Sydney, the supporters, they didn't care about Brisbane and Canberra, Adelaide Rams and all that.

"Newcastle won the comp, we had big crowds, the people were still there in their tribalism. We didn't care, as long as we were getting paid. They could have survived and Super League would have folded because they weren't getting crowds."

And so back to Newcastle.

Schubert says of some of the parties involved in supporting the Mariners: "There was a certain distrust or dislike for what the Knights were doing. The Mariners had some great ideas and some great backers but those guys, in hindsight, probably should have been behind the Knights, not trying to disrupt the Knights."

Brett Keeble says "everyone was always going to hate on the Mariners because they were the News Limited team - even though they had some good blokes in the the team and blokes who had done a lot for the Knights in the case of Robbie McCormack and Paul Marquet and Brad Godden as well as some of the young guys coming through like Robbie Ross and Brett Kimmorley.

"They were obviously seen as an enemy despite doing all they could on the field and off.

"From the *Herald* point of view, we tried to give them equal coverage."

According to former Knights prop Mark Sargent, who joined the Mariners, many Novocastrian officials in 1995 believed the club would be better off at Super League and those officials would follow them across town eventually.

But Newcastle had always been resistant to change, Sargent says - in 1988 many thought the Knights themselves would "destroy the local comp". So those traditionalist forces were simply lying dormant, waiting for a new cause, when Super League dropped.

"Some of the people who pushed back against the Knights entering the comp were still there to push back against that as well," says Sargent, who described the city as "as a place that brought a really passionate supporter base, as a place that was still producing plenty of players - and not only Knights players, across the League".

But until 1997, he says, the town was never properly appreciated."

Shane Richardson: "I remember the day we played the Hunter Mariners. There must have been 11 people there. When the song came on over the PA, you know 'the Hunter Mariners"… I nearly burst myself with laughter.

"I was thinking 'what the fuck is going on here? Where are we?' I've got to take my hat off to them, they played fucking well. They played in the final of the World Club Challenge and they played with a lot of pride and they did a great job with that side."

The CEO at the Mariners was Bob Ferris, formerly of Wests Leagues Club.

"I think in my life, I've had some great jobs, but there's no doubt working for Super League was a blessing," Ferris says. "It was the best thing that ever happened to me."

Ferris has fond memories of most he worked with during this time but adds: "I'm not going to comment on John Ribot because I'm not sure you could say what I want to say.

"All I'll say is I didn't respect John and I didn't respect how he only looked after himself in the finish.

"When John Ribot was making in-roads for Melbourne, I knew we would be washed up.

"He pulled a swifty there. Just before we were going to go away to play the final of the (World Club Challenge), he took a lot of them away down to Melbourne mid-week and broke up their training.

"Behind everyone's back, he offered to pay their percentage fee to their managers for the first year or two years or something. No other club had thought of that. I thought it was very poor that he would take them down at such an important time when we needed to win.

"Ken Cowley told me ... I went to the opening of the RM Williams store up here ... that he wanted to run (the Mariners) one more year but at that stage Lachlan was in charge and Ken pulled out because he thought he was smarter than any other young man he'd ever seen.

"He said to Lachlan he'd like to run it one more year and Lachlan said 'no'."

(Ribot says he had no role in the demise of the Mariners but "the Hunter Mariners were put in there - and he knows better than anyone - for strategic positioning hoping that people would all come back together. They were never going to be long term". Furthermore, he says any payments to managers was above board and declared under the salary cap)

Ferris recalls getting an empty rifle shell in the mail on one occasion. "You'd go up town and people would make comments, hoping to bait you but that only got my back up more.

"I felt 'this is Australia. If I want to shop at Coles, I'll shop at Coles. I don't have to shop at Woolworths. It made me more determined."

It's easy to say that in 1997, everyone was doing what they believed in. But Hagan admits: "When it was conceived, no-one in their right mind ... I didn't understand why you'd even contemplate a second team in Newcastle.

"The obvious choice was to have an independent team at the Central Coast or something like that. It didn't have any commercial viability to me. Why would you want to do that? We knew the environment we were in and we knew how it was going to be perceived. None of it was pleasant.

"The footy and that part of it was enjoyable and Muzz (Graham Murray) and Robert Finch and Sarge and Keith Onslow - we all got on like a house on fire. Bobby Ferris ... in terms of working together as a team and trying to get this footy team up and running, that was the enjoyable part of it all.

"But the actual underlying sentiment around it? It was far from that.

"It was a very ostracised thing. It was considered 'they play over at Birmingham Gardens and don't dare go there'. Some people ... those that a) thought all that stuff was a bit over the top or b) just like a game of footy and wanted to see Canberra, Brisbane and other teams ... It was a bit like how the Knights started. When the Knights started there was no real following for the Knights. It was more about following Saints and Parra and Manly and all those teams coming.

"Brisbane and Canberra, they were sort of the silky teams for Super League with Alfie (Allan Langer) and Loz (Laurie Daley) and all those guys. It was a bit of a novelty, our event. They were trying to put entertainment around it - as you say, John Paul Young and fire crackers and Mariner Man and …

"Deep down I think it was all a bit of a charade, to be fair."

LEAGUE'S HIT LIST

By Steve Mascord, *Sydney Morning Herald*,
Monday August 4, 1997

YOU were just getting used to "financial control" and "joint ventures"? Get with it, comprmise-followers. The new buzzword is "criteria".

That's criteria as in "there is no criteria in place yet so we can't speculate on how it might affect us" (St George chief executive Brian Johnston) and "whatever criteria they set, we're confident we'll be able to meet it" (South Sydney boss Darrell Bampton).

If the much-vaunted "central issue" (ie, financial control) is ever resolved by ARL chief executive Neil Whittaker and Super League's Ian Frykberg, and there is some sort of hyper-premier-super-duper league next year, they'll have to decide who gets in and who misses out.

That's where our buzzword comes in.

As an exercise in creating controversy, as well as hopefully removing a few blinkers, we've applied four criteria to the 22 teams in both competitions and collated them to list the clubs in supposed order of worthiness.

The first three criteria are simple:
Population base: The main reasons that Brisbane, for instance, rank so highly in the other criteria is that they have had 1.4 million people to play with for the past decade. A big population means long-term potential and is consistent with the aims of both leagues to be Australasian in nature. (NB: In Sydney it was too hard to compare club boundaries with suburb-by-suburb census information. The clubs are each given one-eleventh of Sydney, under the assumption that because they share the same media outlets they can each promote themselves to the entire city).

Results: All results since the inception of the ARL's national premiership in 1995 were checked, with wins as a percentage of total games played. Finals were included, World Club Challenge games and 1997 round 18 ARL games weren't.

Attendance figures: All attendance figures home and away but only regular season for the same period were averaged. WCC games were excluded.

The final criteria was, necessarily, subjective. In ranking the clubs' financial strength, we endeavoured to evaluate their overall status, including Optus and News Ltd funding, leagues club support and sponsorships. Because clubs are run and funded in so many different ways, there is no reliable index for their financial well-being. We have spoken to a number of people in the game and have attempted to approximate the clubs' relation to each other with regard to assets over debt and cash flow.

Because Brisbane and Sydney each has more than one club, Perth has the biggest population base at its disposal, with about 1.2 million. If the Crushers were to merge with Gold Coast, as has been mooted, Brisbane would take this mantle with 1.4 million. But for the moment we are assuming there are

no amalgamations and it's survival of the fittest.

Manly are the most successful side of the past three seasons, winning 81 per cent of their games, with Brisbane second.

Despite falling attendances this year, the Broncos average 25,870 spectators per match in that period - a figure boosted by huge attendances at ANZ Stadium in 1995 and into 1996.

Canterbury's rating as the wealthiest club is based almost entirely on its booming licensed club.

Super League officials believe that if leagues clubs are eliminated from the equation, Brisbane and Auckland will be the first to trade themselves back into profit.

We compiled a composite table by adding up the placings in the four criteria and coming up with demerit points, then ranking them in descending order.

CONCLUSIONS: Brisbane finish first overall because they were fourth in population base, second in results, first in attendances and third in financial strength, for a total of just 10 demerit points.

In the top 14 there are seven ARL clubs and seven from Super League, with North Sydney fourth overall even though their proposed move to the Central Coast was not taken into account.

The Bears are the 11th-best drawing team of the past three yearsi and have a powerful leagues club.

Despite calls for Auckland's omission, the Warriors' strong attendances and population base have them finishing seventh, while Adelaide's boom year through the gate won them 11th spot.

Newcastle scrape into the top 14, mainly because of their lack of leagues club support. But a merger with the 19th-paced Mariners would lift them to fifth on the population table and equal 10th overall.

North Queensland and Perth are just outside the top 14, victims of poor results and financial trouble respectively.

In the event of an 18-team competition, Balmain and South Sydney would squeeze in under our model with four non-Sydney clubs Hunter, Gold Coast, South

Queensland and Illawarra missing out.

Illawarra's last place is particularly surprising, considering the region's rich rugby league heritage.

Because of sophisticated modern recruiting, junior numbers were not included in this evaluation.

The Steelers are 21st for population base, 14th for results, 19th for crowds and 18th for financial strength.

The proposed Melbourne franchise was not considered because there are no figures for results, crowds or financial status.

Obviously, more than just four simple barometers will be used to determine which clubs are invited into any new competition.

But be warned, once "criteria" becomes the word on league officials' lips, it is likely to be quickly followed by another buzzword: litigation.

Population
Perth 1.2m
Adelaide 1m
Auckland 855,000
Brisbane 700,000
South Queensland 700,000
Gold Coast 400,000
Balmain 336,363
Canterbury 336,363
Cronulla 336,363
Manly 336,363
North Sydney 336,363
Parramatta 336,363
Penrith 336,363
South Sydney 336,363
St George 336,363
Sydney City 336,363
Western Suburbs 336,363
Canberra 296,000
Newcastle 257,500
Hunter 257,500
Illawarra 211,000
North Queensland 150,500

*Population divided by number of teams in that region

1. **Manly** 54 from 67 81%
2. **Brisbane** 45 from 62 73%
3. **Canberra** 42 from 61 69%
4. **Cronulla** 41 from 63 65%
5. **Canterbury** 38 from 62 61%
6. **Newcastle** 37 from 63 59%
7. **North Sydney** 38 from 64 59%
8. **St George** 38 from 65 58%
9. **Sydney City** 35 from 63 55%
10. **Western Suburbs** 30 from 62 48%
11. **Hunter** 7 from 15 47%
12. **Auckland** 28 from 58 48%
13. **Balmain** 26 from 61 43%
14. **Illawarra** 25 from 61 41%
14. **Penrith** 24 from 58 41%
16. **Perth** 23 from 58 40%
17. **Parramatta** 23 from 60 38%
18. **Adelaide** 5 from 15 33%
19. **Gold Coast** 18 from 61 29%
20. **Nth Queensland** 13 from 58 23%
21. **South Sydney** 13 from 61 21%
22. **Sth Queensland** 11 from 60 18%

*incl finals, not WCC

1. **Brisbane** 25,870
2. **Auckland** 18,226
3. **Canberra** 15,564
4. **Parramatta** 14,601
5. **North Queensland** 14,528
6. **Manly** 14,340
7. **Newcastle** 14,184
8. **Adelaide** 13,425
9. **Cronulla** 12,693
10. **Sydney City** 12,131
11. **North Sydney** 11,800
12. **South Queensland** 11,747
13. **St George** 10,972
14. **Canterbury** 10,967
15. **Perth** 10,660
16. **Penrith** 9620
17. **Hunter** 9484
18. **Western Suburbs** 9448
19. **Illawarra** 9406
20. **Balmain** 8900
21. **South Sydney** 8206
22. **Gold Coast** 7580

*home and away, not including semi-finals or WCC

1. **Canterbury**
2. **Parramatta**
3. **Brisbane**
4. **North Sydney**
5. **Penrith**
6. **Sydney City**
7. **Cronulla**
8. **North Queensland**
9. **Manly**
10. **St George**
11. **South Sydney**
12. **Adelaide**
13. **Hunter**
14. **Canberra**
15. **Auckland**
16. **Western Suburbs**
17. **Balmain**
18. **Illawarra**
19. **Newcastle**
20. **Gold Coast**
21. **Perth**
22. **South Queensland**

*From a variety of sources. Based on cashflow and debt-to-asset ratio.

1. **BRISBANE** (10)
2. **MANLY** (20)
3. **CRONULLA** (26)
4. **NORTH SYDNEY** (27)
5. **PARRAMATTA** (29)
6. **SYDNEY CITY** (30)
7. **AUCKLAND** (32)
8. **CANTERBURY** (36)
9. **ST GEORGE** (37)
10. **CANBERRA** (38)
11. **ADELAIDE** (40)
12. **PENRITH** (41)

- - - - - - - - - - - - - - - -
(cut along the dotted line for uper League-style 12-team comp)
13. **WESTERN SUBURBS** (49)
14. **NEWCASTLE** (50)

- - - - - - - - - - - - - - - -
(cut here for compromise-style 14-team comp)
15. **NORTH QUEENSLAND** (53)
16. **PERTH** (53)

- - - - - - - - - - - - - - - -
(cut here for an ARL-style 16-team comp)
17. **BALMAIN** (59)
18. **SOUTH SYDNEY** (59)

- - - - - - - - - - - - - - - -
some say we'll end up with 18...)
19. **HUNTER** (60)
20. **GOLD COAST** (65)

- - - - - - - - - - - - - - - -
u could cut here, but why bother)
21. **SOUTH QUEENSLAND** (70)
22 **ILLAWARRA** (72)

CHAPTER 17

A Peace Of Me

AUSTRALIAN Rugby League communications manager Geoff Carr boasts he didn't create a single enemy out of the Super League War. "If people had a different opinion to me and they believed in different things to me, I wasn't going to take it personally. I wasn't going to play the man and not the ball."

Carr is one of those people who can adroitly walk the line between professional and social - but it's a demanding role, especially in football. For every schooner sunk, there must be a kilometre run around Sydney's jagged, spectacular coastline.

One morning in the first half of 1997 - he can't quite remember the date but "well into the season" - the former St George chief executive saw, as he pounded the pavement, a familiar, imposing figure - newly-installed News Limited head of sport Ian Frykberg.

"He was walking," Carr recalls in an interview for this book. "The first couple of times - we knew each other from before - we exchanged pleasantries. 'Hello mate, yeah good'.

"One day he sort of indicated he wanted to say something to me so I stopped and we walked for a while.

"What he said was the game couldn't go on the way it was. I was unaware that he'd been brought back at that stage to sort it out. He said 'do you think Neil Whittaker, he might be up for a meeting?'. I said 'I'm sure he would mate, I'm happy to ask him'."

They weren't quite Kerry Packer and Rupert Murdoch but the football peace that the business moguls wanted - needed, insisted upon - had moved off the starting line. (Frykberg, Kevin Neil points out, "had worked for Kerry and had worked for Rupert and was highly regarded on both sides").

Meanwhile, in the *Sydney Morning Herald*'s Goulburn Street offices, the phone rang at the desk of young business reporter Matt Kidman. It was a general of the enemy: Tom Mockridge, who was transitioning out of his role as Ken Cowley's assistant CEO and into the job as Foxtel chief executive.

"He said 'come over'," Kidman recalls. "I kept writing 'it's time that the camps just stop fighting, none of it makes business sense, there's not going to be a winner'.

"Anyway, he got sick of me writing about it. There was this big lounge in his room and he said 'look, I want to give you something to show you something's happening. There is peace being negotiated'. He said 'here's a 10-point plan' and it was signed by Rupert and Kerry and it was from London.

"He said 'you can't write on this' and I said 'you're kidding'. He said 'you can have a look, I'll walk out, go to the loo and come back but you can't write on it. I just want you to know things are happening. You keep writing that it's ridiculous and so-on'. I went back and I said 'you are kidding'.

"So I talked to my editor. What I did was I never wrote it but I relayed it to Anne Davies (who knew Mockridge from Canberra)… she rang Tom and said 'look, you fucked Matthew around showing him this - I'm going to write on it'. He goes 'I'm furious at you two' and she said 'well, you should never have shown us a signed thing. You should have done it a different way'."

Davies - who says "I remember putting huge amounts of effort into finding out if they had done a deal" - had earlier reported that Packer met Murdoch on the latter's yacht in New Zealand's Bay Of Islands right as the warring competitions were kicking off. Packer and Murdoch had first met to resolve the Super League War in London on November 8, 1995.

The 10-point plan, Kidman says, definitely included the Super League War - and ended it. "It stretched beyond football. It was the whole Foxtel scenario with (rival broadcaster) Australis which was the real trigger.

"Who knows how long they would have fought for without that?"

Davies, an award winning investigative journalist, says Super League "seemed like a good idea at the time but the bad blood they created meant they ended up trashing both competitions".

Carr, meanwhile, takes up the story as it appeared to the moguls' minions: "I went back to Neil and explained what had happened and he said 'yeah, we've got to see if we can fix this thing'.

"So I said to Frykers the next day 'Neil's fine', what are the arrangements? He mentioned a couple of dates and he had a mate Tony that was the concierge at the Sheraton On The Park.

"He said 'tell Neil to arrive at the hotel. Tony is the concierge. Tony will give him a room key and just tell him to proceed up to the room'.

"That's subsequently what happened." Where, then, was the NRL born - with the first peace meeting? Neil Whittaker has a bit of a glint in his eye.

"There's only two people who know where they were and one of them's dead."

C'mon mate, it's 25 years ago!

"The first meeting was at the ANA (Hotel). I don't know what it's called now (The Shangri-La). It was upstairs in a room. You know, I'd never met Ian, that was our first meeting and it was obvious to me from that very first meeting that Ian had an incredibly clear grasp of … he understood our issues - and his issues, of course - and he understood the best way through it was to negotiate a settlement and he had to convince his people of that as much as I had to convince my people.

"That's the impression I got from it - that for different reasons we were both in the same position, that News Limited had invested so much money but what was important was that in the year 1998, there was one comp."

Business consultant Bruce Kerridge says he was involved in an advisory role but stresses "the real hard yards were put in by Whittaker and Frykberg because they were the ones who developed, basically, the model.

"Neil was the one developing all of the models and I must admit I was with him when that was being developed - the different options of how it would operate including the finances of it.

"Frykberg, he would then fine-tune that. It was pretty obvious when you started '97 that News wanted to do a deal. They didn't want - I don't think - Super League to actually start.

"The NRL concept was basically 'what are we going to finish up with and it doesn't matter what it's called'. Just some premier entity.

"From my point of view, Neil was the driving force of it. There were a few people involved. For memory, News Corp were using false names and we were using things like venues that people would never think about to have a meeting."

Whittaker recalls: "We just decided we didn't want too many guys like you knowing what was going on. We met in places around Sydney but we'd go there at different times, the rooms would be booked by other people.

"...the reason being ... he had the authority to negotiate but he knew that I had an organisation that needed to be brought along. So we met a bit just on our own until I could work out what we wanted to achieve out of this.

"We had probably four meetings where we met in camera and we talked about what might be able to be achieved."

Further down the chain, in what is affectionately known in rugby league as "clubland", Don Furner - now the CEO of the Canberra Raiders - was just starting out in the Green Machine marketing department in 1997.

"And he called it early," his colleague at the time, Bevan Hannan, recalls.

"He was the one dealing with current sponsors and potential sponsors and he said 'look, people don't care about these other teams. They want us to be playing Parramatta and St George and beating them'.

"'These other new teams - it's just not the thing and it's going to be a long year. We've got to get back together'. I don't think anyone thought it would get as bad as it did. Like World War I propaganda 'we'll be home by Christmas' - you never are.

"Everyone realised pretty quick that there were some winners here but the game's not winning and we've got to move and get out of this somehow."

At this point it's important to draw a distinction. At the corporate level, the war was as good as over. June 20 was later reported as the date Murdoch and Packer reached "an accord" over Pay TV which involved Packer's PBL dumping Optus Vision and linking with Foxtel.

"Rupert was across in New Zealand on his yacht in the Bay Of Islands and Packer came across and met him," says Tom Mockridge.

"It was pissing down with rain. I think that contributed.

"But it was like anything: there was a whole sequence of meetings and it was edging towards that.

"I was very close to Ian (Frykberg), who was not only a friend of mine but someone I regarded as a mentor.

"Even though Foxtel was a joint venture between Telstra and News … it was still part of the News information grouping….

"But remember part of the deal was that PBL came into Foxtel. I was very much a part of that. I was at a bunch of meetings where Rupert

… I remember once we flew down to Melbourne - for some reason - and saw James.

"He was down there trying to create something then and eventually it merged into that deal where News Corp basically gave PBL a 50 per cent option in News Corp's investment across the pay TV business plus a big supply deal of Fox programming into Channel Nine.

"These were all elements of the peace deal. This was through the course of 1997.

"I'll have to be direct about it: the football was only part of a bigger deal around the economics of Foxtel and the TV programming.

"Ian was the frontman in negotiating that and there was a bunch of lawyers certainly across pieces of it and in the end it was Ken (Cowley) and Rupert who were driving it on the News side."

Asked when he knew there would be one competition in 1998, Mockeridge answers: "It would have been when the deal was done with PBL to give them the equity option.

"One guy who was very constructive was Nick Falloon. He was CFO at Channel Nine then.

"There was a bunch of people across the two organisations working on it and in the end it was a Packer-Murdoch compromise that gave us the result.

"And these guys, they can speak to each other at a moment's notice, any time and the rest of us don't know it. There's always conversations going on."

But why did News accept PBL buying into Foxtel? According to Kidman, it was a shrewd piece of business by Packer that really ended the war.

"To me it all pivoted around the fact that PBL out-manouvred News Corp," Kidman says.

"There was no streaming or anything like that. You had to do a deal with the US movie studios.

"Foxtel obviously had 20th Century Fox because that was Rupert's. But what happened to them was a disaster because Australis, which was the microwave dish operation, went and signed all the movie studios up. So it cut Foxtel out of movies in Australia.

"They only had the 20th Century Fox. (Australis) had Warner Brothers, they had Disney. They had the bulk of them. Optus had its own suppliers of various movies but it wasn't strong either. Foxtel virtually had nothing. Foxtel had to buy their movies through Australis and they did a deal with them on the basis Australis … Foxtel always thought Australis would go broke because they had no distribution. They didn't have the money to roll out and get the clients but they tried to send Australis … they sat there and tried to sweat Australis out because what they needed was to get Australis out of the way and have a direct deal with a movie studio. They were just paying far too much for their movies."

Then like the opposite of a thief in the night, Packer swooped to prop up Australis by buying a share of it.

"Once PBL invested, News had lost the game," Kidman says. "Foxtel had lost the game and you could see it almost overnight. They said

'OK … where's Kerry? This is the outline … who do we need over there to get the deal done?'

"They thought they could just win by being bullies and PBL … that was a competition they couldn't win so they had to start negotiating.

"If you ask me, as someone who followed it from the helicopter view and writing about it every day, it was PBL's decision to support Australis that meant News had to change their approach - and Telstra applying pressure saying 'hey, this is a real waste of everyone's money, we just don't want to do it anymore'.

"It was the big guys saying 'we've got to change this' and that's probably … it wasn't the love of the game, it was another thing that was haemorrhaging."

So PBL buying into Australis, Matt Kidman is convinced, ended the Super League War.

Now the footy officials just had to do their own face-saving to come on board. "It was decided above rugby league that there had to be one comp but it took inside rugby league to agree," says Kevin Neil.

And it was not a straight line to peace among footy men.

On July 1, Whittaker and Frykberg met for two hours. "The worst thing we could do is hang up our boots in September and still not know what we're doing next year," Whittaker said at the time. "We've got to make sure there's room for everybody and that we re-embrace the Super League organisation into our game."

But even as they moulded what would become the NRL, Frykberg and Whittaker weren't above flinging a bit of clay in each other's faces in public.

Frykberg outlined the 'stalemate' to me in mid-June.

"From News Corp's point of view, we need to retain control of our investment," he said in a back page lead for the *SMH*.

"We need to be in control of the finances. News Corp has invested hundreds of millions of dollars into the game and the idea is that the clubs should eventually become profitable.

"We are prepared to continue funding rugby league but we need to have some control over how that funding is spent."

Whittaker responded: "It is not in our charter to surrender a community asset" and, when asked about Fykberg's predictions, offered the immortal quote: "I haven't got crystal balls".

Several days later, Frykberg - now speaking publicly on behalf of News despite his innate reticence - hit back. "If they did a better job of managing it in the past, there would not have been a Super League. At the end of a war, there is a victor and a vanquished. The ARL certainly can't claim to be a victor."

The initial idea had News Limited appointing the CEO and Super League still being the competition's moniker. "If we are going to have financial control then it stands to reason we would appoint the chief executive," said Frykberg. "News have already appointed a chief executive – that's (Ribot's replacement) Colin Sanders." Frykberg said the use of the term "Super League" for the new comp was not negotiable.

Fans disagreed. Some 67 percent of Channel Seven viewers, 90 percent of 2GB listeners and 82 percent on 2UE opposed the name "Super League" for the new competition.

News Limited offered $63 million in funding for a 14-team competition in 1998, amounting to an additional $18 million compared to the company's commitment to club funding in 1997.

But $4.5 million per merged club was regarded by ARL sides as a poor incentive, considering they would get $6 million by pooling their Optus grants if they merged in a separate ARL league..

Neil says he had been appointed a spokesman for the Super League clubs in early 1996 while he was out of the room using the toilets.

"There were commercial realities for people. Everyone was burning money, everyone was getting paid too much.

"So the powers-that-be said 'we've got to reunite this' but it needed the support of everyone.

"Frykberg used to, probably, confide in me I think. And I always had open communication with Denis Fitzgerald.

"So sometimes he would feed me, give me some stuff that he wanted to get an opinion on and I could bounce that off Denis and always get a good and honest response from him.

"He did thank me on that day in Sydney when it was all brought back together for the support I provided and all that sort of stuff.

"I'd like to think I played a small part in helping the egg get put back together."

Meanwhile, other pressures were being brought to bear.

While April 1, 1995, was the day the Super League raids besieged the existing ARL-loyal Sydney clubs, April 1, 1997 was the date the siege became more deadly when pubs were allowed to compete with the wealthy league clubs by having poker machines. This provision was accompanied by higher taxes on 'pokies'; Sydney teams had suddenly become especially vulnerable.

"If some of our clubs decide to jump ship now then they are bigger scumbags than the first lot," said George Piggins at the time. "We know Rupert Murdoch was trying to kill us and now we've got (NSW state premier) Bob Carr sinking the boot in.

"The crowds that are coming to the game wouldn't even pay the water boys."

Piggins would later offer qualified support for a promotion and relegation system whereby only stand-alone Sydney clubs could be demoted. That, to him, was preferable to merging.

That idea alone probably seems worthy of a chapter but there was one such concept every second day in July and August 1997. Whittaker warned there would need to be significant progress by the end of July or the ARL would commit to its own competition in 1998. It was therefore in everyone's interests to make out there had been significant progress.

On June 25, the ARL announced it would accept a secondary state cup involving "all Optus Cup clubs." The ARL then revealed it was willing to form a partnership with News. A Super Bowl between the winners of the rival competitions was pencilled in for October 25 at the Sydney Football Stadium.

Who would survive this looming peace?

During a 41-8 win over Manly, Bear Billy Moore mouthed the words "merger my arse" to the crowd at North Sydney Oval. Club chairman Ray Beattie said Norths were moving to Gosford the following year whether there was one competition or two.

Super League placed a moratorium on all player signings in anticipation of a peace deal. ARL clubs refused to join the signing moratorium and Balmain plus Parramatta confirmed holding merger talks. "Parramatta Tigers doesn't sound too bad," said Fitzgerald. "I don't think you'll see Parramatta Panthers." Roy Masters evoked Shakespeare, writing: "Tis time to fear when tyrants seem to kiss".

St George CEO Brian Johnston offered: "St George certainly won't be merging. We will fight to the bitter end to avoid it happening." In early July, when Frykberg said Auckland would be part of a united competition, Perth's Stephen Edwards said he'd like a similar guarantee. When the ARL's National Premiership Council said it opposed a team in Melbourne in 1998, Ribot responded by saying he would love to head up a Victorian franchise in a united competition.

On July 10, it was reported an internal player draft would also be part of a united league.

Back on the field - the was still footy going on - Australia beat the Rest Of The World 28-8 in Brisbane, commentator Ray Warren offering the immortal words "The World is over!"

"It was played like a Test match," Australia coach Bob Fulton recalls. "Put it this way, there was no difference to the approach in a full competition, if everyone was still together. I was coach before that and coach after it. The players applied themselves exactly the same. Can you imagine a team not preparing correctly under Malcolm Reilly? No."

Adrian Lam recalls: "Malcolm Reilly was the coach and It was a massive game. I remember players coming into camp and we were just 'wow'. We got paid quite well for it. Another opportunity - to captain Queensland that year and then the Rest Of The World."

The match being in Brisbane, however, meant the focus didn't stay on that side of the whitewash for long. It was revealed South Queensland and Gold Coast had held merger talks. "If you're going to have a look at it, you'd better have a look at it right now," said Whittaker. "I'm delighted with the leadership role (South Queensland and Gold Coast) have taken."

Next, Manly and Balmain.

But Newcastle chairman Michael Hill insisted rather than a merger with Hunter, the Mariners would "cease to exist" in 1998. Super League clubs nevertheless formulated a plan for the following 12-team competition: Adelaide, Auckland, Brisbane, Canberra, Melbourne, Newcastle-Hunter, North Queensland, Northern Sydney, Cronulla-Sydney City, Parramatta-Penrith, Western Suburbs-Canterbury, Perth.

And a proposal for a 14-team competition: Adelaide, Auckland, Cronulla-St George, Canterbury-Western Suburbs, Gold Coast-South Queensland, Illawarra, Manly-North Sydney, Melbourne, Newcastle-Hunter, North Queensland, Parramatta-Penrith, Sydney City-South Sydney-Balmain.

On July 30, *Rugby League Week* reported Perth had sacked 20 senior players.

Ian Heads wrote: "The 'new' compromise looks much the same as it did 28 months and $500 million ago".

And at the beginning of August, Bob Millward told the *Illawarra Mercury:* "It is getting doubtful now whether we can have a merged competition with a reduced number of teams." Whittaker said: "If we have to have a transit year, so be it."

Then came the cunning and risky political ploy from Frykberg involving ARL chairman John McDonald.

Even though the competition was called the Australian Rugby League, it was run from Sydney and Whittaker had considerable power in the peace process. In time-honoured fashion, this put Queensland's noses out of joint.

John McDonald was the ARL chairman but was effectively a spectator - so Frykberg invited him to a meeting and 'Crackers' went to it.

It was reported that Frykberg and Lachlan Murdoch went to meet McDonald about a sponsorship and television coverage of the Queensland Cup.

Clever. And it had the desired effect for News: the NSWRL board then recommended that McDonald accompany Whittaker to future meetings with Frykberg. Dividing had indeed led to conquest. "Nothing surprised me," said Whittaker. "It was just another thing to deal with."

Slowly, the inevitability of one competition in 1998 had turned the jockeying for position into something of a circus.

Governor General William Deane even intervened in the cause of fixing rugby league, hosting Whittaker and Frykberg at Government House. After further peace talks, Frykberg said some of the demands of the Australian Rugby League clubs were not achievable.

Whittaker announced the ARL was willing to give financial control to New Limited in exchange for the right to run the competition on a day-to-day basis. A three hour meeting between the warring parties in Sydney on August 7 resulted in an agreement which each delegation was confident its board would approve. The meeting was attended by Neil Whittaker, Ken Cowley, Warren Lockwood, Ian Frykberg and John McDonald. The reports emerged on August 8, the 90th birthday of the sport in Australia.

But 2GB reported 19 of 22 clubs were opposed to mergers.

On August 13, Brad Fittler wrote: "Bring on Melbourne and thanks but no thanks Auckland. That is the first step I'd take in the rationalisation process. Let's concentrate on Australia. Clearly going global is not the answer so let's shore up our backyard." In the same edition of *RLW*, Ian Heads reckoned: "Once the compromise (deal) is done, the words "Super League" should be carved one last time in fibrolite and buried in a black coffin, never to be uttered again."

Many feared that peace would fail and the game would continue its inexorable slide into irrelevance. Some - rival sports - probably held this as a hope."I don't want my son to grow up being told his father played for Australia in some sport called rugby league and to think that's not much of an achievement," said Glenn Lazarus

On August 18, Super League abruptly withdrew from peace talks, citing interference from Optus. It was speculated at the time News wanted to force Optus to the Pay TV bargaining table. But News claimed that was Optus' motivation in making demands via the ARL. Three days later Whittaker and Frykberg were talking on the phone again. The ARL had apparently changed its position on Colin Sanders, saying it wanted him answerable to the new competition's board as well as News Limited.

As the end of the month - and the finals of the respective competitions - neared, a stockbroking firm reported the war had cost Kerry Packer $20 million. Lost advertising totalled $10 million to $12 million.

Friday night ratings for men 18 years and over had dropped 53 per cent, the report said.

On August 29, South Queensland and Gold Coast announced what was supposed to be the first joint venture in Australian top flight rugby league history.

It later collapsed.

For their last-ever game, South Queensland threw open the gates and 11,588 saw them beat Wests 39-18. The victory gave their would-be merger partner, who thought their season was over, an 11th-hour reprieve, The Chargers qualified for the finals and eliminated Illawarra the following week.

Gold Coast coach Phil Economidis recalls: "The Crushers, I think I sent them up a couple of kegs of beer. Rather than saying the Crushers got us in … we beat Manly in our last home game which was no mean feat.

"I'll treasure that for the rest of my life - not that there's much of it left!"

Chargers prop Martin Bella, who thought his career had ended with the conclusion of the regular season, offered: "There's not too many people who get a second chance in life and that's what we got."

Still the finals began with only a vague confidence the game would be reunited the following year - and utter confusion as to how it would be achieved.

"Everybody on both sides of the conflict would have been doing their best to make things good," says Mockridge.

"But in the end, it was a split competition, it wasn't generating a new set of fans. It's not like two companies making something and getting more people to buy it. You've got the same set of fans.

"I think everyone through that year realised this wasn't how you wanted things to continue."

The above machinations may have left some readers's heads spinning in confusion. Sorry - but in a book about 1997 it's necessary to recount these multiple deals and no-deals. On the eve of the play-off, it all came down to this: News wanted the new competition to be responsible in some way for the company's $300 million investment in Super League but the ARL refused.

But Australasian rugby league's destiny would not remain in the hands of executives and deal-makers much longer. There was one place in the sport's empire where control had never been surrendered to them.

It was a place that had fallen into financial disrepair under the ARL's watch, and in which Super League had initially taken but a passing interest, offering contracts to only its youngest stars.

As September neared, the Newcastle Knights played their annual intra-club cricket match, sponsored by brewer Tooheys.

"I spoke to Adam Muir, who had announced that he was going to North Sydney, and Marc Glanville who had announced he was going to Leeds," club chairman Michael Hill recalls.

"I said to them 'look, you've got an opportunity here; what I want you to aim for is to get a standing ovation after the end of the last game - you blokes need to play your heart out'."

On Saturday August 30, in front of 22,157 fans at Marathon Stadium, the Knights beat Balmain 37-10 to finish the ARL regular season in second position with 14 wins, seven losses and a draw, three competition points behind Manly and ahead of Parramatta only on percentages.

"As they walked around, Muir and Glanville got a bigger cheer than most. Everyone was down on them for leaving and here they were having this great last year."

And just like that, the peace process was no longer the domain of people in suits.

They didn't know it then, but Muir, Glanville, their team-mates and those 22,000 people - plus more besides - were about to take the very fate of rugby league into their own hands and impose their will upon it.

THE GOOD POINTS TO COME OUT OF LEAGUE'S BITTER WAR

By Steve Mascord, Sydney Morning Herald, Friday, September 19 1997

TOMORROW night in Brisbane, Super League stages its first and maybe last grand final.

The reason it may be the last, of course, is that both the News Ltd-owned league and the Australian Rugby League insist they are confident of a united competition next year. (And presumably, such a competition would have only one grand final.)

Now, it's getting a bit late to significantly reduce teams for 1998, so what we're staring down the barrel of is 20, 21 or even 22 teams.

This, three years after a 20-team competition was torn apart to produce "the best of the best".

Many will tell you that this is final compelling proof that this whole war has been a gigantic waste of time and money with no lasting benefit to the game.

No-one would be silly enough to suggest the Super League war has been good for the sport. But as we near the end of this divided season, it would also be foolish to suggest no good has come out of the schism.

The list of ailments it has foisted upon us is long and well reported: skyrocketing player payments, financially crippled clubs, nose-diving crowd figures and' television ratings.

But there's another list, one not quite as long. It proves that despite all the gloom, there's always an upside to competition:

The Great Clean-out: As it stands, the only major administrator still holding the position he had at the start of the war is British boss Maurice Lindsay. At the ARL's Phillip Street headquarters, the big broom has swept away a lot of the suspicion which the public rightly or wrongly had about certain clubs being favoured.

Decentralisation and amalgamation: Before the war, Sydney clubs would consider merging only over their dead bodies. Now, just about all of them see the need to have a league that is more national in nature. North Sydney say they're relocating to the Central Coast, South Queensland and Gold Coast are merging. Likewise in England, franchising has been introduced and a dramatic restructuring of the game is about to take place.

Increased democracy: Super League offered coaches and players a role in the running of the game before long both leagues had a captain's forum. The resulting united administration is sure to be less autocratic than the old one.

New clubs: Adelaide and Paris are sons of the Super League war. Adelaide has been more successful than all but the most optimistic of leaguies had hoped. Paris? One out of two isn't bad.

Rule changes and innovations: Just as rugby league changed its rules gradually over its first two decades to make it more attractive than rugby union, the two competitions have tinkered with the laws of the game to the same end. It appears the video referee will stay, while the evolution of the play-the-ball has been fascinating. By mid-September, it had reached a truly happy medium in both comps faster than the old ARL, slower than the most breakneck excesses of Super League.

Aggressive marketing and public relations: Before Super League, rugby league didn't need a PR person. By the end of the year, journalists were getting 100-page dossiers on teams when they arrived at matches and were being invited to weekly chats with Neil Whittaker. Pre-match entertainment that was for only the grand final and Origin games until this year. Super League started at one extreme by spending $80,000 on club games. By mid-season, fireworks and a pub rock band were common sights at ARL matches, too.

Better wages for players: Sure, players might be overpaid now but if there's one thing the war proved, it's that they were underpaid before. Why else were they considered so valuable?

Increased international awareness: The World Club Challenge did harm the image of the quality of international football, but at least it had become an issue. Sydneysiders could be excused for forgetting the game was played anywhere else until this year. After all, who was the chairman of the NZRL before Graham Carden?

More quality players: In sporting competitions, if you spread the available talent over a wider area, the standard is supposed to fall. So why were there as many high quality games this year as ever? Easy because younger players stepped into the breach and measured up. Craig Gower and Trent Barrett may have been still waiting for a chance in first grade under a united competition.

Hard-core fans: Most Australians have never had to think of themselves as rugby league fans before. They just followed Balmain, or the Cowboys or Cronulla. But suddenly, this year, they had to stand up for themselves as the transient element of the sports market kept telling them their game was dead. They formed groups like Aussies For the ARL and the Super League Action Movement. For the first time they started writing letters to newspapers and calling open-line programs with complaints more significant than whether the reserve grade five-eighth was getting a fair go.

CHAPTER 18

The Holy Grail

WHILE teams in both competitions were preparing for the finals, Perth Reds football manager Steve Anderson had a secret mission. He was heading to Melbourne.

"I was told in May '97 about the club being formed, by Bullfrog (Peter Moore)," says Anderson, now back in Perth and working in rugby union. "At that stage Ribot had already been working hard behind the scenes. I took up residency in Melbourne in, probably, September '97.

"I remember the (first) day very well. We had a meeting in the *Herald-Sun* building which was our office. There was Greg Brentnall, Michael Moore, Chrissy Johns, John Ribot and Chris Anderson. We had a room, a table and a whiteboard. We had no players."

Just as News Limited and the ARL were about to build the most successful club rugby competition in the world, those six men went on to build the sport's biggest franchise of the 21st century, although not one unaffected by controversy and even disgrace. Early suggestions for the team's nickname were Lightning, Rebels, Jacks, Mavericks, Maulers, Meteors, Gladiators, Vipers or Mercury. Chris Anderson suggested in an early newspaper interview the new club might get players from Hunter as well as from a relocated Perth.

Ken Arthurson, standing on the sidelines, was unimpressed. "John Ribot could not possibly be acceptable to fair dinkum league people after all he has done," he said in the *Sun-Herald* when asked about the team that became the Storm on September 19.

Immediately there was speculation the new team would raid ARL ranks. "Timmy Brasher, the Johns boys and Paul McGregor will be with us until the year 2000," the ARL'S Neil Whittaker countered.

Steve Folkes was appointed to replace Anderson at Belmore.

In the ARL, seven of the 12 teams made the finals. They were: Manly, Newcastle, Parramatta, North Sydney, Sydney City, Illawarra and Gold Coast. Super League employed a traditional five-team play-off series; their qualifiers were: Brisbane, Cronulla, Canberra, Canterbury and Penrith.

On the eve of those finals, Roosters coach Phil Gould wanted to rest seven players against North Sydney - but was ordered to reinstate them. By 2021, there were no longer any scruples about deliberately understrength teams being tendered at this time of year. The Super League play-offs kicked off first, on August 30, with the ARL's beginning on September 5. Fairfax was on strike that day so I ventured out to watch my beloved Steelers at Parramatta Stadium over a beer on a Friday night - and watched their season end, losing 25-14 to the second-chance Chargers, six days after the same teams played in Wollongong with the result going the other way.

"We beat both Newcastle and Manly who contested the grand final," recalls Phil Economidis. "Our budget in '97 was a million. We were playing some teams where it was six to eight million. Parramatta! The players, whenever I asked them for a little bit more, they gave it. It was David and Goliath stuff, to be honest."

Economidis was named the ARL's coach of the year. "Jack Gibson said 'if the club had any money, he wouldn't have got the job'," he laughs. "He took a liking to me after that. He used to send me a book every year with a hand-written message, which I've kept."

Crowds weren't bad on the respective first weekends of the finals but they fell away sharply. Canberra's sudden death major semi against Penrith - at home - attracted just 10,153 people. The focus remained off the pitch and on what rugby league would look like the following year.

On September 3, Players Union boss Peter Moscatt - who used to greet reporters as "Digger" when he returned their calls and who died in 2019 - warned of legal action if players lost their jobs as a result of mergers. On September 4, the Supreme Court ruled the ARL player loyalty contracts were valid.

John Fordham, manager for Andrew and Matthew Johns, said on September 3 that the ARL had formed a secret fund to help certain clubs keep certain stars. Whittaker declined to comment.

In Leeds, the RFL voted in a new seven-man board, which stripped Maurice Lindsay of much of his power. A newspaper revealed an expenses bill of £220,000 over two years. "I like to drive a Jaguar and I don't think the chief executive should have to catch the no.33 bus," Lindsay was famously quoted as saying.

Ken Cowley is reported in the *Yorkshire Post* as having written to Lindsay, chiding: "The only way News Corp will get a return on its investment is if Super League develops into a better product and delivers a new viewing audience to television. An elite national league which is attractive to TV is vital to your future. Your plans must include new areas."

The RFL subsequently announced five new regions targeting expansion: Glasgow, Dublin, Birmingham, the north-east and the south-east including Wales. Glasgow applied immediately. Since then, a Super League team in Wales and one in Gateshead have come and gone and none of these other cities have even got close. Amateur teams from Birmingham and Dublin were in 2020 announced as founding members of a new competition called the Euro XIIIs, which had no affiliation with either the RFL or the European Federation.

Also in September, Peter Moore attended the launch of Ken Arthurson's book (quoted in early chapters here) at the NSW Leagues Club - 'Bullfrog's first visit there since the outbreak of hostilities.

For the average fan who still gave a damn, the signals about what would happen in 1998 remained bewildering.

Frykberg said it was more likely a television truce would solve the impasse than one between football officials. "We made it clear that if we are going to fund the game for as long as it takes to get it on its feet, then we can hardly wipe clean the investment we have already made. You can't have it both ways." News Limited's Super League losses were placed by its annual report at $237 million but this was later revealed to be a gross underestimation.

On September 17, it emerged that peace talks would resume. Frykberg and representatives of the 10 Super League clubs were invited to a meeting of the ARL's National Premiership Council.

But amid the confusion, uncertainty and widespread ambivalence towards onfield events, a cultural tidal wave was quietly gathering force up the F3 motorway from Sydney.

"It started when the finals started," Michael Hill recalls. "There were 70 and 80 and 100 buses. The drama of the finals series and our progress through it was enhanced by the stories about the fans."

Newcastle's first appointment was Parramatta, on September 7 at the Sydney Football Stadium.

Knights assistant coach Steve Dunstan recalls: "As they drew into that finals series, you could feel the impetus of people getting behind the team. It was like this big wave of emotion. It started like a ripple and it just built up, built up."

One of the Knights' ball boys, Michael Maher, says now: "I was only 14 at the time but I was a passionate fan from the time they came in and I can remember some games they blew that year - they were not on other teams' levels.

"They were never a chance against Manly. It looked like they were never gonna get over the top of them."

Meanwhile, former Knights halfback Matt Rodwell became the first Super League player to defect back to the ARL when he transferred from Perth to St George. NSW sports minister Gabrielle Harrison warned: "The government will look less favourably on investing in a ground that may be closed as a result of a merger."

Australian Rugby Union boss John O'Neill predicted a reunification of the rugby codes as a result of the Super League War, something that was again being bandied about in

2020 as Covid-19 hit both sports.

Andy Goodway was appointed Great Britain coach with Australian Shaun McRae technical director. Brewer Bass announced it was pulling out of its Super League Europe sponsorship a year early.

Warrington sacked five overseas players, including Nigel Vagana. Halifax played its last game at Thrum Hall.

Also in September, the ARL launched the threatened legal action against the RFL for what it claimed were unpaid monies from the 1995 World Cup. "The ARL has reluctantly taken this course because they have been unable to obtain any accounts, despite assurances from Maurice Lindsay and the RFL that such would be forthcoming," said a statement issued by the Leeds-based solicitors McCormick. The RFL replied with a media release in which finance executive Tony Eagleton described the ARL's claim as "utter nonsense".

"The accounts actually confirm that the Australians were overpaid. In view of the fact that they have now commenced legal action I have instructed the RFL solicitors not only to contest their claim most vigorously but to start a counter-claim to recover the £75,000 they received as overpayment."

(The following year, Ken Arthurson flew to England to resolve the issue, meeting with Sir Rodney Walker before an out-of-court settlement was agreed … again, on April Fools Day).

But enough of that; back to September footy and the march to the Holy Grail … er, grails.

Super League glamour team Canberra was eliminated 10-4 by Cronulla in the preliminary final.. "We were in it up to the death; through the whole game I felt we were still going to win," says Brett Mullins. "It was disappointing not to reach the (grand) final because I felt we were destined to get there. That's rugby league."

The Raiders' Super League odyssey - now over - had been a vexed one. "You contrast what happened to Canberra with how the season went for Brisbane," said Bevan Hannan. "Everything went to plan for them. When things got back together, they were still a powerhouse. For Canberra, it wasn't the case.

"It was so strident that Super League was about keeping everyone together. But there was this gradual erosion …. Canberra, history shows how long it took them to recover.

"You can't help but ask 'would it have been different if Tim (Sheens) had stayed?' Steve Walters was gone in '97. John Lomax was gone in '97. They'd both joined Tim in North Queensland.

"Would some of these things have happened if they weren't in Super League? It's highly questionable. Don't forget, the (rugby union ACT) Brumbies were on the rise then too."

And so it was the Broncos and the Sharks - the latter still without a premiership since their inception in 1967 - to contest the first and only Super League Australia grand final, at Brisbane's ANZ Stadium. The breakaway's imitation of the Super Bowl - with ticker tape and dinners in the lead-up - was described as "overkill" by Glenn Lazarus in his newspaper column.

Paul Kind says: "We did a street parade and I was desperately worried that along the 3km route we'd have nobody - because there was no way of knowing how many people would come. It was incredible. It was thousands and thousands and thousands of people on a Thursday lunchtime."

Super League's decider was on September 20 - eight days before the ARL grand final. Pre-match entertainment was Jon Stevens and Olivia Newton-John performing the hits of *Grease*.

"That was a coup, I have to say," says Kind. "She was amazing. She hadn't done that sort of live performance in Australia for a very long time. She certainly hadn't performed *Grease* songs.

"With Jon, who was a great talent, she did 'You're The One That I Want' and she did 'Hopelessly Devoted To You' and everyone had their lighters in the crowd.

"She was a proper star. So that was good, that worked."

Shane Richardson, leading the Sharks into hostile waters, recalls: "It was ridiculous, They decided that we were going to go and play in Brisbane. That's alright. They'd probably get a better crowd there because Queensland were onside.

"But they sent us up for the whole week. We spent a whole week in a hotel in Brisbane preparing for a grand final, including a ticker tape parade.

"So the preparation was highly questionable because you're away from your families. You've got wives trying to break into husbands' hotel rooms. It was a ridiculous week.

"But then on top of that, the game …. they didn't think they'd sell it out. Two days, three days before they decided they were going to sell it out … oh, fantastic …. They fucking added more seats, these open air seats along the sideline of QEII Stadium. And that's where they put all our families, because they wanted to sell all the seats in the grandstand.

"And it pissed raining! That's why I ended up with Danny Lee's baby on my knee and his wife next to me, Anne Marie, next to John Lang who's the coach. That's how ludicrous it was. We had to get our wives out of the rain. Still to this day I've never forgiven (Broncos CEO) Shane Edwards. We're great mates but I've never forgiven him. "

Brisbane beat Cronulla 26-8 in the Super League grand final before 58,912. "I reckon it was a plan for the Broncos just to upset us completely. We were in it at half-time but we ended up getting beaten," says Richardson.

John Lang says now: "They were just too good for us. I wasn't disappointed with the way we played. If you look back at the players they had, whoa, they were a great side."

Kevin Walters: "I remember Steve Renouf scoring three tries which was pretty hectic in a grand final."

Darren Lockyer wrote: "I collected my share of the $1 million prize money courtesy of our Super League premiership win and our victory in the World Club Challenge competition, with the 25 members of our first grade squad each taking home an equal share.

"By the end of the year, I walked away with a pay packet a smidgeon shy of what I was paid a decade later as captain of the club, Queensland and Australia and dual Golden Boot winner.

"I used my earnings from 1997 to purchase my first house - a replica Queenslander in Rockbourne Terrace, Paddington, just a stone's throw from Red Hill."

Reflecting on the only grand final held in Brisbane until the Covid crisis of 2021, Kind says: "It had a sense of scale but it had none of the real emotion of the following week.

"It was bright and shiny and successful and it lacked that real emotion of rugby league which came out in spades in the ARL grand final which was not as slick by any means but had substance, that real memorable substance."

Back in NSW, with the peace process spluttering along, that DNA-level bond between sport and community - thought to be on the verge of extinction in rugby league after three years of rancour - suddenly exploded like nuclear fission.

The game's innate ability to compensate for its many systemic flaws with transcendent moments was about to become incarnate once more, on an unprecedented and salvationary scale.

The Knights had two weeks previously trailed the Eels 18-0 only to run them down 28-20. In the hours before the Super League grand final, Knights winger Darren Albert then did the running down himself, stopping North Sydney's Matt Seers with a tackle for the ages before Matthew Johns booted a field goal to end the Bears' last real chance ever of a grand final appearance. The Novocastrians - driven to Phillip Street in a minibus to sign up with the ARL - were to play Manly, effectively the people who were doing the signing, in the second grand final of the split season.

"It was almost meant to be," Knights doctor Peter McGeoch rhapsodises. "There are so many things that had to come together for us to win it. It was preordained, almost."

But back in Steel City on Sunday September 21, there was a confrontation that exposed the dark matter inside the beam of light pointing the Knights towards immortality. The Mariners - still alive in the World Club Challenge - decided to pay the victorious ARL side a visit at a pub owned by Knights football manager Dave Morley.

"Things got a bit hectic, when Mal (Malcolm Reilly) and Sarge (Mark Sargent) looked like they were going to have an altercation," recalls Dunstan.

"I don't think it would have ever happened … but it was pretty close. I think it was more a little bit of adrenalin … having beers, everyone excited, made the grand final…

"There were a few of the Mariners boys who came down to pass on their support, I suppose. As a few beers flowed … Malcolm has a reputation of being a very tough guy and not suffering fools gladly.

"Someone only had to say something. It was always a very touchy situation."

Paul 'The Chief" Harragon separated ARL loyalist Reilly and Super League devotee Sargent in the toilets at Morely's pub.

Dunstan stresses: "(But) in the whole season - and I was pretty close to him (Reilly) the whole year - he never once mentioned Super League. He never gave any indication it bothered him."

Another Novocastrian tale would be played out in front of a much larger audience.

Andrew Johns had broken two ribs scoring a try against Parramatta. Despite receiving a painkilling injection before the preliminary final against the Bears, he had come off at halftime complaining of severe discomfort.

"He was breathing really fast," McGeoch recalls.

"Oddly enough, I'd packed my bag and I ended up with all these quite long needles, which I wouldn't normally have. I'd normally have a needle that was about 2cm long and these things were about 3cm long.

"He wanted a top-up and I'm actually topping it up with this needle I'm not entirely happy with. At some stage … I don't think he actually registered that I'd done it and I don't think I did either...

"We've done this and he's gone to sit down on the other side of the room and I'm watching him and you could sort of see that he wasn't quite right. He started looking in discomfort.

"Suddenly it's dawned on me and I thought 'oh fuck'.

"My life has flashed before my eyes. I've thought 'oh fuck, we're going to miss out on the grand final because of this. I've sat down, watched the second half with my heart in my mouth thinking there's no way we can win without him."

But they did, 17-12.

"And it's just that combination of circumstances," McGeoch continues. "I was absolutely ecstatic at the end of the game. I've never been at a game where I've ridden the highs and the lows so much.

"I thought 'this is going to be terrible because there's players who won't ever get that opportunity again' as a consequence of what happened.

"We got him into hospital and I think it was on the Monday he had the tube put in. He came out on the Wednesday. At the start of the week it was devastating - he's gone into hospital! Maybe we're thinking 'fuck, maybe he will be able to play!'."

Two days into grand final week, Whittaker invited reporters including me to Phillip Street and launched the National Rugby League Championship.

The structure allowed for an eight-man board - five from the NSW and Australian rugby leagues and three from News Ltd, which was designated only as "corporate partner". The National Rugby League Championship would include up to 22 teams. "When News Ltd pulled out of talks, we thought about making public how far we'd come, so people could see what the roadblocks were," Whittaker said. "But I have made a commitment not to discuss what happened in the talks. So we have gone one better - we have put it into practice." Once more, it was stressed the new company would not take on the debt of Super League. News could appoint the CEO but he would be answerable to the NSWRL and ARL boards, not just News.

Yes, things were so bad the governing body willfully detracted from its own grand final week to promise the public a better future. Whittaker had a plan. He just didn't know the degree to which fate would conspire to shake everyone out of their indifference and supercharge that plan.

That indifference, however, stopped at the Moonee Moonee Bridge as you headed out of Sydney.

In Newcastle, an afterthought for both sides initially, 'extremist' pro-ARL groups like Aussies For The ARL had been formed. They threw rocks through the windows of the Mariners with the same arm that held placards protesting the closure of the steelworks.

Newcastle was the only place that still really cared.

But the bubble around the Hunter region sometimes seemed physical to the Knights. "The last couple of weeks of the finals series,' recalls Hill, "Ian Bonnett - the CEO … he and I drove down to see Neil Whittaker about getting some funds because the Knights were rooted.

"And we got to the Hawkesbury River and Neil said (by phone) 'look, I can't help you. I'm in a meeting, go home'.

"So we turned around and went home, won the final which no-one expected us to do, made a six-figure sum out of selling t-shirts as well as everything else we got and rescued the Knights financially.

"For the year '97, the Knights had no money at all."

Opponents Manly - who'd been in the previous three grand finals - had won the last 11 games against their working class opponents.

Journalist Brett Keeble shadowed the Knights for grand final week. Like Hill, he didn't particularly think of them as title contenders until well into September. He flew to Sydney with Reilly and Harragon on the Monday and travelled with the team on their bus again the night before the grand final breakfast.

"All they talked about was they felt a sense of destiny, they felt a sense that this is the time … 'if we're ever going to beat Manly, why not do it in a grand final?'

"You could feel the belief and the confidence growing within the team but rugby league players are confident before they go into any game.

"But the game itself? It was always a long shot."

Newcastle's coach was intimidating Englishman Reilly, a close friend of his opposite number, Manly's Bob Fulton. "At the end of that season, he came up to Darwin for two weeks with myself and my sons and Royce Ayliffe and quite a few others,' Fulton recalls in an interview for this book which was his last before he died on May 23, 2021.

Manly and Australia doctor Nathan Gibbs warned in the lead-up to the grand final at the Sydney Football Stadium Johns might die if he played. When I spoke to him, Fulton had no recollections to share of this iconic grand final week story.

But Gibbs told me: "Chippy (journalist Peter Frilingos) has rung me up. He's saying 'will he play next week?' and I said 'well a punctured lung, it depends how big it is, he might recover'.

"Then he's saying 'will he need a painkiller in his rib?'. I said 'I'm not sure but he probably will. Obviously you should ask their doctor'.

"So he said 'is it risky? You know, they've organised to have an accident/emergency physician on the sideline'. Chippy's telling me this.

"I'm like 'oh, they obviously have some concern about his ribs'. So he said 'what could happen?' and I said 'he could get another punctured lung, it could increase'. 'So what would happen?'

"I said 'well he might have to come off and he might have trouble breathing'. Yeah, so what can happen with that? 'Well sometimes it's a tension in your thorax and sometimes you really have trouble breathing'.

"Well what can happen with that? Obviously you've got to release the pressure. 'So what can happen?' Well if you don't release the pressure in time, it can stop the heart beat.

"'And so what can happen?' He could die.

"So that was the headline. The great Chippy, the great journo that he was, just hammered me and hammered me for 10 questions until I got to the .001 percent chance of sudden death - and that was the bit that was in the paper."

Johns' team-mate Marc Glanville says: "That was probably Bozo telling Nathan 'mate to stir up a bit of that. Maybe it will unsettle Joey'. But he was going to play regardless."

Michael Hill felt the comment from Gibbs was dirty pool. "The club said 'that's just everybody's against us'. It was a typical Manly comment. It was just another piece of evidence that everyone was…."

Peter McGeoch: "Andrew enjoyed it. Subsequently when they'd go away on tour, he'd keep reminding Nathan of the quote. He'd come up and say 'you might die Nathan'."

Was it a conspiracy to put pressure on Johns?

"I was pretty media savvy by that stage in my career," says Gibbs. "I knew what was going to be the headline if I said what I said. I was quite aware where it was going but at the time I felt it was quite funny. I enjoyed it and by that stage I knew Joey pretty well, we'd been on quite a few Origin and Australian trips away.

"And I've got to say, it's quite impressive that he played with it. It was quite dangerous. There's no doubt about it. You talk about the medical thing but it's also performance. It's bloody hard to play with a busted rib and a lung puncture because it's pretty painful."

Reilly, now 73, says of Johns: "Look, he had plenty of injections. How tough can you get? He was an inspirational person. Andrew was just a tough character. Single minded. Joey would have to be the best player I've ever been involved with, at any level."

At one point in the finals, Reilly says, injury was giving Johns so much pain he wanted to come off. "I was on the bench and I said 'mate, we can't win this game without you, get back out there' and he just turned around on a sixpence and went back out and got back into it."

Harragon was also battling pain each week. "He did mostly pool work," says Dunstan. "For a bloke who did that, his performances were phenomenal. He played State of Origin, he played Australia.

"His knees were bad, obviously. He was beyond reproach with his body. He sacrificed himself every game. He couldn't recover enough to do any maintenance, running or ballwork.

"Adam MacDougall was basically the same. The last half of the season, Doogs was in pain as well. Doogs was carrying lots of injuries.

"The coaching staff made a decision in grand final week we didn't have to do much other than a captain's run because the state of adrenalin with the players was … we couldn't train because guys couldn't walk in the stadium, because there'd be a thousand people out front. Everyone wanted to be a part of it. Newcastle was going to be number one in Australia - and it was. It wasn't only for a day. It was for a week, possibly a month. It was the number one city in Australia.

"When we were leaving on Saturday on the bus, they were three-wide up Lambton Road heading out to the highway.

"The tears and the emotion on that bus going down was phenomenal".

Reilly's team was hard and clever and fast but not without its rough edges. English hooker Lee Jackson, the coach admits, didn't quite fit in. "He had one or two faults," Reilly says. "He also had some qualities too. He was a good attacking player, his support play was good, he was quick. He could spot an opportunity.

"He didn't mix. He wasn't bothered about alcohol and his social skills weren't the best in the world, mixing wise. I think that was seen as a bit of a detriment sometimes because the team loved a good time."

'Rivalry' does not do the enmity between the sides justice. Maher once saw Manly's trainers spray water all over their Knights rivals at Brookvale Oval - "even the Manly trainers would niggle the Knights trainers" - and heard the greatest hits of arch Sea Eagles sledgers Terry Hill and John Hopoate at close range. Hopoate, for instance, would call Darren Albert a "baby".

Michael Hill: "On grand final day, buses came from Orange to Newcastle, from all over the country. They couldn't get enough buses to take the people there. There was this great sea of people moving up and down the highway.

"People still tell me stories about where they were on grand final day. There was a bloke who said to me 'I drove from Raymond Terrace to Belmont on that Sunday afternoon and didn't pass another car'. The whole town was captured, absolutely captured."

Two nights before the ARL grand final, the Australian Super League team was stunned 30-12 by New Zealand at North Harbour. On Sunday morning, the *Sun-Herald* ran a back page story announcing a 20-team competition in 1998. It said there would be "two conferences" with "regular crossovers" and a "Super Bowl."

Andrew Johns wrote: "I remember the bus ride down to Sydney from Newcastle. It was so emotional seeing Chief (Paul Harragon) cry as the fans lined the streets to wish us well.

"When Chief called the team into his room the night before the game - no coach or officials, just the players - and went around the room and made every player explain what it meant to him to win the competition, the occasion hit home to all of us.

"I had an attitude of 'whatever' before the team meeting - I just wanted to let rip and play - but when Marc Glanville talked about how hard he had worked to come back from two knee reconstructions and how he'd battled (for) the club for 10 years and how this was the only grand final he was going to play and how much it meant to him, it really united us.

"I was really blown away by it because I thought these big moments happened all the time."

The hotel was the Holiday Inn at Coogee. "Chief had got everyone around and said 'let's have a chat and go up to the room' and we sort of said 'no, we've had enough talks," Glanville recounted when I interviewed him for *Two Tribes*, "and we've done everything' and he said 'no, no I think we should' so we ended up going up there, just the players.

"Chief said when he was in the Origin team, one of the camps, Phil Gould got them all together and said 'if this was your last-ever game of footy, what would you do to win it?' or 'what would it mean to you?'.

"We were going around the room and some of the young blokes were saying stuff and when it came to me … I hadn't really thought about it much.

"When I started speaking, I thought 'shit, this is my last ever game for the club, the club I'd been with for 10 years which is one third of my life' … then, it was. And I hadn't really achieved too much in the game. I had desires to play for NSW, play for Australia etc and unfortunately never did that.

"I spoke around 'when I leave the game, I want to have achieved something and at this stage I haven't really achieved anything'. Then I started getting emotional that it was my last ever game. I sort of broke down. I guess the younger guys, that meant something to them because they thought 'shit he's been there 10 years and played in the ARL for 15 years and this is his only grand final that he's getting the chance to win'.

"I think that meant a bit for the younger blokes, that this is their only opportunity. They may never play in another one and there's obviously been plenty of good footballers over the years who have never won a grand final."

And so to game day. Windy, sunny, high teens, low 20s centigrade.

Hill: "There were only two types of people at that ground. There were Knights supporters and those who hoped Manly lost.

"We shouldn't have got to the grand final but we got there and (John) Quayle sent out a message to all clubs, to the officials, saying 'look, the NSWRL box is the NSWRL box and loud supporting and cheering for the teams is not appropriate'.

"I said 'well shove it up your arse. I'll watch the game out with my family'. So I didn't go in the box. I knew who it was directed at because after we beat Norths we were just ecstatic."

The Knights had taken extraordinary precautions against the possibility of Johns' broken ribs and punctured lung rendering Nathan Gibbs' predictions ghoulishing accurate.

"We had a cardio-thorasic surgeon called Alan Boyd who was a fairly keen supporter," McGeoch recounts. "He got involved, it was fantastic. He put the tube in, got it taken out, gave (Johns) a stress test on the Thursday where he got him to do some work on the treadmill just to make sure that it was intact.

"Alan Boyd rang me after he did the stress test and said 'there's really no reason … look, there's a bit of a risk but I'll be down there and if we need to put a tube in, we'll do it'.

"He actually came to the game. We were so grateful we gave him a signed jumper and I think he got 400 bucks (for it). He sat on the sideline for arguably one of the best games of all time, got a signed jumper and made a quid out of it. Every time I ran into him after that we had a bit of a giggle about how he had the best day in the world."

Let's stop there.

In one of the most famous games of all time, arguably the greatest player of all time could have needed emergency surgery at any time and had a surgeon sitting on the bench just in case.

Yep.

"Basically he would have put a tube in between the lung and the pleura space and taken the air out of it. You have a tube and a suction process. We didn't put a percentage on it but we thought it was extremely unlikely to be necessary but in these circumstances you've got to cover all contingencies.

"It would be in the dressingroom. There's a thing called the tension in the thorax where the hole in the lung acts like a one-way valve.

You're pumping the air into a space and it's not actually escaping and that can be a bit of a medical emergency."

But no-one knew any anything but sketchy details of this outside the Knights' inner sanctum as the teams ran onto the now-demolished SFS.

Maher: "When the Knights came out, it was as loud as Marathon Stadium. Maybe louder. When Manly came out, they got booed onto the field. In a grand final."

Glanville: "Troy Fletcher had a great game and Chief, to start the game, coming out … The story goes that Mal Reilly had said to Chief, quietly, 'no-one gets sent off in a grand final. Go out there and get into them'. We as a forward pack said 'we need to get on top of them if we're any chance to win'."

By halftime, though, the working man's team trailed 18-6. "It wasn't looking good," says Glanville. "It was quite funny, we were pretty relaxed even though we were trailing.

"When we all put our hands in together to say we were going to go back out there and give it our best, I think Butts (Tony Butterfield) or someone dropped a fart and Chief's talking and we've all got our noses buried in our jumpers.

"We sort of broke up and laughed!"

And that afternoon at the Sydney Football Stadium, Joey didn't die.

Instead, he set up a try for Albert in the dying seconds to win Newcastle their first premiership. "I reckon they might have got us if it went into overtime," Johns wrote. "I hadn't played much football. I was struggling to jog, let alone sprint."

Andrew and his brother Matthew had studied tape of Manly - and other teams - leaving a gap behind the play-the-ball while defending with play near the sideline.

"I heard Matty calling for the ball, obviously for one last shot at field goal," Andrew wrote. "I looked over from dummy half and there was John Hopoate staring at Matty and his body language showed he was going to charge out and jump Matty and try to charge the kick down.

"So I said to Darren Albert, who played the ball, "stay alive" and then feigned left and snuck down the short side to the right, dummied again to my old mate Mark Hughes on the right … then took the tackle of Craig Innes and put Alby in for the try."

Fulton: "It was a grand final and every grand final, you've got to be prepared. It was the same as any grand final I've been involved in as a player and a coach.

"It was 16-all until Joey put that try on. The game goes for 80 minutes and there was a try scored in the last five minutes."

Geoff Carr was high in the western stand at the SFS, with his eye on a prominent fan of his old club St George.

"It was generally my job, with security, to work out when the prime minister should go down to the presentation. It was accepted by security: probably seven or eight minutes before the end of the game because it was easier to get him down the steps at the old Sydney Football Stadium rather than wait for the lift because you could be stuck there a minute or two.

"John Howard it was. The idea was to get him down the steps before the crowd start to leave.

"There's eight minutes to go and the security bloke's looking at me and John's really enjoying the game. It was a great game.

"I said to the security bloke 'give it a couple more minutes because he's really enjoying the game and I think it looks as if something's going to happen'. It was one of those games that's going to go to the wire but something's going to break it open.

"Then with five minutes to go I sort of shrugged my shoulders and pointed to Howard. We're sitting there. Then all of sudden there's a couple of minutes to go and it wasn't time to get up and go because he was going to miss it. We waited and as soon as Joey put him over, the security bloke said 'we've got to go' so we went

"And when we got to the steps there was nobody.

"Not a soul.

"Everyone was in the ground. No-one left. Not a person."

The ARL allowed a small group of print media men out onto the field at full-time along with the radio and TV "sideline eyes". One of my most vivid memories in 35 years as a journalist is being embraced by Matthew Johns in the middle of the Sydney Football Stadium after the most important grand final of all time.

Hill: "In fact, I gave an interview after the game out on the field. Craig Hamilton said to me 'what do you think?' and I said 'we beat the fucking lot of them - the referees, the administration."

Johns, meanwhile, told the ABC's Hamilton: "I just want to get nude and sit on the goalposts"

Keeble recalls "Mal didn't want to go on the lap of honour because he said it was for the players" and Reilly says: "After the game I had a bittersweet feeling to a degree. I just appreciated people on the other side … Arko had done so much for the game and Boze (Bob Fulton) … I'd been involved with the club before.

"But mate, I won two premierships with Manly, I won two with Castleford in England, I coached Great Britain beating Australia - very special - but that rates the very highest emotionally. The town was just immense in their support of the team and the players couldn't have done it without them."

Paul Brown, a fan who had driven down from Gladstone for the match and would later be CEO of London Broncos, reminisces: "I never FELT a grand final like it before or since. It was incredible."

McGeoch left his wife to drive back with a newly-born child alone while he joined the players on the victorious bus journey, interrupted by at least four toilet stops. His own place in the sport's folklore was assured - by accidentally puncturing someone's lung while giving them a painkilling injection! "I used to feel really guilty about it," the doctor says, before naming two rival club doctors who committed the same error with key player

Super League lawyer David Gallop, who would lead a united competition in years to come, was sitting at home watching on television. He says he just shook his head in astonishment at "an example of the game prevailing despite the politics around it. And I remembered those two occasions really clearly. One, at the Tri-Series (final) and the other, the 1997 ARL grand final and at the end of it thinking 'wow, the game's done it again'. It's shown us all that it's such a survivor."

Hill: "My memory of the aftermath of it is that I'd never been involved in mass hysteria before. That's how I viewed the crowd. They were hysterical because their wildest dreams had been fulfilled.

"I suppose that's my answer to whether it was building. Not for any of us. It was just a complete shock."

Keeble: "The celebrations afterwards have become part of town folklore. Chief, the Johns boys, Tony Butterfield, Marc Glanville … anyone who is ever interviewed about it talks about people lining the streets when they left the day before and then the long trip home … people lining the streets 50, 60 kms out of Newcastle and the slow crawl from the Wallsend roundabout into the Workers Club."

Glanville: "We got to the two Shell servos at Wallsend there and we had a police escort by then. We pulled up at the lights and Matty and Joey got out and they're up on top of the police car dancing and people are all cheering.

"It took us an hour to get from Wallsend into the Worker's Club in King Street.

"The Sunday night was massive. I got a lift home from someone and had an hour's sleep and then I went back in and we had Mad Monday. Tuesday we had the ticker tape parade. I had a spell Wednesday and then Thursday we were back on it.

"We went out to Cessnock and did the coalfields areas, a bit of a pub crawl.

"There was strong talk we wanted to go down to Manly and do a pub crawl. Luckily, we didn't."

Brett Keeble adds: "Most people seem to think that game and that result were the beginning of the end of the Super League War - and it seemed to play out that way."

Paul Kind has thought a lot about that day in the quarter-century since.

"Fans on both sides just lost the sense of belief that their team was competing against the best other teams because you had that split comp," he says. "I think that Manly-Newcastle grand final was really important because what it did at the end of that season was put it back together … no matter which side of the divide you were on, if you didn't enjoy that grand final, I'd be surprised.

"If you were a Raiders fan or a Broncos fan or you worked at Super League, if you loved the game of rugby league that was a super-important game because it helped what was to come."

McGeoch: "The grand final reminded people how great the game could be and what it was all about. It was about a working class town rather than the glitzy teams winning it."

The only fan base that wasn't willing to quietly let rugby league slide from the centre of Australian popular culture had been serendipitously blessed by a once-in-a-generation, transcendent moment.

And as Harragon will explain in the afterword, the team had been blessed and enabled by them. It was the nobility of the proletariat, writ large.

As they lined the streets leading into Newcastle and mobbed the players who partied with local heroes silverchair and the Screaming Jets, the people reclaimed The People's Game before our eyes. Without this one match, reckons Dunstan, "the game wasn't going to recover".

Neil Whittaker's eyes widen just a little at the memory: "Newcastle winning the comp, in an absolute blockbuster grand final, was the absolute turning point for us.

"I arranged with Channel Nine to be interviewed immediately after the game on the field and I invited all of the Super League teams to join our comp next year.

"And I told everybody that our 12 teams would be playing in the comp next year. I said 'you should go have an off-season, don't worry about the game, we'll all be playing again next year'.

"And Frykers rang me the next day. 'Let's get started'.

"In my view, It's the game that saved rugby league."

BRONCOS FEED ON SHARKS

By Steve Mascord, *Sun-Herald,*
Sunday September 21, 1997

Brisbane 26 Cronulla 8 at ANZ Stadium

ACCUSATIONS of kicking and head-butting flew thick and fast last night after Brisbane survived an early second-half challenge by Cronulla to take out the Super League title they were destined for.

A crowd of 58,912 - a Queensland league record and the biggest grand final roll-up in two decades - saw the Broncos run out comfortable 26-8 winners over the Sharks at ANZ Stadium.

Brisbane were deserved premiers, surviving a determined rally by the Sharks, who narrowed the margin to two points just after halftime, when they led 10-2.

But at least one incident from the game will be examined by judiciary commissioner Jim Hall and there were strong words from players on both sides about opposition tactics. And a Brisbane player, who did not want to be named, said: "I saw a Shark player headbutt. If he doesn't get suspended...

Referee Bill Harrigan placed a tackle by Danny Lee and Les Davidson on Broncos replacement John Plath on report.

The tackle ended with Davidson throwing punches at Plath.

"I thought he kicked Danny in the head that's why I got involved," said Davidson. Plath was in the thick of the action throughout, admitting he goaded Cronulla winger Mat Roger at halftime leading to the other major incident of the game, a shoving match between Plath and three Sharks on the sideline.

"That's the way he plays - we should have realised that and not retaliated," said Davidson.

"I try to play with my head and not my heart these days, and unfortunately I played with my heart"

Plath admitted he used "my mouth and my smile as my weapon" against the Sharks. But he insisted he only had an accidental head-clash with Lee.

"I don't think anything should come of it," he said. "It was a tough game of rugby league. Things happen in the heat of the moment and what happens on the field should stay there."

Not that there was unbridled acrimony after last night's game, played in intermittent rain. Cronulla coach John Lang admitted the Broncos were the best side in Super League, as they happily embarked on what should be a tireless celebration of their $500,000 windfall.

Brisbane's only try of the first half came after 34 minutes, winger Steve Renouf crossing for the first of his three tries.

A wayward pass from Broncos winger Wendell Sailor presented the Sharks with their chance, winger Geoff Bell soccering the ball into the in-goal and centre Russell Richardson claiming the try.

But when the Broncos presented Cronulla with opportunities immediately afterwards, they were penalised twice for incorrectly playing the ball, Cronulla couldn't take advantage.

And with 25 minutes remaining, Cronulla fullback David Peachey caught a bomb on the tryline but dropped it in a Peter Ryan tackle.

The Broncos sent the ball wide and Renouf scored. The conversion by outstanding fullback Darren Lockyer widened the margin to eight points and Cronulla's tilt at glory was lost.

Renouf scored again, off Lockyer, in the 68th minute and a wonderful pass from lock Darren Smith to winger Michael Hancock completed the champions' account Super League officials were crowing afterwards, Broncos chief executive Shane Edwards saying: "In 1995 the ARL couldn't see any merit in bringing a grand final up here. Try telling that to the 58,000 people here tonight."

Broncos coach Wayne Bennett confirmed afterwards that skipper Allan Langer's groin injury was indeed serious and that he was no chance of playing for Australia against New Zealand at Auckland's North Harbour Stadium on Friday night.

The Australian side will be named in Sydney tomorrow. Langer is also rated unlikely to play much of a part in the Broncos World Club Challenge finals campaign, which begins in two weeks against St Helens.

Lang described the Broncos as the best team in Australia but Bennett and his players were reluctant to buy into speculation about a Super Bowl against the winners of the ARL competition.

Reflecting on the Sharks' season, Lang said: "Rome wasn't built in a day."

BRISBANE 26 (S Renouf 3. M Hancock tries; D Lockyer 5 goals) bt CRONULLA 8 (R Richardson try; M Rogers 2 goals) at ANZ Stadium. Referee: Bill Harrigan. Crowd: 58.912

CHAPTER 19

Wayne Bennett

THE game that saved rugby league? "It's bullshit, mate," says the sport's most decorated coach, Wayne Bennett.

The striking dichotomy of the year of two tribes is that to this day, below the veneer of entente cordiale, the tribes remain.

Maurice Lindsay insists Phillip Street came back on bended knee. Paul Langmack says Super League was months away from collapsing because no-one cared about it. The players won. Super League won. The game won. The ARL won. Packer won.

And so, almost 25 years after he told Rebecca Wilson he'd been standing up for press conferences his whole life and would continue to do so, Wayne Bennett does not swallow the narrative that the Newcastle Knights stopped The Greatest Game losing its greatness.

"They were the greatest promoters of themselves," he tells me from the NRL bubble in Brisbane, where he's coaching South Sydney.

Of the 1997 ARL grand final, Bennett insists: "It was a great game and it had a tremendous finish but rugby league was strong and healthy. Super League had 60,000 people at the game in Brisbane here, at the grand final.

"It had everything a grand final could have. It had a great atmosphere, a great build-up, a pretty exciting time. But again, we look like criminals because we won our premiership. The ARL, they made out they were in a superior competition and we were an inferior competition. It was the agenda which was absolute bullshit again.

"We went to Newcastle the following year and it was packed out, the ground. There's no doubt that they were on and we were on and they wanted to show everybody that we wouldn't have beaten them if we played in the grand final.

"But we beat them in Newcastle mate. It took 60 minutes to get on top of the bastards but we got there."

The fact that high profile people can have such contrasting views of a single series of lived events is what sets 1997 apart in the entire history of the sport. And Bennett, of course, was there at the very genesis of Super League.

"What I do remember is when it all started, with (co-owner) Paul Morgan - in particular - at the Broncos ... being privately owned, they were about making profit and at the time they felt the NSW and Australian Rugby Leagues just weren't making that happen - particularly because they were tied up with Channel Nine for the rights and pay TV was coming and that was the Murdochs," Bennett says, early covering ground which we have until now avoided.

"They went to Sydney to have the meeting and Kerry Packer addressed them and he told them that there was no way he was going to let anyone else have the rights, etc, etc. They could all stick it up their arse. He had a contract and that was it.

"That was the moment that Super League was born."

Brisbane took out the two titles on offer in Super League and in the first NRL grand final on September 27, 1998, they comfortably bettered fellow breakaway side Canterbury 38-10. The Broncos, instigators of the schism, hadn't just survived it but thrived and grown during it.

But to many casual fans, particularly in Sydney, the ARL premiership was the 'real' 1997 competition, even though those in the other camp subsequently dominated a united league that was largely bankrolled by News Limited. It was necessary to convince these very people of this very worldview in order to win them back. But it clearly sticks in Bennett's craw that the establishment controlled the narrative and enjoyed a PR victory that in some respects endures today.

"The thing I've learned in life is that there's a group of people out there who will always have an agenda," Bennett comments.

"We had an agenda too. We all thought we should be paid better. Well, I was happy with the money I was getting, actually. I didn't become a part of it for the money, for the extra pay that I got. Most of the players didn't but that's what was on offer. We had a bit of a belief that the game could be stronger, could be better run.

"I was on a hundred and ... I don't know what it was at the Broncos. Anyway, they rang me up and said 'oh listen, we're going to Super League. We're going to give you a pay rise. I said 'what for? I don't need a pay rise. I'm happy with what I'm on'.

"They said 'nah, nah, nah we've got to give you a pay rise. We're going to give you $300,000'. I said 'gee, I don't want $300,000. I didn't want it. I wasn't coaching for the money and I was getting well paid.

"'No, no, no, you've got to take the $300,000. Take it'. I said 'righto' and then about two weeks later, a month later, I get another phone call. 'We're going to give you another $50,000'. I said 'what?'. They said 'yeah, Tim Sheens has been hanging out and we've increased his salary. We believe you should be equal to him so we're going to give you another $50,000'. I said 'Jesus mate, you're too good for me'."

Gorden Tallis and Anthony Mundine, who held out for varying periods at St George because they wanted to play under Bennett, were also what Peter Mullholland would call "intrinsically motivated".

Bennett recalls: "Gordie came up and we paid him that year (1996) to sit out because that's what he wanted to do. He refused to go back to St George. And the other controversy for us was Anthony Mundine. He decided to go to Super League and he didn't have a club because the Dragons weren't in Super League.

"He was to go to Canterbury and he didn't want to go anywhere near Canterbury. He bucked the system and came to Brisbane and of course there was a helluva blow-up about that. Jesus. It was like the Third World War, that was, him coming to Brisbane.

"We had a real strong team. He elected to come to us. The club weren't paying the salaries. Super League were paying the salaries. They didn't have an alternative because he wanted to play in Brisbane."

During the period, Bennett says, "there was a huge amount of distractions. The players were being distracted. There were headlines every day. We spent a lot of time in Sydney (in 1996) at meetings holding it all together when it looked like it might fall apart with the court case and all that type of stuff.

"But I made sure the players weren't too distracted. I kept giving them the security and the sureties that they needed. I was talking to John Ribot and we were pretty focused. We kind of didn't miss a beat because I kept the players out of it as much as I possibly could.

"Chris Johns became our advocate. He was at the end of his career and so it didn't impact on him.

"I dealt with John Ribot because he was the CEO, right? We didn't know much about the peace deal mate. It just got dropped on us. I think we were all happy for it. None of us were disappointed. Me personally? Paul Morgan was in it up to his eyeballs. And the Broncos board. But we were just playing footy the best we could. We won the premiership and we won the World Club Challenge."

Have those achievements been cheapened by the romance of Newcastle's ARL victory? Before and after, Brisbane were the better side...

"Because we were all playing rugby league and they were trying to muddy the waters enormously, that we were the bad guys," Bennett says. "Because of Super League everyone got a pay rise - the ARL players and the Super League players. There were no losers there.

"No-one said we want to play a quicker game or anything like that. It was never on the agenda. But again, NSW and Phil Gould and a few guys down there … it was like 'we're playing the real game'. It was bullshit. It was absolute crap. The football was good, we played some great games and there was never an instruction that the game was to be quickened up. It was the same refs that had been reffing the ARL but they took that choice. They wanted to find fault with us and that was their agenda."

But as it turns out, Bennett does believe Newcastle saved the ARL, if not rugby league itself.

However, it happened 18 months before Darren Albert's try, he says.

On March 31 1995, the Broncos played their new crosstown rivals South Queensland at Brisbane's ANZ Stadium. The next night in Townsville, Canberra players signed en masse with Super League (Bevan Hannan still has the chips he used that night as props as he worked the floor at Breakwater Casino finding out what was happening upstairs)

"We probably lost it the day we lost Newcastle," Bennett says of why Super League was not a bigger success.

"When the strike was on, the pre-emptive strike about getting these clubs to sign up before the ARL could do anything about it, we were one of the first clubs to sign up. The Cowboys hung out for a few days and that didn't help.

"I said to John Ribot - I knew it was happening - 'if this gets out before the players know about it, mate I'm not going to support us on this'. I said 'I'll convince the players that it's not right... because we could all lose our jobs here'. I said 'if we ended up being isolated here, the ARL will say 'you get stuffed, the Broncos don't exist anymore'.

"We were supposed to sign on the Friday night and they were supposed to be at Newcastle on the weekend. They didn't have enough people. They had a few football people but they had too many lawyers and solicitors and accountants involved. They didn't have enough rugby league people talking to the clubs.

"Anyway we played on the Friday night and I remember saying to John 'I'm not saying anything to the players. I'm going to tell them until after the game. I'm not saying anything to these players until the Monday. There's a headline today in the Sydney papers because they couldn't keep their mouth shut that there's going to be a breakaway league' and there was. And we were at the forefront of it.

"They came and signed us on the Monday and by the time they got that done, they were about to go to Newcastle and Paul Harragon had put them on the bus. They'd gone to sign with the ARL.

"The bottom line is, that's when we lost it."

All of which suggests Newcastle didn't save the ARL. Wayne Bennett did.

CARROLL: ENJOYING THE FRUITS OF HIS SUCCESS

By Steve Mascord, Sydney Morning Herald, Saturday September 27, 1997

THERE'S an apocryphal story about the dressing-room scene at Manly before they play arch enemies Newcastle.

Bob Fulton is circling the room, talking to players one by one. With some he speaks harshly and directly. With others he is tactically technical or quietly consultative.

When he reaches the Sea Eagles' 110kg prop, Mark Carroll, Fulton says: "You're playing Chief today. He's 10 times the prep you are, he'll have you for breakfast."

"No he won't, Boze!" Carroll replies. "Yes he will Spud, he always gets the better of you". "No he doesn't, I'll show ya, Boze."

It's a conversation which has, perhaps, never taken place. But when told by those familiar with the culture at Brookvale, it's a fable with two morals.

One, Bob Fulton is without peer when it comes to what is known in rugby league as "geeing-up". And two, when it comes to falling hook, line and sinker for a gee-up, no-one bites like Mark Carroll.

"I'm one of the best biters here," Carroll said during a break in grand final training at Brookvale. "I've learnt how to control it, you know.

"They used to deadset throw lines out with no bait or nothing and I used to take it. But now, they can still rile me up."

When footballers are described as big kids, a lot of people think of it as a slight on their intelligence. It's not.

Even the smartest footballer is different from everyone else in the same way that teachers are: they have spent their lives in an institution that everyone else has grown out of.

As a result, social customs that die in the rest of us are preserved among them.

Having spent their lives in schools, some teachers have a tendency to talk down to others. Having sperit their lives in footy teams, your average 28-year-old player is still prone to wrestling, playing practical jokes and calling people names.

And there's that other thing kids do, that a lot of us leave behind at school or in the under-15s: habitually picking on people, zeroing in on weaknesses and imperfections, testing the resilience of one's character.

Nowhere is this schoolboy custom more lovingly preserved than at Manly.

"That's part of Manly, bagging or whatever," Carroll says. "People can't believe when we're out there as a side, we're as one."

The old saying "it's a tough school" could have been made for coach Bob Fulton's extremely tight little shop at Brookvale.

Perhaps that's why Fulton is so successful: thin skins are quickly removed and hung out to tan. And of course, Manly players need thick skins anyway, just to deal with the outside world.

"You get used to the bagging everybody gives you," says Carroll, who signed from South Sydney in 1994. "If people don't like you, they heckle you.

"You hear the boos. I love boos more than cheers now, so they can boo as much as they want.

"It's just the Manly thing. I love being part of it"

But no-one is more out of step with the Sea Eagles' insidious image than Carroll. A straight-forward, affable big man who clearly loves football, there's nothing hidden or contrived about him.

When picked in a representative team, Carroll regales reporters about how excited he is to get the tracksuits, blazers, jerseys, shorts and socks.

"Some blokes give them away," he often says, "but not me. I'm going to keep it all. I love that stuff."

In many ways, it seems ordained that Carroll and Harragon should collide in big games and take turns in knocking each other out.

They each have wives and families now but you suspect little has changed in their characters since they were running around during their lunch hours, skinning their knees as they charged through walls of hapless classmates in scratch games of footy. Sure, they're living what many of their contemporaries would regard as dream existences, but they know it, and they are grateful for it.

Carroll was knocked out two weeks ago when the Sea Eagles played Newcastle, the victim of an untimely collision with Harragon's knee.

A couple of years ago, when the roles were reversed and a full-bodied tackle was the cause, Carroll stood over Harragon at Marathon Stadium, in his words "as if he was my prey".

After this month's game, Carroll sought out his NSW and Australian teammate.

"I saw him after the game and I waved to him and said see you in two weeks. And that's the way it's turned out," Carroll says.

If only life was like that for everyone. You knocked me out, I couldn't stand up, look forward to playing against you again, mate.

The most refreshing thing about meeting people like "Spud" and "the Chief" is that it takes only five minutes of conversation for it to be apparent that their childhood enthusiasm hasn't been extinguished by years on the nine-to-five treadmill.

It still burns, you can see it in their eyes.

"In 1995 before the grand final against Canterbury, I was ecstatic to make a grand final because that's what I came to Manly for, to win a grand final," Carroll says.

"I got too excited too quick and by the time the game came around I was stuffed.

"It's a mental thing. You start the batteries going early, it's pretty hard to stop them." Carroll was kept awake then by his new son, Joshua, but now, he says, he's got a "routine" in order at home.

"I just bought this massive TV, 135cm TV, and I bought a Playstation with it," he says. "I'm playing *Rage Racer* and all these sorts of games.

"And I'm just like a big kid."

CHAPTER 20

Meanwhile, in England...

IT was at the Sydney Football Stadium on Sunday, February 5 1995, that Gary Hetherington first heard about the possibility of a European Super League - the one that survives to this day.

Hetherington, now the Leeds CEO and one of the most powerful men in the British game over the last two decades, was manager of a Great Britain team that was dumped out of the World Sevens a day earlier with a loss to St George after a win against Penrith.

"I went along on the Sunday; that was the day when the Packer organisation were at one end of the ground and Murdoch group was at the other," Hetherington says now.

"Before I flew home, Maurice Lindsay, he said to me - there was plenty going on, there was speculation about Super League and such - 'I'll give you something to think about on the plane back'.

"He says 'confidentially, what would we do with £50 million in the game?'

"Of course, it transpired that we ended up getting £87 million."

It was a helluva way to earn the extra £37 million, the British game's past in some of the country's most impoverished regions forming a tectonic plate against Murdoch's global ambitions.

"The first plan was to have 10 Super League sides which meant people like Wakefield and Castleford would merge," decorated Australian referee Greg McCallum, the RFL's head of match officials at the time, explains.

"Hull and Hull KR would merge. There was a riot. People just wouldn't wear it. It also meant the death knell of the Second Division clubs.

"For the game to agree to sign with News Limited, those 22 clubs had to be accommodated as well.

"That's where it raised from £50 million to £87 million if you believe the stories. Maurice went back to Rupert and said 'they won't cop £50 million but they'll take £87 million'.

"The £37 million basically paid off the 22 clubs who weren't part of Super League. That's what happened."

Historian Tony Collins says there was another stage between the two offers.

"At the meeting when the first offer from Sky was made, £77 million … the clubs lower down the leagues just basically wanted to accept it straight away.

"It was Maurice who said 'hang on: first law of negotiations - never accept the first offer.'"

Chris Caisley, a former Super League chairman, recalls: "There were stories I heard about the directors of clubs outside Super League using the money to get off for a week in Barbados. I'm sure that happened.

"I remember one time we were off to play Paris and we ran into the directors of one club. We said 'where are you going?' They said 'we're off to Spain'. They said 'where are you going?' 'Oh, we're going to play a game of rugby league in Paris'."

The Centenary 1995-96 British season that followed looked as bizarre as the Covid-interrupted 2020 campaign. It started in August, was halted so England and Wales could host a World Cup, and resumed in time to finish in January ... so the first summer Super League season could kick-off just two months later, in late March.

The switch to summer was posited as the most revolutionary aspect of Murdoch's investment in the Northern Hemisphere game. But Neil Tunnicliffe, who would later become CEO of the RFL, says this was merely spin.

"...the switch to summer actually got ridden through on the basis of the Murdoch money (and) I think there was a bit of ... a slight untruth peddled, which was that a switch to summer was a condition of Murdoch's funding of the game," Tunnicliffe says.

"...which I don't think it ever was but it was used as a mechanism to fulfil the agendas of those who actually wanted the game to switch to summer because they thought it would be easier to market.

"A lot of the thinking behind the switching to the summer season was that an alignment with the Southern Hemisphere game would make it easier to play something like a World Club Challenge and Test series ... and to align the broadcast and marketing and sponsorship deals ... so there was this sense of this global game."

The real reasons for the switch to summer, according to Tunnicliffe?

"There was an awareness at the time that the product wasn't great. Certainly the facilities in which the product was delivered were substandard. The marketing of the game was poor. There were all manner of solutions being sought to this. There was a research project done to work out exactly how much it would cost to renovate, upgrade the stadium facilities in the premiership at the time, which came to tens of millions of pounds - which the game just didn't have.

"There was a debate beginning as to whether (instead of) just trying to find that money to renovate the stadia, it would be easier just to flip the game to a summer season so that you were watching the game in rubbish facilities but in warmer weather ... to make it a little more tolerable."

Caisley recalls: "I was running a small committee that was formed somewhat earlier to look into summer rugby, to transfer the season from winter to summer. Gary Hetherington was involved in that with me.

"The report was published, it went to the rugby league board and it was just gathering dust until such time as the News Corp interest came about. That, then, brought that report into the spotlight and we moved the season."

There are now some great new facilities in Super League, such as the MKM, DW and Halliwell Jones stadia. But there are still arenas such as Mend-a-Hose Jungle and Belle Vue for which "dilapidated" would be a compliment.

McCallum confirms Tunnicliffe's recollections, saying: "The day that the Super League offer was announced, we were actually meeting at Headingley to discuss the change to summer!

"So it was actually on the table. Then of course the famous phone call came that Maurice took in one of the side rooms. He shuffled over, took the call, shuffled back and said 'oh, I've got some good news'.

"It was sold as a wonderful surprise. That's how it was sold."

Obviously Hetherington's recollections at the start of this chapter contradict that. "I never bought that it was a surprise," says McCallum. "Neither did Ken Arthurson and John Quayle.

"The change to summer got pushed through on the back of Super League at a time when it probably would have taken time to convince everybody. The amateur game wanted no bar of going to summer.

"Looking back on it, the significant changes at Red Hall at the time were getting ready for something to happen. If you look back, someone had prior knowledge of what was happening."

'Super League II' was the official moniker for the elite competition in 1997 but the championship was still awarded to the team that finished the regular season first - it was the last year before the introduction of a grand final, which ended 100 years of tradition in that area - and which still has its critics all these summers later. Bradford Bulls were the champions but Wigan took out the end-of-season premiership, beating St Helens 32-20 in front of 33,389 at Old Trafford on September 28.

London and Paris, bolted on for Super League's 1996 debut, remained. PSG finished 11th, the Broncos a creditable second.

The team representing the capital had so many Australians, player Josh White recalls, "we trained in Yeppoon, in north Queensland for 10 weeks before we went over. It was like having a week away at the start of the year! We trained hard and we partied hard."

"From what I can remember, the standard of football was dreadful," says Collins. "It took teams a long time to adjust to playing in the summer."

All 12 Super League teams took part in the Premiership, giving rise to the unusual situation of Castleford narrowly avoiding relegation and almost playing in the final within a matter of weeks. The coach of the Tigers was Stuart Raper, son of Australian Immortal and ARL hard-liner John.

At the end of '96, Stuart recalls, "I was coaching reserve grade under John Lang (at Cronulla) and assistant first grade coach.

"(Brother) Aaron decided to join Parramatta and the ARL. Dad was very keen for me to join the ARL and I nearly went to North Sydney and joined Peter Louis as his assistant coach. A few family dinners throughout '96, there wasn't a lot of footy talk going on because Aaron had decided to go to Parramatta and I'd decided to go to Cronulla.

"In April I got the call to go to Castleford. I think it was Greg McCallum who was over there as refs boss who recommended me to the club and they did some research."

The Wheldon Road side had sacked club great John Joyner (only a few months earlier sounded out to replace Peter Mulholland). The ambition for the season was simple: avoid relegation.

"I couldn't get a visa. I mentioned to Richard Wright over there 'my mum's Welsh' and he said 'you can get what they call Right Of Abode'. I said 'righto' and I hung up the phone and thought 'how am I going to get this'. Dad said 'what's up?' I said 'I need this Right Of Abode and it takes about six weeks to get'.

"He said 'hang on a minute, I'll make a phone call' and he just gets on the phone and talks to this girl, Wendy I think her name was, and he says 'can I speak to John please?'. Dad says 'hello mate' and tells him the whole story. 'He's got to go there? Right.' He hangs up and says 'you've got to go down to Canberra tomorrow, go to the consulate' or something, 'see this bloke and he'll get you the visa'. I said 'who you talking to'?.

"It was John Howard. John Howard was the prime minister at the time and he was talking to him like it was one of his mates, just some bloke he knew! He gave him a number, I went down and got the visa and I was on the plane five days later!"

On the flight - of course Raper senior got him an upgrade too - Stuart wrote out his coaching philosophies for the first time. "People were desperate, they were desperate to win. Castleford was one of the only sides that had never been relegated. I didn't realise how bad the place was and (if I did) I probably wouldn't have gone.

"I got there and we lost a couple games. My first game was St Helens and we played at Anfield and got flogged. I made some big changes. I started sacking some off-field staff. There were just people there who weren't right for the place and had to move on. I remember getting called into the board and they asked me to stop sacking people because they were coming back to them and trying to get payments.

"We won a game, we beat Sheffield at home and people were crying, people were hugging me and it was like we'd won the Challenge Cup. The day we avoided relegation was the day that Lady Di died. They didn't play any soccer but they did play rugby league. My assistant coach was Shane Flanagan. It pissed down raining. He piggybacked me out on the field to hug the players because we avoided relegation. We had a party out on the field and it was hilarious."

After a trip home to Australia for the World Club Challenge (see previous chapter), it came time to play the Premiership. For

Australian readers, it's important to understand the big title was the Championship, which was first-past-the-post, and the Premiership was a post-season league. "We came seventh and we had to play Bradford at Bradford. Adrian Vowles' wife was pregnant and if we lose, they're on the plane the next day going home. If we win, they have to stay and have the babies in England. We didn't think we were going to win. We went to Bradford, who had just been crowned the champions, and we ended up beating Bradford so Vowlesy and his missus had to stay and have twins over there."

Elsewhere, in the British game that year Ian Blease - now the CEO at Salford - was banned for life for hitting touch judge Nigel Dickenson in a reserve team game between Salford and Bradford on May 29. However, the life ban was later lifted and expired on March 31 1998.

Wigan and St Helens were each fined £15,000 for a brawl in February which started with a high tackle by Bobbie Goulding on Neil Cowie. In June, Keighley Cougars complained to the RFL about monies they claimed were owed them being withheld. Keighley were a boom team but unwanted in Super League because it was a small town. The High Court upheld the Cougars' injunction against the RFL in December. In July, the RFL faced investigations into the misuse of foundation money.

Joe Lydon and Tunnicliffe returned, meanwhile, from their overseas fact-finding mission requesting a reduction in the overseas player quota. They got their way - three for Super League clubs and two for the other two divisions.

Over the course of a couple of weeks in July and August, the sport lost superstar winger Martin Offiah and then marketing whiz Peter

Deakin to rugby union. Also in August, Goulding was sacked as St Helens captain for disciplinary reasons.

In September there were reports of a new winter league backed by the ARL. November saw the opening of the Halton Stadium on the site of Naughton Park in Widnes. Rugby League (Europe) became Super League (Europe) in November.

"Ian Frykberg…," Hetherington says, rolling the name on his tongue the way you do a word you've not uttered for some time.

"I remember a small delegation - me, Maurice Lindsay, Rodney Walker and Chris Caisley - all travelled to the Lake District to see him. He was in a hotel retreat.

"…to basically talk through the plan and the progress."

On September 3, the salary cap - still in force and still criticised today - was introduced to the British game and set at 50 percent of income, not including transfer fees. On October 16, the RFL and British Amateur Rugby League Association called a truce when a joint policy board was formed, a peace that endures.

Virgin entrepreneur Richard Branson bought a share of London Broncos at the end of the '97 season too, acquiring 55 per cent from previous owner Barry Maranta. Branson had earlier taken a 15 per cent share - in February 1997. He memorably took them to Wembley in 1999 (I flew over for the weekend). Branson departed in 2001.

But the largesse of the Murdoch money was over.

At the end of 1997, three professional clubs folded: Paris Saint-Germain, Carlisle Border Raiders and Prescott Panthers. The Panthers had been around in some form since 1880. Oldham Bears were liquidated but replaced by another Oldham club. Hull KR also went into administration.

Clubs going broke, being bailed out by fans, and then going broke again remains an abiding tradition of British rugby league. Warmer weather has not proven to be a cure for this particular malady.

And as the British game reeled from an Australasian-mandated World Cup postponement in late 2021, it was again grappling with the idea of profound and get-wrenching change to avoid an otherwise inevitable slide into part-timism. Increasingly, there is a believe that tougher decisions should have been taken a generation ago.

McCallum says a hallmark of Super League's introduction to England was "no consideration given to planning for the future in terms of investing money" because "we had clubs who were weekly attendees at Inland Revenue to try and keep their doors open..

"It's very difficult when a significant amount of money comes into a business that's got debt. The first thing you've got to do is fix your debt up. People don't want to do that, they want to spend on, as if there's no debt. So it (money) erodes at double the rate.

"The game (in England) went from having this unfounded confidence from the fact that all of a sudden someone wants to pay us a lot of money to the reality of it kicking in.

"I think it was a period of time in the game when people were second guessing themselves all the time."

Hetherington concludes: "We as a game made a complete mess of it in terms of managing the money that we got.

"We went from a million quid a year to 17 million. In terms of creating the Super League, we had a 16-team competition and we had to get it down to 10. It had to include London and Paris.

"That's when all the talk of mergers started to surface. It ended when the Rugby League Council decided on just the top 10 from the previous year and gave a load of money to clubs who formed the Championship.

"So a load of money was squandered in England. We had no idea how to move to full-time. We didn't manage it well. With the benefit of hindsight, we were confronted with something we'd never come across before.

"Maurice Lindsay wanted to do the right thing for the game. He was a bit of an autocrat, were Maurice. But as a game we were ill-prepared for it. There was only one fulltime team, remember, which was Wigan. There were teams in the Super League in that year one … we got Halifax, we got Workington and Oldham and teams who just weren't…

"You had bigger teams. You had Bradford. You had Leeds at that time, they were hardly progressive, they were nearly bankrupt. Wigan were on the verge of going bankrupt.

"We didn't have the infrastructure to cope with such an influx of money.

"There were some good things that happened quickly. We got the play-off system up and running and the grand final and so-on.

"The crowds increased and over the next 10 years we built better stadia and bigger clubs came into the competition but I'd say, fundamentally, we weren't geared up to be able to manage the transition either as a game or as individual clubs.

"It was a struggle. It probably took us four or five years to be able to get to grips with it."

Almost no-one in the British game argues that Super League was a bad thing. "There was no other option, really," Collins points out. "There was no other deal on the table. Murdoch was the only game in town." But almost everyone in 2021 believes it was nowhere near as good as it could - or should - have been.

Collins adds: "There's a bit of a mythology that's grown up that if Super League hadn't happened then the game would have gone bankrupt and it would have died.

"But 'the game is dying' is a trope that's been around for as long as the sport's existed.

"It was going through an overspending crisis, basically, which was brought on by Wigan going full-time professional and buying all the best players from the mid-eighties.

"Then, of course, Wigan ran out of money because they were living beyond their means and so Maurice became poacher-turned-gamekeeper and decided that the game had to cut its suit according to its cloth.

"Rugby league had to change because the world was changing. It couldn't have stayed the same. The idea that we could have gone on as we were and played in winter and things would have been better or the idea that things would have collapsed if we hadn't switched - they're kind of meaningless speculation.

"This was just the latest cycle in the development of professional sport around the world."

But rugby league still had responsibility for how it spent the windfall - and few argue it chose wisely.

"The smart thing to have done," says Collins, "would have been to say 'the RFL has got £87 million. If you want to play in the Super League next summer, here are the criteria for applying'.

"The entire structure of the game could have been revolutionised if the governing body had have used the money to set down clear professional criteria. Call it franchising, call it what you will.

"As far as Britain's concerned, that's the missed opportunity. It should have been used to clear out the dead wood, bring in a new way of thinking, new structure.

"The money was just used to perpetuate what already existed."

So the good? "The move to summer has been a good thing," says Collins. "I don't think anyone can deny that there's nothing better on a warm sunny evening to be standing on the terraces watching rugby league. That's how it should be watched.

"Attendances have actually gone up. Until we got to the 2008 financial crash, for the first time in over 40 years the average top division attendance was more than 10,000 which would have been a good target.

"Even though they've dropped back down now, they're still at a higher level than they have been since the 1960s - so that's a success."

And the bad…"What's happened with Super League is it's brought back a lot of the bad tendencies that rugby league suffered from before the 1970s.

"In those days the game was governed by the RFL council and every club had a vote and so nothing ever happened. They never got a two division structure until '73, '74.

"That whole structure of everyone getting a vote was thrown out - but now the current structure of Super League means we've got exactly the same problem.

"Clubs vote purely for their own self-interest."

Expat Australian coach and administrator Steve Simms points out: "There was so much allocated for you to buy your players, there was so much for your ground improvements and so much on youth development. Well none of that happened. When they were given the money, they just spent it all on players."

Nigel Wood insists: "In 1996 at the beginning of it all, there were great success stories - Bradford being the biggest one.

"Bradford and St Helens were trailblazers at the beginning. The Broncos had made advancements in 1996 and 1997. They were strong.

"Wigan and Leeds recovered from their traumas at the creation of Super League to become heavyweights. If you remember, Hull - who are one the biggest clubs - were not even in the original competition.

'… the emergence and consolidation of Warrington, the inclusion of Catalans … the game has got more big, strong clubs than it had in 1996 but it's troubled by what critics would call having quite a long tail.

"And I think some of the events of the last two years, or three years in particular, haven't served the game well - but that's just a personal perspective."

Simms is less diplomatic. "The officials, they don't know what they're doing here, realistically.

"Just take this year at Leigh. They haven't played for 12 months. They need a new team in Super League so they pick someone. They pick Leigh. Then they expect them to compete and give them half the money everyone else is getting. What sort of administration thinks they can be successful?"

Chris Caisley adds: "I was chairman of Super League for a few years and I only intended to do it for a year.

"I think there were some successes. I think the grand final and the play-off competition, which didn't exactly replicate what was happening in Australia but was very similar, I think that was a good success, a great success.

"The one thing we alway struggled with was getting people to sing off the same hymn sheet in terms of getting some consistency of approach to things that would drag the spectators in.

"Gary at Leeds did it. Wigan and St Helens did it and then there was underneath all that. We had problems in London. There was this perception you had to have a club in London because that was the only way to get people involved in the City, big companies.

"London tried various things …. Moving grounds, got Richard Branson involved … London never really took off despite whatever we tried to do.

"So we always had problems with expansion. Paris went after two seasons which, again, was disappointing. If Paris had taken off that would have been a tremendous shot in the arm for the game over here."

Any new blood that the switch to summer and the infusion of funds gave to the British game has long since fallen victim to the vampire of reality. What is left is little more than a husk, one which Sky in 2021 saw fit to give only just over half the sum of TV rights fee it had previously paid for the sport.

For all the progress marked by rising attendances, a couple more big clubs and new events like the grand final and Magic Weekend, the British game is once again desperately looking for a saviour.

As this book went to press, private equity investment and abbreviated versions of rugby league were being widely touted as panaceas.

And - perhaps partially as a result of a very short-lived 2021 soccer uprising that went by the same name - the Super League brand itself may soon finally be laid to rest.

KNIGHTS PACT TO WIN FOR FANS MAKES HISTORY

By Steve Mascord, *Sydney Morning Herald*,
Monday September 29, 1997

NEWCASTLE 22 MANLY 16 at Sydney Football Stadium

NEWCASTLE winger Darren Albert sealed arguably the greatest grand final of all time with six seconds to go yesterday - but his teammates claimed victory had been assured 24 hours earlier.

Albert sent an entire city into delirium when he backed up a risky blind-side dash by injured halfback Andrew Johns to touch down before a 42,482 Sydney-Football Stadium crowd dominated by the Knights' faithful.

The try sparked the most emotional scenes at a rugby league game in recent memory, as players dedicated their triumph to their tragedy-affected home town.

Afterwards, players spoke of a pact made after thousands of people lined the streets of Newcastle to farewell them on Saturday.

"It was lined with people for 20 kilometres and three or four blokes who had been there for 10 years, since the club started the Chief, myself and Mark Glanville we were in tears," veteran prop Tony Butterfield said.

"There were kids, women, men, young and old. They weren't just cheering us on, there was just a passion you could see on their faces.

"We knew we had to do it."

Ebullient fullback Robbie O'Davis, who scored two tries to clinch the Clive Churchill Medal, admitted: "At the beginning of the week, we were just content that we made the grand final.

"The Newcastle people, they changed us. They made us believe in ourselves, they treated us like champions."

Words like "emotion" and "passion" were thrown around like blue and red confetti as Knights captain Paul "Chief" Harragon lifted the Optus Cup 200 years after his city was founded, 10 years after it rejoined the game's top flight, and just months after it lost thousands of jobs in its steel mills.

But those words seem inadequate to describe the scene in the middle of the Football Stadium at full-time, as footballers embraced and spoke of having their lives fulfilled in just 80 minutes.

Better, then, to let the gripping final eight minutes speak for themselves.

72 minutes: Manly are leading 16-10 and look set to win.. Every time Newcastle take the ball out of their half, they drop it.

73 minutes: Manly five-eighth Cliff Lyons misses with a field goal attempt 74 minutes: O'Davis slides between defenders, performs a double pirouette, and plants the ball at the base of the goalpost pad for what referee David Manson rules, after careful consideration, to be a try. Andrew Johns converts from in front for 16-16. Extra-time looms.

77 minutes: Five-eighth Matthew Johns's forlorn field goal attempt

from 40 metres out falls into Manly hands. 78 minutes: Another Matthew Johns field goal attempt fails, this time bouncing agonisingly off the right upright before being fielded by Lyons.

79 minutes: An Andrew Johns shot is charged down and the Knights retain possession. With 17 seconds remaining, the ball is played to Johns, who darts down the blind-side, draws the defence and passes inside for a flying Albert to flash over near the posts with six seconds left.

The siren sounds, players pile on top of Albert and Newcastle have won their first premiership.

Andrew Johns converts. Newcastle 22, Manly 16.

"I think it's only a game, you might as well have a go," said Johns, who played despite puncturing a lung a week before.

"I could have been a goose, I might have been the villain of the city."

For most of the match, the grand final looked as if it would go the same way as the previous 11 between the arch-enemies:

385

Newcastle starting with fire and brimstone, Manly winning.

The collisions in the first 15 minutes were brutal, but in customary fashion Manly eventually found space out wide.

Sea Eagles winger John Hopoate taunted O'Davis after crossing for a converted try in the 10th minute.

And Kiwi centre Craig Innes finished off a dazzling blind-side manoeuvre, in which Lyons handled twice, to make it 10-0 after 25.

Andrew Johns pegged the scores back to 10-2 with a penalty goal in the 29th minute. Then O'Davis, helped by a dummy, shimmied past Geoff Toovey and Terry Hill for a converted try which made it 10-8.

But O'Davis had scarcely finished performing his victory dance in goal when Harragon spilt the ball

in his own quarter up the other end and Manly fullback Shannon Nevin scored a try and goal for the Sea Eagles to appear firmly in control at 16-8 at the break. The margin was narrowed to 16-10 through a 58th-minute penalty goal to Andrew Johns - then came the finish that will be written into the game's history.

"They made pledges to themselves they weren't going to come back without the Optus Cup," Newcastle coach Mai Reilly said.

"Goodness knows, they left it a bit late."

CHAPTER 21

Neil Whittaker

JUST as some people have a voice that leads them almost inevitably to hosting radio, others have a characteristic that makes them good electronic media guests.

It's a pause for thought that, paradoxically, happens without thinking. Neil Whittaker always had it. Because we were used to him stopping in the middle of sentences, regardless of whether he was talking about the result of a match or the very future of the sport, we weren't really conscious of it.

During my visit to Maurice Lindsay, he remarked on Arthurson: "Ken would always put his tongue up against the inside of his mouth when he had something important to say". Whittaker would always pause, sometimes starting a word and sucking it back in.

But it never signified indecision. Just carefulness.

Neil Whittaker along with the late Ian Frykberg basically invented the NRL, the most powerful club rugby competition of either code on the planet. Yet the NRL does not espouse its own origin story and nor do its fans, prepared to gloss over conception, pregnancy and the way it came kicking and screaming into the world at Moore Park in December 1997.

The reason for this reticence can be summed up in one word: Souths. The NRL's birth is permanently stained because it was the result of an agreement many perceive as unholy: that the number of teams would be forcibly reduced.

And in 2000 and 2001, South Sydney were excluded.

Whittaker oversaw this whittling of teams from 22 down to the current 16 and then - as if it was part of a Machiavellian plan to obscure his role in the eyes of the competition's history, like a deadbeat dad being written out of someone's childhood (or, with a bloodied Reggie Rabbit on the sidewalk, an assassin in a getaway car) - he disappeared in a puff of smoke.

"So, that's exactly right," he says when I use that exact expression, "puff of smoke" during our interview. We are in an office building in downtown Sydney with sprawling city views. The sun streams in, obscured by towers of concrete and steel.

"But there were reasons for it. It's really simple….

"I played the game from when I was five. I loved the game. I was chairman of Balmain when we said 'no' to going to Super League because I didn't think it was right and we were probably one of the most broke clubs.

"But the board unanimously agreed we stay.

"I'd never wanted to be a sports administrator and I never wanted the job but when a number of people including George (Piggins) and Quayley and others approached me and said 'one of us has got to take it', I took the job.

"At the end of 1997, when the deal was becoming obvious, I offered to both sides that I'd resign. When the deal was signed, I thought the appropriate thing for me to do was to resign as well and get away from it to allow processes to roll on without people worrying about whose side I was on.

"There was a lot being written by some of your colleagues about me and News Limited which was very unfair and completely wrong. It was in a Sunday paper that I'd been paid a million dollars! Something ridiculous.

"Everyone was looking for what my agenda was and I didn't have an agenda and no-one could accept that. In rugby league, you've got to have an agenda and I didn't have one.

"Because I was a Tiger, that's fine when I was chairman of the Tigers. But if I take on the job to run rugby league, then that's my job. No-one could accept that either."

There's no pausing now, none of that trademark caution...

"So anyway, I then went into '98 and '99 and I became very disillusioned with people, generally, and it was clear they wanted me to stay on and be the fall guy in all this. I decided: best thing for me to do is to do a really professional job, do it well, have it so that smart people could understand what we were doing and why we're doing it and the outcomes that were going to happen.

"...and then, in August of '99, I told them I was resigning but I would stay on until after the announcement of the criteria for the restructure of the comp, to give everyone the ability to blame somebody, and then I would leave.

"The last thing those guys, the following people, needed was old former blokes sticking their nose in. So I've stayed right out of it. I didn't disappear off the face of the earth. I didn't want the publicity and I didn't need it. And afterwards, I've certainly avoided it.

"And this interview is the only interview I've ever done since then."

This is a passionate monologue that I felt needed reporting without interruption.

But we're beginning at the end of a poignant personal story at the heart of *Two Tribes*, a story of service and sacrifice.

We previously touched on the end of the beginning; his appointment, Whittaker's approach to the role, the fact peace talks began almost as he walked through the front door. "I'm sure News Limited thought they would get a result a lot cheaper and a lot quicker and Arko and Quayley did an unbelievable job," he says.

"There's no way I would have been able to do what they did. Them having fought that fight, it was probably right they didn't try to be part of putting it back together again. News Limited were smart enough to throw Ian Frykberg in so that we could start afresh."

As mentioned previously, I remember clearly being one of only a handful of journalists invited to Phillip Street in September 1997 to see a blueprint for what was then called the National Rugby League Championship. Whittaker had us all around a table and handed out a photocopied presentation, a copy of which I was unable to locate in the summer of 2019-20. Around the same time, according to Paul Broughton's book, Whittaker had got up in front of the ARL clubs and said "I have met the enemy and it is us".

That visit to Phillip Street seemed historic to me at the time, as the moment the "National Rugby League Championship" was conjured up. As it transpires, I was deluded. Whittaker and Frykberg had been talking for months. When News pulled out of talks because, it seems, the ARL board had come back with some hard questions, those still interested in Australian rugby league gasped. For Whittaker, it was merely a blip.

"It happened, and they pulled out, and I remember what we did afterwards.

"We wrote …. I think we got all our clubs to sign an agreement to stay. They were chipping away at the clubs to get them to jump and we got our 12 clubs to all sign.

"So we just then went back to running the comp because you can only watch Brisbane on Friday night so many times."

Frykberg died in 2014, aged 68. His loyal executive assistant Lisa Masters had a front row seat in the creation of the NRL but remembers him as such a private man he may as well have been planning a moon landing or plotting to overthrow the government.

A former girlfriend of Penrith's Greg Alexander, she got the job after a referral from John Ribot's assistant by answering in the affirmative just two questions from Frykberg: "are you organised?" and "do you have shorthand?"

"He was a man of few words and he taught me everything I know," Masters - who now works for former News Limited CEO John Hartigan - says. "He was like a second father to me.

"When I went for the interview, he was so intimidating but I cracked him. I was still working for him 11 years later. I start and his desk is just covered with documents. He says 'I'm going out. Can you just sort this out?'

"He was head of sport for News. So anything that News owned, he was in charge of. I'd never heard of SANZAR and stuff like that because I grew up with rugby league.

"He comes back and I go 'who are you? What do you do?' He did this really rough chart and said 'I'm in charge of all of those'.

"I remember going 'oh my God, what have I got myself into?'

"I've got Mr Packer on line one and I've got Mr Murdoch on line two. Oh my God, who do I put through first?' and I ran into his office. He says 'tell James I'll ring him back and put Lachlan through.'"

Paul Kind - who also worked under John Quayle - says of Frykberg: "Honestly, I think he was a reluctant leader. He wasn't accustomed to sports admin. He was one of the great deal-doers in broadcast, legendary in his ability to cut broadcast deals and from a News Corp view he was the guy that they absolutely trusted to get deals done.

"So not surprising, I think, is that one of the most important things he did in all that time was cut the peace deal and he was the exact right person to do that.

"He said very little. I think if he said a lot, you were probably in some trouble rather than doing well.

"He was there because they asked him to be there, I think. Not necessarily because he was the best sports administrator running around."

John Lang observes: "That's why he went so high in business. He listened, he thought about it and he made a decision and moved on. When I said the News Limited blokes weren't smarter than us … he was."

Trevor McEwan says "Frykberg is the unsung hero because he's the one who picked up very early that this is not going to work, these two comps. A lot of us didn't know how much work he was diligently doing in the background to sort things out. He kept it from a lot of us.

"He just gave nothing away. I think it was one of his absolute attributes. You just couldn't read him. You just didn't know what was going on. He used that to good effect when it helped him. My suspicion is it was Rupert or Ken Cowley but someone told him 'this has to end, everything has to end, your job is to go and sort it out'.

"I got the impression that he did that pretty much autonomously.

"I think he could tell that people reacted emotionally to whether there were compromises … Frykers worked that out pretty quickly. I don't know Neil. I don't know too much about him. It might be that he had similar qualities and they might have been the right two guys to get around the table but I recall a lot of us thinking and talking amongst ourselves, saying 'what's Frykers up to, what's going on, he's out of the office a lot, he's not saying too much' That's when he was getting all that done. And God bless him for doing it because it had to be done."

ARL chairman John McDonald, feeling left out of peace talks because he was from Queensland and NSWRL identities were driving those talks? He went to have his own meeting with Frykberg. "That was just another day, when it became obvious that that was what was happening," said Whittaker. "It came out in a board meeting at the Australian Rugby League. It was just another issue to be managed."

But some things were bigger than blips. Some things perturbed or even consumed Whittaker. When Optus provided funding after the

October 4 court defeat, it was for one year. The ARL never really admitted publicly that was the case, preferring to let the public think the telecommunications company had committed long-term.

"So I've never revealed what the actual situation was and I probably won't now," says Whittaker - before pretty much saying what the situation was.

"I can tell you when we got to the middle of the year - I think it was a bit later - when (Optus CEO) Peter Howell-Davies announced they were going to continue the funding - was a good day."

And how did Whittaker convince Optus to continue that support?

"So, it was difficult. It was unbelievably difficult.

"We kept playing well. The emotion around the game … it all came down to how well our comp was going and the emotion at the grounds. I took some Optus executives out to the games so they saw how we were going. They could see how the game was travelling, the comp. At the end of the day, they all needed content and we had content.

"We'd backed ourselves on clubs and the ability to run the sport. We had better rules and we had a game that people could recognise."

Would the ARL have folded had Optus not stumped up beyond 1997?

"Rugby league had existed like that for years - 'what would happen if it didn't happen?' It had always happened.

"Look, it was a disaster. But it was a disaster at the beginning of the year. I always liken it to … we were playing bluff poker with Packer and Murdoch with a pair of twos. No money and a pair of twos.

"It wasn't really like that but it was tough because we had no money and sponsors were jumping out, using it as an opportunity to go and clubs were anxious and everybody was anxious. The funding was very, very important from every angle.

"But again, as you say, no-one said that Optus weren't going to fund us!

"Nah. I was confident. I was confident that we had enough if we could run the comp, in our bag of assets, that we would be important to an outcome. And as the comp went on, it became more and more obvious that a negotiated settlement, a fair negotiated settlement, was becoming more and more possible.

"I was getting good advice from the television people, and by television people I mean content people via Optus and Nine and American cable places .... that the only thing I should focus on was content.

"OK? So that's all I did. I just focused on the content so when they (News) said they weren't negotiating, I think … we just said 'fine'. We were coming up to the finals series and our ratings would get better through the finals series. We were going really, really well. We let them have that grand final so we didn't clash and we played our grand final a week later and it was a screamer."

Thanks to Joey Johns, punctured lung and all, Whittaker had played Blind Man's Bluff with a billionaire and won. As previously recounted, after the grand final he went on TV and invited the Super League teams to join his competition in 1998.

In six months, the peace process had gone from in camera to on camera. Whittaker had decided on the stunt a couple of weeks before. But he could not have dreamed of such an iconic moment.

"It's a funny thing," he says, shaking his head just a little. "It was hard for people like Arko and the Manly guys because they got beaten. Newcastle won their first comp ever. It's just such a shame that there had to be one side lose and one side win. It was just the game we needed, the finish we needed.

"And it was, I think, a good reward for us staying focused, what we were meant to do. Because the opportunity to be distracted was unbelievable."

It was a triumph, an achievement worthy of eternal veneration for any sports administrator, nevermind an old hooker who never wanted to be one in the first place.

But the expulsion of South Sydney from the NRL in the 2000 and 2001 seasons seems to be something Neil Whittaker believes erased his place in the game's pantheon. Perhaps his old club merging on his watch hurt too. Like John Quayle, Whittaker seems to me embittered and - as a result - distant from the sport to which he devoted a lifetime.

"The whole process we went through over that two year period was debilitating," he confesses, in reference to 1998 and 1999.

"Once we went through the 30th of June, 1999, it was unstoppable. I thought, and from what I'd seen and from what Frykers' view was as well, that there was enough activity around for us to get down to the number we needed without ever getting to a September 1999 announcement.

"But it just so happened that as confidence grew that with cutting the clubs, the comp was going to thrive, everybody started not wanting to merge.

"It got harder and harder and probably my greatest regret would have been to not push harder for a different …. I was just so pleased to get everybody playing again in 1998 and give everyone two years to get themselves organised and let them see that News Limited weren't going to steal the game, that they wanted it to be a successful comp and that it settled down.

"I thought it would sort itself out over the two years, that there'd just be a natural .. that there was that much activity going on that we'd get there without having to …. We got down to 17, unfortunately."

The careful pauses, the grasping for the right words, are back. I ask Whittaker if you still need an agenda in rugby league. "I don't know, I've got no idea. I mean, I've been away a long time.

"All I know is that it's gone from … you look at what we put together, Frykers and I, the view that we came to and how we could get it going, and how it could be structured and how it could ultimately be restructured, it's all happened. We've got strong competitions, a great game. I don't know how many multiples of income (it is now) over what we got when we first started. "

But still as we bid goodbye I am left with the overwhelming impression that South Sydney haunts Neil Whittaker. Those trademark pauses are put to good use in avoiding actually saying the name of the club and what happened to it: "Souths", "kicked out".

I don't recall him uttering the name of the Rabbits in the room a single time.

"Um, yeah … the lowlights for me all came afterwards, honestly. In 1997, it was easy. We were in a war and we knew who the enemy was. In 1998 and 1999, we weren't in a war and you had no idea where the enemy was.

"The hardest year was not 1997. The hardest years were 1998 and '99.

"Other people saw, better than I did … as soon as it looked like it was safe again, the old agendas come back out again. A lot of people picked better than I did that it was going to be harder than I thought to get through the next two years.

"And most of them made it harder.

"That's alright, I get that. It was a case of doing a job I'd agreed to stay on and do and the sport's got on with it. To me, it looks now to be set up with the commission, it's run well, and certainly as a game, it's thriving.

"I pushed hard but I would have preferred now if we had not had … if we'd just allowed an economic outcome. Let clubs sort themselves out. "

There is it again: regret. But the event which is too painful for him to directly describe did what the Super League War could not - get Sydneysiders to march in the streets the way Novocastrians lined theirs' before and after the grand final.

Kicking Souths out actually had the same cultural impact in Sydney as Joey Johns' blindside raid had up the freeway two years earlier. It fished out those who still harboured an emotional connection to the sport and it swelled their number.

South Sydney lifted their 21st premiership in 2014, 43 years after their 20th. The bunny rabbit logo, unseen for two years at the beginning of this century, is now burnished by Hollywood actors, models and pop stars.

Whittaker's guilt is, to me, profoundly misplaced. In the popular imagination, his name resides a fair distance from that entire episode. The taxi drivers who refused to service Fox Studios blamed Rupert, not him.

Those who sought to set Whittaker up as the fall guy, frankly, failed.

The NRL's first CEO poses for a couple of photos in front of the window and answers a question for social media before we bid goodbye.

"Most people forget," he says as we eye the door of the meeting room.

"You're the only person I've met who wants to talk about the three years of the Super League War. Whenever the game has been talking about itself, it doesn't mention that period.

"'It didn't happen' - when in fact it was the redefining of the game."

PERTH: So much for Super's vision

**By Steve Mascord, Sydney Morning Herald,
Friday October 3, 1997**

PART of the problem is they have different aims. Super League aspires to be a national game, whereas the ARL doesn't" - Super League chairman Ken Cowley, *Rugby League Express,* September 8, 1997.

Mr Cowley, can you therefore explain why it was the ARL which set up a team in Perth three years ago, and your organisation which closed it down on Wednesday? Wednesday, October 1 - less than a month after the above statement was published - should go down as one of the blackest days of the rugby league war, a day when the game ingloriously abandoned an entire state and crawled back east with its penny-pinching tail between its legs.

What if the AFL had pulled out of Sydney after three years, when the Swans were struggling?

Certainly the Reds' results and crowds stack up against the rest of rugby league better than the Swans did with the rest of the AFL in the early 1980s.

Super League will, quite rightly, point out that the ARL has,

in effect, closed down South Queensland by merging the Crushers with Gold Coast and, almost certainly, playing most of their games at Carrara.

But there is still a team in Brisbane - the Broncos. Rugby league is not walking out and leaving a town to its competitors.

Besides, two wrongs don't make a right. Both administrations claim to agree there are too many teams in Sydney, yet they have both used their financial stranglehold over expansion teams to shut them down.

Why?

Didn't Super League say something about the ARL not being able to make the tough decisions in the interests of the game?

So October 1 should also go down as the day when it became apparent that any vision Super League ever had - national or global - was declared clinically dead.

The reason Super League deserves, or deserved, a fair go is that there are a lot of idealists involved in the breakaway movement who were determined to spend the money Mr Murdoch gave them to make the game better.

But this week's distasteful piece of economic expediency proves the idealists have been well and truly overruled by the bean-counters.

Sure, the Reds were losing S10 million a year. Rugby league has cost $300 million. Should we just close that down as well because it's losing sponsors, and crowds are down?

Whose fault is that?

If having a presence in Western Australia, if matching it with other professional sports, was as important to Super League as it is to the game, it would have been considered money well spent.

But Perth is far from the game's heartland and therefore unable to garner too much sympathy, so why not give it the chop?

Super League's interest in developing and promoting the game in new areas is summed up by the fact that under the peace plan with the Australian Rugby League, all of that is handed back to them.

And do you think the ARL can afford to pick up the tab? Western Australia is the tip of an iceberg which has the potential to make a Titanic of rugby league.

Melbourne is more important because it is a "head office town" where sponsorship decisions are made.

Perth has some good juniors and a hard-core group of fans, that's all.

Sure, News Ltd has honoured some pledges to the game in developing areas. National under-19s and under-17s competitions have been run at great expense and the World Club Challenge has been run at much more.

But Perth made the grand final of that under-17s competition, with only four players from outside Western Australia. They are the products of enormous strides made there by rugby league at junior level in the past decade.

Maybe all the Reds' elite players' contracts will be honoured - but what happens to these kids?

Like the fans who have shown up in greater numbers for three years than those of some Sydney teams, they'll go to Australian Rules, rugby union or soccer.

And so they should.

Rugby league doesn't deserve them.

CHAPTER 22

Fear the Reaper

IN bedrooms around Perth on the morning of October 1, 1997, hung pristine, classic dinner suits.

The Reds rugby league team had endured a poor season in Super League, winning just seven of 18 games to finish third-last. But, recalls prop Robbie Kearns, director Peter Moore had stood in front of the group in the preceding weeks and said "listen guys, you have my word. All this speculation and all this talk of the club closing is full of shit". The season over, the Reds were at home with their families while they waited to head to Burswood Casino, now the Crown Casino, for their black tie presentation night. Then the calls started coming. "My recollection is it was just one of the girls from the office," says Kearns.

The club was closing - immediately. "Boys, presentation's off, take your suits back and good luck for your future," hooker Matt Fuller recounts. "We were over in a one-team-town, miles from anywhere. Players went into panic mode. It was just every man for himself. It was unbelievable scenes."

In April 1995, a fairy Godmother bearing fistfuls of cash had tapped rugby league players on their shoulders. In October 1997, the Grim Reaper came calling on the game's clubs. The period of terrible reckoning for the excesses of the previous two years began in earnest with the throats cut of the Reds and the South Queensland Crushers. The Mariners would just slip away in their off-season slumber.

Western Sydney-raised Fuller played more games for the Reds than any other player and had set his sights on being the first to a century of appearances.

"I thought when I came over for the Reds, we all assembled in '94, that that was the last club I was ever going to play for," the former Canterbury, St George and South Sydney hooker recalls. "I couldn't believe another club I'd play for would fold or amalgamate."

The Reds had an accumulated debt of $26 million; their closure came on rugby league's 50th birthday in Western Australia. "Another year would have given us time to consolidate," said chairman Stephen Edwards at the time, "as I think we did in a competitive sense this year, as well as make substantial inroads into a new venue. We were being funded by someone else's money and they could withdraw that money whenever they wanted."

When South Queensland threw the gates open in the final round, beating Western Suburbs, they knew it would be their last game because of their own debts. The result of the game, however, helped keep the season of the Gold Coast Chargers, their intended joint venture partners, going for at least another week.

Gold Coast would prove to have the power of life and death during the carnage of late 1997 - not only over the Crushers but also over the Mariners.

But on the back of the choices made when they thought they had the whip hand, the Chargers ended up six feet under themselves.

"I approached the board of the Chargers with the suggestion that we consider a merger (with South Queensland) or absorb the club, given that the ARL or QRL would have to pay out contracts anyway," Paul Broughton, who was Chargers CEO, wrote in *One More Walk Around The Block*. "I went public with the suggestion and the chairman censured me with a motion fully endorsed by the directors, that only the chairman could speak to the media on the matter."

The Chargers board, says Broughton, turned down the chance to sign the likes of Trevor Gillmeister, Travis Norton, Clinton Schifcofske and Mark Tookey - which they could have done without taking on any of the Crushers' debt.

Broughton had always been an ARL man. In his book, he contends News Limited just didn't understand the sport's traditions. He had been placed in charge of the club by the ARL administration, which owned it, and survived the debacle of Jeff Muller's brief ownership. But in 1997, Broughton was placed in a position which required him to choose between the club, the city and the ARL. He chose the city and the club.

Sitting with wife Bev in a Broadbeach Cafe, he tells me: "News Limited offered us $5 million for us to merge with the Mariners. You can say half of the games would have been played at the Mariners but the Gold Coast would have won in the end."

Bev then interrupts. "Is that when we registered Gold Coast Rabbitohs?"

Broughton: "Yes. Gold Coast Rabbitohs. George (Piggins) is going to kill me. Anyway, I said to Tom (Bellew, chairman) 'we have to do this (with the Mariners)'. I said 'forget about rugby league, we owe this city. They've put their hand up for us, the mayor, the council, the whole lot. They gave us a free ground, they gave us all this free stuff so the Chargers could survive. Tom says 'I'm ARL, I'm appointed by the ARL, and that's it'.

"So I resigned."

Gold Coast officially pulled out of its merger with South Queensland on October 31. Bellew, who died in 2001, said: "We had what we thought was a successful club this year and, who knows, if we merge and the club wasn't travelling well next season, it could be disastrous."

Hunter CEO Bob Ferris recalls: "We went up there and I thought we'd done the deal. I knew one of the directors up there and he thought we'd done the deal. We got up the next morning. A bloke called Malcolm Noad was a director of News Limited and he was the director I reported to.

"We got up the next morning and he said 'we're aborting this' and I said 'why?' and he said 'I've been instructed to."

The Hunter Mariners couldn't be closed because they still had a game to play - the World Club Challenge final against Brisbane on October 17 at Mt Smart. Their final game was for a world title - the marker of a bizarre era if ever there was one.

"We were at the Park in The Bar pub afterwards, we had a massive night," Michael Hagan recalls - name-checking a favourite Auckland haunt of footballers that once had perimeter advertising at Brookvale Oval - "...and news started to come through."

Everyone knew the club was gone - but officially, the Mariners were still on the table when peace talks resumed. Their star halfback Brett Kimmorley didn't realise they were dead until he returned from the Australian tour of England in late November. Local reporter Ben

Drzyzga recalls final confirmation of the club's death on New Years Eve - as he had during the World Club Challenge, he interrupted his holidays to cover it.

"I remember going down to the Prince Of Wales (pub) in Mereweather and all the boys were back there and had a chat to Muzz (Graham Murray) and we got a few photos and had a beer and that was it."

Frykberg claimed the ARL had made it clear in peace talks there would be no place for Perth in a united competition, a comment Whittaker described as "completely inappropriate". "From day one in our talks, the ARL said categorically there was no place for Perth," Frykberg said. "I have seen an ARL document that has a competition structure and Perth is not in it. Nor was Auckland, although they seem to have changed their minds on that one."

The day after the Reds' demise, the Industrial Courts upheld the ARL loyalty agreements of Anthony Mundine, Phil Adamson and Carl McNamara. Rod Silva, Robbie Beckett, Danny Farrar and Steve Carter were cleared to stay with their Super League clubs because they did not receive sufficient legal advice at the time of signing their ARL contracts.

Peace talks had resumed a few hours before the hearing.

At News Limited's Annual General Meeting in Adelaide on October 7, Rupert Murdoch addressed the situation, saying: "We are certainly working to see if it will be one competition next year. But there are many, many complications, the least of which is the danger that we would become the ham in the sandwich, the meat between Telstra and Optus in arguments on telephone interconnect charges.

"Overall, we are very optimistic we can get the competition back together." He said News would share the TV rights to the new competition with Optus.

On October 8, Anthony Mundine signed a three-year, $2 million contract with St George and pulled out of the Broncos' remaining matches in the World Club Challenge. Super League gave Melbourne Storm the first four "draft picks" from the disbanded Perth Reds, with North Queensland and Adelaide getting the next two before the Storm were granted unlimited signings from the dead club.

Western Suburbs banned prop Harvey Howard from playing for Great Britain, even though he did not have an ARL loyalty contract. A rift between the Raiders and Ricky Stuart emerged when he was dumped as captain. The ARL confirmed helping Newcastle retain Andrew and Matthew Johns even though under the convention at the time, they were not supposed to do so.

On October 26, the *Sun-Herald* announced that peace talks had broken down once more. It was said that Lachlan Murdoch had told the Super League staff the differences between the sides were "insurmountable". Frykberg, however, said he would be surprised if talks had broken down for good. Rugby league, with 13, had more drugs positives than any other Australian sport in 1997. Glenn Lazarus signed for the Storm as their likely captain.

Rupert Murdoch and Cable and Wireless chief Dick Brown are reported to have sealed a deal in London guaranteeing a single competition in 1998. Peace was on the horizon, now clearly visible.

Geoff Carr and John Brady, meanwhile, were travelling around addressing fan forums, usually of loyalists like the Aussies For The ARL organisation.

"We went out to Campbelltown," Carr recalls "We did this presentation, it went really really well.

"Everyone sat there and listened and Wests were obviously one of the teams that were in danger. We started taking questions, that looked like finishing.

"Brades said 'one more question' and this bloke got up and said 'if Western Suburbs aren't playing at Western Suburbs, at Pratten Park, you can all get fucked' and the joint went into uproar!"

The Yang of the Super League experience for players had been an exponential increase in earnings. The Yin was the dreadful reckoning that began in October 1997 for clubs and continued on for many years, right up until South Sydney's readmission in 2002. Or even until right now, given Peter V'landys' avowed opposition to readmitting Perth to the NRL.

Fuller has no doubt he would trade the Yang for the Yin.

"From a selfish money point of view, it was fantastic. To be honest, my payments went from $100,000 to $225,000 to $244,000 in two seasons. It's massive money. I played the most games for the Reds with 59 and I was the 10th lowest paid player in the club. Some blokes were on astronomical money and it was just ridiculous.

"But in saying that, Super League - outside the money side of it - destroyed the competition, it destroyed a lot of families and all for the sake of getting the television rights - which they accomplished.

"Marriages broke down. Most people were settled in WA. They'd bought houses, they'd made financial commitments to the state, had kids in school. It was a very, very stressful time. Even though there was a lot of money around, suddenly you find yourself without a club to ply your trade. I went back to England and played again for Wakefield Trinity.

"Then I came home from there and it wasn't long after that that my own marriage broke up. I went to Sydney and played for Tom Raudonikis in the Magpies' last-ever flight. It was just horrible times."

Kearns says the fears on the part of club officials that players would get drunk and rip up the casino in anger the night of the abortive presentation were unfounded. Fuller says the club was doomed from the start, damned to a vicious circle: forced to pay for all visiting teams when it entered the ARL, pushed into News Limited's arms by the financial burden that created, then slaughtered partly due its disloyalty to the ARL.

The presentation night eventually happened - 22 years later when a State Of Origin game was played in Perth and the Reds alumni flew in from around the country for a five-day get together.

Fuller is still in Perth with his new family. He still firmly believes the game needs a team there.

Kearns went on to play 169 games for the Melbourne Storm and represent Australia 26 times. He spent the bulk of his career in cities that are frontiers for the sport.

"Bad publicity, players doing the wrong thing - that really hurts us in these new markets," he reflects. "The Melbourne Storm have been pretty successful since day one. Any new team in any area of Australia that could be happening in the future, they've got to get off to a really good start. To do that, you've got to have good administration, you've got to have a good coach and you've got to have good players.

"Australians like a winner and if you're not winning they won't follow you. That's exactly what happened in Perth. We were playing out of a shit stadium. For the three years we were there, we didn't play finals football.

"If they started over there now and had a successful side like the Melbourne Storm playing out of their new rectangular stadium, I reckon they'd have a future."

Walking across the WACA on the evening of March 12, 1995, I could not have envisaged such an inglorious demise for the Reds just three years later. They had just beaten St George 28-16 before 24,932 fans in their first competition match and kids were flooding the field to back-slap Mark Geyer and Brad Mackay. Sure, the Red Rooster mascot was attacked by some young scoundrels and had to be rescued by the Paddle Pop Lion, but still….

That morning in Kings Park overlooking the city, John Quayle and Ken Arthurson had planned a media conference to celebrate their success that weekend in launching a trans-continental and trans-Tasman competition with 20 teams. It was to be the ultimate valedictory moment for the Pope and his Monsignor. Instead, Quayle had to answer reporters' questions about reports from back east that News Limited's breakaway competition was about to happen.

The Reds started life as a party spoilt - and that's how they died as well.

BIG JOE'S A WEIGHTY FOE

By Steve Mascord, *Sydney Morning Herald,*
October 10, 1997

AT the beginning of 1996, Australian Martin Hulme took up the head trainer's post with Auckland.

He had a problem.

A young prop called Joe Vagana stepped on the scales for him and the needle settled at 128 kg.

Hulme approached coach John Monie, saying: "He can't play at that weight!"

Monie's reply was simple: "He's your problem."

For the past two Fridays, Vagana has continued to be a problem for opposition forwards.

Only 22, he made as big an impression in New Zealand's 30-12 win over Australia at North Harbour Stadium two weeks ago as a young Kevin Iro did almost a 15 years earlier during a similar boilover at Lang Park.

The sight of Vagana, now a "slim" 113 kg, holding the football out in one hand while swatting big-name Australians with the other like King Kong, will live long in the memories of Kiwi fans.

And he followed it up with a terrifying performance against Bradford last week. "He can turn it aggression on like hot and cold water," Warriors coach Frank Endacott said yesterday from Brisbane, where Auckland meet the Broncos in a World Club Challenge semi-final tonight.

"He's a real smart cookie who is always smiling. You can't get the smile off his face.

"A couple of years ago, I said he could be the best prop in the world. He's still got a long way to go, but I believe he's on the way."

What turned Monie's overweight interchange forward into one of the most feared props in Test football was more than a diet.

"Being a prop is very demanding, and as a young bloke, Joe was up against some very experienced players," Warriors football manager Laurie Stubbing said.

"And he'd only be on for 10 minutes and he'd be back off again. He'd just had time to get warmed up."

When Vagana arrived in Brisbane on Wednesday, his teammates noticed something strange. The media swarmed to Big Joe.

Insiders say it's usually the outgoing front-rower who calls fellow players' rooms pretending to be from a newspaper.

So when the *Herald* called him yesterday, he didn't return the call because he thought it was some big-name Warrior seeking revenge.

"It all started in the Tri-Series," Vagana said of his rise to prominence. "Graeme Norton left me on the field for a while.

"Then I got back to the Warriors and Frank started doing the same."

The result is best summed up by Brisbane hard man Gorden Tallis, who told AAP yesterday: "He's so strong, you just can't stop him."

CHAPTER 23

Going out with a bang

"I HAD a sore head and a sore back and they said some bloke's kicked my door in and belted me."

The last time an Australian team played under the Super League banner was Sunday, November 16 1997.

John Lang's national side spared themselves the embarrassment of becoming their country's first side in nine years to lose a series to anyone (and in 25 years to lose a series to Britain …. and in 38 years to be beaten in the UK in a series) by winning the deciding Third Test at Elland Road 37-20. It wasn't as close as the score suggested; the tourists actually scored seven tries to three.

This was the end of a long and stressful year for all concerned. The future was uncertain but peace - whatever that meant - in Australia looked overwhelmingly likely. Players, staff and media from both countries gathered in the Roundhay Bar at the Crowne Plaza, where months earlier Jason Death had performed a nude dance called 'the Helicopter' in front of members of the Australian cricket team and their families and been sent home.

The next morning, Australian fullback Brett Mullins would wait in the foyer for a rematch with GB prop Dean Sampson, who had beaten him up in his own hotel bed. It was a helluva way to end a helluva year.

Laurie Daley says that until the final blow-out after the Third Test, there couldn't have been a bigger contrast between the frivolity of the World Club Challenge and the Lang-coached tour. Two years earlier, an ARL-only team had come to England and won the World Cup. Personal pride dictated that the Super League-only green and golds had to be as successful.

"That was the motivator for us, to not be that team to come over here and lose," Daley says. "So the pressure was on from day one: we needed to win."

Before the tour, Great Britain chose Gary Connolly and Jason Robinson - despite both being contracted to the ARL. Robinson ended up playing in the series and Connolly did not.

A look at the venues - Wembley Stadium, Old Trafford and Elland Road, all soccer citadels - gives an indication of rugby league's strength in Britain at the time. All three games attracted 40,000 people - just a little fewer than the ARL grand final in the preceding months and a roll-up that would have delighted the RFL had the 2020 Kangaroo Tour gone ahead.

"I just remember there was a lot of pressure on us - they had a good side," says Robbie Kearns. "Adrian Morley was one of the young blokes coming through.

"I can recall plenty of times hanging around the hotel room and watching big Wendell (Sailor) and Gorden (Tallis) wrestle. I'm not too sure why but the Broncos, they were right into their wrestling. They loved a wrestle.

"It was my first experience of an overseas tour. Johnny Lang was the coach and he turned me down a couple of years prior at Cronulla Sharks. The group we had was made up of a lot of the Canberra Raiders, they were on song back then. The Brisbane Broncos … Alfie (Allan Langer) was crook, Kevvy (Walters) was the same.

"Gorden was new in the ranks. He had an unbelievable series. I roomed with him.

"I was in awe of all these players because I'd been looking up to them for such a long time. It was a fun group. Johnny Lang was all footy, as he always was, but he let us let our hair down a couple of nights there."

Lang recalls: "I never got to play in England and I never got to coach (a club) there but I had four games with the Sharks in 1997 and then three Test matches. It was a really good experience.

"They only wanted to send 20 players over. I said 'it's bloody ridiculous. We've got to play three Test matches in three weeks and you can be short of players after the first match.

"Ian Frykberg said 'what's this bullshit about wanting 22 players?' I went bang, bang bang, this is why. He said 'OK, you've got 'em. You'd better fucking win."

British Gas sponsored the series for a reported £250,000. Australia won the First Test 38-14 at Wembley Stadium. During the series Paris Saint-Germain, the club of GB coach Andy Goodway, was kicked out of Super League. A team from Swansea was to be added in 1999 - but (obviously) this never eventuated. On November 7, troubled former Test star Peter Jackson died of a drug overdose in Sydney.

Britain tied the series with a 20-12 Second Test victory at Old Trafford and during the following week Maurice Lindsay visited the Australian team hotel and tabled to touring reporters what seemed an audacious idea - instead of tours, more than one national team would gather for a series each year. The first Tri-Nations was played two years later.

Lindsay also offered to stand down as World Board chairman if it helped the cause of peace in Australia. "I don't need any more labels on my jacket," he said.

Back home, the ARL was accused of going soft on performance enhancing drugs; one positive swab star - not named - reportedly played all three State of Origin games for Queensland after receiving only a warning letter.

Daley says he remembers a little of the aftermath of the Third Test but has fond memories of the match itself.

"I've got to do my top five venues … obviously Wembley and Old Trafford are in it and I'm thinking of putting Elland Road in as my number five ground that I've ever played on," he says. "Lang Park is in there.

"Elland Road was a fantastic ground, it just felt like everyone was on top of you.

"I actually liked Langy. He was different to Sheensy (Tim Sheens). He was very big on the basics whereas Sheensy was more analytical. Sheensy was more into picking apart the opposition and designing plays around that whereas Langy was 'this is the way we're playing and this is the way we're going to play it.'"

And so to the Roundhay Bar. "It was a massive relief for everybody - a relief and a release," says Lang. "We'd started with trials in bloody Samoa in February and here we were still going.

"Some of the guys had played in the club competition, the World Club Challenge, the Tri-Series, the finals and then the Test series.

"Back at the hotel, all the pommies came. It was a bit of a celebration really. Not a victory celebration, just a celebration of the season being over."

Mullins takes up the story of that wild final day of Australian Super League. "I'd done my thigh the game before, I was out, so me and Peach (David Peachey), we got on the bourbons in the morning and watched the Third Test.

"The next thing you know, I wake up. I think it was Luke Priddis and Locky (Darren Lockyer), they come in and go 'you alright?" and I go 'yeah, what's going on?'.

"And my door's been kicked in.

"Obviously they told me what had happened previously. From what they told me, I got what I deserved."

Let's fill in the gaps, then. "On the last night, Brett Mullins went nuts," Debbie Spillane recalls. "He had too many drinks.

"He didn't play that day, he'd obviously been on the turps."

I was there too - and clearly remember Mullins smashing the heads of BBC commentators Dave Woods and David Oates together after calling them "pommy bastards" or some such, causing them to spill their drinks all over themselves.

"I really felt sick," Spillane recalls. "I'd never heard people's heads smash like that. He did it hard. There was stunned amazement. What the fuck just happened? Laurie Daley came over and shooed him away."

At some point later in the night, Mullins turned his attention to Sampson, allegedly spitting at the Castleford prop's wife.

"I was there that night. I was right in the middle of it," said Stuart Raper, Sampson's club coach but there to visit his countrymen.

"Diesel (Sampson) came over to me. I was standing with ET (Andrew Ettingshausen) and a few of the Aussies. Diesel said 'I've got to tell you that I'm going to have to go and smash Brett Mullins'. He was cool and calm. I said 'what'?. He said 'he just spat at my missus'.

"I said 'mate, you can't do that'. I knew if he got in a fight, all these blokes are gonna jump on him and what am I gonna do? I'm gonna have to go in and try and help him and I don't want to get in a fight here.

"We'd had a few drinks and I went over to ET and said 'Ett, if there's a rumble … and I just grabbed him and … 'just start pretending to fight'.

"I calmed him (Sampson) down, he didn't do anything, which was great. I went home and didn't realise … I got a call the next morning and found out the door had been kicked in and Mullos had copped a bit of a bashing."

Sampson wrote about the incident in his biography, *My Shangri-La*.

"I looked across to where Lorraine was sat and saw she had her head in her hands and seemed to be crying, her friend had her arm around her and knelt in front of Lorraine were two Aussie players, Wendell

Sailor and Gorden Tallis. I made my way over to them and asked what the hell was going on. 'There's been an incident but things are OK now.' Wendell replied. "Everyone was apologising for what had happened, John Lang, Wendell all of them, but I was still no wiser as to what had actually gone down. 'I'm going home are you coming?' Lorraine said.

"There was a brief moment when Lorraine looked straight at me; 'One of the Aussie players … he spat on me. … 'I went to hit him but he spat at me again'. Whatever the reason no one was willing to give up a name. I decided to be patient and sober up a little, just to be on the safe side, I needed to be sharp and clear headed. The night wore on and people began drifting off to bed, then bingo, they say everything comes to those who wait, the guilty party swaggered back into the room unknown to me until someone let it slip. 'I can't believe he's come back after what he did.' It was just loud enough for me to overhear.

"Thirty minutes later when the bar was practically empty, I started making my way down to reception. I asked the night porter if he had an envelope as I had something to return to one of the Aussie players and wanted to put it under his door along with a note to make sure he got back what I owed him. The porter handed me an envelope and asked which player it was, I gave him the name and he replied, 'let me see for you sir, ah yes he's in room 216.'

"I came across room 216. What luck, the door opposite was ajar. Opening it fully I looked in the room, a player lay comatose on his bed, I walked to the back of the room turned and ran back across, into the corridor, hitting the door to room 216 with my right shoulder. There was a sound of splintering wood as the door and the casing collapsed into the room. Quick as a flash, I stepped into the semi-darkness, the offending player shot from his bed, eyes like saucers, seeing me stood before him, his jaw dropped.

"He cried out. 'Wait, no, no, hold on.' But my self control had gone. I rained blow after blow on him until he flopped onto the bed face down and unconscious. Then in sheer frustration at him, I smashed my fist into his back. I thought to myself 'that will hurt when he sits down on the plane tomorrow', I hoped a reminder on the long journey home of the disgusting way he had behaved toward my wife.

"I had taken retribution but I had gained little satisfaction and I was still in a thunderous mood as I turned away from the prone torso only to find Wendell Sailor stood in the doorway. To say he looked shocked was an understatement, an unconscious team-mate, a smashed door and the room in disarray was probably not what he expected, especially if it was his room. 'I'm done with him.' I said.

"This long corridor was full of Aussie players in all differing states of undress with their eyes transfixed on me. Talk about walking the gauntlet but I'd made my bed and I had to lie in it. I walked through the throng of Aussies who collectively could have given me the mother of a hiding. A couple postured and another shouted but no-one stepped forward.

"I apologised to the night porter, handed him my credit card, told him what had happened and told him I would return at 10 o'clock.

"It is alleged his behaviour when drunk had left a lot to be desired on previous occasions. Well, he should cut down or stop because none of his team-mates defended him or sought retribution, for reasons known only to themselves."

Another key part of the tale is recounted by Greg McCallum. "I was there that night and he was lucky Dean Sampson didn't break his legs because he'd actually collapsed between two single beds.

"Dean Sampson found him (that way) in the room and it actually crossed his mind to jump on his legs and it would have snapped them in half and that would have been the end of him."

Mullins reflects: "I deserved what I got, apparently. But I did ask, after I got told that, 'you get the bloke back here in the morning and I'm quite happy to face him one-on-one' but the bastard didn't turn up.

"I was just a naive kid. I'm happy players have guidance these days. I didn't have any of that. I had people around me that took advantage of me, outside of rugby league. I thought I'd play rugby league for the rest of my life, that it was my job.

"Anyway, we waited for this bloke to show up. He didn't - so we went to the karaoke and got back on it."

As reporters at breakfast that morning, we had to decide whether we chased a story. Spillane says "eventually I got a letter from him apologising. Obviously he'd been told he had to do it" but at that stage Mullins' misadventures were still a rumour. I was on holidays that morning, ready to head up to Edinburgh with cameraman Anthony George. I wasn't going to stand around in the foyer, door-stopping hungover footballers on my first day off after covering the Super League War for three years.

As far as I was concerned, it was over.

And it was.

POSTSCRIPT: Ian Schubert was one of the team managers on the tour and recalls: "There was a trophy. No-one knows where the trophy is.

"The trophy was at the airport when we left Heathrow and I'm pretty sure someone had it in the Qantas lounge in Singapore. It never got back to Sydney - and if it did, someone's got it and they're not going to say.

"I was looking for it because I thought we'd better take it back to the office. "Well I didn't put it on the plane. Did you put it on the plane?"

"No-one knew where it was. Whether it's still in the lounge in either London or Singapore, no-one is sure."

Meanwhile, Lang couldn't believe that trainer Paul Watson did not wake up for the entire flight home, except for the short Asian stopover. "He slept for bloody 25 hours!"

It had been that sort of year.

LANGER IN TOUR PLEA AS BRONCOS TRIUMPH

By Steve Mascord, *Sydney Morning Herald,*
Saturday October 18, 1997

BRISBANE 36 HUNTER 12 at Ericsson Stadium

BRISBANE captain Allan Langer last night pleaded to be selected for Australia after making his comeback from a groin injury in the Broncos' world championship-clinching win over Hunter.

Langer played the full 80 minutes as the Broncos survived a second-half revival from the Mariners to win the World Club Challenge final 36-12 and $1 million prize money before 10,000 spectators at Ericsson Stadium.

It was the veteran half's first outing since the Broncos' Australasian Super League grand final success on September 20 and while he was far from his best, Langer refused to leave the field and got through a mountain of defence in the seven tries to three victory.

"It feels sore, but not as sore as it was before," Langer said after the game. "I've trained alright this week and I got through the game, so I've got my fingers crossed about being selected.

"This could be my last tour. I've had a couple of ordinary tours over there in the past and I'd really like to go."

Brisbane coach Wayne Bennett supported Langer's bid, saying his performance was better than in the grand final, when he was "restricted".

The side is due to be announced around 3 pm today in Sydney, with Canberra's Ricky Stuart and Hunter's Brett Kimmorley the other scrum-half contenders.

Three-try centre Darren Smith was the star of the Broncos' victory last night, which installed them as world champions, replacing Wigan, who beat them in the previous international decider, at ANZ Stadium in 1994.

Brisbane had raced to a 12-0 lead when Smith started his hat-trick in the 20th minute He scored again in the 24th and 29th, and at 26-0 the Mariners, tipped to be relocated, merged or shut down, were gone.

The crowd, officially 10,000, had lost interest, but the Mariners hadn't. They scored through winger Nick Zisti in the 35th minute.

In the second half, the video referee disallowed two Hunter tries and when winger John Carlaw and Zisti, again, scored, the game became interesting again.

But the Broncos killed off the Hunter resurgence with late tries to winger Wendell Sailor and centre Steve Renouf, finishing the evening with a lap of the sparsely populated arena.

Hunter coach Graham Murray rated Brisbane the best team in either Australasian competition. He was proud of the Mariners' last 45 minutes but said they were a bit nervous early.

He confirmed having fielded a number of offers from Euro League clubs in anticipation of the Mariners' demise.

Bennett said he would be recommending to Super League that the WCC be retained next year but as a four-team competition pitting the top two from Europe and Australasia teams against each other.

"The reason this competition was introduced was that we only had 18 rounds of the Super League competition and there was a void we had to fill," he said.

Super League chief executive Colin Sanders supported Bennett's idea. And he contradicted claims from Gold Coast City Council that Super League had told council officials it was considering relocating the Mariners there.

"We've said nothing at all to them about the Mariners," Sanders said. "They have placed a few conditions on the ARL and are unhappy with some things, and we have been speaking to them about that"

BRISBANE 36 (D Smith 3, K Walters. J Plath, W Sailor, S Renouf tries: M Devere 3, B Walter goals) bt HUNTER 12 (N Zisti 2, J Carlaw tries) at Ericsson Stadium. Referee: G Annesley. Crowd: 10,000.

CHAPTER 24

Versailles

AS if things couldn't get any worse, on the morning of Friday, December 19, 1997 - despite it being the height of summer - drizzling rain greeted media representatives as they arrived in the Moore Park precinct of the Sydney Cricket Ground and Football Stadium.

That day, a series of meetings framed with Spartan precision would determine if the ARL would make peace with Super League, if there would be one competition in 1998 or two.

If two, each ARL club would - reportedly - be $300,000 worse off - but still there were doubts. "What concerns our club is that we are handing over our destiny to be determined by a company whose directors we don't know, whose powers and functions we don't know in any detail and who will be deciding - on criteria we don't know - our futures as clubs," Gold Coast's Tom Bellew said.

"If there's no additional money, we won't be going ahead with the peace plan," said North Sydney's Bob Saunders..

Slowly the cars started to pull into the scene of Newcastle's dramatic triumph two months earlier. Knights chairman Michael Hill was late because of traffic - but not late enough to avoid the rain, which didn't clear until 9am.

Then it started to warm up, literally and figuratively.

The first meeting at the SFS was of the NSWRL board; 8am. This comprised Neil Whittaker, Warren Lockwood, Nick Politis, Bob Millward and Denis Fitzgerald.

At 9am, the ARL board met. At 10am, a meeting was scheduled between four representatives of the Country Rugby League, two referees' representatives and the 10 vice-presidents of the NSWRL board.

Whittaker was to address all three meetings on the proposal.

"I was on the Australian Rugby League board and I was on the New South Wales Rugby League board and it was in one of the corporate boxes," Millward recalls.

"I'd heard most of it but there was always an update, on every report back. The clubs had come in at nine. Over that four-hour period there was variation … I wouldn't say on the hour but there were plenty of meetings and then reports back and then responses to those reports."

A 20 minute walk away, in the very same hotel where they had "partied like there was no tomorrow" 441 days earlier, Super League club representatives had gathered to receive the news.

"We were like a cat on a hot tin roof, waiting," says Kevin Neil. Ian Frykberg took multiple calls from Whittaker and vice versa.

Millward recalls: "On the day, they wanted every club executive, their full board if possible, to be in attendance.

"Neil and John McDonald were the two that took it around.

"There were relays going back to the boxes. They would have 20 minutes discussion and deliberation and they would then come back and deliver what they thought of - I've got to say - the 'latest' proposal.

"Because there was proposal after proposal, change after change, going on."

At 11am, the chairman and chief executives of the 11 surviving ARL clubs (after the death of the Crushers) were to gather. The general committee meeting was at 2pm, with everyone together. During a break in this meeting, the board of every club met individually in different corporate boxes. "We have 60 minutes to make decisions which will affect a club that has been in existence for 60 years," an unnamed official was quoted as saying in that day's *Sydney Morning Herald*.

Then, when that was over, everyone met one more time. The players association had no vote but referees did, a small indication of the paradigm that was being left behind.

"Money wasn't the greatest consideration," Millward recalls. "From an ARL point of view, we wanted a date when News Limited would exit the game. To form the NRL, it was a partnership between Super League and the Australian Rugby League but we were looking for a timeframe when News Limited would exit the partnership.

"They started at about 20 to 25 (years). We said 'let's start with one'. I think it ended up at 'within 20'. It didn't go 20 of course. But they weren't giving any commitment of a shorter period.

"I think both parties were desirous of forming the NRL but in hindsight I'm sure that News Limited, with their financial backing of the Super League, held a lot of the cards - as is the case in most negotiations in regard to forming partnerships or takeovers or whatever you want to call them.

"I think both parties wanted it to come out that it wasn't a takeover, that both parties were winners, but I think most of the losers ended up on the ARL side - particularly the clubs."

Including, perhaps, Millward's club: the Illawarra Steelers.

Damien Kelly, who was working for 2UE on the day, recalls: "We were there all day. No social media, it was made for radio. We were giving updates, it was fantastic.

"I do remember this most magnificent game of cricket that all the media played. We were waiting there for hours. There were cameramen and reporters."

Contemporary accounts tell us one fan was present for what would become the birth of the NRL. He identified himself to media only as "Balmain Tiger" and carried a placard that read "It's time. Peace with honour. The ARL must control. Let's get on with the game." Michael Cowley, who wrote one of those accounts, tells me now Balmain Tiger was "one of those guys who, like many at the time, was pissed off with the way the whole thing had played out and wanted the game he loved back the way it was."

At midday, Balmain Tiger announced to all and sundry he was going to Balmain for a beer.

It had been a quite a month.

Whittaker and Frykberg met twice during the final week of November. The ARL surrendered its majority on the proposed joint board in exchange for continued News funding. Late on December 4, it was reported that Optus and Foxtel had settled the rugby league war between them. The ARL premiership (run by the NSW Rugby League) lost almost $4.5 million in 1997.

"We'd send off Neil with responses to various things over months," Millward recalls. "'Yes', 'no', 'we'll accept that but we'll reject that'.

"Look, it had gone on for months and months. They were down at the Sheraton on the Park. We used to have a meeting, they'd have a meeting, we'd send Geoff Carr down there and they'd send … sometimes it would be, what's his name, (Kevin) Neil from Canberra, he'd come and talk to us.

"It went on for weeks until … it was News Limited's desire, and ours, that we should have a merged competition for 1998.

"And we left it a bit late. It was Friday the 19th of December, 1997."

A NSW bid to unseat John McDonald as chairman of the ARL early in December had been thwarted. McDonald appeared to have been saved by the vote of Bellew, who was retiring. From Brisbane, McDonald, Lockwood and Whittaker then flew out - together - to continue meetings with Super League in Sydney!

A $20 million upgrade at Campbelltown Stadium was touted as guaranteeing Western Suburbs' future. It was reported ARL Sydney clubs wanted to be guaranteed two years in the new competition or they would vote against compromise.

And so back to the old SFS, demolished in 2019.

"There was a bit of standing around between meetings," John Brady recalls. "Separate rooms had been organised at the SFS and Cricket Ground - a lot of thought had gone in to scheduling the legal order of the decisions

"No club could have fairly said they were dragged into it. The mood was one of both an opportunity to end it and a chance to get going. They all knew the terms of the deal so there was a bit of apprehension about how it would play out but mostly I reckon a bit of relief that there was some funding ahead.

"I think some were of the view the criteria could never end up putting them out so 'do the deal anyway'. Others were thinking more long term about the opportunities that might come. Others were looking for less teams not more. They all knew how much they were struggling financially. Souths knew that more than anyone.

"Most of all I think it was relief that the war was over, no matter how much they did or didn't trust the other side."

Over at the Super League hotel, Kevin Neil recalls: "Frykberg got a call to say 'yeah', it's all agreed to. He came up to me and thanked me for my efforts. He could have done that to everyone in the room, I don't know."

Finally, mid-afternoon, It was announced at the subsequent media conference that peace had been made; 20 teams would compete in 1998, to be reduced to 14 by 2000. Balmain and South Sydney voted against the proposals. "I honestly believe … that if the ARL clubs had stuck together and toughed it out one more season, in 1998, that Super League would have fallen on its face and News Limited would have packed up bags and departed poorer, but wiser," George Piggins later wrote.

"That belief is the reason we voted against the 'amalgamation' plan.

"By the end of '97 the ARL was no more than a Clayton's organisation because the game belonged to Murdoch.

"I did my best to convince the ARL clubs that we were in front and should keep going.

"There was plenty of wheeling and dealing going on in the background and I doubt we were being told the full story at any stage as Neil Whittaker (ARL) and Ian Frykberg (Super League) worked in secret.

"There were a lot of lies at the time about the inflated financial standings of ARL clubs.

"I have no doubt many of the ARL clubs saw the prospect of News Limited money in a united competition as a godsend, as something that could rescue them from the deep shit they were in.

"The amount of double dealing that went on in the lead-up to the 'historic' meetings of December 19th, 1997, which sticky-taped the game back together, was bloody breath-taking."

McDonald, not Whittaker, had the honour of making the announcement.

Kelly recalls: "Word leaked out eventually from the Football Stadium that it looked like there was a deal and then we all had to rush into the city for this big announcement that a deal had been done and then News did one (a media conference).

"And the ARL did their press conference at the footy stadium.

"Later we heard anecdotally from a number of clubs who were at the Football Stadium that they had the radio on and they were listening to what we were saying. They didn't feel they could trust the other clubs, they didn't know what was going on with the other clubs.

"They were five corporate suites apart and the deal was that no-one was allowed to go in and try and influence them. They had to come to their own individual decisions."

The National Rugby League Championship Company would be owned equally by News and the Leagues. The Hunter Mariners were closed down ("I had a very good financial controller," recalls Bob Ferris. "Her husband was an insolvency expert. She was able to wind the company up and sell everything off with ease, without going for expert help. One day we just got up and walked out. I thought it was a sad day but I look back on it and I think it was the best time of my life. We sent everything back. We had half a store room of Nike shoes. Because I wasn't from football, I didn't think about taking anything. I don't have anything except memories."). There would be a maximum of eight clubs from Sydney in the final 14 and a minimum of six.

Brisbane, Newcastle and Auckland were immediately granted five year licenses. Clubs which merged would receive $4 million in 1998 and $3 million in 1999 and get five-year licences. Licences for 2000 were to be issued on July 31, 1999.

Lachlan Murdoch said in a statement: "What we have done today is ensure the survival and prosperity of rugby league. This is the best outcome for all parties - clubs, fans, players, the ARL and Super League."

The salary cap was to go down to $3 million. Before the war, clubs were spending between $1.2 million and $3 million.

The *Herald* reported an afternoon phone call in which News agreed to a $100 million payment over the following 12 months had been the clincher. The vote was 36-4. Uncertainty over Optus funding beyond October 1998 was a key factor in the ARL clubs voting the way they did.

The agreement guaranteed the ARL clubs $3.5 million each the following year.

"It was made clear to us that we've got seven months in order to get a licence to be one of the 16 teams in 1999," Balmain's Keith Barnes said. News received first and last rights of refusal on TV rights for 25 years.

Norths members, in December, had voted in favour of the club moving to Gosford. As a North Sydney fan, Professor Andrew Moore claimed in a scholarly paper that the ARL had "capitulated" to News. North Sydney managed to be considered a regional club - but Illawarra were not.

(Millward explained that the Steelers had been forced to surrender their regional status in order to be accepted to the Sydney premiership in 1982. They were allowed back into the Country Rugby League and yet to this day are considered by the NRL to be a Sydney club, meaning Newcastle can host finals on weekends that Wollongong cannot.

"We had the best of both worlds," Millward argues. "We could be city when it suited us, we could be country when it suited us.")

News was barred from providing additional funds to help their own clubs survive. Packer's pay TV contract with the league, which started the war despite him not having a pay TV station, was due to expire in 2000. Matthew Kidman wrote at the time: "One thing is for certain: rugby league is not going to drive subscriber numbers higher for Optus or Foxtel in the immediate future - and supposedly that was what the rugby league war was all about."

Ken Arthurson commented: "The deal is not what I would have liked but in a compromise you can't get everything you want." Agents and lawyers were reported to have made more than $30 million from the war since 1995.

"We had to get this home today," Whittaker told the media. "Providing Optus, Foxtel and Channel Nine can confirm additional funding packages, we will have a 20-team competition in 1998."

The Sweeney Report had discovered league fans wanted to know the future of junior league development was in good hands. People no longer cared who was to blame. "A tinge of sadness exists over the need to finally sell half of this great game to a media organisation in order to survive," wrote Phil Gould

The *Herald* reported Fykberg would receive a success fee if he could negotiate a united competition of which News were at least half owners.

"Congratulations" shouted reporter Tony Peters at the start of the media conference.. "Yeah thanks," responded Whittaker.

High above Sydney 25 years later, Neil Whittaker tries to deconstruct what happened that day.

"There were two stories to a lot of clubs," Whittaker says. "There were the people who knew how well the clubs were going, what they wanted and there was what they were saying publicly.

"So there were a lot of negotiations behind the scenes on getting mergers together … when I got there, there were merger talks happening between clubs. They were down to memorandums of understanding on what they were going to do. That was happening at a pace.

"During that year I did not spend so much time on that because it was only if you wanted to do it, you could do it. I think St George and Illawarra were the only two that joined together towards the end of that season (actually in '98)

"There was a lot of politics."

But why did the Sydney Super League clubs survive as stand alone entities? Even the CEO of the ARL in 1997 will eventually admit the stark truth of that.

Because they signed with Super League.

"There was a whole lot of …. It's hard to condense down to a short sentence but we had 22 teams and we had to get down to 14 or 16. It was a process where we just worked our way through.

"We eventually got to a point where we understood what News Limited's position was and why and then the Gold Coast and Crushers … another southern Queensland team would have been good but they were casualties.

"The Mariners closed, Adelaide and Perth went (at the end of '98), Auckland stayed and commercially that turned out to be one of the better decisions that was made and Frykers knew that. The value of the TV rights in New Zealand was outstanding in the early days and it got better and better."

Staring straight back at me after further quizzing, Whittaker says bluntly: "Everyone who wants to sit and judge what happened didn't understand that I was sitting there with 12 clubs and a comp with no money and there's 10 other clubs sitting there with News Limited with plenty of dough. How was it going to be fair?

"We had to try and come up with an idea that got everybody back in and being looked after in the same way. The merged clubs got a lot of money. That money was paid for by News Limited.

"And that was after the event. The ones that had jumped, there were obligations for (News) to look after them. But they pushed hard. I can tell you that mergers between News Limited clubs were pushed as hard or harder because they didn't want to keep putting the money in. So there was an issue that the money might be there but there was also a big driver, to not have to put another cent into rugby league.

"Have a look at the comp now. Have a look at how successful rugby league has been since that time. It's still got 16 teams, I think.

"There was a really strong view, supported by people on both sides, that it should have been 14 and it should have been (two rounds), home and away. We got down to 16. The process we used to get down to 16, I would not recommend to anybody."

Fykberg, Whittaker says, had originally championed a far-reaching and, depending on how it would have affected you, brutal approach.

"Frykers wanted to restructure the whole game, right through, all the way down. My view was that that was too hard. We had to get the comp working first and then restructure the game later … there wouldn't have been rugby league played in 1998.

"Turns out, it took 15 years to do that but we got to a commission which is probably where we were meant to be and I had their (News Limited's) word that they would work towards (further rationalisation) but they wouldn't put a timeframe around it.

"That's when we agreed we would form some competition and there were a number of names thrown around for it but the National Rugby League is what came up in the end. That's how it got set up, with rotating chairmen and board seats and all that sort of stuff. Ken Cowley said publicly that I shouldn't be chief executive. He was quite clear on his position."

As I've said repeatedly here, one of the major negotiating points was whether the new body took on News' debt and, says Whittaker, "we didn't. We didn't take on any of their debt. They kept their debt and we ran the competition.

"He (Frykberg) was using that to negotiate with us, to get control. We said 'you've invested that money and that's your business'. But it did mean we had to give them an opportunity to make their money back, so...."

And does THAT mean the NRL gave News favourable commercial conditions as part of the peace deal? They did get first right of refusal on television rights, after all, and it was years before the NRL could be truly regarded as being independent of the media company....

"No, no. Not really. They may have but we didn't do it deliberately. Look, they got the terms they needed to be able to manage their investment and we got a game that was unencumbered by that investment and it was an unbelievably good result.

"We didn't have money to pay for our legal fees so they paid those too. "

Whittaker now reveals, several months of the 1998 season were played without a written television contract in place.

Even on the day the NRL was formed, the ARL delegation went away having to find hundreds of thousands of dollars in a matter of days. "The announcement was made that there were some funding issues to be resolved," Whittaker says now. "Frykers wouldn't have allowed us to say that if he wasn't confident that we'd get there.

"There were some caveats on me and our team, that we had to go away and get more money for the ARL clubs. There was an appropriate concern that the Super League clubs would continue to be funded by News Limited and would have all the money and our clubs would struggle financially.

"That was on the Friday and I had until Monday to do that - otherwise the mandate I had expired … at the end of Monday.

"And on the Wednesday, which was Christmas Eve, we still didn't have it done.

"Geoff Carr and I and Johnny Brady were sitting in a coffee shop in Martin Place looking at the window of our lawyers MinterEllison and at three o' clock on Christmas Eve we got the signed documents from News Limited … from the parties, there were a number of parties that had to provide funding.

"We got the money and we got the documents signed."

Shane Richardson reflects: "Brave decisions had to be made but the decisions were not about bravery, they were all about just trying to patch it back together.

"So you sell off your mate over here to save your mate over there. Going broke is the reason they got rid of a lot of clubs - the Crushers, Adelaide, they would have all gone bust. The peripheral players just didn't have the money."

And at 2.55pm, as the media conference to announce a new era in rugby league concluded, the SFS was engulfed in a wild electrical storm.

POSTSCRIPT: Damien Kelly insisted I must interview North Shore restaurateur Stanley Lee for this chapter. "The late great John Brennan who was the boss of 2UE at the time said to us ... we had six or seven reporters who were on the story that day ... 'head to Lee's Fortuna Court ' - which is still a favourite of media people but it was a big 2UE haunt because it's just down the road from 2UE.

"We used to go there all the time. We had Christmas parties there. It was the sort of place ... it's got all sporting memorabilia on the walls, the West Indies cricket team would go there. It's this famous media and sporting restaurant. Stan Zemanek had his own bottle of scotch there that he'd just leave there.

"Brenno said 'I'll pay the bill as recognition of the job you've done' so I've walked in and Stanley said 'you guys have picked the wrong night to be here' and we said 'no, no we're celebrating, peace in our time and all that'.

"He said 'no, last night was the night to be here'. I said 'what are you talking about?'.

He said 'that table over there - Neil Whittaker and Ian Frykberg did the deal and we toasted it with a glass of port at the end of the night'."

Alas, when I contacted him in mid-2021, Stanley Lee has no direct recollection of that momentous toast.

"It's probably true because Frykers would come here all the time," said Lee, who counts Ken Arthurson as a regular.

"As you come in the restaurant, he would sit in the corner, on the left hand side and he always wanted two chairs, one to sit on and one to put his arm on."

He is taking reservations for the same table on December 18, 2022 if you're interested.

MY REGRETS

By Steve Mascord, *Sydney Morning Herald,*
Friday November 14 1997

TELL Laurie Daley that his rugby league career is to reach a pivotal moment at Elland Road on Sunday, and he blinks and pauses.

"Maybe so," he says after a little while. "But I'm not thinking about that. I'm not letting it enter my head, I'm just thinking about playing."

There can be few more significant occasions, even in a career as stratospheric as Daley's, than to captain Australia in a deciding Test against an unchanged Great Britain side - 80 minutes that will decide if a 38-year winning streak is to end.

That's how long it has been since an Australian side has lost a series in Britain. And, as has been recited ad nauseam this week, it's 27 years since the Lions won an Anglo-Australian series anywhere.

Thanks to the war that has ravaged the game, Australia, the team Daley leads on Sunday (Monday morning, Australian time), is drawn solely from the Super League competition and is full of rookies who are so young they don't even know how to misbehave on tour.

"That's the big difference," the 27-year-old Canberra five-eighth says, sitting in the foyer of the team's Leeds hotel and reflecting on his previous national tours of duty here, in 1990 and 1994.

"On those tours, there was a lot of experience. Some of these blokes, I've hardly played with. I don't know how they react in certain situations, under pressure, and I'm still learning to play with them," he said.

If the game in Australia is to reunite next year, then Sunday's Test at Elland Road will provide a telling postscript to three years of recriminations and sheer carnage during a sport's dramatic fall from grace.

Have the reverberations from the war been such that Australia's four-decade domination of the international game will be brought toppling down?

That will have happened to a degree if Great Britain win,

although the ARL are deserved holders of the World Cup.

The ups and downs of rugby league over those three years of division have been inextricably linked to the fortunes of Daley, arguably the sport's brightest star.

He was one of the first players signed by Super League, in a Townsville hotel room in early 1995, and when the ARL won the first court case, he swore he'd never go back.

The establishment, he said, had treated players "like dogs".

Eventually, he went back, and displayed enough professionalism to enhance his reputation as a player of rare flair and courage, the archetypal "natural".

When Super League did kick off, it was fitting he should be its player of the year, just as Brad Fittler won the equivalent in the ARL.

Reflecting on the stormy early days of 1996, when the game was hit by a players' strike and he and his fellow elite players were wheeled out by both sides as spokesmen, Daley says: "Yes, I have regrets.

"I regret some of the things I said. I look back and think: 'I should not have said that'. "But we all got caught up in the emotion of it. It was a bad thing, what happened,

and I can only hope it never happens again."

Asked if he lost friends because of his stance, Daley says: "Not friends. Not real friends. I lost people I knew, people I was acquainted with.

"But yeah, I know there are people who don't like me."

Despite all this, there are not enough people who don't like Laurie Daley for it to matter.

A *Rugby League Week* poll of first graders this year on who should captain a united Australian side under a compromise, was won by Daley.

His influence on this Australian side is subtle but goes something like this: if your captain, your best-paid player and biggest star can say hello to everyone, sign endless autographs and greet everyone he encounters with a smile, what right do you have to be a prat?

"It makes me feel good that fellow players think I should be captain when we get back together," said Daley.

"It's one of the reasons I wanted to be captain at Canberra, so I'd have the experience of doing it at both levels."

That brings us to the Canberra captaincy controversy. Some

people who know Daley were a bit surprised he accepted the Raiders captaincy when he knew incumbent Ricky Stuart would be aggrieved.

After all, Laurie is such a nice bloke and alL "It's easy to go with the flow," Daley says, also referring to the game's schism, "but if something tells you you've got to go in a different direction, you've got to take a stand."

But, the Test captain says, enough is enough when it comes to two competitions. Peering out at empty stands this year made him feel "sad . . . but I understood why people were staying away. No-one wants two competitions, everyone wants them to get back together and just get on with it. But I can also understand that there is a lot to work out

"One of the things I learnt last year was don't get involved in politics."

Cynics say players can't possibly be as motivated when they earn $500,000 a year as when they signed for $20,000 and were on incentives. Surprisingly, Daley says that's true in some cases.

"When you get out on the field, I think you want to play and do your best. But for some players, it may have affected their preparation."

Preparation is not something Australia will lack when the national anthem is played at the sold-out home of Leeds United soccer club on Sunday.

Coach John Lang has devoted the entire week to minutiae.

"Let's face it, if we do happen to lose and I'm the losing captain, it will be a great disappointment to me but you've got to roll with the punches," he says, eyes ablaze. "Obviously it's hard because you know about the history, it's in the back of your mind. But the more times you think about it, the more pressure you put on yourself.

"I can't control it. All I can control is going out there and playing well."

For most of this decade, that has been enough to get teams including Laurie Daley past the post.

If it is enough on Sunday, the horror movie that has been league in Australia these past three years will have a happy ending.

CHAPTER 25

"Peace"

The day this project was conceived is well documented in my first book, *Touchstones.*

Pre-Christmas 2016, the Brighouse Rangers - a foundation club of the Northern Union - took on the Toronto Wolfpack, then preparing for their debut season in League 1. It was cold and wet and uplifting.

This was the 'Pack's first-ever match, featuring North American trialists whose adventures were being documented for a reality show. And it was a life-affirming day if you were a rugby league dreamer, the sport's glorious, grimy past meeting its gleaming trans-Atlantic future right in the heart of the land that gave it life.

Nigel Wood, then CEO of the Rugby Football League, sidled up to me on a muddy touchline and suggested I should write a sequel to Mike Colman's *Super League: The Inside Story.*

There is a sublime poetry to the fact that, in the time that it took to complete this project about their sport's appetite for self-destruction, the Wolfpack themselves have lived and died.

What we learned about rugby league from the Super League War is the same thing we learned from the Wolfpack's story.

"I think of rugby league as a small sport that is wildly over-exposed in NSW and Queensland and which will never completely go away," broadcaster Debbie Spillane told me during her interview for *Two Tribes*.

"But it will keep going around in circles - whether they are ever-decreasing circles, I don't know. Perhaps they are."

A clue about rugby league's propensity to walk repeatedly into the same electrified fence, forgetting the agony each time, lies in our surroundings that day: overgrown traffic islands, run down semi-detached cottages, beat-up old sedans in the carpark.

Firstly, and above all, rugby league can't afford *not* to keep making the same mistakes over and over. It was created specifically in 1895 for those who could not afford to play rugby otherwise

And it is still played and followed by the descendents of those people, without having made much headway at all in other parts of society in the five generations since.

"It is a game built by, played by, and watched by working class people. They may not have much in their lives but what they have is that treasure," Jim Quinn, the CEO at Oldham, said at the height of the merger protests in 1995.

To me, there is one subject at the centre of any serious discussion about what Thomas Kenneally called "the supreme code, a cellular structure comprised of 13 players which mimicked life and art and war so exactly that it became them."

It's the fatal flaw.

That is, the elusive DNA strand that makes rugby league great and simultaneously holds it back - the strength that is simultaneously

445

its weakness, the nobility that has a symbiotic relationship with pettiness, which lies in the red hot nucleus of the sport.

This is a book about that nucleus, about the people who loved a game so much they almost destroyed it - but also so much they managed to save it.

In 1997, rugby league tried to be something it wasn't: global, glitzy, up-market, national. When it was left floundering, it was rescued by the same core demographic that had shown its disdain for those aspirations.

We see this regularly in our sport. Rugby league's existing support base is often like a passionate, devoted but maniacally and violently jealous partner. It will do absolutely anything for its paramour - aside from share it or allow it a life of its own.

"if you do things at the right pace for the right reasons and they're well thought out, then people will come on that journey and that's been evidenced by some of the things that are still in the game now that were introduced during that period. You've got to be very careful that when you do it, (that) you've consulted widely, there is general support for it and that you've been through a process where you can confidently predict that there's going to be more support for it than opposition to it. You'll never get universal support for some of those things because there's too much passion in the game to get everyone feeling the same way. But you just have to be careful to be sure you do things a) for the right reasons and b) you've got the right levels of support to be able to do it."

On March 21 1996, colleague Peter Fitzsimons wrote in the *Sydney Morning Herald*: "After all this distance traversed and all this blood spilled, it is equally obvious now that the ARL is never going to be able to carry the future with Parramatta v Souths matches.

"If those games were never much in recent years, they're going to be looking all the more pathetic now against the backdrop of the mighty Super League 'vision' that the Murdoch crowd have spent all those millions promoting."

I agreed with Fitzy back then. We were, of course, both horribly wrong - South Sydney v Parramatta in 2022 is a blue riband event.

We were wrong because we simultaneously over-estimated and underestimated the sport of rugby league.

We dramatically over-estimated its ability to appeal to new demographics and present enough of a united front to operate on a level playing field with other sports.

And we just as dramatically under-estimated the dogged determination of the very same people whose infighting retards its growth to prop it up over and over again in their own enclaves.

Why we were wrong is what the Super League War taught us.

Like most adult eccentricities, rugby league owes its most abiding trait to its childhood - in fact, to its birth.

Because of its origins as being a reaction against something - rugby union - league is tied to class and regional identity more than other sports. They are its sole reasons to exist, in fact. When it loses its identity, it loses literally everything.

In 1997, it lost much of its identity and much of itself.

Those running the game discovered its limitations the hard way. It was not easily translatable to strangers. It relied absolutely and utterly on the communities that begot it and it lived or died at their whim.

To my mind, it doesn't go far enough to say rugby league is 'a working class game' in England, Australia and New Zealand. It actually IS the working class, or a branch of it.

Don't expect rugby league to do anything the working class won't do. And its glass ceiling is the fact that the A-B demographics in these areas are already enamoured with another code of rugby.

League's path out of its role of selling mixed drinks and home improvement tools to western Sydney is, it would seem, permanently blocked by the circumstances of its birth.

The traditionalists saved rugby league by coming back to watch it from '98 onwards; and the game's debt to them makes it fearful of ever doing anything that might upset them again.

The NRL's football operations manager Graham Annesley confirms how carefully administrators now treat - but argues progress is still possible.

"If you do things at the right pace for the right reasons and they're well thought out, then people will come on that journey and that's been evidenced by some of the things that are still in the game now that were introduced during that period," he said in his interview for this book (see next chapter for more).

"You've got to be very careful that when you do it, (that) you've consulted widely, there is general support for it and that you've been through a process where you can confidently predict that there's going to be more support for it than opposition to it."

In the fullness of time, the greatest service anyone can do for rugby league is to be its Oppenheimer - to split that atom at its heart and let it operate free of its cultural history without killing that component during the operation.

That can, perhaps, hold be done with new frontiers and new formats of the sport - which will again be mortally challenged by the deeply considervative constituents the sport relies on to draw breath each day.

What the preceding pages tell us is that all the money in the world won't help unless that atom is one day split. Because money can, and will always, be wasted by desperate people.

Born out of the hunger for money - even if it was just money to relieve hunger - rugby league is stuck in an interminable loop whereby that hand-to-mouth imperative will repeatedly tear it apart.

How can something demand loyalty that owes its very existence to disloyalty?

In 1995, many of the game's dreamers saw their fantasies made manifest: Nines, Tri-series, Brisbane grand finals, expanded World Club Challenges, more big city teams.

They were the game's left, the constituents who looked enviously at other sports and believed rugby league could be 'better'. Even though I worked at Fairfax, I was a rugby league leftist.

And guess what? We got a billionaire to fund our city in the clouds.

No matter what you believe about who 'won' the war from a business perspective, there is no doubt our floating metropolis came crashing to the ground.

The right won the cultural war - by knockout. Their prize was controlling the game's destiny for the next 25 years. There aren't enough leftists in rugby league to nourish it. I would posit that, by definition, it is a 'right' sport - in almost all the senses we now use that word: conservative, traditional, even religious.

The Super League War should have taught us rugby league lefties that we can have our grand experiments but unless we have laying around the $80 million it has so far cost the Melbourne Storm to stay afloat, they are destined to fail.

It is, fellow progressives, not our sport. We will always be in the minority. We are guests in their midst.

I once argued with an NRL executive that State of Origin had been over-commercialised with even the national anthem performance a plug for the cast of a stage show, movie trailers on a loop on the big screen and car dealerships parading their wares on a lap of the perimeter fence. He looked back at me aghast.

"State of Origin IS a commercial entity - that's what it IS!" he responded.

Likewise, we might say that a sophisticated rugby league that looks outwards to new territories and moves suburban teams around the country like chess pieces while abhorring violence makes about as much sense as communism itself opening a chain of fast food stores or God himself taking up atheism.

For those 12 years from 1895 that it looked the same as its parent game, the things that set the new sport apart were many of the same things that Super League in Australia wanted to change.

But it could not. As the Toronto Wolfpack might now tell you, no-one can. It comes down to that DNA.

Dump old-fashioned tours: Lindsay

**By Steve Mascord, Sydney Morning Herald,
Saturday November 15, 1997**

AUSTRALIA"s three-Test tour of Great Britain, which ends on Sunday with the Lions attempting to secure their first series victory in 27 years, may be the first and last of its kind.

While Super League's decision to scrap matches against club sides and scratch France from the itinerary was seen as a radical break with tradition, World Board chairman Maurice Lindsay wants to go further.

Lindsay said on Friday that he would be calling for league to follow the lead of rugby union and have more one-off Tests against a variety of countries.

That means in future Australia and New Zealand may be in Britain at the same time, playing against the likes of England, Wales and leading clubs but meeting Great Britain just once or twice per visit.

"I think we should restructure what was an old-fashioned system," Lindsay said. "All we ever did was Great Britain went to Australia every four years and Australia came here every four years. I think you've got to play each other in short spells, more often.

"The expectations of the public are now much higher than they used to be. They now demand international sport."

Lindsay's comments are certain to upset traditionalists, but league is desperately trying to keep up with rugby union in Britain, where tickets for an All Blacks Test have been sold out after having 20,000 empty seats for Super League's Second Test last Saturday at Old Trafford.

Conversely, the Australian Rugby League is thought to favour a return to extended tours should there be a compromise with News Ltd.

"I think you should structure it so you play each other more often," Lindsay said. "At the moment you've got three visiting touring sides playing the rugby union boys.

"In a month, you've got England playing the All Blacks, Australia and South Africa. They're all sellouts. When you get that money, you can use it to develop your game." The Elland Road Third Test is a sellout, though.

And officials of Britain's Rugby Football League have said more than 120 journalists had sought accreditation. This exceeds 1995 World Cup levels.

Australia's preparation has been clouded by injuries to centre Ryan Girdler (knee) and winger Brett Mullins (leg), who face late tests.

Girdler trained with the side on Thursday, but Mullins jogged only lightly and is unlikely to play.

"I don't want crocks out there and I don't care who they are," Australian coach John Lang said. "That's what I've told the medical staff."

Rival coaches Lang and Andy Goodway were waiting on Thursday night for responses to queries they have put to Kiwi referee Phil Houston.

Houston, who was criticised by British manager Phil Lowe because Australian second-rower Gorden Tallis was not sent off in the Second Test, returned from a brief European holiday only on Thursday night.

Lowe has said he feared the match might become violent as a result of several isolated incidents at Old Trafford.

Goodway was open about instructing his players to test Houston, but Lang said: "That's not my style, I'd rather us rely on our own ability. If you go out there to test the referee and get penalised out of the game, you've only got yourself to blame."

Brad Clyde, to play his first game since late September because of a calf injury, said he would need a rest at some stage. Lang plans to replace him with Matt Adamson after about 30 minutes.

CHAPTER 26

For better ... or for worse?

IN January 1998, delegates of clubs on both sides finally met to consummate their marriages.

"All the CEOs of all the clubs went to a meeting at the Sydney Football Stadium in one of the suites there," recalls Kevin Neil. "There was thick air between a lot of people - it wasn't an easy meeting to go to.

"But it ended up fine and most people agreed we had to move on and that's when (Ian) Frykberg informed us 'NRL' was what the logo was and what the competition was going to be called.

"Everyone went there with good will. I remember Neil Whittaker said 'there's a lot of people here with a lot of baggage, we've got to put that to the side and move on'.

"It all happened on that day. I think that when it's 25 years (since) they should get everyone who was there together for a drink."

The war started with Kerry Packer refusing to surrender his pay TV rights - even though he had no pay TV operation - and it ended with Packer jumping into bed with Murdoch - something the ACCC originally forbade.

In the last chapter I offered some of my general impressions of what it all may have told us about rugby league. Now it's time to turn it over to our 100 interviewees.

What does it say about the sport that there is no real consensus on any of the answers? Why can't people address this issue dispassionately after such a long time? Is it that the story has never been properly told?

Or are agendas just such an integral part of that game's culture that objectivity is nigh on impossible?

What Was It About?

BOB FULTON: "I'll put it this way. Ken Arthurson and John Quayle basically built a product that two of the biggest media moguls in the world were fighting over. Simple as that."

SHANE RICHARDSON: "It was one of those opportunities to spread the game and really make big changes in the game. But it wasn't about that. It was about compromise to put the game back together. Murdoch had had enough of running out of money, the ARL were on their knees."

GEOFF CARR: ""It was all about - as we know - TV. If Packer and Murdoch would have sat down and solved it earlier… The game was flying in '94. The '94 Kangaroo Tour … everything was flying. But Brisbane had come in and caused a lot of tension because they were privately owned. When I say tension … all these little things were antagonistic but it was about entrepreneurial people trying to get more money. They started behind the scenes to pick up other creaks and strains in the way the whole system operated and then there was a group of people … the Roger Cowans of this world.

Roger, he wanted to take pressure off his leagues club. There were different motivations for people to do what they wanted to do. The financial incentive was appealing to a lot of clubs. The little cracks that were there in '94 became bigger cracks. People started to meet and take sides. Everyone knew (News Limited's) David Smith was going around … in the background discussing things with clubs. There were all these rumours about which clubs would be invited in and which would go. People were manoeuvring to do the right thing by their particular club."

MARK SARGENT: "Ultimately it was a pissing contest between two multi-millionaire media barons. Those two organisations had historically done deals both before and after. They were always going to work something out so in some ways it was a monumental waste of time, money and caused everyone a lot of grief."

PAUL KIND: "My primary observation right the way through the entire exercise was what a great waste of opportunity it was for both sides. Because both sides of the equation had to throw everything they had at trying to prove that they were better than each other and trying to - effectively - bury each other. There was a view on both sides that a couple of successful years and one or the other league would ultimately make the other one get on its knees. There was so much at stake."

GARY PEARSE: "This whole time, it seemed to be Murdoch was the villain when to me, Packer was really the villain. Here he was marching into that room full of CEOs and telling them they were the greatest brains in rugby league in the world but 'if you go near News I'm going to sue the arse off you. I'm going to take your car, your boat, all that stuff'. He was controlling the game with a two week (warning) of when games were played. He looked, during that time, to be 100 per cent with the ARL but within 24 hours of us winning the court case he went straight in and brought Monday night Super League."

LINDSAY YOUNG: "I'd say rugby league had been going since 1908 and it had got to the point where it had got stagnant and there was a media organisation who came up with the idea of creating more clubs and having a Super League and making it worth a lot more money. But a lot of people didn't trust that. Better the devIl they know, I think. It didn't work but it rattled the chain of the incumbents and they had to make certain concessions so the media organisation didn't get what it wanted. And the NSW Rugby League couldn't keep it the way they had it so there was basically amalgamation of those - which theoretically has been good for everybody."

GEOFF BELLEW: "The idea that a game that's played on the eastern seaboard in Australia and in a few counties in the (UK) and a bit in France and a bit in New Zealand is going to be taking the world to the point where Chinese 13-year-olds are going to be buying Ricky Stuart shirts is ridiculous, when you think about it. It's just absurd. But there were some who genuinely believed that was the case. One of the bad fallouts was that international football suffered, I think - badly."

JOHN LANG: "It was all about content for TV, that's what it was about. Channel Nine had had the rugby league for years and had done well out of it. It was to sell Foxtel, from News Limited's point of view. It was always going to happen in one way or another. I just think it was part of a technological revolution really. From free-to-air to Foxtel and now we have all the streaming services. Things had been the same for a long time."

JOSH WHITE: "My young bloke asked me what it was about and I said it was something that had to happen but it was wrong how it happened. I think they did it all the wrong way, doing sneaky deals behind backs. A lot of blokes made a lot of money out of it but the way it was run was really weird. Clubs got swallowed up, which is sad. I've got two of them, Western Suburbs and Steelers, so it leaves a sour taste in my mouth that way. But in another way, it made us a lot of money. I was on $40,000 at Wests plus a car and I ended up signing for nearly $300,000 a year! Graham Murray signed me to Super League and he was my cousin."

ROB WEAVER: "Survival. That's what it was all about for us (Penrith). That was how we were focused, both on the field and off it. The coach knew it. All the players knew it. Most of us knew it. We had a few people on the board who thought otherwise. Either they thought we'd survive regardless or they wanted to go down screaming."

JIM MARSDEN: "A lot of people will say it was about these media people, Murdoch and Packer, and their egos and flexing their muscles. I think that under-rates them. I think it was a power struggle. Murdoch saw an opportunity the same as Packer had seen an opportunity with cricket previously and he thought 'I'm going to take that opportunity'. Packer, I don't think it was about his ego. It was his opportunity being undermined, his control of the League being undermined, television and everything else".

ANNE DAVIES: "These days people wouldn't be that shocked by it but in those days football was a community activity and this turned it into a multi-million-dollar business that was designed to drive other businesses, like the roll-out of Optus or telecommunications. People were really shocked that the teams that they loved could be sacrificed on the altar of business."

STUART RAPER: "There's big things in our game, real landmarks. They went from unlimited to four tackles, they brought in six tackles. When they changed the rules from five metres to 10 metres … but this was as big as anything - splitting the game and then bringing it back. That just changed the game from semi-professional to full-time professional. It changed everyone, from on-field to off-field people."

SAM AYOUB: "Super League thought they could just railroad in and take over the game and be custodians of the game with the administration being the ARL. There wasn't much right with that. The product was always good. For that reason, the war happened. It was fought over TV rights. Who knows whether it would have organically grown more, nationally?"

RODNEY OVERBY: "One of the first owners of a sports team in Australia was Michael Wrublewski, God rest his soul. He went up against the grain of what Australia was normally used to. People who want to change the game, you're not going to change it without people not liking it. Change is difficult for people to accept. Michael Wrublewski was one of those type of dudes, he taught me a lesson. 'Have a go, mate' is what I learned here in Australia and Murdoch, he was having a go."

BOB FERRIS: "It was about some clubs not getting a fair deal (from the ARL) - all over. Some clubs were getting a better deal than others."

WAYNE BENNETT: "It was about pay TV. Who's the biggest promoters of rugby league now? Pay TV. What do they rely on?

Subscribers. It was about subscribers. Paul (Morgan) and people at the ARL could see the amount of money that would come into the game if they bought into it. Packer didn't want that. He had Channel 9, he realised what was coming and he wanted to have them excluded from rugby league. That's what the shitfight was about - nothing else."

KEVIN WALTERS: "For mine, it was about trying to grow the game of rugby league. That's what I believe. Trying to grow the game into an international sport, including the Super League clubs in England in the competition. And trying to bust down some barriers that possibly could have been there with the Australian Rugby League."

MARC GLANVILLE: "I'd explain it like mum and dad had split up - but then they got back together. It was a bit rough - but they got back together and they live happily ever after."

Who Won The War?

MATTHEW KIDMAN: "Probably Nine … they had a big voice in what happened and probably didn't have to fork out anywhere near the amount of money. They ended up getting quite a good deal … I think part of the Australis settlement was Super League but they also got a stake in Fox Sports for it. News had to give up a lot. PBL weren't funding the roll-out of cable. Well they were, but in a very small sense. What did News end up with? Nothing. It's not as if News got anything cheap. They've had to pay full tote. What did they lose? Was it $600 million in the Super League War? They owned a few clubs for a while which is just another liability. Nine ended up with the free-to-air rights and there was always the anti-siphoning thing they (News) never really got on top of, never won that battle. I think

News Limited lost. I think it was poor strategy, it was bully-boy stuff. They'd done it in the UK. They thought they were going to win again. They thought they could watch Australis die. So it was a schmozzle, the whole pay TV war. It was a debacle. The Australian market's not big enough. There was very little commercial sense put to it. The only ones who played their cards right - it seemed to me - was PBL who took bits and pieces, spent some money but never overly committed and it didn't drain them. At the end of it, Lachlan had to resolve the issue, didn't he? It was a disaster. And Rupert probably said 'right, we need to change, we need to build bridges again and get a deal done, Kerry wants to do it, we did it in London, now do it on the ground, get it done' .The News Corp lieutenants in Australia were hopeless, absolutely hopeless."

JIM MARR: "Super League won hands down didn't they? At the end of the day it was a business fight and a business decision and I'm saying that Super League won and I stick by that but I only say that in sporting terms. I feel that their business ideals have won and they have taken advantage, have taken control. The most evident thing about that for me is there are too many non-footy people in administration. You have to have business acumen and you have to have business knowledge but it needs to be subservient to the main thing. I have a fear that after old bastards like me and you shuffle off their mortal coils, I don't know who's left for it. You struggle, you really do struggle, to find any pub in Sydney showing rugby league now. It didn't used to be like that."

DENIS FITZGERALD: "I'd have to say that the ARL won the war. I think the clubs that went with News, they got money. They won the lottery."

KEVIN WALTERS: "I think the game won, really. The explosion of two competitions, that certainly made rugby league a topical event in papers, in magazines … on television. It certainly created a lot of headlines around the world with what happened. In one way, and I'm trying to keep things as positive as I can, the winner was rugby league because it was in everyone's faces. There were some things I'm sure a lot of people from both sides regretted that they actually did do but it was great for the game because it's evolved now into a sport that can cater for everyone."

GEOFF BELLEW: "In a sense the ARL won because they managed to preserve the fabric of the game. News had this idea they would just steamroll them, particularly when all the international countries went with them. I don't think there were any winners."

GEOFF COUSINS: "I think it does (have a simple answer). There is no Super League, it doesn't exist. It was furphy, a phantom. It didn't last. The game basically went back to pretty much the same clubs. It didn't go to Asia. It didn't do any of the things that the Super League said. And, who did it cost the most? Since it was a war about money, who did it cost the most? Well it cost News Limited hundreds of millions. I've read $300 million, $400 million. Amazingly it never appeared as a line item in a News Limited accounts, which is pretty incredible. What did it cost Optus? Nothing like that. A mere fraction of that. I can't remember the figure but about $30 million I think is about probably where it was. So who won it? If it was a business war, I'll tell you who won it and it certainly wasn't News Limited. It was about pay TV. When you say Kerry won, well it wasn't about free-to-air. Kerry … he had about five per cent of our company. He was a very small shareholder. He didn't put up a lot of money. Optus put up 95 per cent of the money, even at the start. I think it's silly to say

Kerry won because it was a pay TV war. How could he win? All he owned was five per cent. News Limited owned 50 per cent of Foxtel so the losers were Foxtel - meaning News and Telstra. And the winner was Optus, at that time. Yes, I was passionate about the sport and really the ethical questions involved and I thought News Limited's behaviour was appalling and I still think it was and they should be roundly condemned for it in every respect. I'm glad they lost all the money."

MALCOLM NOAD: "Not surprisingly, I'd have to say that News Corp won. But I say that because: look where Foxtel is these days. If we hadn't had the rugby league and Optus had the rugby league, perhaps they'd be where Foxtel is now. It would be hard to say that News Corp wasn't the winner out it."

KEVIN NEIL: "No-one. Commercially, probably News Limited. The TV revenue they're generating now, if you took that $8 million that Kerry Packer was paying in 1995, I think he owned the pay TV rights for another million. If you CPI-ed that and added it to what it's generating in TV revenue now, it would be way, way way above CPI (Consumer Price Index). Did anyone win? News Limited and Foxtel maybe? Clearly it didn't deliver what it promised (for Canberra) but it probably delivered a financial windfall for the organisation because … all the expenses of the football team were funded by News Limited for seven years. The Leagues Club group basically put $1 million a year into development and didn't have to put anything else in. Clubs like Parramatta and the Roosters and probably Canterbury at the time were probably putting seven or eight million dollars a year into their football teams. The leagues club group, they say it's great management. They sort of forgot.. That turned into a windfall for the club, that's probably why they're one of the wealthiest groups in the league now. They were really well managed, but… they didn't have to spend any money for seven years. They just put it into the bank account."

JOHN LANG: "Who won? The players. They made a motza. They won financially. I'm not sure that full-time professional sport … a lot of people, it doesn't serve them well over their lifetime. Neither the ARL nor Super League won. In the end, Channel Nine kept the rights and Super League got it for Foxtel."

SAM AYOUB: "I wouldn't say the players won a war. They were beneficiaries of the war. There's no way you could say the players won the war because they didn't partake in it. They were the commodity. In the end, no-one really won. It was a war that wasn't won."

BOB FERRIS: "Did anyone win? I think rugby league did win because it has become a better game and a cleaner game and more ethical in some ways."

LAURIE DALEY: "I don't think anyone really won. There was a lot of money spent and a lot of hurt and pain caused but I think when you look at what Super League was trying to achieve, people would say that's nearly the right model to have if you were starting the game today …starting with those teams and maybe progressively adding another one or two and having that 12- or 13- or 14-team comp. There's a lot of disenchanted people still … a lot of money spent."

ANNE DAVIES: "The ARL won in the end. Super League in my view lost the public relations battle but many of the Super League clubs emerged stronger. Whether it was the injection of funds … the News Corp accountants came in and said 'this is how we're going to operate."

ADRIAN LAM: "I strongly believe it helped develop and grow the game and make it better. I know there was a financial massacre to the whole sport over a short period of time and we had to rally really hard but from there I think the game's only gotten better and bigger because of some of the things … when it got back together they had brought some of those ideas in."

JAMIE MATHIOU: "I'm a business person and I always believe … whether you're a developer, a builder, progression's got to happen. If someone else came in and turned it upside down and there was an opportunity for a lot of people to go professional, to make a lot of money … have a look at the game. Who thought athletes would run this fast, be that powerful? When you're working (a job), trying to be a professional athlete is pretty tough mate."

TOM MOCKRIDGE: "It caused a lot of tension and activity in its time but nearly 25 years later, the NRL today is not only the leading rugby league competition in the world but I'd say it's the leading rugby club competition in the world … better than anything union's putting on in the northern hemisphere or across Super Rugby. I think it's a legacy of unambiguous positivity. It's really pushed the game to a new level and given it a future and something that has to constantly renew. I hope everyone keeps an open mind and we keep things moving forward positively."

PETER MULLHOLLAND: "I really think players won the war. They got better terms and conditions out of it. It turned us into a full-time professional sport. I think players and coaches were the benefactors of it. If you want to go down to cold hard business facts, I guess you could say 'Fox are still alive, aren't they?' They got the game. Someone gave me some figures of how much people are paying to watch footy and how many million had it and all of a sudden it made sense why he spent $700 million to get the NRL."

PAUL LANGMACK: "There's players who were on $50,000 and overnight they were on $400,000. There were players who were one-and-a-half graders getting first grade money. There wasn't enough good players for all those teams, for the 20 teams. So they were lucky that they got the money. They got paid under false pretences. If there wasn't a Super League War they still would have been playing second grade. You say boom or bust. I think they were kissed on the arse by an angel. They should be grateful. If it happened now, they wouldn't be playing first grade."

NOEL GOLDTHORPE: "Murdoch? What it was all about was getting the footy on Fox. He did what he wanted to, he spent what he wanted to. The players won financially."

MICHAEL HILL: "The war was the vehicle that enabled the Knights to jump to the next level because the competition wasn't as strong and consistent. That's what war did for Newcastle in the first instance. It split the competition. We then were growing a terrific team. We had a bloke in Malcolm (Reilly) who got them to play. The basis of the club - 'be the player that everyone wants to play with' - that Allan McMahon created was built upon by David Waite who was a theoretical coach. He spent hours drilling them and then Malcolm got them to play. Malcolm inspired them to play. But it was all against the background that half the competition wasn't there. We jumped. That's what the war did. It allowed us to get to the top."

PAUL KIND: "I think the ARL lost the control they had had bestowed on them for 100 years so I think they lost the war in that regard. They had a lot more to lose in making peace, I reckon. But they had no choice. The clubs, it was not really good for a lot of the clubs because they took a long time to recover from the money that disappeared, and then the new money that came, and then it all went. News won, of course, because they got TV which is what they wanted. I don't know if they would say they won if you asked them because there was a pretty big consequence for them. For a long time after, people didn't trust their involvement in the game. They got TV but corporately they suffered for a long time and I think when they finally got out of league in 2012, they were probably really happy."

WAYNE BENNETT: "Nobody won. It destroyed the game for 18 months. We had people on both sides of the divide. Most of us got on with our lives. They put it back together again. Why did they put it back together again? Because it was about money. It was about doing a deal. They were both hurting themselves. Who put the deal together? Kerry Packer and Rupert Murdoch. Because the game can't survive without the TV rights. It wasn't complex. I didn't have any complexities in my mind about what was going to work and what wasn't going to work and why we were doing it. Nor did the players. It changed the game in that their incomes were changed forever. That wasn't a bad thing because the money was in the game to do that. Look at the TV rights we get today because of that. We wouldn't be getting those TV rights today if that didn't happen."

PHIL ECONOMIDIS: "My belief in the whole thing was that the game belonged to the people, not the media moguls. A few years later, most of the ARL coaches from 1997 were out of a job and most of the Super League coaches still had jobs. There was hardly any of those ARL coaches still coaching. It cost me a job at Leeds. (Gary) Hetherington flew to Sydney and told me I had the job. Then he rang me to say it was purely a business decision that Super League were paying Dean Lance and it was costing them nothing. So obviously, they took Dean Lance."

NEIL TUNNICLIFFE: "Had the money not come into the game, then the game would have died a slow death - so it has to be seen as a positive. Was all the good got out of the opportunity that could have been got? No, I don't think it was. There were several missed opportunities, reflecting back. Is the game in a better position now than it was back then? Again, a qualified answer. Yes and no. I think there are some bits that are stronger but there are some bits that are no further on. As many problems have been caused as there have been solutions. Who won war? A draw probably."

GRAEME NORTON: "I think it was the beginning of a period later on when New Zealand did really well. You had all these players emerging. Your Sean Hoppes, your Stephen Kearneys, all these guys were coming through. It changed the face of New Zealand professional teams, where all the players were professionals. The Nines, we won that a couple of times, and the team we played against, the Australian teams, were the heroes of the day. When Super League arrived, it brought a new energy to New Zealand rugby league because there were opportunities appearing everywhere. There used to be 20 New Zealand players in the Australian competition. Now there might be 100. A New Zealand team can compete now from one season to the next against all the strong nations. Super League at the time certainly brought enthusiasm and interest and captured a whole lot of new people."

SHANE RICHARDSON: "If Super League hadn't come along, Cronulla were gone. We'd had that champion Under 21s side but we were going to lose those players. The Roosters and these guys were going to sign them. We had no money to retain them. Once we got involved with Super League, not only did we retain them, we became stronger. Built grandstands, good lighting, all these things. On the other side, they became weaker. What happened was they just just didn't have any funding. They were promised a lot of funding but it was never delivered to them. They were weak anyway. They were struggling. North Sydney were struggling with the leagues club. So were the Crushers. It was like signing a pact to commit suicide - which is what they did.

"It was financial suicide, what they did."

ROY MASTERS: "I believe the Packer family were the winners. On the ARL side, Optus were the biggest spenders, Packer intimidated the ARL into spending its $25 million reserves and Packer didn't contribute much. When the Super League comp began in 1997, he got TV rights for bugger all, I suspect. He therefore televised both comps. When the war ended, as part of the peace treaty Packer was granted 50 per cent of Fox Sports and 25 percent of Foxtel. When Murdoch wanted to own Fox Sports outright, it was valued at $2 billion and Packer received half. So, he gets $1 billion for minimum investment."

What Did We Learn?

GRAHAM LOWE: "The whole game underestimated the value and the wisdom of blokes with broken noses and cauliflower ears."

NATHAN GIBBS: "I don't think the game is any different now to how it was before the war in the sense that it's still run by money and Covid was a good example of that. Once games weren't on, there was no money. You need the broadcasters to actually make money. Super

League was all about who was going to get the rights to broadcasting football. It hasn't changed the game. It hasn't changed anything about anything, really."

JOHN BRADY: "It showed a lot about the game and about its importance to people. The number of sports that could come through that at all is incredibly few, I'd suggest. So it showed something about the psyche of the game, it showed something about the psyche of the people who followed it. When you talk about getting the game back together, Carry (Geoff Carr) and I went around talking to the clubs, trying to see if we could get the game back together and trying to get people around the frame that we have to start talking at some point. You would get people saying 'I sat at Pratten Park when there was no-one else there and it was pouring down rain'. And you say 'how many people were there with you?'. 'Oh, just me - but that doesn't matter'. Carry always had a line - what News never quite grappled with in understanding was the ability of clubs to live when no business sense said they should, just on being them. It was organic. It doesn't mean they could always stay that way but... (it was) their ability to defy reality and survive. It showed a certain inner strength of the game as much as it showed its problems. The recovery work under (David) Gallop, particularly, I don't think people have ever really understood. The head start everyone had had around that ... AFL had had this massive head start, rugby (union) had had this head start... For the game to have got back within the period of a short number of years to be setting records again... It's not something you'd like to go through again if your life depended on it but it is something that showed a strength of character and a sense of community. Community is the word but ... just organic connection with people. It's quite amazing."

SAM AYOUB: "Greed was created and the coercing of players into breaching contracts became a bit of a norm for everybody, which was uncomfortable. I found it uncomfortable. But you had to act and you had to act quickly to achieve the result. Sometimes it evolved. A bit like now: clubs blame the players and they blame the agents when it suits them but, mate, there's more clubs that punt players than there is players wanting to be released from clubs. I think that is a direct result of what clubs started to do then because they were supported by their respective leagues. 'You get him to jump over, we'll play his legal costs'. Caps were introduced and policed - not like they are these days. The ARL probably owed a lot of gratitude to people like Bob Fulton, Phil Gould, Nick Politis who was probably the most staunch in the initial stages. Being a successful business man he probably wasn't afraid to take on the big boys.

People like Phil Gould, Ken Arthurson, John Quayle, Bob Fulton, they cherished the ARL because it was giving them a product, a game. To them, Super League were the aggressor and the enemy so they dug their heels in and without people like Packer behind them, who knows where it would have ended? In any war there are people who you could call heroes and they were probably heroes of that war."

MARK SARGENT: "It's the most profound thing you can ask about the whole thing: what did we learn? Where did we get to? When you reunified it and you dressed it up differently, it looked more like Super League than the ARL and everyone adopted it.

It's the power of marketing - how you put the message across and how you present the product. Both sides put their stamp on it so it's OK. One of the stated aims of Super League was that the players were the heart and soul of the game so they should have a bigger slice of the pie. That's probably come to pass."

JIM MARR: "I think we learned that the dollar is king and that all those fibs we tell ourselves about the purity of rugby league and its innate moral superiority are just that - they are sort of fibs that have a basis in fact. But in the end, Super League showed us that when push comes to shove, they are fibs."

IAN ROBSON: "When we got through the course of the year, we actually got a whole heap of research done. We went to heartland places like Canterbury Leagues and Penrith Leagues to do it. It was clear that one of the things that had died in Sydney in 1997 was footy tipping. It had imploded because if you and I both worked for Qantas in the maintenance shop at Mascot and you were a Cronulla fan and I'm a St George fan, we actually don't have anything to talk about anymore. We did a whole bunch of focus groups. Frykers (Ian Frykberg) saw it and we sent it up to Holt Street. What it told us was that no matter how much money News Ltd was prepared to throw at this … mate, they bought a lot of properties. They bought players, they bought coaches, they created this new IP. There had been a lot of things they'd been able to buy. But one thing they hadn't been able to buy was hearts and minds. When you start to see, through those focus groups, not anonymous surveys or 45 percent of people said this, just hear the words, hear the way they say it, it was just a hearts and minds issue that could never be resolved. It couldn't just be about the fact that the players were on this and the coaches were happy to go along. The engine room, the economics of the model, was always going to be driven by fans. It hadn't really stuck and it was slipping which was very different to World Series Cricket. It stuck immediately. In saying that, it started very slowly. That first ever World Series Cricket game at Waverley Park, that people still talk about, there were literally 10 people there. Two of them were Kerry Packer and Jeff Kennett. But once they got it right with a bit of tweaking, it became very quickly apparent that it was the real deal. "

KEVIN NEIL: "It's a tribal game, isn't it? And you can't manufacture tribalism. That was clearly demonstrated by Souths. The game can never allow that to happen again. I think there are agreements in place … it's 20 years since I left the Raiders … but I think the club agreements are much tighter and they don't allow that to happen. Player contracts are probably much tighter. We were foot soldiers in a bigger war but didn't realise it until afterwards."

ANNE DAVIES: "All those clubs who were struggling, everyone had to address their financial situations. So it certainly hastened the rationalisation that was going to come anyway. Super League completely underestimated the value the public placed on teams and they (the public) were really reluctant to face the fact that football was a business. It is! Now we're less shocked at that. Every football code has an underlying economic basis and that's how it works. At the time, rugby league was just the sport of working class people. I don't think (News) understood the value of, like, Balmain Tigers and the Bunnies."

LAURIE DALEY: "We still haven't really got to where the game needs to be here in Australia. We haven't really got a plan of what rugby league looks like in, say, five years, 10 years. I don't think we've ever had a plan to say 'this is where we're going to be', 'this is where we need to be', 'this is how we're going to do it'. I haven't seen that. I think that's the frustration of everyone. It's basically the old 'oh well, we'll see what happen, if someone goes broke we"ll look at getting someone else to join, we're not going to bail them out or we'll try to bail them out as best we can'."

BRENT READ: "Was it the war we had to have? Probably not. I think the game's become more professional. Players obviously started earning a lot more money but with that comes a lot more responsibility and I reckon players are still getting their heads around that part of it - what it means to their profile. But it hasn't eradicated the factionalism and the war in the game. All that stuff is still around. There's still a lot of grudges. There's a lot of suspicion. The selfishness. Clubs more often than not act in their own best interests. It's almost an every-man-for-himself attitude that hasn't changed. The thing is now, the clubs are members of the game. They own the game. The commission is an independent body but the clubs have got the power, if they're not happy with how the game is being run, they can just vote the commission out and appoint new commissioners. They don't need to (break away) because the clubs have got that power anyway. There doesn't need to be an uprising. They can just keep removing the eight commissioners until they get the ones they think are best for the job. I think everyone realises how much damage that did to the game and I don't think they'd do that again. I don't think they're that selfish that they'd do that again and push the game to the brink of destruction to serve their own ends."

SHANE RICHARDSON: ""Greed and money hasn't changed since '97. It was all about greed and it was all about money then. For the last four years ever since the other television deal it's all about money. There was no chance when they put those two comps together that there was going to be realistic business plans for the clubs to survive but the players were just paid such ridiculous money and they were locked in for long terms. The idea of setting up the ideal world was never going to happen. It was all about exposure and television. That went on and on and it never cut back. The last time this deal was done it became the worst of all. You tell me another deal where you pay 130 per cent of all the players' wages to the clubs and then put very little back into development. More importantly, you don't change the way the business is done or the structure of the business. It's the opposite of Super League. It's a world now where players and people realise you can't be paid the sort of money you're being paid now, you can't have $10 million salary caps. The whole game is going to have to reduce itself by 30 per cent. In my opinion, that will make the game so much better, if it's redistributed the right way to grassroots. There was an opening up of minds about what we could do in the game but you didn't have to throw out the baby with the bathwater. I'd come in from outside so I always felt it was a closed school. I was surprised how it happened but it didn't surprise me that it needed to happen. The greed got so much involved in it and it just went straight over the top, giving out millions and millions of dollars to people for ridiculous reasons. It was an unreal world at an unreal time. Dealing with some of those guys, the South Afriicans and their dogs … Tiann Strauss … I never would have believed that I could be involved with all that stuff at the highest level … sitting cross-legged with Lachlan Murdoch on a bed in a motel speaking to the St George players about changing over..."

MAX COWAN: "There's a more inclusive approach to running the game than there was prior to the war. I think there's a recognition that each of the clubs needs to have a voice and not just an elite few. Prior to that event there was an inner sanctum and an inner-inner sanctum and the rest. It became much more democratic, if you like. That, in itself, has its own problems but I think it's far better. It's far more collaborative. But at the time when there was a potential for making really hard decisions about the game, particularly as it is in Sydney, I don't think there was enough daring to make those decisions because it would have upset lots and lots of people. But by now, 20 years later, those dissatisfactions would have dissipated and the game would have been a lot stronger."

RODNEY OVERBY: "The Players' Association started growing and knowing what it was like to get paid your worth. I certainly got more loot than the average (ground announcer) was getting. The players were getting peanuts back then. Now they're getting millions."

JOHN LANG: "I think it shows: whoever is running a sport like rugby league, you've got to keep moving with the times. Peter V'landys says you've got to look 20 years ahead. I don't necessarily agree with everything he does but I think he's right. The lesson is: you've got to keep moving with the times or someone else will come and try to take it off you."

DEBBIE SPILLANE: "I get so tired of meeting people who've got this black and white view that Super League was bad and rugby league was ruined by it. At the time, I totally understood the game going to Super League. Basically, we were just getting an hour replay on a Sunday night. That was it. I know what happened was not because Rupert Murdoch cared more about rugby league than Kerry Packer. I'm not an idiot. But he saw the market wasn't being properly treated and he tried to take advantage of that. People say to me that since Super League, they don't care as much about rugby league. I say 'I feel the same - but it's because Super League didn't work'. We needed a team in Adelaide, we needed a team in Perth. The AFL just wore it. They wore the discontent and the shit and kept their interstate teams supported and viable and it's been to their advantage and the disadvantage of rugby league."

LUKE DAVICO: "There were a lot of good things in Super League as far as players earning what they were entitled to but also it had so many teething problems and initially we just had too much time on our hands, I think. All of a sudden we came into this windfall of money. With idle time, you have too much time to get up to mischief or probably not be focused in the right direction. Maturity is a wonderful thing but when you're a young guy and all of sudden you come into all this money it's very hard to not get carried away and over-excited."

NEIL CADIGAN: "It was a massive line in the sand for rugby league. Trust was betrayed so badly between people. It became about business and finance rather than the sport itself. All of a sudden you didn't trust people that you normally would trust. The media coverage of the game changed significantly because of what happened with Super League. The coverage of the game went far beyond the game, the sport and the stories around it. It became scandal, off-field issues. It became contracts, player managers … they took on a whole new powerbase. There were agendas galore all through media and administration. That was the start, I think, in the media of 'us versus them'. That's when, media-wise, journalists and commentators became part of setting the agendas. They became part of the scene rather than reporting on it. They started to think they were, and became, personalities whereas before they were observers. Ray Hadley was a big part of that. Peter Frilingos was in a tough situation on the News side of things. Roy Masters. They became part of the scene, driving what they thought."

IAN SCHUBERT: "I met Reebs and he said 'what do you think's wrong with the competition now and how it all works?' and I mentioned things like the unfairness of the judiciary and I thought the international calendar and how that's all run should have been a bit fairer. I knew all the other nations didn't have any say in what went on except Australia and England. The judiciary was prone to have decisions made before you actually got in there. He said 'well, you can start tomorrow'. I thought 'how great?' You're starting from the ground up and trying to right what I thought as an ex-player were some of the wrongs. I never had any qualms doing what we did. I just saw it as an opportunity for the game to move aside and reassess and still progress. I don't think we went backwards. We had two competitions for a year and I thought the outcome of all that would never have happened if it hadn't been for the turmoil of that 12 months. We always, as a game, spent beyond our means in relation to players. That hasn't changed. It's just the numbers are probably bigger. Without our leagues clubs we'd have a four or five-team competition and that's always a big concern. We keep saying 'this can't go on forever' but it seems to keep going on forever. Clubs can be artificially propped up by their leagues clubs which is gambling money and alcohol. The game is so flexible. We've twisted and turned it on its head and upside down and it just keeps coming out smelling like a rose. We've had some atrocities ... and they've put some dents in the armour but those dents polish out pretty quickly in rugby league. In rugby league, we're quick to forgive those who make mistakes. In some aspects that's a good thing - not in the eyes of all of the public. Rugby union is more at the elite level, where they concentrate. We're down with the grassroots. That's what we do. But they don't like change at the grassroots. As much as we try to do Hunter Mariners and an Adelaide Rams and a Perth Reds, the reality was ... common sense in the end said 'we haven't got enough players to go to all those places'. All it would have done - and it did - was weaken both competitions. We haven't got the number of people to really be able to afford a good second tier competition where you could possibly have promotion and relegation. They even knocked the 20s on the head. It's a lot about the numbers in our sport. Even though we've had a big influx of money, we're still financially constrained enough to keep it where it is. We try to make it stronger every year. As much as rugby (union) 'don't like' the fact they're the elite … don't worry, they like it. Rugby league don't like to be considered poor but that's what we are. We don't have to be snobs. We don't have to wear tweed jackets. We can go to the footy in our tracksuit pants and have a great day and abuse everybody and go home. I love our sport!"

TOM MOCKRIDGE: "OK, it was a big - literally - shitfight at the time but the crucible of that change was that it did generate a new outlet and the best of both inputs - rugby league traditional values but a new commitment to commercialisation that recognises in the end that all these things have got to compete for people's time. There are two scarce things, time and money, which you're competing for all the time."

WAYNE PEARCE: "The negative of the Super League war from my perspective was the exposure of a lot of values that were selfish and greedy but the selfish side was that it really forced the game and the administrators and everybody involved at the clubs to start looking at ways to do things more effectively and better rather than just doing the same things over and over again, the old way."

GAREN CASEY: "People just don't like change: the 'don't fix what ain't broke' mentality. But it was broke. It had to happen, maybe not to that extreme. You feel bad for Souths supporters and Norths supporters but at the end of the day those things have happened and built the market. You look at it now and it's one of the biggest followed sports worldwide, continues to grow because it's been able to play through a pandemic. The supporters are always going to be there because it's in their blood. You can't really walk away from that kind of sport."

MALCOLM NOAD: "I think it also says a lot about relationships within the game because there were very heated relationships between people on the ARL side and the News Corp side but a lot of those people became very good friends. I became a very good friend with Denis Fitzgerald and he was probably one of the most vehement people against Super League at the time and News Corp at the time. But over the period of a few years, I think people wanted to put that behind them and move on and make it a more successful game. I think that's happened. The ARU (Rugby Australia) would be in a much better position now and rugby league would not be in as good a position now without the war. They didn't have a war but they did become professional and we did (have a war) but we became professional much faster because we had to. The players were getting huge amounts of money. In the long term I think that's been beneficial.."

BILL HARRIGAN: "If anyone says to me 'oh, they wrecked the game' I say 'no, the game is what it is today because that war happened'. We got what we've got now because of that war. Now we're professional referees, we're on good money. Back then mate, we were always the afterthoughts. Things that we changed and things that we did in '97 were not perfect but it certainly opened up the door to the game as it is today with the introduction of referees becoming full-time, video refereeing, different technology as far as our communication goes on the field, some of the rule changes that were brought in … If someone said to me '97, you can write that off, I'd say 'no way'. Ninety-seven was important for me and it kicked off my career again and so I was very happy for Super League to come along. I have no regrets about it whatsoever."

BARRY RUSSELL: "I believe there were all good intentions … way back then there was a view that there were too many teams in Sydney and ultimately to expand and grow there needed to be amalgamation and what-not. I just look back on all the money that was spent and think 'holy shit' but sometimes you need to have a crisis like that to grow stronger."

BOB FERRIS: "Because I came from the business side of things, what I didn't like was it was 'win football at all costs'. Murdoch got one of the big top commerce companies to come around and audit all the clubs. They went through all your books and they came down and they sat down with me and my financial controller. They said 'what's your goal this year' and I remember saying 'my goal is to make money'. He said 'gee, you're refreshing. You're the first one that's said that. Everyone's else's goal was to win the competition'. They would go close enough to working together but if they could get a player off you or something else, they'd do it. It can be a dog-eat-dog world. The driving force to win a comp is so strong. I don't think (cronyism) disappeared but they realised it was a dinosaur attitude they had and it just got less."

TREVOR McKEWEN: "It's a tough old game. How it's survived is quite incredible and shows the strength of the game itself. Can it ever achieve what they were looking to? I don't know about that.

I think rugby (union) is just too powerful and it's got too many funds. For all the issues that it's got, I think rugby (union)'s going to break through in the US before league does ... if, in fact, either of them ever do. I doubt either of them ever will. But the tribalism was underestimated by News Limited. I think News Limited were probably strongly influenced by the American model, that it is possible to create new franchises from zero and create tribalism. That's not really the Australian or the Kiwi way and there wasn't a firm enough understanding of that. I think it's in pretty good shape now though mate. I watch so much of it now. It's become the thing that keeps me going in terms of my sport interest which has waned over the years ... but it's a pretty bloody good product in my view. It continues to refuse to die and bounce back. The one thing I've learned from covering other sports is that rugby league is almost out on its own in terms of taking entrenched attitudes and refusing to waiver from them. There's people who've arguably contributed a lot to the game on different sides who still won't talk to each other. It's quite astounding. You haven't necessarily seen that in other sports where there's been a schism or a rift like this. Rugby (union) went through quite a bit when it went professional, the whole Cavaliers tour and that sort of thing. Over time they seem to be healed. Those people talk to each other. A lot of time they're working alongside each other in paid roles now. It doesn't happen in rugby league."

JIM MARSDEN: "If Wests Tigers had focused more on southwestern Sydney, it would be absolutely massive by now. The biggest lesson is the game is a massive business and if we let business people run it, we will lose a bit too much of the tribal nature of the game."

PAUL KIND: "My big observation out of it was: if you could have invested all that money in the game of rugby league when AFL was where it was and league was where it was, if you could reinvent that two years … God knows where we'd be today. It really challenged the rugby league fan, young and old, who trusted the game, that what was going to be delivered in future would come back to being as kind of raw and emotional as rugby league was before. People continued to support it because they wanted to see it keep going but the passion disappeared, I reckon, on the Super League side. It felt like those teams weren't as authentic as they had been before. The people-power in that was the fans of the clubs in Super League continued to support them but there was a sense for me of there being a massive job ahead for whoever took on that challenge to really mend all those broken bridges. I've seen that first hand as a young guy. I came into the game in ''92. We did Tooheys Challenges, we did Melbourne Origin in '94 and Tina and into '95 with expansion and the 747 around the four new teams. It was incredible what was going on in the game at that point. Then l lived through '95, worked on rugby (union) in '96 and by the time of '97 I was worried how it would ever get back to being what it used to be. Ninety-five, that year working in the ARL as a 22-year-old, watching players come through and Bozo (Bob Fulton) and Gus (Phil Gould) in their corner offices signing guys up, wild celebrations when Adam Ritson signed back across to us… that was awful. It was awful. You know, just a money grab and a PR war and watching poor old Quayle and Arko who had built this incredible opportunity for the game see it get ripped apart was amazing. I mean it was sad. I remember writing a press release in '94 about a $12 million profit from the year. I remember everyone in the NRL being elated in 2014 when we made $40 million. Now that doesn't seem like it's that much different to 12, really. I think the game would have been in an incredibly strong position (without the war). The fact that that TV deal existed with Packer on an exclusive basis … if you could have changed that moment and News and Packer could have agreed on television, I think the game would have been incredible. You would have gained subscription television and it would have maintained free-to-air. It would have been in expansion markets where it had support and finance behind it. Melbourne was an inevitability, regardless of whether Super League came along. Adelaide was probably the wrong decision and just a dot on the map. I don't think that would have changed but I reckon we'd have a national comp that still had lots of old archaic elements to it. It really did clean out the old ARL boards, God love them all. There was a need to clean out that old structure. They probably would have got there on their own, to a commission-type structure. I think the game would have been infinitely better if it (the war) hadn't happened. The upside of it was it did clean up that governance in the next generation of the NRL and it made it abundantly clear to everyone that from a television point of view, rugby league was always going to be a winner. It set up our TV value. It stunted our TV value because News had those last rights but when News lost their last rights in 2012 … when Dave (Gallop) left and John Grant claimed he'd done the deal. Internationally, I don't think it would have been vastly different. It would have evolved. Super League did nothing, really, for the international game other than probably inflate the reality in the Pacific Islands and places like that by putting false money into those markets. I think at the end of the day, we'd been better off without it and I thought the game was really flying. Being inside it and seeing it operate; Quayle was an incredible leader and probably would have stuck on longer than he did. There was more downside than upside for me."

MALCOLM SPEED: "It shook up all of sport in Australia and I think everyone was looking over their shoulders there for a while about what might happen with the aggressive push for pay TV rights and TV rights. It was quite a bizarre time."

STEVE SIMMS: "The game (in England) has got better but it's still not the same game as back home in Australia. They're miles apart."

DANNY MUNK: "If you jump past the end of '97 to now, you've got some (licensed) clubs in the NRL putting in anywhere between five and $10 million a year to keep their football teams afloat. I've got no idea how that makes any sense and I've also got no idea how they haven't learned from the past .... having a game that isn't able to support itself without outside sources such as licensed venues being the prime cash cow has always made the game fragile. That's one of the primary lessons they never learned. I think the other thing was … the Super League War was about too many clubs in Sydney, not enough use of the Australian market. That was one of the prime reasons for the battle, it was too much of a NSW-Queensland story and mostly NSW. Because of the Super League War, we started expanding. The worst thing was when the war ended, we lost Western Australia, South Australia. We really ended up with only one team in Melbourne, one strong team in Brisbane and a team up in north Queensland. Once again, we've come up primarily eastern states. If it wasn't for the money from the Super League fight, if Optus hadn't have put in and Telstra hadn't have put in, most of those clubs wouldn't have got to the other end of the war. We were in a situation where you had the Easter Suburbs, you had the Parramattas, you had the Canterburys, We couldn't compete against those. So when the war broke out and Optus started putting in the money, it kept us in the game."

GEOFF BELLEW: "I think the game is well run but I also think the seeds for that were planted in the eighties when they got rid of that 42-person general committee and introduced a nine-man board. That's still the model they're using. It's a commission but it's an eight-or-nine person commission made up of people, some of whom have a background in football like Wayne Pearce, others who don't. Financially, in terms of television rights and all that, the game's fantastic but there is a core of people who have been lost. I'm 61 and I remember it well but I have two daughters, 19 and 22 … the youngest one follows it. She hasn't got a clue what all this is about. I show her old videos of dad doing interviews in the eighties and the nineties and she wonders what it's all about. The one group which might have come on board to a greater degree is women. I think there are more women following the game. My daughter comes with me when I go and watch a game. She's grown up with it to a certain extent. She's got mates at uni who follow it. That wasn't the norm when I was a kid. The boys followed it. The reality is, if the game had been going badly, Murdoch would never have been interested in it. There were powerbases, there's no doubt about that. There always are. I don't know Peter V'Landys at all well and I haven't spoken to him since he took the top job but I'm sure he's got a particular powerbase because that's how all those sorts of things work."

JOHN HUTCHISON: "There was a camaraderie around back then that money changed and I feel like it's worse now. You could just see the change in the attitude of the players. It became more about 'what can I get?', all about me, 'if I can't get what I want, I'll fuck off somewhere else'. I know professionalism comes into that but I still think that was a hangover from the Super League era, that players got an expanded view of where they sat in the world. I thought it was quite sad because footy was about connecting people. It didn't matter if you were from the wrong side of the tracks or black or brown or what colour you were, as long as you were a decent bloke and you had a go, the game had a place for you. Money changes people's views."

KEN ARTHURSON: "I think the game is still terrific. I really love the game. I'm probably the worst person in the world to say what their thoughts are about rugby league because it's been my life and always has and will be. It's becoming a little bit … you sort of know what's going to happen. The ball's kicked off, someone takes it, a forward rushes out and charges ahead. Five tackles they'll take it up and then kick the ball. The opposing fullback will take the ball, the opposing forwards have rushed up and got him. They'll do the same thing five or six tackles and then they'll kick the ball. That's become a little bit repetitive. But generally, it still is a terrific game and I saw some terrific games of football last year. I really did."

GEOFF CARR: "In any upheaval out of anything, the compromise out of it may produce a lot of better things … but it nearly killed the game. Our newspapers were full of the politics of rugby league rather than the sport itself. The easy way for a lot of people to cope was just to disengage. And they did. It could have been dreadfully, dreadfully … it was a very painful way to bring in a couple of improvements, if you ask me. I still remember John Hartigan asked to address the ARL clubs, as the editor of *The Telegraph*. And what it was about was … Sydney was ARL, pretty much. They stopped buying the *Telegraph*. It was a protest against Murdoch, number one, but number two they got sick of reading about all of this crap that was happening to their game. I still remember Hartigan saying 'look, we promise you we'll give you equal coverage. We promise you we'll promote your game'. They knew. They were starting to bleed financially because people just turned away from the *Telegraph*. It's a pretty painful way to improve the judiciary."

GRAHAM ANNESLEY: "What you do learn is that, firstly, our game - no matter which way you look at it - does have a degree of tradition to it. We had a lot of rule changes and they were intended to make the game more attractive. In hindsight, they went too far. There was all the criticism about Super League basically turning into touch football because of the speed of the rucks and all that sort of thing. Some of those things that were innovations at the time ultimately had to be pared back a little bit. But it was the opportunity to actually do some of those things that, in some ways, were ground-breaking in terms of rugby league tradition and history. Some of it was very good, some of it was not so good. People don't like to move too far from that tradition and if you do move from that tradition people generally like to be taken on the journey slowly. You can't completely turn things on their heads and just expect people to adopt it, adapt to it. And when I say people, I don't just mean players. I mean fans and the general public. So you've got to be careful not to change the fabric of the game too much. You can at times do things that are too radical, too quickly. But temper that by saying if you do things at the right pace for the right reasons and they're well thought out, then people will come on that journey and that's been evidenced by some of the things that are still in the game now that were introduced during that period. You've got to be very careful that when you do it, (that) you've consulted widely, there is general support for it and that you've been through a process where you can confidently predict that there's going to be more support for it than opposition to it. You'll never get universal support for some of those things because there's too much passion in the game to get everyone feeling the same way. But you just have to be careful to be sure you do things a) for the right reasons and b) you've got the right levels of support to be able to do it."

487

WAYNE BENNETT: "Bugger all mate! We learned nothing! Absolutely nothing! We learned that greed is still the driving force in life for a lot of people. Everybody got more. The pay TV and the normal TV are now working together and getting on with life. I don't know how long that would have taken us (otherwise). Five clubs went out at the end of that debacle and clubs amalgamated. The original idea, which they couldn't agree on because of the politics of it all, was to have 12 teams. That's what they wanted. I wouldn't like to see the game do it again. I'll tell you what the fans want: they just want to see their footy team play every weekend. They don't want the politics of it all. That's their life, their life is full of politics. That's why they go to sport, that's why they gravitate towards it. That's what I learned: don't play around with what the fans love: the tribalism of their team. There'll be no administrator in the game that will survive if he disbands a team now. If the club becomes dysfunctional because they can't pay their bills, that's a different matter. But there is no-one in the game now or in the future who will ever pull a club out, whoever it may be, and say 'you're not playing in the NRL anymore'. Because, mate, they won't survive."

JOHN QUAYLE: "Was $800 million worth it? I don't know whether it was"

CHAPTER 27

Vignettes of Change

What happened next?

Originally at the Toronto Wolfpack game in Brighouse, Nigel Wood had suggested that while Mike Colman's book had covered just 14 months, this one should encompass 25 years.

I soon discovered that such a volume would be little more than an encyclopedia - with the colour and humanity drained out of the story. But it was hard to get my interview subjects to shut up when they got to December 19, 1997.

Two Tribes was deliberately limited in its focus - but many of my interviews cast light on events which occurred later, especially in the fields of mergers, club closures, relocations and - in the case of one particular inner-city Sydney team - expulsion.

So may I present vignettes of change: things that happened, almost happened and shouldn't have happened from the perspective of those who were there, from the toast at Lee's Fortuna Court Chinese Restaurant on December 18, 1997 to right now.

This is almost the end of a book but … who knows? It may be the beginning of another one.

December 1997: Hunter's merger with Gold Coast is aborted and the Mariners fold.

NEIL CADIGAN: "It was December 29 1997 - that date always stuck in my mind because it is my sister's birthday - when News - Malcom Noad as chief negotiator - called 'no go' on the merger with the Chargers. That was when I received his call while in our caravan at Bateau Bay and I said they'd killed two clubs in the one day. So it was (10 days) after the 'compromise had been struck'. I said 'they won't survive another year, the Gold Coast'. I said 'they're a financial basket case, they won't survive the cut'. They only played one more season and then we ended up having what we laughingly call the Melbourne Mariners. David Barnhill was on the board of the Gold Coast and he was dead set against (the merger with the Mariners). Tom Bellew was crucial there. (Graham Murray) didn't know what was going on. He had to take the offer to go to Leeds. There had been discussions about who would get what positions and (Michael Hagan) was thrown up as a possible coach. We'd done the full compromise. Phil Economidis would be coach and Hages would be the assistant. We'd even decided Graeme Foster from the ARL, he was doing the marketing. They said 'Caddo, you go up there for a while and Foster's going to hang on. He won't last long, you can take over'. The players were going to be divvied up. Robbie Ross had already signed with Melbourne. (Brett) Kimmorley) hadn't committed, Scotty Hill hadn't committed, John Carlaw … all those guys would most likely have gone up there. They'd gone through and worked out what a combined side would be and very few of the Chargers players were going to survive. It was a Mariners-dominated side. Phil Economidis, he was all for it. 'It's a much better side than I'm going to have here, let's do it.'"

490

PHIL ECONOMIDIS: "That's when I was required to front the board with my reasons why we had to accept the Mariners merger. I presented a case as to why we had to and unfortunately at that time we were getting ex-directors from the Crushers onto our board and some board members were going to lose their place because the Mariners would have wanted nearly 50 per cent of the board members as well. They flicked it, which was really sad because the majority of those players went down to Melbourne Storm and they won a comp within a couple of years. I'd already met Michael Hagan, we'd flown him up and he was going to be my assistant for a year or two and then I was going to step back and he was going to take over the reins. We missed out in all ways. That signalled the end of us when we didn't do it, I thought - even though David Barnhill kept reassuring us that our future was secure. That wasn't the case at all."

GEOFF BELLEW: "It was geographically ridiculous, really. There was no rhyme or reason in terms of that. (My father) copped a lot of criticism for that because they said if they had gone ahead with the merger, the Gold Coast would have been like Melbourne. I think that he thought - and it may have been false hope - that as a consequence of their success in '97 that they were strong enough to go it alone. I think that was his philosophy. In hindsight, that probably wasn't right. I think he was probably unjustifiably buoyed by the fact they made a finals series in a reduced competition. With hindsight, that mightn't have been the greatest judgement call."

MARK SARGENT: "Willie Mason went to Canterbury instead of Newcastle. That's fucking crazy. Because he'd been at the Mariners, they wouldn't have him."

January, 1998: A single set of rules - on-field and off-field - for the NRL is formulated and referees reunite

GEOFF CARR: "It was quite a tense time. There were different rules. We set up a rules committee. There was me and Gus (Phil Gould).... We had to thrash out, decide what ball we were going to use. They used a different ball in Super League. There were all these discussions before the game could go ahead in one competition about how it was going to go ahead. We got people like the Johns brothers to take home different balls to give a critique on them, how they like to pass, how they liked to kick. All those logistical things had to be solved. We kicked off (in 1998) without the partnership agreement having been signed! Me and Peter Jourdain had to go around to the clubs and come up with notional salary caps. There was a salary cap of $2 million and clubs had player payments of $6 million and $7 million. We had to go around and value all the players and get them under this notional cap and then when players came off contract it was a guide to the club and what they should be signed on. There was all this massive dislocation to try and get the thing back."

BILL HARRIGAN: "When the animosity really hit was when we came back in 1998 and they brought us back together and they tried to broker deals between us where we weren't going to be at each other and all this and I remember they took us to the City of Sydney RSL. Fair dinkum mate, it was blokes on either side of the room and there were daggers being thrown across that room left, right and centre. It did not do anything to diffuse the animosity. It wasn't all of the squad. Some of the squad had the attitude 'well, good luck to you blokes, I understand what you did and the reasons you did it'. Another thing, bonding, that they tried to do: they took us to one of those paintballs and split us up. There were some Super League and some ARL blokes on each team. I had (Steve Betts) on my time and Bettsy was one of the antagonisers. We were good mates but he was 'piss off, don't talk to me', all those sorts of things. I remember he got shot and you know when you get shot you've got to put your gun above your head, turn around and walk out? You're off the action. I'm standing near him and mate, I unloaded my gun into him. He was on my team. As he was walking off, just from the side, I went 'I'm going to let you have it' so I unloaded every pellet and then got kicked off the paintball for doing it. But mate, I hit him in the balls, everywhere you weren't supposed to hit him, I hit him. It broke things down a little but which was quite good. Then we went away to a training camp down in Bulli and we wiped the floor with them. Out of the first five spots in the run, we won it and the only bloke who broke the five of us up was Sean Hampstead coming in fourth. That antagonised them even more because they said 'it's not fair because they're full-time and we're not.'

March, 1998: The NRL kicks off with 20 teams - and no signed TV deal or partnership agreement. Fearing a criteria based on fudged data, Penrith photograph the crowds at other Sydney clubs.

ROB WEAVER: "We knew pretty well how we were travelling and it became obvious after not terribly long that there were a lot of people out there who wanted to send us somewhere else, like Western Australia or Adelaide or anywhere but western Sydney. (We) would sit around a table and look at these photos and count the crowds and then someone else would recount them. Then we'd look at what the club was claiming and we'd have an idea whether that was bullshit or not. At the Roosters, the photographer got a photo of an attendant spinning the turnstiles several times."

493

MAX COWAN: "We thought it was an ideal opportunity for the administration of whatever came out of it to rationalise the game so it could be structured in a way that really suited a national competition. But they weren't really daring enough to head down that path. They could have said 'we're going to have this many teams in Sydney - four, five, six but not nine - and this is how we're going to structure it'. They could have been the bad boy so none of the clubs would look like they sold out. I don't think it would have been easy but I do think it needed to be done. Even now, there are clubs that must be struggling financially. It was a matter of the weather and a bit of luck that we managed to stand alone. I kept a tally. They issued that criteria and for some of the criteria there's publicly available information. Some of it we couldn't really get hold of. I ranked all of the clubs according to the information that I could get, each week for the season. We wouldn't have made the cut. The fortunate thing for us is that North Sydney didn't have a home ground and it rained a lot. As the season progressed, I was able to watch North Sydney's ranking go down, down, down and we jumped them. That didn't take us out of danger because if they decided to do a joint venture with someone they would be given exemptions from any cuts. We were concerned right up to the last moment, really."

March, 1998: As half-owner of the NRL joint venture, News Limited conducts a charm offensive.

MALCOLM NOAD: "I was going to almost three games a weekend. One of News' ambitions was to try and … to let people know it was more than just a business. I mean, the league was something that we were really quite enthusiastic about and wanted to be involved with. I wasn't instructed to do it or asked to do it. I just felt we had to try and get some credibility back to the fact it wasn't just all about the dollars. There was a genuine interest in rugby league as well. It was more than me. I'm not saying there was just me going to lots of games to look good. There were other people going to lots of games as well from News. One of my surprises was how enthusiastic the clubs' supporters were about the football."

April, 1998: In their first international with a united team after the war, Australia are beaten 22-16 by New Zealand. Brad Fittler beats Laurie Daley to the national and state captaincies.

LAURIE DALEY: "Once we came back together and Freddie was captain, once he did an outstanding job, there was no way in the world I was going to get it back. That's all part of it, isn't it? That's part of life experience, that's part of the decision. You've got to stand by what you've done and you've got to pay any consequences that might come from that. I'm not bitter about it. I've moved on a long time ago. At the time you're obviously disappointed - 'oh, I should have been allowed to play, I wish I was playing, I wish I was still captain'. Over time you move on and get on with it. I still had a fantastic career, I was still able to play football, I still captained my country, I played NSW, I won comps and rugby league's given me everything. I can't complain about too much."

September, 1998: Gold Coast unable to repeat their giant-killing of the previous season and fold.

PHIL ECONOMIDS: "We had an influx of Crushers players and directors. We went from being a tight-knit group to … there was a bit of a faction there, to be honest. Everything we had built, it fragmented. Also, I'll take some of the blame too. Paul Broughton said to me at the end of that year 'if you want to go to the next level, you've got to be ruthless'. Well, ruthless doesn't work mate. You've got to have the raport with the players. It gave us that little bit of success. I should have just built on that. That was my relationship with the players, it was very solid. People don't realise that even during that (brief owner Jeff) Muller fiasco, we won the only trophy the Gold Coast has won. The rumour mill was in full swing in '98 that we were going to exit."

GEOFF BELLEW: "Despite having quite a bit of money in the bank, they were targeted for exclusion and of course ultimately they were (excluded). The thing that (my father Tom) was upset about in particular was that that was then used to prop up other clubs who were not doing financially so well. That was one of his great bugbears. They had all this money, which had come about because they were financially responsible, really. Newcastle, in particular, were really in trouble financially then and he was very upset about the fact that … I remember him saying 'we don't exist anymore, we've been financially responsible and the money's been used to prop up other clubs'."

September, 1998: The St George Illawarra Dragons are founded.

BOB MILLWARD: "We started to stagger a bit in 1995 when we had to sack our best-ever coach because of policy, again. Graham (Murray) knew our policy. He took it on his own bat, before training one night without our knowledge, to … Lachlan Murdoch and John Ribot came to Wollongong, unknown to me… he said he felt the players were entitled to hear what was on offer. So he was immediately sacked. We ended up great mates and you've seen me around the world with Muzza. I've stayed at his place in England and Townsville and all of that. But we had to do it. With that, we lost some players and a lot of our players … probably our best era was '92 and we probably would have still be good in '95 and '96 but it disrupted the club, it disrupted a lot of our players. They were confused. When you get players like (John) Cross, (Neil) Piccinelli, players of that nature ... then there were five or six players that did sign on that night. At 8 o'clock the next morning I drove them back to News Limited with their cheques. It was a traumatic period for our club and it was a traumatic period for rugby league in Australia. We didn't think we had the financials to stack up going forward. We'd just lost BHP. They gave us 18 months' notice that they were discontinuing and one of the reasons - and I don't believe it was the reason - was that there was uncertainty where the money would end up. 'Give it to the Illawarra Steelers and it could end up at News Limited'. But I do believe that was a very minor concern overall. There was a bit of a downturn in the steel industry at that time. We lost MMI Insurance. Our three big backers, of course, were BHP, WIN Television, MMI and a lot of assistance from Cleary Brothers. That was our reason for talking to St George. Their reason, of course, they would not have met the criteria in relation to juniors and pathways areas. They've still got the same problem today. They didn't have any nursery there and they were concerned about the famous St George maybe being under scrutiny and maybe under danger of missing out. We were every bit as concerned. We were the first. Then followed Wests and Balmain. Then followed Norths and Manly. When we went in (to the rationalisation period), we were warned by other people we didn't have enough money. Before we formed the joint venture, Peter Newell and I called a public meeting down at the Novotel. There were a lot of business people there. We said to them 'we're $2 million short' and I'll never forget the response. A chap stood up and he said '$2 million? We'll have a whip around here tonight and we'll raise $2 million'. And I said 'no, hang on. It's $2 million annually. It's not $2 million tonight'. We went with the concerns, the disappointment and a lot of good wishes from the people in Wollongong. The game of rugby league, through the joint venture, is back to six games in Kogarah and six in Wollongong again. We had a hiccough there. We were well supported by Bruce Gordon. We would love to be back on our own as the Illawarra Steelers but we still fulfilled our charter: we brought world class rugby league to Wollongong on a regular basis. It's 21 years now. We have our moments. We've sold our shares to WIN TV. WIN TV bought the shares to ensure the games remain being played at Wollongong and look, the Steelers are in junior reps. We won two of them (in 2019). We're still the nursery of rugby league. When you look back on it, we've come out of it as good as we could under some trying circumstances."

KEVIN NEIL: "At one stage the Steelers and the Raiders were both sponsored by WIN TV. Bruce Gordon, the owner of WIN, invited me down to head office and I met with both him and Bob Millward. There was a concept, a proposal put on the table that the Raiders and the Illawarra Steelers merge, with half the games in Wollongong and half the games in Canberra and to be sponsored by WIN TV. The meeting certainly happened because they flew me down there by helicopter. It was before the judgement on the fourth of October. That never got out anywhere."

October, 1998: Adelaide are excluded after one year in a united competition.

GEOFF CARR: "There were all these meetings initially about 'these teams can't go because they were good for us' and one thing or another. But News were the ones who could make those calls because they owned most of the clubs."

CHRIS QUINN: "What saddens me a little bit is that if you look at the Sydney Swans and what they've done as far as how they started to where they're at now. Because it doesn't happen overnight and we already had a good establishment of a fan base that would have just built and built and built. Everyone was there for the right reason. We had a great time and we were a pretty tight group, even though we were only there for a short time."

December 1998: A syndicate comprising the Tainui Tribe, Graham Lowe and Malcolm Boyle, takes over the Warriors

TREVOR McKEWEN: "That peace deal that was struck, it required both sides - News Limited and the ARL - to exit certain clubs financially over a period of time. They had to exit their propping up of them. The very first one cut by News Limited was the Warriors, which to me made absolutely no sense at all. I still believe it to this day ... if News Limited had thrown their weight behind the Warriors in the same way they did with the Melbourne Storm, the Warriors would have become the juggernaut that everyone expected that they would. It was corporate pride that drove them in Melbourne, as you know. They couldn't afford for the Storm to be seen as a failure. Everything the Storm got, the Warriors didn't get and the thing I found ironic is, and probably even now, a lot of those Storm players can walk down the middle of Flinders Street and nobody knows who they are. At the time News Limited owned pretty much every newspaper in this country as well as Sky. From a commercial point of view, it absolutely made sense that they prop up the Warriors. It would help Sky TV, it would help their newspapers. Instead, along came the Maori tribe that didn't know what they were getting into and boom, let's get out of here. The Warriors are still paying the price 22 years on, 23 years on from when that decision was made. It was

499

when Lowey and Malcolm bought them at the end of '98. When Mark Graham fell out with Matthew Ridge and they wanted to pay him out a year early, Frykberg helped us with paying that contract out but by and large we were gone. The Warriors have never had a correctly focused owner. Even through the Eric Watson days, they never really invested any money in the club or did what they needed to do. We're still paying for it now to the degree that the Warriors are still struggling. They should have been a Melbourne and I believe they would have been a Melbourne if News Limited had taken a commercial view towards it rather than a parochial 'we can't be seen to not succeed in Melbourne'".

August, 1999: Western Suburbs take their second consecutive wooden spoon.

JIM MARSDEN: "We were thinking 'stand alone' (at the December 1997 peace meeting) and one of our biggest concerns was going to be the ground. Then eventually, in the years to come, we discovered that we had no choice but to enter into a joint venture or merger. But we gave it a good shot. Wests didn't have the support of someone like Souths. Wests had some good corporate support - one was (Australian Olympic Committee president) John Coates. He did some great things but we realised we were not going to get that level of corporate support. We couldn't take the fight on - a little bit like Norths."

September, 1999: Balmain merges with Western Suburbs to form Wests Tigers.

DENIS FITZGERALD: "Prior to '97, of course, we had discussions with a number of clubs, being Penrith as well as Balmain and I think Balmain would have been far better off now if it had been the

Parramatta Tigers as opposed to the Wests Tigers. That's a whole other story. I was always confident we could stand alone but didn't want to lose the opportunity of getting stronger. If we joined with Penrith it could have been a very dominant club for a long, long time, given the resources of both our licensed clubs and the juniors and the growth. With Penrith it was that Roger (Cowan), and presumably his board, took the gold rather ... basically sold the team out with the fans. With the Balmain situation, the fact that they joined with Western Suburbs later, we were nearly there as Parramatta Tigers but it turned around on a Balmain players reunion. Kevin Humphreys still had a degree of sway there at Balmain even through ... when I first got on the NSWRL that was in the wake of the Royal Commission that involved Humphreys and Neville Wran ... Humphreys, I never trusted him right from the start. That's another story. He was a very good orator. Fortunately a few of the amalgamations didn't work - or didn't work as well as they should. North Sydney and Manly hating each other and trying to be lovey-dovey. And Wests and Balmain have always struggled, even though they won the comp in 2005 so I copped a bit of flack over them winning the comp. But it made sense for a stronger club on the field and especially financially to join with a weaker club so that you had one club that maybe had 60 percent of the amalgamation so it was 60-40. It never seemed like it was going to work well when they were 50-50 and both sides struggling financially and that happened a bit with St George and Illawarra even though St George were seen to be far stronger, in an actual sense it was always that Illawarra were going to have all the juniors and basically all the south coast even though they didn't have much in the way of a licensed club financial support. St George have struggled a bit as far as the licensed club was concerned."

DANNY MUNK: "Denis had put forward a nice enough proposal and we could see the validity in the proposal but we had asked that the conversations be kept (secret) until we could work out 'was it a good arrangement or wasn't it? Literally that day when we had the meeting with (Parramatta chairman Alan Overton) and Denis, it got out into the media. I remember we were playing St George down at Illawarra. By the time we got down to Wollongong I was getting calls from the media going 'are you going with Parramatta?' Our board just went 'nah - if this is the way it's going to be, rather than die on our knees, we'll die standing'. Jim Marsden gave us a call going 'I gather you're about to be raped and pillaged'. I went 'yeah, sounds about right'."

WAYNE PEARCE: "We didn't get any real benefits from the Super League War in terms of players who came across. For us, we were probably a casualty of the Super League War. The black and white facts were that Balmain didn't have the money to stand on their own. Some clubs were advantaged because they were aligned with Super League during the Super League War and they got bundles and bundles of money which helped them get into a better position post-the war. We at the Tigers certainly weren't one of those clubs so that was an inherent disadvantage of not being one of the Super League clubs. We didn't have the money to compete in this new world, and it was a new world of rugby league. It would have been a battle to even field a team, let alone try to win a competition. Then the rugby league put a big bundle of money on the table to incentivise teams to merge."

JIM MARSDEN: "At the time that was all on, my business partner was John Adam, the old Norths centre. They (Norths) actually wanted a joint venture with Balmain and I undercut them. I shouldn't say 'undercut', more like cut them off at the pass. I knew they were talking to Balmain because John Adam had told me. We talked regularly about what was happening with our various clubs. Ray Beattie was the chair at Norths and he was a friend of mine. And of course John Adam was one of my best mates and business partner. We talked about the problems. I had some very unpleasant negotiations with Canterbury. Gary McIntyre started on a fairly friendly basis but after about four meetings it got down to the level where the only aspect of the Wests Magpies was the name 'Western' so it became Western Bulldogs. And it wasn't Western Tigers, it was always Wests Tigers. That was always at my insistence. And I stormed out of the meeting after Gary McIntyre had gone back on his words half a dozen times. He had just shown me the latest jersey and I said 'what I suggest is a little more black, it's all blue and white'. He said 'what do you suggest' and I said 'what about a little black arm band for the death of Wests' and he said 'what?' and I said 'a black arm band - the death of Wests - see you later'. I had a beer in Queensland with John Singleton and Kevin Humphreys. At that time or not long after, Singo gave me a call and said 'have you thought about Balmain?' I said 'mate I really haven't. He said 'that's because you're too Campbelltown-focused'. He said 'Wests and Balmain traditionally share boundaries' He said 'Balmain are in a difficult situation. They don't want to be taken over like you don't want to be taken over. You want to go into a joint venture'. I then started talking to John Chalk and at the same time - nobody knew this - I was also talking to Kevin Humphreys. Kevin, while he didn't have any positions, he was still fairly influential. Kevin was giving me guidance and also John Chalk guidance. He was certainly giving me a helluva lot of guidance - knowledge about their board and knowledge about our board as well. Without the instigation of

John Singleton, without the guidance of Kevin Humphreys, I don't think it would have happened.

September, 1999: Melbourne win the grand final.

PAUL KIND: "When you had St George (Illawarra) and Melbourne in '99 with 110,000 people, the team that should have won didn't win and Melbourne won … it created some interesting outcomes and I think inevitably Souths disappearing showed how fragile it was. Souths and Norths … the consequence of the reality hit the game even harder in some respects than while the war was on because of the rationalisation of money and teams and …"

November, 1999 : Manly and North Sydney name their impending joint venture the Northern Eagles. The club folds in 2002, leaving North Sydney dead as a top tier entity.

GEOFF BELLEW: "There were bad, really bad consequences (of the war) like North Sydney. Sure, they were run into the ground by their management and they had this insurmountable debt they couldn't get over but they're a casualty and they're a permanent casualty. They'll never come back. Forcing clubs into merging was never the answer. The Wests Tigers are still there but the Balmain side of the joint venture has no money so therefore they have very little say. Wests have the money because they have the leagues club. St George, to a greater or lesser extent, is the same. And the Manly and Norths one could have worked but there were too many people with too many agendas. I was put on the North Sydney board to fill a casual vacancy in August 1999. The first board meeting I went to, they started talking about this debt that they had. Ray Beattie is talking about this debt and there's no board papers. I said 'how much is the debt?'. "Oh," he said, "we've got an approved overdraft with Westpac of $1.5 million but they've extended that at the moment to 1.9'. And I said 'right, you're not going to make the semi-finals this year. When's your next round of player payments due?' He said 'October' and I said 'how much are they?' and he said 'oh, about $2 million'. I said 'OK, you've got no revenue coming in at the moment of any significance. That means your debt's really about $4 million'. He said 'oh, if that's the way you want to look at it'. I said 'there's no other way of looking at it, I'm brand new here'. The meeting after that, we had this accountant's report to say the company was insolvent. I said 'well, that's the trigger. Once it's insolvent … if you trade while you're insolvent, you're committing an offence, you're rendering yourself personally liable. That's the end of it. It was at that meeting they went under'."

DANNY MUNK: "We thought about the Central Coast. The only reason we didn't do it was when we investigated it, outside of (John Singleton) there wasn't a lot of corporate support up there. As the Bears found out, or the Manly Beagles as I call them, when they went up to the Central Coast that was a quick starvation."

GEOFF CARR: "Player payments … clubs like Manly footed the bill while clubs like North Sydney never paid a zack of their own money. The League signed the contracts so they expected the League to pay it all. There was a fair bit of that going on - 'how much can we benefit ourselves' - across the board. They had a real attitude about a lot of that stuff. Norths got Jamie Goddard and he was an Origin hooker. I think he was on $200,000 to $250,000. I said 'we'd rather have him go somewhere else but if you're going to have him, you're going to have to make a contribution. They initially refused any contribution at all and in the end I think they paid something like $10,000."

July, 1999: Souths are excluded from the premiership.

KEVIN NEIL: "Well, it happened - and it happened because a couple of accountants came up with a formula. News Limited might have driven it but John Hartigan, when he became CEO, he pushed pretty hard to have Souths back in. It shouldn't have happened but it did happen."

SHANNON DONATO: "Mate, absolutely the club was struggling. I can tell you unequivocally. In fact, I remember at the beginning of Steve Martin's reign (in 1998), all the players ... one of our first sessions ... we spent an hour, half of us, cleaning out the weeds. They obviously couldn't afford quality groundspeople. The surface was terrible. I don't know whether history has been rewritten or not but I can tell you the club was struggling at that time. It wasn't flash. People might not like to admit it but you need to hit rock bottom before you can go up. Maybe the Super League and being kicked out expedited that. Otherwise we may have limped along like a maimed wildebeest for a long time before we got put out of our misery. It expedited that and it expedited the rebirth. Maybe it did put us out of our misery and expedite our resurrection."

October 1999: Rugby union administrator David Moffett is appointed NRL chief executive.

DAVID MOFFETT: "I was only there two years and there were two things that happened. The first thing was the way I found out about News Limited doing a deal with South Sydney (to bring them back). They didn't involve me in that and I was the chief executive. In actual fact, David Gallop found out before I did. I didn't think that was very good form, to be perfectly honest with you. The next thing was: I suppose with that in the back of my mind: I woke up one day and

I said 'if I had my druthers, would I work for News Limited? And the answer to that was 'no' because I found it really quite difficult to understand how come... The journalists would hammer the hell out of the NRL and yet they owned 50 per cent of it. I'm talking about News Limited journalists. I mean, I understand why. I understand the personalities, I understood the reasoning behind it but it most likely made the job a little more difficult. You know what I'm like. I accept the brickbats and if you want to have a crack, go right ahead. But I was a little bit perturbed by that sort of behaviour. And at the same time, I was approached by Sport England to do the job there so those three things all came together and I decided that's what I'd prefer to do."

July, 2001: South Sydney is readmitted to the premiership.

STEVE SIMMS: "It was just elation. After they got back, it was like winning a war realistically."

SHANNON DONATO: "The other thing that's not popular: even when we came back into the competition we were an effing basketcase for the first few years. It wasn't until we privatised and got our shit together off the field in terms of management, commercial programs, proper governance that we really started building to where we are now. Regardless of which metric you use, whether it's membership numbers, merchandise sales, ratings, we're either number one or two in the NRL now. Back then we were pretty much last in all those metrics."

February 2002: David Gallop replaces David Moffett as NRL CEO.

PAUL KIND: "I worked in the Gallop era for 10 years, which were the repair years really. We mended the game in that 10 years after, from '99 to 2009. They were really the years where the game got sort of put back together again - financially, emotionally, clubs working together openly, all those things. It took years to recalibrate."

February, 2012: The ARL Commission is formed.

PAUL KIND: "I saw a lot of people in Super League when I got in there … they had a lot of belief in what they were trying to do. I was a bit surprised by that. I saw a lot of passion for the game in a lot of those people. But I also saw people, whether they be in clubs or wherever, who had self-interest as their primary motivation. Interestingly, I think the game went there (again) when the commission started in 2012. There was a lot of self-interest between 2012 and 2015 when I left. There were a lot of people not there because they loved rugby league. They were there because they wanted to further themselves. I can tell you honestly there was no interference from News for the 10 years I worked there after (the war) inside the business but there was always a belief that they were fiddling with the game."

March, 2021: Super League Europe turns 25 with little fanfare. Expansion attempts in Paris, North Wales, Gateshead and Toronto have all failed.

GREG McCALLUM: "Maurice (Lindsay) was a very dominating character and basically nothing got through or passed or changed unless Maurice gave it the thumbs up and a number of the clubs felt he'd taken over, basically, the RFL. The RFL was like the ARL. It suffered significant financial damage because of Super League, because the Super League clubs got the money and the RFL didn't. The RFL survived on the basis that it had the 22 other clubs, it had the Challenge Cup and it had free-to-air coverage of the Challenge Cup on the BBC. The RFL, once it stabilised and Maurice was removed from the RFL, it strengthened its position and ended up drawing significant funding through the sports lottery because it was recognised by the sports lottery as being the governing body. "

October, 2021: The NRL considering "expansion" … ie: reclamation.

GEOFF CARR: "In '95 they introduced four new teams. They introduced Perth, who are no longer there. They introduced Auckland, they introduced North Queensland and they introduced the Crushers. Where are we now? We want a second team in Brisbane. Well, we already had them. We want a national comp. Well, we already had Perth. North Queensland became important and they're still there. And Auckland are important. We had all those things solved 25 years ago. Now we're back to trying to solve them again. We got a team in Melbourne out of it - which is a plus. But they may have been next in line if nothing happened. That fast-tracked Melbourne. Losing the second Brisbane team and losing Perth was a real backwards step."

JOHN LANG: "We've still got the same thing: too many clubs in the Greater Sydney region. I think those clubs now … clubs like the Rabbitohs … they are the South Sydney Rabbitohs, that's where they come from and that will always be their home but they're really an Australia-wide club. The Sharks: will they be able to survive? They've got to look outside the Shire I think."

October, 2021: The NRL considered buying a stake in Super League (Europe), which could extend or end the brand's 25 year lifespan.

BRENT READ: "The visionaries like Richo (Shane Richardson) are just floating around the periphery of the game now. Pete V'landys, one of the things V'landys has wanted to do is improve the international game. One of the things (Andrew) Abdo has wanted to do is buy a stake in Super League. I reckon those guys have got that vision but at the moment, because we're in Covid, they're just fighting to save their own backyards, they can't afford to be visionaries. The plan was they'd have money in the bank and they'd be able to do that. They've got to keep the money now because every day's a rainy day."

AFTERWORD

The Chief

"ALL THOSE northern English coal-miners who broke away because they couldn't get paid, couldn't work if they got injured in a game, a lot of them came to the coalfields out here at Kurri and Cessnock.

"No wonder when this Super League War broke out the way it did … Newcastle people, it was already in 'em."

To give Paul Harragon the final word in a book about 1997 is to have Luke Skywalker himself explain Star Wars. For the Newcastle Knights captain to speak like Obi Wan Kenobi - tying together the micro and macro aspects of our story so eloquently - was completely unexpected. I get goosebumps reading those quotes back.

It was well into the second half of 2021 when I tracked down 'The Chief' by phone. Our conversation over the course of an hour, at times, made me feel like I was in that hotel room on grand final eve, ready to do battle. His voice trembled with emotion, his words carried ethereal authority and the impact on the listener was profound.

"This is the biggest thing, I reckon, that's happened to rugby league since its inception. The big reset. How it happened and who did what and why is really important to document. I'm so happy you're doing this.

"I've heard distortion of it, misrepresentation of it, and it hurts me because I put myself out on a limb."

The high point of our conversation is a six minute soliloquy; a dissertation on being at the centre of something created by pure human energy and spirit a quarter century ago. We'll get to that a little later.

Until now I've deliberately avoided covering the period described in Mike Colman's seminal *Super League: The Inside Story*. This has been a very different book, almost an oral history, but it's also an attempt at a sequel.

But if anyone can break the rules, the premise, the expectations of anything, it's The Chief. Paul will soon tell us how he shouldn't have even been playing for most of '97, let alone leading the storming of corporate Australia's gates. He remembers the chaotic first week of April 1995 with clarity and gives us a narrative that differs in some respects with what is already on the public record.

"I have no qualms talking about that because to me the Super League thing was a juggernaut moving at lightning speed that gobbled up club after club and we were next," the 52-year-old says.

"I remember the phone call. I was living across the road, basically, from Marathon Stadium. My brother (and manager, Mark), rang me. He said 'I've just got a phone call from the Super League and the ARL. In the morning, we're going to Sydney, we're going to talk to both'.

"I stayed on the phone to my brother for hours. He said 'mate, the whole world's been turned upside down - it's on'. We dissected it and talked and I rang up every one of the players. It must have been two o'cloc before I pulled the pin and then had four or five hours' sleep and we're off.

"I forget the hotel, my brother remembers it - but I remember walking out of this lift on this thick carpet, going into the room and there's (Ken) Cowley there and there's young Lachlan Murdoch and there was another guy.

"They sat down, told me the story, used the word 'vision' a lot and every question I asked … 'what do you mean you're going to do another team in the town? You won't be able to use Marathon Stadium' … he said 'no, we'll build another one in the town, on the BHP site, we've already sussed it out'.

"And my brother starts to go in depth about 'what about Paul and his career later on and he said 'we're taking the game to America, we're' doing this and doing that. He can be part of the commentary team'. I got a full glimpse. They were wonderful people. I walked out of the door thinking to myself 'how on earth am I going to tell everyone else back home - and John Quayle and Arko who I'm going to see next - that I'm going to Super League?"

"It was just the most mind-blowing thing. Then the dollars came into it. Nothing was a problem."

But then, at Phillip Street, Harragon was reminded about Origin, about the Australian jersey, about grassroots.

"'Because you won't be playing for Australia, you won't be playing for NSW. They're all ARL. And all the grassroots? They're not interested in the grassroots. They just want TV rights'. So when everything was even, I just looked at it with my own conscience. I looked at what was right and wrong. What I was really passionate about?" He signed for the ARL.

What happened next is what Wayne Bennett identified in his chapter here, as News' biggest early defeat. And it's what Paul referred to as putting himself "out on a limb". Like it or not, it's a huge part of his legacy.

In *Super League: The Inside Story* it is claimed that John Quayle called Harragon the next day to say he would not be able to get away from Sydney to meet the Knights players and Harragon would have to bring them to Phillip Street.

That is not the way The Chief remembers it.

"I worked it out that it was only me and Ricky Stuart in the whole competition that had heard both sides of the story," he recalls.

"I went home and said to the boys 'listen, there's only one thing I want. I've had the opportunity to talk to both teams. I was gone, I was going to Super League and after I spoke to them it changed my mind and all I want is for you guys to have that same opportunity'.

"Every other club, the hierarchy has made the decision for the club and the players followed. What about we're different? What about the players get to hear both sides and make up their own minds?'

"They were like 'yeah, alright'.

"I knew that the Knights hierarchy - all of them - were already with News Limited, already infiltrated, so to speak… they'd organised everything, the deal. But they wouldn't come out and say it.

"We were at training and (I thought) the ARL said 'we're going to come down to Newcastle and we'll talk to the boys so they get both sides of the story' because by that time, New Limited had spoken to most of the key guys individually and was like, belligerently pestering the Johns boys and all our other great talents, like, on the half hour.

"They were under maximum pressure. Every trick in the book, the businessman's tricks. 'The deal's off in half an hour', all this stuff.

"I'm going 'when's all the ARL blokes coming down, they're coming down today' and Malcolm Reilly said 'I just got a phone call from Bozo (Bob Fulton) and he said something like 'where are ya's?' and I said 'what are you talking about?'.

"I said (to Fulton) 'I just spoke to the Knights hierarchy, I think it was Brad Mellen, and he said you guys were coming down here, you were getting choppered down' and he said 'mate, that's a lie'.

"He said 'they're in bed with the other mob, they are dead set blocking you guys'. He said ' .. no-one can leave, we've got our hands full ... you'll have to come to us'.

"I said 'you're kidding me' so I hand the phone back to Mal Reilly and I said 'what am I going to do?' We just got together and had a chat and I said 'listen: one thing I'll guarantee you is: no-one will sign. No signing. Just hearing'.

"The end result was I had to, with my own cash, get the lowest bus you've ever seen. I just happened to have a license to drive it. No-one else was going to do it so, yeah, I drove the boys down.

"Finchy (Robert Finch), who was our football manager, very much with Super League ... he came down, probably to make sure that nothing was going to get signed. We're about half an hour out of

Newcastle and Mark Sargent said 'guys let me off'. He got the phone call from Super League to get off the bus.

"I came back. No-one had signed. I said 'there ya go, I've done, as a captain, what I wanted to do.

"I was passionate in wanting everyone to get the same opportunity to hear both sides of the story and they did. Half went one way and half went the other. That's happy days."

Court papers later showed Harragon was given a sign-on of $650,000 and a four year contract totaling $1.5 million. The implication, especially from Super Leaguers, is that he was paid to deliver his team-mates to Phillip Street as much as he was for his own talents.

But Phil Gould did make the trip to Newcastle - with an almost open cheque book - to sign the creme of the Knights in the following days and leave Super League's Malcolm Noad and Michael O'Connor twiddling their thumbs in a hotel room.

"Obviously, to everyone else, it's looked like 'Harragon's just copped a big wad and he's just the lackey boy for the ARL and he's drove them all down," the Chief says.

"I won't compromise myself. At the end of the day, the proof's in the pudding. Your mates, the people around you, they know if you're doing the wrong thing. I hung myself out there but I did the right thing for my own conscience and when people get it wrong or they say the bus driver thing, yeah, it hurts.

"But at the end of the day it doesn't because I don't care. Everyone who was there knows."

Let's move on, then, to the start of 1997.

"Early in that year, we were playing a trial in Coffs Harbour against Manly and I had, like, a seizure, a weird episode. Like an epileptic fit, but not one. I couldn't describe all the symptoms. I didn't play, it was before I even played.

"I had a tough month … played the first game against St George and I got a knock on the head and I went into a seizure on the field."

There are aspects of that experience Harragon does not wish to discuss. "Anyway, it kept happening. I went to the neurologist, the specialist. To cut the story short, he said 'look, my advice to you is to retire now'. He said 'I'll give you these tablets. They're strong, very strong epilepsy tablets'.

"He said 'I'll give you one month's worth'. He said 'if you have one seizure in that month, you're gone. I'm recommending to the club you're gone and I know they're going to do the same thing (I recommend)'.

"It was a dark year … on a personal level, where I think 'I'm finished, I'm not even playing' and the game's turned upside down and all that sort of stuff'. It felt like there was no light, there was no way out, it was gone.

"I had a month of the tablets, it stopped them, I never had one seizure in that month. I came back pretty well straight into the rep scene.

"I did notice that every time I got tackled I was getting … I felt like I was getting knocked out a little bit. Anyway, I worked through that."

Paul Harragon, the on-field hero of 1997, the man who - at least symbolically - allowed the people to reclaim their game, was advised before the season even started to retire. I think I can hear myself gasp on the recording of our conversation at this point.

You already know how this story ends. But you haven't heard Paul Harragon tell it; six solid minutes during which his voice cracks once or twice. Yes, a sporting soliloquy.

"You go into the year, everyone's arguing. It's so tumultuous. The whole town is turned upside down. There's two teams and it just goes on and on and on all year.

"We're trying to concentrate on what we're doing, the legitimacy was a question, about which comp's the best and thankfully we had Manly in the comp, who won the year before. They're still the premier team and the Bronc's were obviously strong from '92, '93 and they've had a great run.

"We were just … as I said, it was really tough, really hard, strained friendships. In the town, the main provider BHP has announced it's leaving.

"There was just bad news everywhere and it was going on and on and on and on.

"But there were underlying things! Like the Aussies For The ARL, like the crowds coming out stronger than ever. There was more feeling and more purpose in all of our lives.

"You don't improve, you don't evolve, as a person unless you struggle to some degree. We were all on edge. We were all working extra hard and eating and sleeping this thing together.

"We were galvanised. Every team tries to get that edge in bringing the team together. Well, there's nothing like a purpose, where your livelihood and the whole game looks like it's not going to happen anymore, it's going to just tear itself apart … to pull you together.

"And that's when the magic happens. That's when extraordinary circumstances create…there are moments in time where you do more than you thought you could do, things go further than you ever dreamed of.

"We were in a dark spot for a long, long time and then all of a sudden a few weeks out from the semis, we're going to be in it and we're looking OK. The year's going good.

"We roll down to Sydney. I remember the first week we went down to Sydney and we win, we come back. We're starting to have fun. We're getting momentum. The crowd's getting behind us but still, there's not a thought about victory. There's not a thought about anything else except for 'we're in the semis and that's good'.

"But the North Sydney game was just one of those pivotal games. We were doing OK but Matt Seers takes off up the sideline and I swear to you, if he scores that try, we're not in. Everyone talks about Darren Albert' grand final try but for me … he had no right to even chase. He was on the opposite wing, on the other side of the field. He turns and runs … he's the fastest man in the universe. When you slow motion it, Matt Seers left the ground to dive, he was only inches from the ball touching the grass and his hand clips in-between and rolls him over. He doesn't score and of course we go on to win. By that time, everyone was really happy.

"People come from everywhere! We go into the grand final and the celebrations were amazing. But I could tell, apart from people making the sausages red and blue and the cakes and the pie shops red and blue and painting their houses red and blue, all that stuff … that no-one really thought that we'd win because this mob had beaten us 11 times or 13 times in a row.

"But it was about halfway through the week where we all had a shift.

"I really felt that: you know what, to me this is way surpassed the game and I don't feel any nervousness. I don't feel like there's an expectation hanging over me, weighing me down. I felt like I was so privileged. I was a fitter and turner at BHP in a hard hat and overalls. That's my apprenticeship.

"That I had this opportunity on the biggest scale to bring some happiness home to our joint that had been so ravaged by all this shit for such a long time....

"I felt like I was on cloud nine and again, raised to another level. I know that everyone else started to get that shift in the mentality and that's when I started to think 'some magic can come here'.

"I reckon the people started to believe in it a little bit as well.

"I fast forward it to ... on the Saturday we leave the Knights' ground and there must have been 10, 15,000 people there to see us off. You couldn't get in. They moved us all into the grandstand just to get away (and I could see the scene). One person was standing there signing autographs and there was a kaleidoscope of colours around them and there were little dots with like 500 people around each player until they moved us out the back.

"It was fever pitch because everyone needed hope. Just like now in the pandemic here, everyone's looking for something. Well, back then, everyone latched onto the team, the team latched onto each other and this game was written for us.

"It might seem like an exaggeration but in that little cocoon it was like the epicentre of the whole world. We had two ways to go: getting overawed and getting pumped again by Manly or our whole world was going to change.

"We felt it then. I was in the bus and I was howling. I couldn't help it. I know Marc Glanville, he's the tinniest bloke, he doesn't cry MG, he had tears in his eyes. We drove out of there with people …. I could feel it, like a vibration in my heart. It was amazing. I'll never forget it, as long as I live.

"As we drove out of that street, on Griffith Road on the way to the link road and out onto the freeway, there were - and I swear this - people all the way along. On top of their cars … Hughesy (Mark Hughes) reckons one of the greatest omens was when a couple of sheilas drove behind us in a car and one of them jumped out and took her top off to the bus. He reckons after he saw that, he knew we were going to win! It was just incredible. All the way to Sydney, people followed us.

"I know it's nothing compared to when we came back. The place exploded. But that's what I felt. This is something like we've never been involved in before and it was up to us to lift for the occasion. I knew that was now or never, that was our time.

"And we had a wonderful meeting the night before. We spoke about the Super League War. We spoke about what happened. We spoke to the point of 'what does it mean to you' and 'where are you at now' and we really brought it right into where we come from and who we are and we just knew that in this one moment in time we could either own it forever or it was going to be lost.

"But it was said that it's not about us anymore. And I tried to portray that it's not about us winning anymore. It's about what we can do for everyone at home. And what it did, for me anyway, was it took the pressure off me. The winning and losing and all that sort of stuff, I wasn't nervous going into the game because we weren't doing it for ourselves that much. I hope that makes sense. It really played to our advantage.

"That game was going as per normal. They were out-muscling us a little bit out wide, they scored a couple of good tries, but we were in the moment. We just went play after play. We didn't get flustered when we were behind and it was one of those…

"I think the terminology is the ideal performance state, where you're in the moment and you're actually enjoying your biggest moment on the stage. You've actually got this attitude where you think 'I don't want to be anywhere else in the world right now. I'm happy'. Usually, you're under stress and pressure but to a man we weren't like that. To a man.

"Before the game, the boys are listening to CDs and dancing and laughing and carrying on. I thought to myself 'I'm already having the best time of my life anyway. The rest is just a bonus'.

"All that, to the fact we won in the last six seconds and how we won and all the rest of it, was all on the back of what everyone - all those mums and dads and all the people that live around here - did. They turned our mental attitude around and all of a sudden, a little bit of magic happens.

"That just happened to be the exact right … a wonderful script writer, a wonderful playwright, could write the script where the ARL gets that hope it needs, that glimmer, that rugby league and passion and what we all stand for is still alive a little bit.

"…that the hope was still there."

(exhale)

"When I think of all that," he The Chief continues, "I think of the immense pressure and the turmoil that went on for years and years - and the uncertainty and questioning yourself about loyalty and all of that.

'What are we fighting for again?'

Harragon admits he again found himself asking that question when peace was brokered.

"Yeah, we didn't win," he says ruefully. "The ARL didn't win. The game got run by News Limited - poorly - for a long time. We were negotiating with Foxtel for the TV rights and the AFL are getting twice as much. No-one won that. Nobody won that. Honest, it was a shitfight."

That's question two that we asked everyone else two chapters back, right? Question one: what was it about?

"It was two rich families who wanted the rights to this new pay TV, to protect their business interests. It turned our game and the lives of many people upside down and was a detriment to our game. It pulled us apart. We imploded. We went backwards as a game. The AFL careered forward and put a huge stake in the race for a geographical advantage, spreading the game nationwide.

"Everything that happened … the players got pay rises and all that sort of stuff … mate, you'd give it all back just to keep it the same. Our game would be through the roof. We would be the number one sport by a long way. I truly believe that. It was about people protecting their interests and despite all the working class and everyone who loved the game, I was left a bit empty at the end."

As we near the end of our story, there is no better person to draw out its true significance than Paul Harragon, who helped rugby league regain its meaning for hundreds of thousands of disillusioned people 25 years ago.

"You know the story: we were trying to celebrate our bicentenary (in Newcastle) and BHP said 'it's over', the lifeblood of the town as far as employment is concerned - 'we're out of here'," he begins.

"I think '97 just showed, in sport, the dualities of life where there's darkness and light. Everything looks terrible, it starts to look good again, there's the hero, there's the villain, in different eyes, it's different people.

"To me it showed the game of rugby league could be stretched like an elastic band forever and it will always come back in. We got stretched to an inch of our death.

"The old saying that in the worst situation comes out the best of men and great things can come from when you struggle, it was one of those things. I supposed what I learned was human nature, the negative side of human nature whether it be greed or power, always is there in some form, in sports or in business.

"But ultimately, the good always overcomes the bad and ultimately the game … it can go through anything and come back. It's in its DNA to struggle. We know how to fight. We know how to get down in the ditches and hang in there and that's what people want. That's what the players do every week.

"You can take everything away from us. A rich bloke can come and try to take our jobs or take our game away.

"For a player or any athlete, you always ask yourself: what's the reason? Why do I do things I do?

"Inevitably in life, obstacles are always going to come. If your reason is not stronger than all those obstacles that come your way, you're not going to make it. Why push though? Why dedicate your whole life … as a player, or supporter or admin or any part of it … what is the thing? What is your reason?"

"Some people are really, really struggling in life. Whether they are looking after someone who's ill, whether they're ill themselves, whether it's financial. Eighty minutes every week, they watch their team and they forget about everything. All those worries go. And when they win, they feel better. The world's better.

"We just wanted to bring some happiness to our town and we knew it was the best way to do it and it worked. It may have saved the game a little bit as well. I don't know. But that's all we wanted to do."

To be part of something bigger than yourself and ride that wave of human-generated energy as often as you can until - like those we remembered at the beginning of this book - your time is up. And to protect - or improve - the mechanisms that allow us to experience that precious, visceral thrill.

This compulsion, it seems to me, drove the people of the Super League War. Who knows? It might even be the actual meaning of life.

To The Newcastle Knights On 1997 Grand Final Day

By the time you reach the centre you'll be half a million strong, the roar will rumble down the coast from back where you are from.

Through the city and the suburbs, through the coalfields to the west, in every town and village every soul has joined your quest.

In the weatherboards and rented flats, the hospitals and homes, there will be a rolling thunder… like our valley's never known.

In the lounge rooms and garages, in the pubs and clubs and bars, in the convents and the coalmines we'll be with you every yard.

We'll be there in every tackle, in the heart of your defence, we will be your source of energy and give you inner strength.

You will hear the voice of every woman, man and child as one, inside you every moment until this war is won.

You'll overcome the danger, for in you these hearts believe, our blood is red and blue just like the colours on your sleeve.

We will be your inspiration, you will have us in reserve, and together we'll reach out as one … and take what we deserve.

Go bravely then, enjoy the challenge, faith in every stride, take us out there as your spirit…for today…. you are our pride

Lindsay Young

Lightning Source UK Ltd.
Milton Keynes UK
UKHW020628311221
396440UK00010B/629